WAP Integration Professional Developer's Guide

Srdjan Vujosevic

Robert Laberge

Wiley Computer Publishing

John Wiley & Sons, Inc.

NEW YORK · CHICHESTER · WEINHEIM · BRISBANE · SINGAPORE · TORONTO

Publisher: Robert Ipsen
Editor: Carol A. Long
Assistant Editor: Adaobi Obi
Managing Editor: Geraldine Fahey
Associate New Media Editor: Brian Snapp
Text Design & Composition: Thomas Technology Solutions, Inc.

Designations used by companies to distinguish their products are often claimed as trademarks. In all instances where John Wiley & Sons, Inc., is aware of a claim, the product names appear in initial capital or ALL CAPITAL LETTERS. Readers, however, should contact the appropriate companies for more complete information regarding trademarks and registration.

This book is printed on acid-free paper. ♾

Published by John Wiley & Sons, Inc., New York

Published simultaneously in Canada.

This publication is designed to provide accurate and authoritative information in regard to the subject matter covered. It is sold with the understanding that the publisher is not engaged in professional services. If professional advice or other expert assistance is required, the services of a competent professional person should be sought.

Library of Congress Cataloging-in-Publication Data:

Laberge, Robert, 1961-
    WAP integration / Robert Laberge, Srdjan Vujosevic.
        p. cm.—(Professional developer's guide series)
    Includes bibliographical references and index.
    ISBN 0-471-41767-X (pbk. : alk. paper)
     1. Wireless Application Protocol (Computer network protocol) 2. Web site development. I. Vujosevic, Srdjan, 1961- II. Title. III. Series

TK5105.5865 .L33 2001
004.6'2—dc21

    2001045397

Printed in the United States of America.

10 9 8 7 6 5 4 3 2 1

To my parents for encouraging all my endeavors over the years
- Bob.

To Darija, Nikolina, and Tara - three queens of my life
- Srdjan.

Professional Developer's Guide Series

Other titles in the series:

- *GPRS and 3G Wireless Applications* by Christoffer Andersson, ISBN 0-471-41405-0

- *Constructing Intelligent Agents Using Java* by Joseph P. Bigus and Jennifer Bigus, ISBN 0-471-39601-X

- *Advanced Palm Programming* by Steve Mann and Ray Rischpater, ISBN 0-471-39087-9

- *WAP Servlets* by John L. Cook, III, ISBN: 0-471-39307-X

- *Java 2 Micro Edition,* by Eric Giguere, ISBN: 0-471-39065-8

- *Scripting XML and WMI for Microsoft (r) SQL Server(tm) 2000,* by Tobias Martinsson ISBN: 0-471-39951-5

CONTENTS

INTRODUCTION

S ince we had both been in the computer industry for decades, we thought we had seen or heard it all. Not much was capturing our attention anymore, and we had long passed the wow stage. Or so we thought until one day out of the blue came this really interesting wireless Internet technology called WAP. Wow!—our techie senses were alive once again. We played with the tools and technology, created Web sites, and built WAP applications, integrating wireless devices into older legacy systems. We were hooked!

Over the last couple of years, we learned HDML, the many flavors of WML, iMode, MME, VoXML, and VoiceXML. We got started just before the big wireless craze began back in 1999 with HDML. We saw the industry jump-start almost overnight, and we knew that we were on the right path. Today, there are many wireless sites, portals, forums, and ventures but until several years ago this was *really* new stuff (and still is). So, we thought we'd put together something that Web programmers could pick up, reference, and start developing—something with functional code, diagrams, explanations, and, finally, here it is.

Is This book for You?

If you're holding it, it's for you, unless you just like holding technical books. This book was written for programmers, technical managers, technical architects, and anyone wanting to learn about WAP. If you want to learn the basics, this book will certainly help you do that. If you're looking for a reference book or a how-to manual, this book is what you need.

The idea of this book was to not only create a reference manual but also to include many working functional programs and applications in as many areas of wireless usage as possible. With some HTML and ASP programming knowledge and the examples in this book, as well as with the program code on the attached CD, you should be able to start programming within a few days.

Covered Material

We've created many types of applications, mainly using HTML, JavaScript, ASP, Perl, VB, VBScript, HDML, and WML. We walk you through most program code line by line, explaining all the pieces. As you progress through the book, you'll find the examples becoming slightly more difficult but all the basics will have been explained in previous chapters.

- Chapter 1 introduces WAP, along with its architecture and components. This chapter is the basis for the entire book since it discusses the fundamentals such as the networks, gateways, devices, and the software development toolkits. If you're learning WAP, this chapter is a must.

- Chapter 2 introduces the wireless languages. Since much of North America uses HDML, this chapter describes the HDML language and the more popular WML. The two major WML flavors, from Openwave and the WapForum, are both discussed and compared.

- Chapter 3 begins the application development with HTML Web scraping. The idea here is to develop programs to screen scrape HTML Web pages for any Web site on the Internet. It discusses the pros and cons of performing this type of process and shows exactly how to do it with a Perl CGI program.

- Chapter 4 introduces a very important programming requirement for any Web developer and wireless application. This chapter discusses dynamic WAP, which deals with a back-end database retrieval and update application. A working application is detailed, showing specific functional code.

- Chapter 5 consists of topics such as browser detection, how to send and receive emails on wireless devices, location-based services, and short messaging services. Each has its own working programs that can be copied from the CD and function immediately on your own server.

- Chapter 6 describes what is sure to be the future of WAP—personalization. Since devices are personal, the underlying applications should be too. Here you'll learn how to make personalized dynamic WAP menu systems, add cookies for bookmarking and security, learn how to create pull applications as well as push systems for a well-rounded development cycle.

- Chapter 7 introduces VoiceXML, a language and technology that voice enables Web sites. This is sure to be extremely popular in the future so we demonstrate its ability via an imaginary voice-enabled eCigar Web site. Use the code provided, set up your server, and enjoy this small, yet advanced, application.

- Chapter 8 discusses our views on the future of wireless technology. We cover some interesting topics and provide some personal insights.

- For your reference, we have provided a detailed glossary and many language references in the appendices.

The attached CD has all the programs and applications described in this book, plus several more bits. Review them, copy them, and modify them. We created them for you to learn and use as templates for your own development efforts.

We hope this book, its material, and associated programs will help you learn and develop your own WAP applications. Once you get the knack, you should be able to integrate your newfound knowledge with existing Web sites and legacy back-end systems, allowing your viewers many different portals to your Web site and its information. If you have any comments or questions, please feel free to email us at authors@wavedev.com. We would certainly enjoy knowing your views and hearing about any specific applications you've built using these templates.

Enjoy,

Srdjan Vujosevic

Robert (Bob) Laberge

Getting to Know WAP

T he Wireless Application Protocol (WAP) came about only several years ago back in 1997. For the first 2 years no one really heard too much about it, but in late 1999 something clicked and the world suddenly became very interested in wireless Internet technology. Was it because a similar technology called *iMode* was making it big (real big) in Japan? Or was it because the big cellular companies were getting their infrastructures set up and investing more funds into huge marketing campaigns?

As with any new technology, as WAP became more understood, acceptable, and feasible, people began thinking of potential revenue-generating opportunities, which led to research and development funding. With more financing available, more discoveries were made, more advancements were accomplished, and the wireless Internet evolution was under way. Some call it the Internet's second phase; others coin it as the merger of the Internet and telecommunications, but whatever you call it, it's definitely here and it's a major step in wireless mobile Internet communications.

This chapter describes the basic components of WAP and its Internet integration components. First we provide an introduction to the WAP evolution, generations, and architecture, followed by a look at wireless networks, physical units, and WAP gateways. Then we'll detail the setup requirements for your own wireless development environment.

We do not pretend to present all aspects of WAP but simply to introduce you to the overall concepts in hopes of getting you developing as quickly as possible to be productive with this new technology.

What Is WAP?

Wireless Application Protocol is a method of global open wireless Internet standards for real-time communication of wireless mobile devices such as Web cellular phones,

Personal Digital Assistants (PDAs), and the Internet. WAP is not only a language but also a platform for development and interconnectivity.

WAP components are:

- Multiple programming languages such as Handheld Device Markup Language (HDML), which is really pre-WAP, and Wireless Markup Language (WML).

- Physical units or wireless devices also known as *Web Phones*, Web-enabled devices, or WAP devices built specifically with the ability to access the Internet. This additional built-in feature is called a *MicroBrowser*. Note that the primary purpose of the individual device, at this stage, is still to function as a telephone or PDA.

- Gateways that handle the transition of data from the wireless network through to the Internet network and vice versa.

- Software Developer toolKits (SDKs) for the development and testing phase of the WAP applications.

WAP Evolution

Mobility first came about from the telecommunications industry. It allowed individuals to communicate via wireless cellular phones, which gave us the ability to walk and talk—hence the term *mobility*.

The Internet infrastructure has also been around for some time. This infrastructure allows anyone with a computer and a modem to connect to any other computer with a modem and gives us the freedom to transfer or browse data from anywhere that is connected to the Internet. However, unless you have a wireless modem, the communication must be wire-based and hence only *portable*.

Mobility and portability are now easily possible through the use of WAP, which is the merging of these two industries and technologies. Through the use of wireless telecommunications and the Internet via wireless Internet devices, anyone can now access information anytime, anywhere.

With the world rushing toward a standardized telecommunication infrastructure, network, and protocol along with the ever ongoing increase in wireless device capacity, memory, and functionality, more people will be accessing the Internet via Web phones and PDAs than from any other method. While personal computers will always be our personal base stations at work or in our homes, wireless Internet technology will evolve into our everyday portable and mobile interconnectivity medium. The future potential is unlimited as it only has today's boundaries to overcome.

Growth Predictions

As seen in Figure 1.1, the forecasted number of cellular phone subscribers will increase enormously in the first half of the current decade. This will be due to several factors:

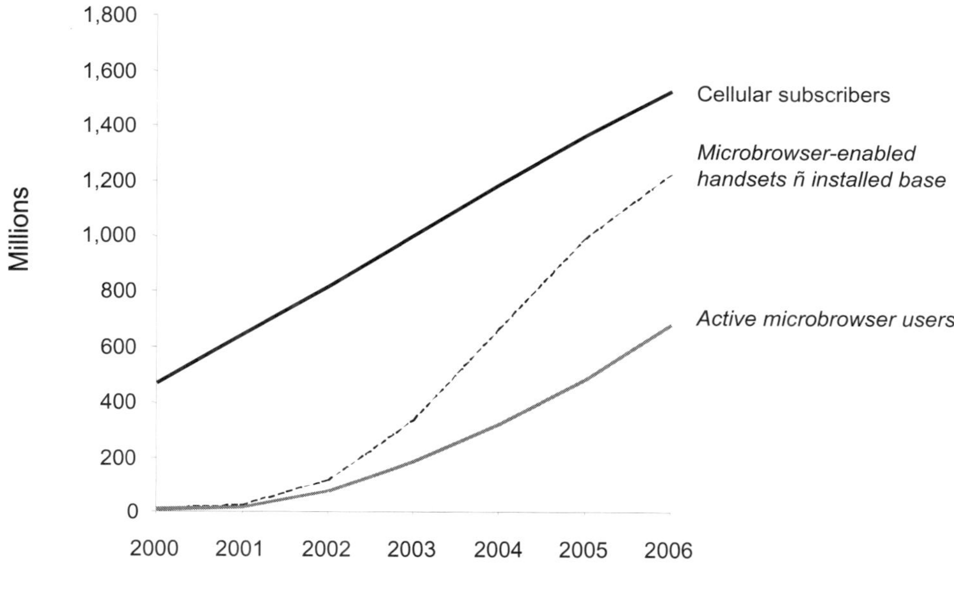

Source: Ovum (WAP/A)

Figure 1.1 Wireless subscribers.

first is the ongoing trend of individuals wanting to be connected or available whenever they wish, anytime, anywhere. The second factor is that many countries currently have poor telecommunication infrastructures.

Many people in third-world countries still do not have telephones, let alone cellular phones. Interestingly enough, telecommunications companies in these types of regions find it more cost efficient to simply erect cellular towers with relay base stations supplying wireless communications rather than laying the groundwork to install cables throughout their cities. The cost difference between erecting several cellular towers and base stations compared to telephone poles and wires throughout thousands of miles of undeveloped rural regions is considerable. Based on these facts and the population growth of many world regions, the number of cellular subscribers will dramatically increase in the coming years.

With the knowledge and foresight of this new wireless Internet technology growth, wireless device manufacturers are beginning to distribute cell phones with microbrowsers in hopes that many individuals will subscribe to the service. Of course there is a partnership between the microbrowser vendors, cell phone manufacturers, and the major cellular providers since they will all profit from this new technology. The number of people who will subscribe to the wireless Internet service via their cellular phones will far surpass the number of individuals currently accessing the Internet via personal computers.

Of course the applications available today are few, but we are in the infancy of the wireless Internet potential. In 10 years, many won't comprehend how we could have lived without wireless access to the Internet.

In the near future, we'll have the ability to contact others as well as have any information we desire at our fingertips. We'll carry our wireless mobile devices with us all day everywhere we go and have unlimited access to any Internet item. The only foreseeable problem will be with wireless network and physical device capacities.

With so many individuals accessing the Internet, will the cellular carriers be able to cope with peak access periods as Internet Service Providers (ISPs) do now? Will the physical unit processors be able to cope with the mass influx of information at our fingertips? Look at the personal desktop computer; every year and a half a new bigger and better CPU chip is released. Instead of megs, PCs now come with gigs. As it stands, the Internet has only really taken off in the last 5 years and look at what's happened to the typical home and work personal computer. Personally, I remember trying to justify the allocation of a 10-MB database only 8 years ago and now a gigabyte single database is not unusual. The processing power of the computer in my office today can easily replace the entire computer center of a typical company just 15 years ago. We've come a long way and the same thing will happen with wireless devices but at a much quicker pace. In 5 to 10 years, we'll have all the capabilities of our desktop computer on our cell phone or wireless device, as they'll be known.

Note: As I was writing this section, a news report on the radio mentioned a very interesting statistic. One out of five U.S. residents who wanted to learn more about the 2000 federal election between Gore and Bush obtained poll results and other information from the Internet, as compared to only 4 percent during the last election. That's an increase of Internet usage of over 600 percent in 4 years, which goes to show the amazing growth of this information age.

Wireless Generations

At some point during conversations about wireless networks, terms such as *2G*, *2.5G*, or *3G* are likely to pop up. So, what are they? Well each refers to a generation of advancements in wireless network capabilities and capacity. Each generation has higher speeds than the one before. With higher speeds comes the potential for more data (or voice) transmissions and more potential for bigger and better applications of wireless technology.

Phone companies began their existence on the concept of one person talking directly to another person. This is now called *real-time synchronous analog communications*. These analog transmissions are based on wave technology and are not that great for data transmissions since there can be many enroute errors due to geographic limitations and so on. The second evolution in the development of wireless technology is called *digital processing*, which is based on circuit switching and packet transmissions.

Think of wave technology as you and I simply having a face-to-face conversation where our voices are simply sound waves traveling back and forth as we speak. Think of digital technology kind of like having a conversation with a robot. You know, short bursts of speech: Hel-lo - my - name - is - Rob-bie - the - ro-bot. - Dan-ger - Dan-ger - Will - Rob-in-son. Now if the robotic conversation were sped up, it would sound much more like a regular wave (or voice) conversation. That's what digital technology is all about, well kind of, but you get the idea—right?

So, as two people carry on a conversation over a cellular phone, the conversation behind the scenes is broken up into a heck of a lot of little bursts called *chunks* and sent over the airwaves to the receiving party. Since data is not really voice but a bunch of data in a bunch of packets, the digital networks can easily handle both data transmission and voice conversations with fewer errors.

Today telecommunication networks involve wires, fiber optics, satellites, cellular towers, ground-relay stations, and much more. Still the main goal is communication, not only with personal conversations but also with data transmissions. Analog conversations are no longer the sole and main use of telephone networks. These days, the wires and airways contain more ongoing transmissions of data than of regular voice conversations. And of course the more data we get, the more data we want. The airwaves are pretty busy in this day and age, full of wireless conversations and data transmissions, and yet we want more capabilities to increase the number of transmissions we can perform. And we want those transmissions to be faster and more efficient than ever before. I want my information now, not in 3 minutes!

The following is a quick look at the evolution of wireless network generations:

The first generation (1G) of wireless services began back in the late seventies. It used analog technology and was strictly for voice usage. 1G uses single-band analog cellular and supports voice communication only.

The second generation (2G) of wireless services began in 1990 and is still around. 2G is a digital wireless network using mostly circuit switching. This means each call requires its own cell channel, which is known to be slow. 2G is more commonly known as Personal Communications Services (PCS) in the United States. PCS uses three competing technologies, which divide the airwaves to allow for more traffic. These are Code Division Multiple Access (CDMA), Time Division Multiple Access (TDMA), and Global System for Mobile Communications (GSM). More on these technologies a little later on. Europe and the United States both use GSM but the versions are incompatible, which is why a U.S. cell phone won't function in the United Kingdom. Japan uses Personal Digital Communications (PDC), which is a packet-switching technology whereby messages are split into packets of data and reassembled at their destination very similar to the Internet. Basically, 2G systems are digital with single-, dual-, or tri-mode phones capable of voice and data transmission.

The second and a half generation (2.5G) is still fairly new. This generation is completely based on packet switching, which saves space and increases transmission speeds. Upgrading from older generations to 2.5G is quicker and cheaper than going directly to 3G even though that is all the rage. Many carriers in

Europe and the United States will make this intermediate transition rather than spending large amounts of money to rebuild their infrastructures and go directly to 3G. Japan, however, does plan to go directly from 2G to 3G in 2001 or early 2002.

The third generation (3G) is supposed to become the world standard, thus allowing roaming anywhere. The problem is that it will cost billions of dollars to create the infrastructure and many carriers are reluctant to spend or are incapable of spending such amounts. 3G offers speeds up to 2Mbps, which would allow for great high-quality wireless audio and video. The United States is supposed to attempt the implementation of 3G in 2003, while European carriers are already bidding on 3G licenses. 3G is multimode and multiband.

Fourth generation (4G) is still a long way off in the future. Software-defined radio, as some call it, encompasses all standards everywhere and will hopefully be available in 2010.

WAP Architecture

To look at WAP architecture, it's a good idea to know a bit of history about the cellular industry. In the United States, one of the first cellular services was launched in Chicago in 1978 and a year later in 1979 the first commercial cellular service started in Tokyo. Full deployment of cellular services in the United States did not really start until 1984.

Cellular technology allows a telephone to become mobile by using 800-MHz FM radio airwaves rather than conventional phone lines to transmit conversations. A cellular network is comprised of individual coverage areas called *cells*, each with its own *tower* or *base station* as it's called since the tower is controlled by the station at its base. Geographic coverage of multiple cells is possible by calls being handed off from one cell site (or base station or antenna) to another automatically via a special relaying process. Each base station is connected to the regular telephone network (land based) via a Mobile Telephone Switching Office (MTSO), which converts the radio signals to a landline network or another cellular network and hence on to the customer's phone. If a subscriber travels beyond the operator's coverage area (meaning the cellular provider has no towers servicing the area) and makes a call, another carrier will provide service. This is called *roaming* (or *no service* if no other provider picks up the signal).

WAP requires a wireless network, consisting of cellular providers, a WAP gateway, along with special cellular phones. This is just one of the basic requirements for an operational WAP system. Of course Internet access is also required as is some sort of middleware to connect these two worlds, which is where the WAP gateway fits in. Think of it this way: the cellular network speaks one language, the Internet speaks another language, and the gateway is the interpreter and translator.

Figure 1.2 shows the high-level components of the entire architecture from end to end.

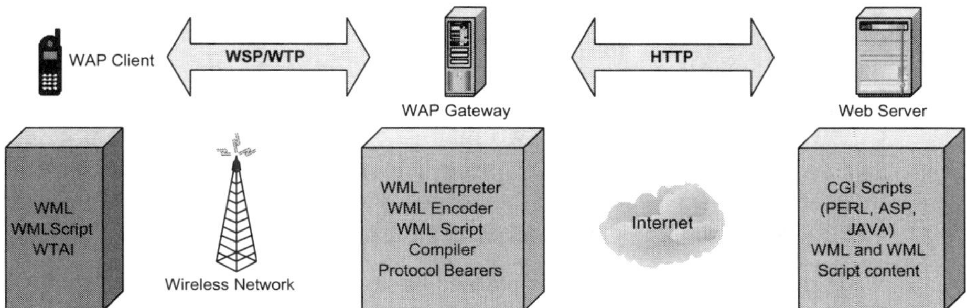

Figure 1.2 WAP architecture.

WAP Stack

The wireless application protocol was created in response to the need for wireless Internet communication standards and for the need to deliver extended services (content and applications) to technologically limited mobile devices.

WAP was designed based on the existing Web OSI model of layers and protocols but it has its own distinct structures. These WAP protocols and layers are designed to overcome mobile device and cellular infrastructure limitations such as poor data quality and reliability (latency) mostly due to transmission problems, latency, and low bandwidth.

Figure 1.3 shows the similarities and differences between the WAP and Web architecture layers.

The WAP layered architecture provides a scalable application development environment where each layer can be individually accessed. Let's take a quick look at each of these layers.

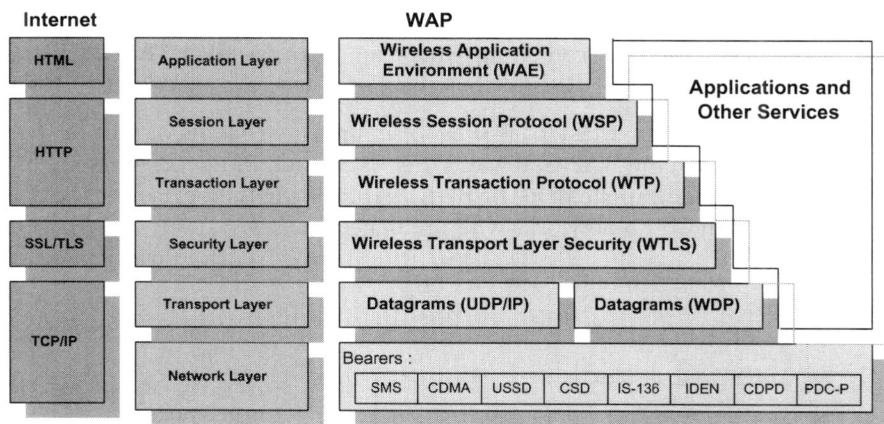

Figure 1.3 Internet to WAP mappings.

Wireless Application Environment (WAE)

This layer is WAP application specific. The *Wireless Application Environment* (WAE) specifies requirements for the WAP language such as text and image formats. The application environment contains two major components: (1) a markup language, in this case WML, used by application programmers to provide a device-independent user interface and (2) a scripting language, WMLScript, which allows programmers to embed executable logic in their applications.

WAP-enabled devices are WAP enabled because of the WAE client. The WAE client conforms to WAP guidelines because of its three components: (1) WAE User agent (microbrowser), (2) WTA User agent (best described as an interface to the physical phone functions such as calling and answering), and (3) the WAP Stack (WAP protocols to connect to the WAP gateway).

Together the WAE client provides the following:

- Wireless Markup Language (WML)-a language optimized for WAP-enabled devices yet similar to HTML (used mostly in the Internet "wired" world)
- WMLScript-wireless scripting language, similar to JavaScript
- Wireless Telephony Application (WTA, WTAI)-telephony services and programming interfaces
- Connectivity protocols to connect to the gateway

Wireless Session Protocol (WSP)

The *Wireless Session Protocol* (WSP) layer is equivalent to HTTP in the Internet world and offers two protocols: connection session services and connectionless session services. The connection session service basically provides a means to manage a session, making it possible to talk or transmit data between the client (WAP device) and server (WAP gateway). The connection session handles communication interrupts and capability negotiation and can be suspended and later resumed. The connectionless session is a thin layer that WAE uses when there's no need for reliable delivery of messages.

The most important task of WSP is to set up a connection, or session, between a wireless client and the WAP Gateway. Wireless Session Protocols are built on services suited for browsing applications (WSP/B). Protocols in this segment of WAP are optimized for low-bandwidth networks with prolonged latency.

The following functionality is provided by WSP:

- HTTP/1.1 functionality and semantics in a compact over-the-air encoding
- Long-lived session state
- Session suspend and resume
- A common facility for reliable and unreliable data pushes

Wireless Transaction Protocol (WTP)

The *Wireless Transaction Protocol* (WTP) runs over the datagram service and functions as a lightweight transaction-oriented protocol that is suitable for implementation in mobile devices. This protocol operates on secure and nonsecure wireless datagram networks.

WTP provides the following three classes of asynchronous transaction services:

- Unreliable one-way requests (message sent without a reply).
- Reliable one-way requests (message sent and an acknowledgment message is returned).
- Reliable two-way request-reply transactions (message sent, got it message returned, ok got the got it message sent back).

Wireless Transport Layer Security (WTLS)

Wireless Transport Layer Security (WTLS) is a security protocol based on the industry-standard *Transport Layer Security* (TLS) protocol TLS formerly known as *Secure Sockets Layer* (SSL). WTLS is intended for use with the WAP transport protocol and has been optimized for use over low-bandwidth communication channels. WTLS can be activated (and is therefore optional) in the same way as a Web browser uses HTTPS as the protocol instead of HTTP.

WTLS provides the following features:

- **Data integrity.** WTLS provides a mechanism to ensure data integrity at the communication endpoints (between the terminal and application server).
- **Privacy.** Encrypted code can be seen but decrypted code cannot.
- **Authentication.** WTLS contains facilities to establish the authenticity of the terminal and application server.

Wireless Datagram Protocol (WDP)

The Transport Layer Protocol is referred to as the *Wireless Datagram Protocol* (WDP). This layer provides a consistent interface between the higher layers of the WAP architecture and the multiple wireless networks that are available. Because of WDP, other layers are able to function independently of the underlying wireless network. This is done by adapting the transport layer to specific bearer features that are used to connect to the network. The Internet's equivalent to WDP is TCP/IP.

Bearer Networks

The WAP protocol suite is designed to operate over a variety of bearer services such as SMS, CDMA, CSD, and USSD packet data. Each bearer offers its own level of quality of service with respect to delays, throughput, and error rate. The WAP protocol suite is designed to tolerate or compensate for these differing levels of service. The list of supported bearers will change over time with new bearers being added as the wireless market evolves.

Wireless Networks

There are many types of wireless networks within countries and among countries around the world. A big problem facing the many cellular providers all over the world is the incompatibility among the wireless network infrastructures. As it stands, European phones can't operate on U.S. networks and vice versa. When cellular providers laid out the groundwork for their networks, the architects and designers never dreamed of one day having to worry about the compatibility issues between their networks and cellular networks in foreign countries halfway around the globe.

To summarize the evolution of the wireless networks, as mentioned in the wireless evolution section, the first generation (1G) began in the late seventies and was only analog. 2G began in the early nineties, and its main characteristic is the use of digital voice encoding.

In our efforts to understand the main incompatibility issues, we must first understand the basics of each type of wireless network available as explained next.

Analog (1G)

The analog cellular system, called the *Advanced Mobile Phone Service* (AMPS), was the first wireless system in commercial use. The downside to analog is that these cellular transmissions, or networks, have relatively poor sound quality and offer few features such as call waiting and voice mail. Analog cellular calls can be intercepted, pirated, and are also prone to lost or incomplete calls due to congestion and interference.

Other analog systems include *Enhanced Total Access Communications* (ETACS) and Nordic Mobile Telephone System (NMT). All three analog systems have been around longer, are more established, and have more coverage than digital networks, but digital is quickly catching up.

AMPS operators in the United States include AirTouch, AT&T Wireless, Verizon Mobile, Southwestern Bell, GTE Wireless, BellSouth Mobility, Ameritech, and Western Wireless.

TDMA (2G)

The next evolution in cellular was digital technology that changes the human voice into computer language. Digital is more efficient than conventional analog because technically it handles three calls for every connection over the network via circuit switching and allows for data transmission.

Digital technologies such as *Time Division Multiple Access* (TDMA), which is built upon the AMPS (analog) framework, adds capacity to the system by letting multiple users share a radio channel without interference or sacrifice of voice quality. TDMA service is available at 800 and 1900 MHz. Digital at 800 MHz offers much improved sound quality over analog on the same bandwidth, as well as better security and calling features such as caller ID. A TDMA phone works in both analog and digital so that if digital is unavailable, the phone automatically switches to analog, hence the term *dual-mode*. TDMA is the dominant standard in the United States today and in Latin America, New Zealand, parts of Russia, and in some Asian-Pacific countries.

TDMA operators in the United States include AT&T Wireless, BellSouth Mobility, Southwestern Bell, and AirTouch.

CDMA (2G)

Code Division Multiple Access (CDMA), first deployed in 1995, also offers both digital and analog service. Like other digital networks CDMA serves multiple users on a single radio channel. Technically, it differs from TDMA in that CDMA channels are about six times wider and the system assigns each subscriber a unique code. To ensure that enough information gets through to accurately describe the voice, each coded bit is repeated many times, thus ensuring parity. Think of this as raid technology for the network. With CDMA, when calls are relayed from one cell site to another, there are potentially fewer noticeable interruptions.

CDMA operators include AirTouch, Verizon Mobile, GTE Wireless, Ameritech, and U.S.Cellular.

GSM (2G)

Global Standard for Mobile (GSM) communication is the most widely subscribed standard for wireless systems. GSM is digital and encodes, transmits, and decodes bursts of information in a fraction of the time required to produce the sound. Eight subscribers can share time on the same channel because GSM is much more efficient at sharing the radio frequencies. GSM permits advanced encryption techniques, strongly securing calls against eavesdropping. GSM phones use a removable *Subscriber Identity Module* (SIM) card containing the phone's number and subscriber account information. GSM transmits data and fax messages at speeds up to 9600 bps (bytes per second).

- GSM 800 MHz is Europe's main digital network, and is also used in Asian-Pacific countries.
- GSM 1900 MHz is used in Europe and Asia but has not been so widely adopted as GSM 800.
- GSM 1900 MHz is the GSM system used mainly in the Americas and Canada.

GSM operators include Pacific Bell Wireless, Omnipoint, VoiceStream, and Powertel.

PCS (2G)

Personal Communications Service (PCS) is digital transmissions at 1900 MHz. PCS-capable phones are usually small, lightweight, offer excellent security, and have longer battery life. PCS is available on TDMA, CDMA, and GSM networks.

PCS operators include Sprint PCS, PrimeCO, and U.S. West.

Tri-mode

Although not a wireless network, it is often spoken of as if it were. Don't be fooled: Tri-mode refers to the ability of a mobile handset to function on three bands: 800 MHz analog or AMPS, 800 MHz TDMA, and 1900 MHz TDMA. This results in seamless uninterrupted service when the user travels from one part of the country or region to another or from rural to urban settings. The phone will still function even when the underlying wireless network changes.

GPRS (2G)

General Packet Radio Service (GPRS) networks and phones has hit the wireless markets. GPRS is called the "always connected" technology and provides higher bandwidths in the range of 171.2 kbps.

We calculate 171.2 kbps from the result of eight timeslots, which is the number of channels on each frequency in GSM, multiplied by the bit rate when using coding schema 4 (CS-4), which is 21.4 kbps. Mind you, eight timeslots in one direction, while feasible, is not probable as the terminals then need to have more than one transceiver since one transceiver can only handle up to four timeslots in one direction. Also, CS-3 and CS-4 coding schemas are not really likely to be implemented in the current networks since many existing infrastructure upgrades would be required. So, using a CS-2 schema with four timeslots, we get a maximum throughput of 53.6 kbps. But chances are that transmissions would only reach 20 to 30 kbps. Since resources are shared, providers may choose different network settings, and retransmissions would clog the bandwidth.

You may have heard of the *always connected* concept and how great it will be. This means that once the phone is turned on, it is *always* connected to the Internet. No hassles with dropped Internet connections or having to redial and wait for a new connection to be established. An important part of the concept is that since the system is packet based (data sent in short bursts), the user will theoretically only be charged on a per-packet basis rather than flat connection time rates. This means more everyday usage of the wireless Internet technology since service charges are based on the amount of packets sent and received rather than overall connection time. This allows users the freedom to relax and take all the time they want to create or read emails since they only pay to send and receive information. Japan initiated this general idea of charging only for packets sent or received, and their iMode technology literally boomed in only 1 short year.

This method is very similar to the 2.5G EDGE network configuration.

EDGE (2.5G)

Enhanced Data rates for Global Evolution (EDGE) is a further enhancement of GSM. Although based on GSM networks, it offers speeds approaching 3G standards. Since EDGE is GSM based, many carriers are making the transition from 2G to 2.5G since it only requires an upgrade to the existing network rather than a complete infrastructure change, which could cost millions and possibly billions of dollars. EDGE is based on packet-switching networks as described in GPRS and allows for overall higher bandwidth with expectations to reach 384 kbps.

WCDMA (3G)

Wideband Code Division Multiple Access (WCDMA) (or IMT-2000) is an International Telecommunications Union (ITU) standard derived from code-division multiple access (CDMA). This new technology offers much higher data communication speeds to mobile devices than is currently available today.

WCDMA can support mobile voice, images, data, video, and other multimedia transmission at up to 2 Mbps (local access mode) or 384 Kbps (wide area access mode). The input signals are digitized and transmitted in coded, spread-spectrum mode over a broad range of frequencies.

UMTS (3G)

Universal Mobile Telecommunication System (UMTS) is expected to reach 2Mbps—imagine what you could do with that much transfer potential! This will allow for images, audio, video, television, and much more on the individual wireless devices.

UMTS is the European implementation of the 3G wireless phone system. It provides service in the 2-GHz frequency and will offer standardization for global roaming and personalized features. Designed as an evolutionary system for GSM network operators, expectations are for 3G to be available, most likely starting in Europe, by 2003.

Network Statistics

To give you a better understanding of current wireless network availability and usage, Figure 1.4 shows the prevalent network infrastructures currently in use within the United States.

WAP Devices

A WAP-enabled device is a portable mobile wireless device containing a WAP microbrowser and capable of accessing the Internet via a cellular network.

**U.S. Subscribers by Technology
from Ericsson.**

GSM	4.7%
CDMA	12.0%
TDMA	13.8%
AMPS	69.5%

Figure 1.4 U.S. subscriber usage.

Popular WAP-enabled devices are Web phones, PDAs, and other types of devices. Web phones are cellular phones with special microbrowsers built into the phone itself. You can't use just any cellular phone to access the Internet since not all phones have the special WAP microbrowser. Microbrowsers are basically simple Internet Web browsers designed and built specifically for these devices. We're all familiar with Web browsers such as Netscape or Microsoft's Internet Explorer used on personal computers; microbrowsers basically do the same thing for cellular phones and PDAs. There are several types of microbrowsers on the market with the two most popular being from Openwave and the other from Nokia. Web phones usually have only one microbrowser built into it (except MME), and given this restriction it's understandable that each microbrowser vendor has made partnerships with cellular phone manufacturers to include their microbrowser on specific phone models. Although one microbrowser is available per unit, that microbrowser may very well be able to handle multiple languages, for example, HDML or WML.

Openwave has its Up.Browser microbrowser and Nokia has its own proprietary version. Each has its own flavor of WAP, as we'll see later.

Physical Units

Figure 1.5 illustrates some of the Web phones available in the marketplace that use Openwave's Up.Browser microbrowser.

Figure 1.6 shows two popular Nokia Web phones; of course Nokia has many more models. Notice the roller button in the center of the 7190 model beneath the display window; this is used for scrolling through the information displayed on the screen. The keypad buttons are hidden underneath the bottom half of the phone, which unfolds.

The second image is the Nokia 9210 communicator. This phone is more of a James Bond device. Not only does it function as a cell phone but when flipped on its side, it opens like a personal organizer with a screen and keypad. The screen is huge, taking up almost the entire device width. Functionality on this unit is quite good and with a keypad resembling a small PC keyboard, it is easier to type in messages than with typical Web cellular phones.

Not only are Web phones popular but so are PDAs. There are many WAP-enabled PDAs and Figure 1.7 shows two popular units with built-in microbrowsers. We've included the Blackberry unit and the popular Palm VII model from Palm, Inc.

Initially Openwave (formerly known as Phone.com and prior to that as Unwired Planet), in cooperation with cellular phone manufacturers and cellular carriers, created this new wireless Internet portal. Openwave created their own microbrowser and managed to have it included in the physical cellular phone unit directly with the

Figure 1.5 Web phones with Up.Browser microbrowser.

Figure 1.6 Nokia Web phones using Nokia microbrowser.

cooperation of the cellular phone manufacturers. The third component was a cellular carrier that incorporated the WAP gateway into its network, and a fully functional wireless mobile WAP system was created. The important point here is that Openwave was the only supplier of microbrowser and gateway technology at the time.

Every month more and more cellular phone manufacturers are adding microbrowsers to their phone units. See Figure 1.1 for an insight into microbrowser-enabled cellular phone statistics. It's almost getting to the point where all newly built cellular phones have microbrowsers included. The idea is that if a phone has the microbrowser, individuals will purchase the unit specifically for the included feature. The software vendors creating the microbrowsers are prospering, the manufacturers have new selling

Figure 1.7 PDAs with microbrowsers.

points, and the carriers are receiving new business from the increase in airtime from individuals accessing the Internet. Everyone is profiting.

Carriers are generating revenues from this new technology because individuals must still use valuable airtime when accessing the Internet via the Internet feature on Web phones. Currently, as long as the unit is connected, the charge is the same as if the person was making a cellular call. With this new WAP technology, if the user surfs the Net on a cell phone, the carriers will make quite a bit more money since the user is using up airtime. So when purchasing a wireless Internet subscription plan, make sure it includes as much free airtime as possible for one specific price per month.

Microbrowsers

As previously mentioned, there are various types of microbrowsers on the market but we'll only have a look at the top two: Up.Browser from Openwave and Nokia's proprietary version. In Figure 1.5, which only represents phones with Up.Browser microbrowsers, a Nokia model is included. Some Nokia phones include the Up.Browser microbrowser rather than their own proprietary Nokia microbrowser. In North America, the majority of Web phones use Up.Browser from Openwave.

Different manufacturers supply microbrowsers each with their own WAP abilities. For instance, if a WAP program, called a *deck*, were to run on Web phones using Up.Browser, you might see a completely different representation than if the same deck were executed on a phone that has a Nokia microbrowser. And it isn't unusual to see the same program run on a different phone model from the same manufacturer and produce different results. You can see why it's so difficult for developers to tune their programs to have the same functionality on many different Web phone models.

The WAP deck (program) in Figure 1.8 was executed on many different Web phones (well, actually on different versions of SDKs, which will be explained later).

Notice the screen results on the phones in Figure 1.9 and how they differ. All these displays were created from the exact same WML program.

Microbrowser Versions

Microbrowsers, just like Web browsers, have different versions with the latest usually able to handle more features than the previous ones. Some Web phones can only handle WML while others can interpret both HDML and WML. It's important to know what microbrowser version is on your phone, especially if you're a developer. You wouldn't want to develop an application that can only function on the very latest microbrowser version, which is probably not the most common version on Web phones in the marketplace.

Figure 1.10 shows a quick reference chart from Openwave for Up.Browser. (The diagram still mentions the old Phone.com name.)

```
<?xml version="1.0"?>
<!DOCTYPE    WML        PUBLIC "-//WAPFORUM/DTD WML 1.1/EN" "http://www.wapfo-
rum.org/DTD/wml 1.1.xml">
<wml>
  <card id="home" title="My Menu">
   <p>
     <select name="type" title="Choose a topic">
     <option value="automobile" onpick="automobile.wml"> Automobile </option>
     <option value="bookstore" onpick="bookstore.wml"> Bookstore </option>
     <option value="contacts" onpick="contacts.wml">Contacts</option>
     <option value="financial" onpick="financial.wml">Financials </option>
     <option value="flight" onpick="flight.wml">Flight Info</option>
     <option value="goto" onpick="goto.wml>Goto URL...</option>
     </select>
   </p>
   </card>
</wml>
```

Figure 1.8 Simple WAP deck.

Notice in the Up.Browser versions that HDML is generally available on all WML Up.Browsers. This means that developers don't have to worry too much about upgrading their existing HDML applications to WML since the Up.Browser microbrowsers are upwardly compatible.

Technical and Design Limitations

Buying a cellular phone is no longer just a quick purchase. Individuals are interested not only in a simple cellular phone but also in all the possible features, including Internet access. With added functionality, the buyer must wade through the many physical unit issues, especially device limitations. Even after deciding on these physical device issues, the buyer is faced with wireless network configurations and limitations from the carrier.

Of course, everyone wants a Web phone that operates in his or her area as well as in neighboring regions without having to worry about roaming costs. Today, with people traveling more often, buyers are also interested in compatibility issues in using their phones in neighboring regions as well as in other countries. You certainly don't want to buy a Web phone in Chicago and find out it doesn't function on your monthly business trips to the United Kingdom.

As this technology continues to grow, wireless devices will soon be treated like computer software. Buy one device today and upgrade it tomorrow. Every year or two you'll be wondering if you should junk your existing phone and purchase the latest version. Wireless technology is definitely becoming more interesting.

OpenWave UP.Browser

Nokia Microbrowser

Motorola Microbrowser

Ericsson Microbrowser

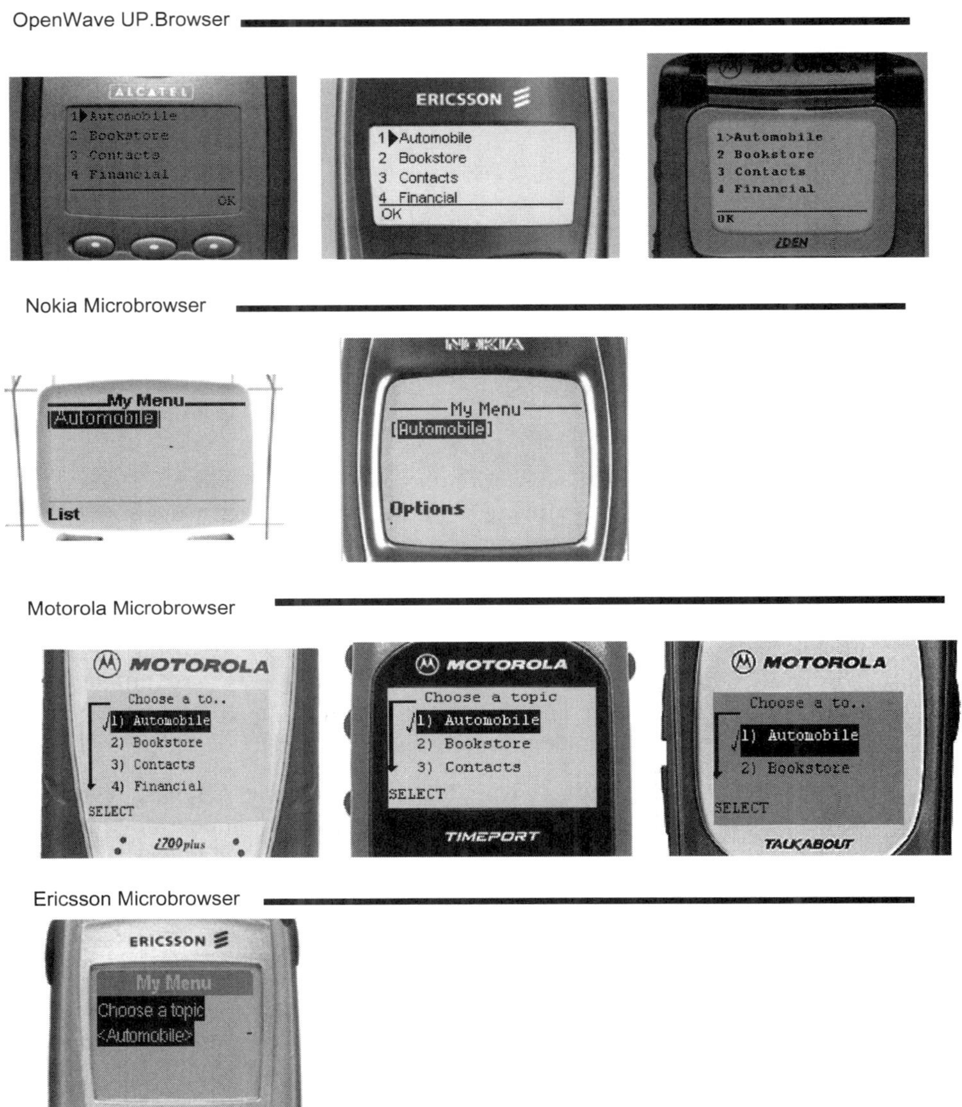

Figure 1.9 Microbrowser examples.

Physical Devices

The limitations of Web phones are straightforward. First, the physical size is important. We don't want to have a huge device that requires its own straps to carry, and yet we still want all possible functionalities. The big problem here is battery size and life span and therefore device power consumption. With increased device usage from Web surf-

Vendor Browser	Browser Version	HDML 3.0	WML 1.1	WML 1.1 with Phone.com Extensions	WMLScript 1.1
Phone.com UP.Browser	4.x	Yes, via UP.Link translation service	Yes	Yes Recommended	Yes Recommended
Phone.com UP.Browser	3.1	Yes Recommended	Yes, via UP.Link translation service	No	No
Phone.com UP.Browser	3.0	Yes Recommended	No	No	No
Other	Any	No	Yes Recommended	No	Yes Recommended

Figure 1.10 Up.Browser versions.

ing, the batteries must still allow for hours and hours of usability. The problem with this is that batteries must be quite big to allow for such lengthy usage, which also affects the unit's size. This then propagates to a weight issue. We all definitely want small, lightweight cellular phones with all possible functionality.

The next limitation to overcome is the unit's small display window. Most cellular phones have very small display windows that only show three, four, or five lines of text. This really limits the application possibilities. It becomes very difficult to show logos, many options on a menu, and so on. The user ends up continuously scrolling up and down menus, which is time consuming and frustrating.

But the most limiting and annoying factor to overcome is typing. With the exception of most PDAs and the Nokia communicators, typing almost anything on a cellular phone is very difficult. Keypads on these phones were designed for numeric input, not to type out a long Web address. To enter a number, simply press the number button but to enter the letter C, the keypad button must be pressed three times, and if it's done too fast, you must start all over again. Don't get me started on typos. If you suddenly realize you mistyped a word, for example, five, six, or more letters back, you must backspace to the typo, losing all input from the error position to your current spot, and then you have to retype everything over again (hopefully with no new errors). Hopefully in the near future technology will advance to the point where we'll be able to simply speak to the device rather than manually type input. The speech-to-text interpreter on the device would accept our commands and dictation and convert it directly in the device.

Another technical limitation to consider is the device memory or cache size. Currently, most Web phones can only handle a little over 1 kb of data, but this does vary considerably among devices. With this limitation, programmers are constantly worried about program size. If the program is larger than the phone's cache size, the phone simply won't be able to load the program and the device will receive an error. The end result is that the applications will not function and you potentially will have lost another customer. This is why we recommend that every HDML or WML program should be no larger than 1200 bytes. Make menus small and don't include many cards in one deck. The software development tools may function but the real physical phones might not, so beware.

Networks

The main differences between Web applications accessed via a personal computer and a WAP application via Web phone are bandwidth, latency, and connection reliability. This is apart from the obvious graphical user interface (GUI) and other Web side features.

Current available bandwidth for WAP devices is quite low with transfer rates of 9600 bps and in the best of scenarios 14.4Kbps. This limits the type of data being transferred to the devices and back to the networks to mostly character-based information. However, with the coming 2.5 and 3G technology, potential rates will be much faster, allowing the transfer of images, audio, and streaming video to be more common.

With data traveling not only over the Internet infrastructure but now over the cellular networks and airwaves to the phone, latency issues have arisen. The data must now travel over more networks, switches, and gateways than before. When a person moves from one cell region to another, there is latency. When transmissions are interrupted, there is latency due to recovery. There are many reasons for this problem but advancements in technology will evolve reducing many latency limitations, allowing quicker transmissions of data to and from the WAP devices. Currently, latency varies from as short as 100 milliseconds up to several seconds, which may seem like an eternity when waiting around for 2 to 3 seconds every time you press a selection button.

Connection reliability also plays a role. Low connection stability depends on the user's location relative to wireless network. For example, you may lose your cellular connection if you're in the basement of a large concrete building, traveling in a remote region, driving between two high hills, or in a tunnel. Unpredictable availability is also related to the geographic location of the wireless user. While in the large cities you are almost guaranteed a good connection, but rural areas may not be as well serviced. Again, wireless network and infrastructure will improve in the future improving connection reliability.

Content Limitations

From the WAP device content point of view, there are many issues and limitations.

First, with all the technical and design issues, many WAP sites on the Web are not compatible with all phone models and microbrowsers. In America, many developers are creating their sites in HDML, which will function on Up.Browser but not on the Nokia microbrowser. Other developers are creating content specifically designed for Nokia with completely different functionality on Up.Browsers, which many times simply won't function at all. The trick here is to develop applications with just the basics and test on all development toolkits available. Remember, your content is available wherever someone has Internet access via a wireless Internet device. This means that people in China, the United Kingdom, Italy, South Africa, the United States, or wherever can all access your application and so it must function on as many devices as possible around the globe.

But the largest content limitation is when carriers who sell Web phones specifically block Internet surfing on their systems. When you purchase a Web phone, the Internet access portion usually has a predefined menu to select from. There may be weather, news, email, horoscope, or whatever on the menus all supplied freely by specific developers in partnership with the carrier. The good part is the Web phone is delivered with existing content; the bad part is it might be a *walled garden*. This is when the carrier doesn't allow the user to surf the Internet. There is no menu item or feature on the phone allowing you to type in a specific WAP site unavailable on the default menu.

Security Issues

Since WAP devices are wireless and function over cellular airwaves, there are also mobile security issues. Is the content that travels from the Internet to the cellular system, over the airwaves to the physical device and back again, really secure?

Figure 1.11 shows the flow of information throughout a wireless application. The Internet portion is as usual with Secure Socket Layer (SSL) security. However, this is now only half the story. In the wireless world, data must now pass over the airwaves to the cellular phone and back again, which involves more security via some type of data encryption. The security used for WAP between the device and the WAP gateway is Wireless Transport Layer Security (WTLS). As with HTTPS, WTLS is optional and therefore must be explicitly coded to take effect.

Future

In the future, networks are going to be more reliable with much higher "delivery" speeds to the wireless device allowing images, audio streams, and video streams. Geographic coverage will be much wider, allowing the device to function in more regions. Devices will be much more powerful. Remember the personal computer evolution. Not so long ago the Commodore-64, Amiga, and Sincler ZX with 48 to 64 Kb of memory were the height of personal computing and look at us now. Memory, CPU speed, and processing power in the actual wireless devices will all increase in the near future and will continue to regularly do so.

The most important change in the near future will be the standardization at all levels within this technology, especially from the major cellular carriers. Wireless devices will become our most used method of performing financial and trading transactions, which will lead to much advancement. New content will drive progress, as will higher versions of software as shown in Figure 1.12. Higher versions of WAP will bring about more

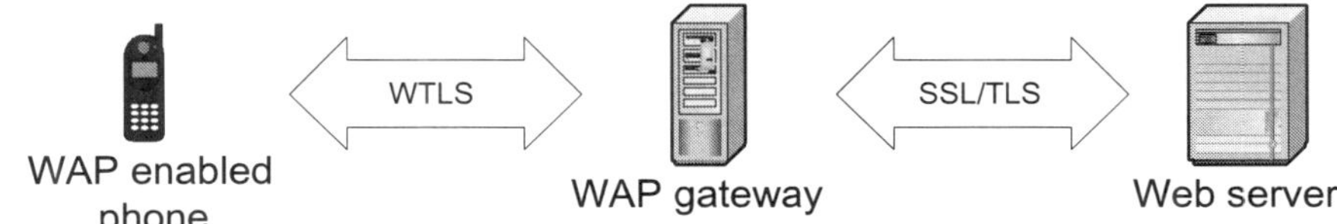

Figure 1.11 Security.

functionality, which in itself will allow more content features and the circle will continue to feed itself.

WAP Gateways

WAP gateways are vendor specific. Normally you will not be required to set up a gateway and if you do, the vendor documentation should definitely be referenced. If you are a WAP application developer, like most people in the WAP world, you won't have to know too much about WAP gateways but you should be aware of what they are and have a general understanding of how they function.

What Is a WAP Gateway?

A *WAP gateway* is software installed, usually, on a dedicated server located somewhere between the wireless network and the content server (WAP application server, Internet,

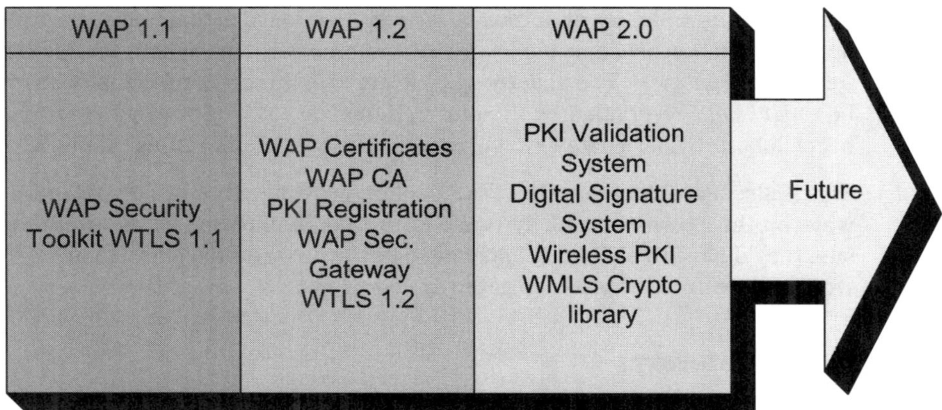

Figure 1.12 WAP versions.

etc.). Its purpose is to facilitate a connection between the Internet network with the wireless network so that WAP devices can (indirectly) access the Internet and therefore access WAP applications on Web servers.

Sometimes the WAP application, rather than being on a Web server, is located on the same server as the WAP gateway. In this scenario, many call the WAP gateway a *WAP server*. A WAP server could also include billing systems, development tools, and other application-based functions.

Reasons for merging both onto one server might be for a corporate Intranet or for security concerns. With both servers acting as one, the WTLS and SSL security conversion remains within the same server at the client's side (actually the same memory region), which minimizes potential security vulnerabilities. In a regular two-distinct server setup, the security from the WAP device must be converted for transmission over the Internet to the WAP application server. This security is encrypted on the device, decrypted on the WAP gateway, and again encrypted on the same gateway before sending it over the Internet. Having the decryption and encryption on the WAP gateway leaves room for potential security infringements since the firm owning the machine can see all the decrypted data.

Types of Gateways

There are several possible reasons for having a WAP gateway. First, as just mentioned, you may be a corporation very aware of security and hence want to control security issues. Second, perhaps a large organization wants to create its own wireless mobile Intranet. A third purpose could be to create a WAP gateway portal in the same sense as a regular Web search engine like Yahoo. Another method could be from a cellular carrier, which is by far the most common setup.

Private Gateways

As in the first example, a specific corporation or institution may wish to provide its own content for any number of purposes. We just mentioned a common security concern for large corporations such as banks or m-commerce ventures, which would be one reason for a private gateway. The underlying problem with this scenario is that Web phones must be *individually* reconfigured to point to the private WAP gateway rather than the original cellular provider's gateway, which would be the default setting on the WAP device.

This is also a problem for other WAP content providers that want to position their gateways on their own network systems. Each time Web phone users want to access that site, they'd have to choose the specific gateway on their devices. Hopefully, the device would allow for multiple WAP gateway selections.

Public Gateways

These are similar to private gateway content providers but are set up for the general public. Public WAP gateways are out there (www.waptunnel.com) but again this requires that the WAP device be reconfigured to point to the specific gateway. If you plan your business venture on public gateways, you may want to take a second job because you will need additional revenue. The reason is the wireless Internet is still young, and it's one thing to get the end users to use your WAP site but quite another to get them to reconfigure their personal phones to use your WAP gateway. Then again, I bet someone said this about Yahoo and AltaVista 10 years ago!

If your WAP application is specific for, say, a fleet of delivery trucks, you could distribute specifically reconfigured WAP devices to those drivers. These devices would then default to your WAP gateway. The same idea could be used for small tourist regions or shopping malls. These devices could be configured to view specific shopping mall store advertisements, specials, information, etc.

Network Providers

By far the most common WAP gateway setup is by the cellular network operator who handles all the specifics. If you purchase a Web phone from one provider, that phone will be configured to use that provider's specific WAP gateway only.

This can be a good thing or a bad thing, depending on the provider. The great part is that the WAP device is usually ready to go. Simply purchase the phone, subscribe to the service, and WAP menu and content are immediately available. The bad part is while some phones do allow for multiple gateway connections, consider your WAP phone dedicated to your provider and therefore bound to its default WAP menu and content. As mentioned in the Content Limitations section earlier, if the provider has no area for the end user to manually enter a specific WAP site on the Web phone, the user is locked into using only the content provided. Imagine if you could only access Web sites found on Yahoo; they're good but not that good, which is why Web browsers have the free-hand URL address line.

What Does a WAP Gateway Do?

The main purpose behind a WAP gateway is to connect the wireless network and the Internet. While there are many steps involved, the basics are from the wireless WAP device to the WAP application on the Web server via the WAP gateway. See the Glossary for acronym definitions:

- The WAP device sends a WSP request for a specified WAP application, connecting to the WAP gateway by using one of the bearer services. Bearer service is the wireless connectivity service. The Internet uses TCP/IP and the wireless world uses UDP/IP, SMS, USSD, or any IP bearer such as CSD or GPRS.

- The WAP gateway:

    Converts the WAP device WSP request to an HTTP format request

    Serves as adapter between WDP used in WAP environment and TCP protocol used in Web world

> Translates WTLS security encryption used in WAP world to SSL security used on the Web side

- On the way back from the Internet to the WAP device, the WAP application sends ASCII WML code to the WAP gateway for conversion to binary (compressed) format for transmission to the WAP device.

- The HTTP request is sent over the Internet to the proper Web server having the WAP application. Connection to the Internet is done by using any of the common Internet connectivity methods (dial-up, ISDN, Frame Relay, ATM).

The gateway also encodes (compresses) WML content for more efficient use of the wireless network bandwidth by reducing the size and number of packets traveling over the network. The gateway compiles WMLScript on behalf of the WAP browser relieving the browser from this CPU-intensive task.

Some gateways also provide additional features such as the mobile device specifics (subscriber's telephone number, geographic location, etc.). In some cases, the gateways are also used to collect billing information, which can be a great service to the WAP application partner. The Ericsson gateway provides such a feature where Charging Data Records (CDR) are created on the gateway machine.

Server Environment Setup

For a WAP application, there's not much to set up on the application Web server other than the *Multipurpose Internet Mail Extensions* (MIME) types. MIME types define data formats sent over the Internet. They were originally created for sending electronic mail over the Internet.

To send information over the Internet, each HTTP response must have a content type defined. The content type is the MIME type value. When the receiving WAP gateway receives a response with a valid content type, it knows how to handle the data within the data file. If the gateway receives an unknown content type, it doesn't know how to process the information and sends an "Invalid content type" error message to the WAP device, which is what the user ends up seeing.

The WML data file (called *program* or *deck*) is sent from the application Web server. The file's extension is then compared to entries on that sending Web server. If the .wml extension is found, the HTTP response content type variable is automatically created with that extension's associated MIME type. If the extension is not found, no content type value is set and the receiving server (WAP gateway) will not understand the contents. This is why it's important to set up the MIME types on the sending Web server.

MIME types are used for all types of data files not just WAP files. You can check your own personal computer to see what MIME types are set up. For Windows-based systems, get into Explorer, click on View, Folder Options, and then File Types. Scroll down the list of registered file types until you see one with a MIME type and you'll see the file extension and its associated Content Type (MIME). Try looking at "Microsoft HTML Document 5.0" if it's defined on your PC. A common MIME type for a plain HTML document is "text/html."

If the WAP application is dynamically generated from a Perl or ASP program (or whatever), as we did for many of our examples, the content type must be explicitly specified before the HDML or WML code. The ASP file extension will be properly mapped from the sending Web server box but the WAP gateway is expecting WML not ASP code. So by explicitly setting the content type variable for the HTTP response header, the WAP gateway will know exactly what to expect and the application will be interpreted as expected.

The simplest MIME type setup required on the sending Web server for HDML and WML, respectively, is shown in Table 1.1.

This is the absolute minimum requirement for a Web server to serve WAP content. However, to send WMLScript, compiled WML, compiled WMLScript, or special .wbmp image formats, you'll have to add the additional MIME types listed in Table 1.2.

There are other MIME types required for other services but those are more advanced and you should refer to the vendors' documentation.

TECHNICAL NOTE:

If the WML and WMLScript source code files are precompiled, then the loading process on the devices will be faster since the WAP gateway won't have to do the compiling itself.

The two most popular Web servers these days are Apache and Microsoft IIS with the Apache Web server being by far the most popular on the Internet. Let's have a look at how to set up MIME types on these two servers.

Apache on Linux

There are three methods of adding MIME types to an Apache Web server. The method to use depends on your control of the server and on how the server is to be used.

The first method is to change the *mime.types* file, which is a global addition for the entire server. Second is another global server addition by adding the entries to the *srm.conf* file, and the third is via the *.htaccess* file which only affects the directory in which it's located.

Table 1.1 Basic MIME Types

FILE	EXTENSION	MIME TYPE
HDML	.hdml	text/x-hdml
WML	.wml	text/vnd.wap.wml

Table 1.2 Additional MIME Types

FILE	EXTENSION	MIME TYPE
WMLScript	.wmls	text/vnd.wap.wmlscript
Compiled WML	.wmlc	application/vnd.wap.wmlc
Compiled WML Script	.wmlsc	application/vnd.wap.wmlscriptc
WBMP	.wbmp	image/vnd.wap.wbmp

The mime.types file is located in the /usr/local/etc/httpd/conf/ directory. This file contains all MIME types currently defined to the server. Simply edit the file and add the required MIME types in the proper alphabetical order. For the changes to take effect, the Apache server must be restarted. Do this by killing the current executing process, kill-HUP 123 where 123 is the process ID found in either the httpd.pid file or from the ../logs directory. The server will restart automatically. The second method is by adding to the srm.conf configuration file located in the same ../conf/ directory as the mime.types file. This method differs from the first in that it allows the tweaking of the mime.types file via server side include statements.

Simply locate the "AddType" section in the srm.conf file, and add the lines as shown in Figure 1.13.

As before, save the file and restart the Apache Web server. See Figure 1.14.

The last method is to use the *.htaccess* file. Create the file as seen in Figure 1.15 and include it in the directory that contains the WAP application. This is particularly handy when you don't have full control over the entire Apache server and yet would like to set up MIME types for a specific directory. Simply add the code shown in Figure 1.15 to an existing or new .htaccess file.

The .htaccess method must be repeated for each directory in which you'd like to enable WAP-related MIME types.

The first line in the file tells the server that the index file for this directory is called *index.wml*. Be warned that some ISPs do consider this last method a security issue and will configure the server so that this file cannot be read. You'll have to check with your ISP to determine which of the above methods is the best for your situation.

```
DirectoryIndex   index.wml
addtype text/vnd.wap.wml wml
addtype application/vnd.wap.wmlc wmlc
addtype text/vnd.wap.wmlscript wmls
addtype application/vnd.wap.wmlscriptc wmlsc
addtype image/vnd.wap.wbmp wbmp
```

Figure 1.13 Apache MIME types for WAP.

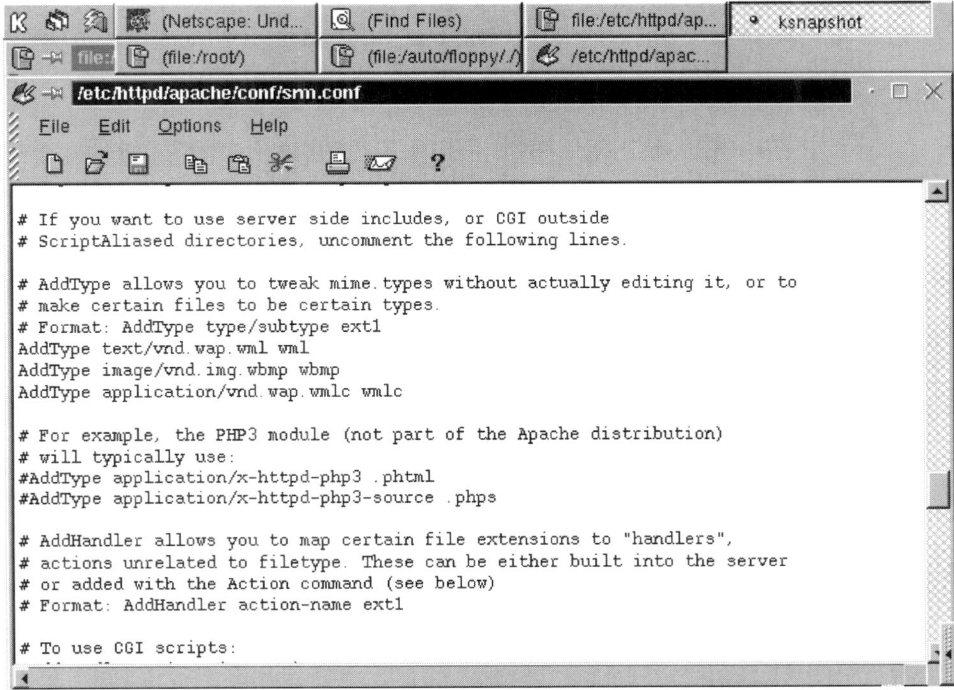

Figure 1.14 Apache srm.conf file.

Microsoft IIS 5.0 on Windows 2000

For IIS 5.0 running on Windows 2000 there are only two methods of adding MIME types. Both are via the GUI IIS Management Console. The first method is to set up the MIME types globally on the server and the second is for a specific directory.

Access the IIS Management Console (Start menu, Programs, Administrative Tools, Programs, and Internet Information Services). To make a MIME type available to the

```
# MIME Types for WAP
AddType  text/vnd.wap.wml  .wml
AddType  image/vnd.wap.wbmp  .wbmp
AddType  application/vnd.wap.wmlc  .wmlc
AddType  text/vnd.wap.wmlscript  .wmls
AddType  application/vnd.wap.wmlscriptc  .wmlsc
```

Figure 1.15 Apache .htaccess file entries.

entire server, right click on the server bringing up the "home properties" window and click on the Edit button in the "Computer MIME Map" section. Click on the "New Type" on the "File Types" window and then simply enter the associated extension (file extension) and the content-type (MIME). This is a very simple process.

To add the MIME type to a single directory, perform the same steps, except right-click on the directory you want to add MIME types to, then Properties, HTTP Headers tab, File Types, New Type, and finally add the MIME type at this point.

Figure 1.16 shows the global server setup windows.

Development Toolkits (SDK)

WAP *Software Development Kits* (SDKs) and *Application Development Kits* (ADKs) are tools of the trade. They're used to develop and test WAP applications. You could use a regular text editor like Notepad, upload your program to the Web server, and actually run each program on a real WAP device but that would be very time consuming and not too productive. Instead, download an SDK from one of the top vendors and you'll be able to quickly develop applications on your PC. Actually we recommend testing your applications on several different SDKs.

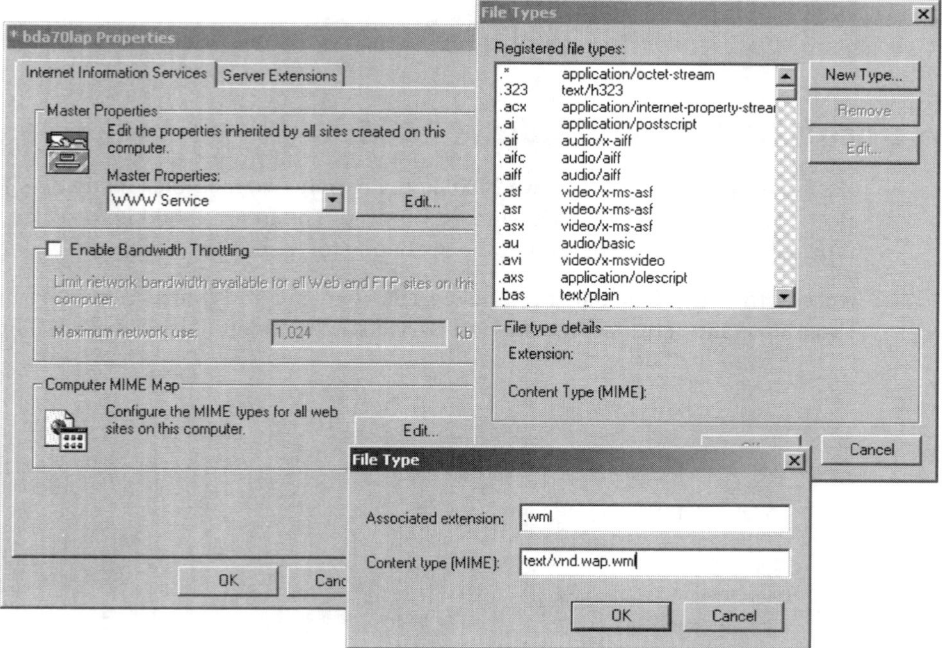

Figure 1.16 IIS MIME type addition.

An SDK is an emulator and simulates your program code results. Many emulators do not provide a true representation of how your code may appear or function on a live WAP device, but they come very close. For this reason we recommend you finalize all your development in a live environment. SDKs usually include user guide documentation, detailed viewing of cache contents and history stack, as well as other features.

Let's start with a look at the current popular development toolkits.

Openwave UP.SDK 4.1

Openwave offers its software development toolkits free of charge; simply visit www.openwave.com and download the SDK of your choice. The latest UP.SDK 4.1 toolkit supports WML 1.1 and all previous WML versions. If you wish to develop HDML applications, download UP.SDK 3.2 for HDML. Openwave toolkits work on Windows 95, 98, NT 4.0, and 2000 (SDK versions 4.1 and 3.2) and Solaris (SDK version 3.2) platforms.

The installation of the toolkits is straightforward; simply download the SDK of your choice and execute the file. Very little intervention is required.

The SDK doesn't contain a WML editor but does include the UP.Simulator, reference and developer guides, tools, and other interesting items. We use Notepad for all our editing needs. UP.Simulator simulates the UP.Browser on a mock WAP cell phone and comes with its associated information window as seen in Figure 1.17. Enter the URL of any WML site in the cell phone emulator "Go" line and you're in business. Almost all that transpires behind the scenes in the execution of the WAP URL is shown in the information window. You can also view source code, history stack contents, cookies, variables, and much more. This is quite a nice tool.

Figure 1.18 shows the different Up.Browser (formerly Phone.com) WML and HDML capabilities. When developing applications, it's important to test your application on the appropriate SDK that is compatible with the most popular Up.Browser version on WAP devices in the marketplace.

The UP.Simulator has two modes found in the Settings menu:

HTTP Direct. In this default mode, the UP.Simulator loads WML or HDML directly from a Web server, bypassing the UP.Link WAP gateway server. This mode is great for testing your WML code because it requires no special setup.

UP.Link. In this mode, the Up.Browser microbrowser interacts with an UP.Link Server just as a real Web phone would. So, obviously you need access to an UP.Link Server and register the UP.Simulator on that server before you can use it. This mode is used to test UP.Link features that run on the server, that is, bookmarks, fax services, and notifications.

If you wish to test your application on another phone model, since Up.Browser is on many different WAP phones and phones do differ in window size and keypad layout, change the current configuration settings in the configuration files.

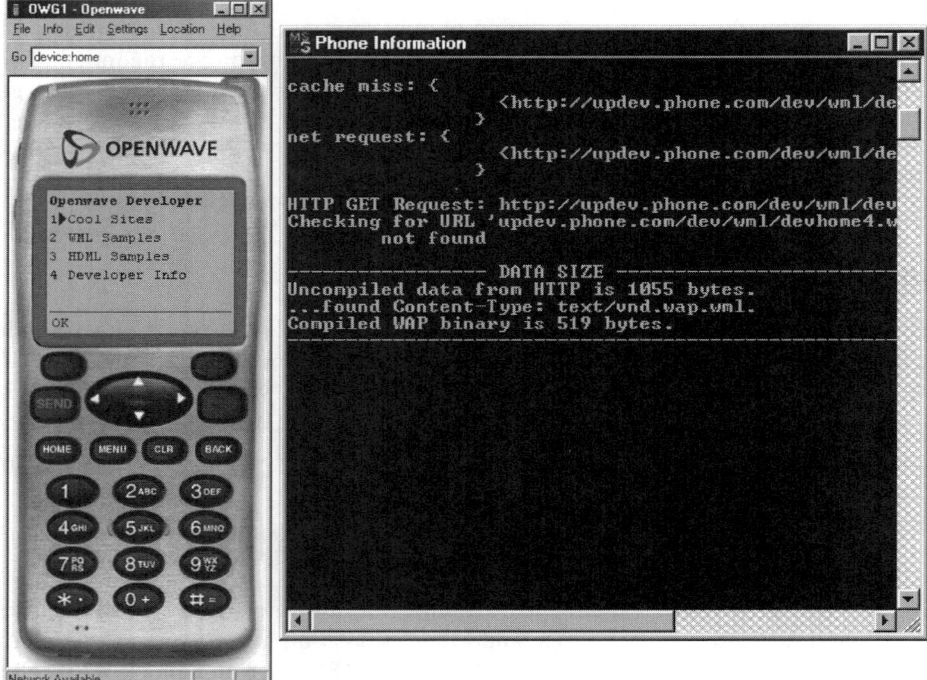

Figure 1.17 UP.Simulator, UP.SDK 4.1.

The great thing about using the UP.SDK is that Openwave includes many examples and actual WAP sites as a default. If you're unfamiliar with WMLScript or some WML tag usage, simply navigate to the examples on the SDK and see how the items are used in a working program. By pressing F5 (show source) on the emulator, you'll see the entire deck source in the information window.

Nokia WAP Toolkit 2.0

The Nokia WAP Toolkit 2.0 is a freely distributed SDK that is downloadable from www.nokia.com. The minimum requirements to run this toolkit on your PC are 30 Megs of available disk space, 64 MB of memory, a 266-MHz Pentium processor, Windows NT 4.0 with SP3 or Windows 98 (I use it on Windows 95 without any problems), and a high-resolution monitor (1024x768 16 bit). We've also used it on Windows 2000 and it works just fine but Nokia does not officially support the tool on this OS platform. Another important requirement is the installation of Java™ Runtime Environment (JRE) 1.2.2 or higher on your personal computer. This can be downloaded from Sun's "Java Developer Connection" Web site.

The toolkit has a server simulator based on Nokia WAP Server and is another great PC-based product for developers to build their applications. The Nokia WAP Toolkit

Vendor / Browser	Browser Version	HDML 3.0	WML 1.1	WML1.1 with Phone.com Extensions	WMLScript 1.1
Phone.com UP.Browser	4.x	Yes, via UP.Link translation service	Yes	Yes Recommended	Yes Recommended
Phone.com UP.Browser	3.1	Yes Recommended	Yes, via UP.Link translation service	No	No
Phone.com UP.Browser	3.0	**Yes** Recommended	No	No	No

Figure 1.18 Browser versions from Openwave.

includes tools for creating WML and WMLScript content, debugging WAP applications, and simulating the WAP content on WAP-enabled devices. The latest release of the toolkit offers three different WAP phones for testing applications: Nokia 6210, 7110, and the Blueprint phone for WAP 1.2.

As you can see in Figure 1.19, the Nokia WAP Toolkit concept is similar to Openwave's SDK. The tool has two windows—one for the phone simulator (right side), and the other is the emulation window (left side).

The nice part about this tool is that it includes a WML editor and has the ability to compile the WML deck before it's actually run. This compilation feature actually generates WMLC code on your PC ready for uploading to the Web server. The WML editor feature is quite nice since it allows multiple decks to be opened at the same time and highlights commands, options, attributes, and user text in different colors for easy viewing and recognition. The tool also offers several WML editor views such as the *tree* view of your deck, which is great for viewing the structural design of decks and cards.

The bad part about this toolkit is that it takes quite a while, once invoked, before the tool actually appears on the PC. And there is a lack of additional phone skins, which does limit the development results testing.

All in all, this Nokia WAP Toolkit 2.0 is a must for developers since Nokia does have quite a large number of users in many countries using the Nokia microbrowser. Be sure to test your applications on this SDK as well as on Openwave SDK.

Motorola ADK 2.0

From all of the toolkits reviewed in this section, Motorola's Mobile ADK 2.0 covers the most wireless development areas, including WAP, VoxML, and VoiceXML. Because of all the languages this tool covers, Motorola has called it an *Application Development Kit* (ADK) rather than a *Software Development Kit* (SDK).

This tool provides an Integrated Development Environment (IDE), which helps in the management of project and file structure, source control, code compilation, debugging, and online testing of individual programs or entire systems. With the Mobile ADK, you

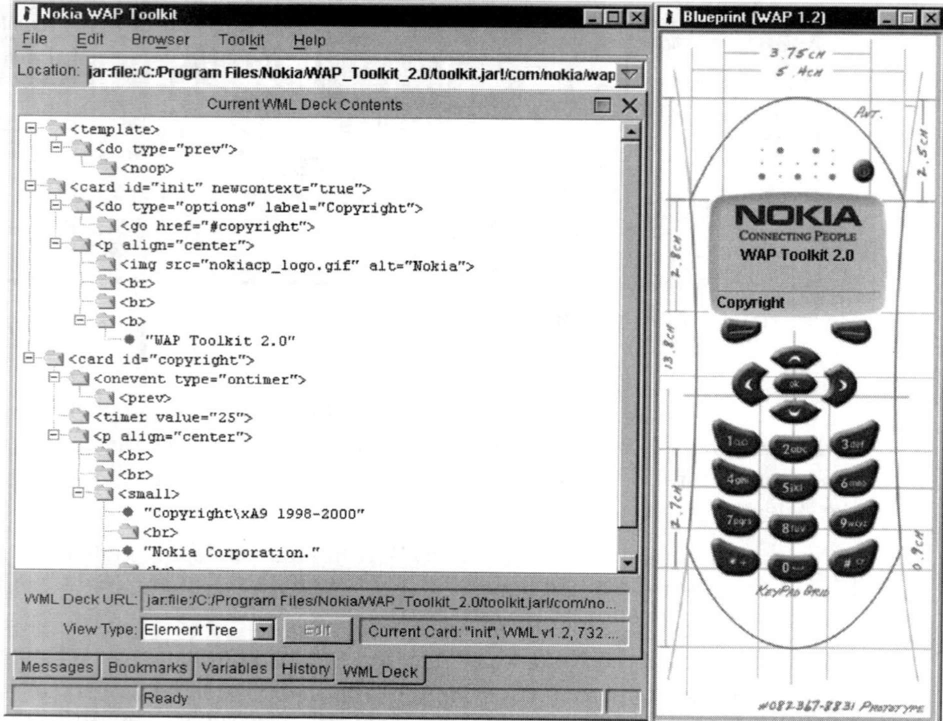

Figure 1.19 Nokia WAP toolkit 2.0.

can create wireless applications with multiple end-user views, including voice views constructed with the VoxML language, data views based on WAP's WML language, and applications that incorporate both voice and data.

The *Motorola Applications Development Kit* (MADK) provides templates, guidelines, robust documentation, online help, and sample applications for simple and fast development. Applications developed within the Mobile ADK will run on Motorola's MIX platform along with other standard compliant WAP and/or VoiceXML gateways.

The free toolkit is downloadable from the Motorola Web site and runs on Microsoft Windows 95, 98, NT 4.0, and 2000. System requirements specified by Motorola in the toolkit documentation show:

- IBM or compatible system with an 80486 processor or higher

- 32-MB RAM

- 256-color SVGA monitor (800x600 minimum resolution)

- Windows 95, Windows 98, or Windows NT 4.0 (Service Pack 3)

We strongly suggest that you not install this tool on a PC with less than a Pentium II processor and 64-MB RAM. Otherwise this excellent tool, with its wealth of features, will be too slow to function properly.

The installation of this toolkit takes slightly longer than others because of its many components required for VoiceXML/VoXML. VoiceXML and VoXML portions include voice recognition, speech recognition, grammars, VoiceXML, and VoXML parsers. As such, this tool has the highest disk space requirements of all other WAP toolkits.

Installation includes two products, the *Integrated Development Environment* (IDE) and the *User Interface Simulator* (UIS), free after registering at the Motorola site. If you have an earlier version of the IDE installed on your system, it's a good idea to completely uninstall it before installing the new one. The simulator comes with the following device configurations:

- Motorola Timeport P7389-Leap Phone
- Motorola i500plus™ Phone
- Motorola i700plus™ Phone
- Motorola i1000plus Phone
- Motorola ST7867W-StarTAC® Phone
- Motorola Talkabout® T2267 Phone
- Motorola V. Series V2282 Phone
- Motorola V. Series V8160 Phone

The IDE is a Windows-based, 32-bit visual development tool that allows you to perform such functions as managing your project and accessing project components from a consolidated and straightforward interface. The IDE makes it really easy to create and manage a project. It provides tools that enable you to manage and navigate through project components, enter and edit source code, and package your applications for distribution. Additionally, integrated tools such as the debugger and simulator help in the test, trace, and monitoring of the development and execution processes in your applications construction.

Figure 1.20 illustrates the Motorola MADK. This is well-rounded tool that provides Application Project Management and includes an online syntax checker and nice code editor. If you are looking to provide a central development point for WML, VoxML, or VoiceXML and also to implement these additional delivery channels to your customers, this would be the tool to use.

Ericsson WAPIDE 3.0

WapIDE 3.0 is an SDK designed to assist developers with WAP application development and testing. It can be downloaded from the Ericsson developer site at www.ericsson.com.

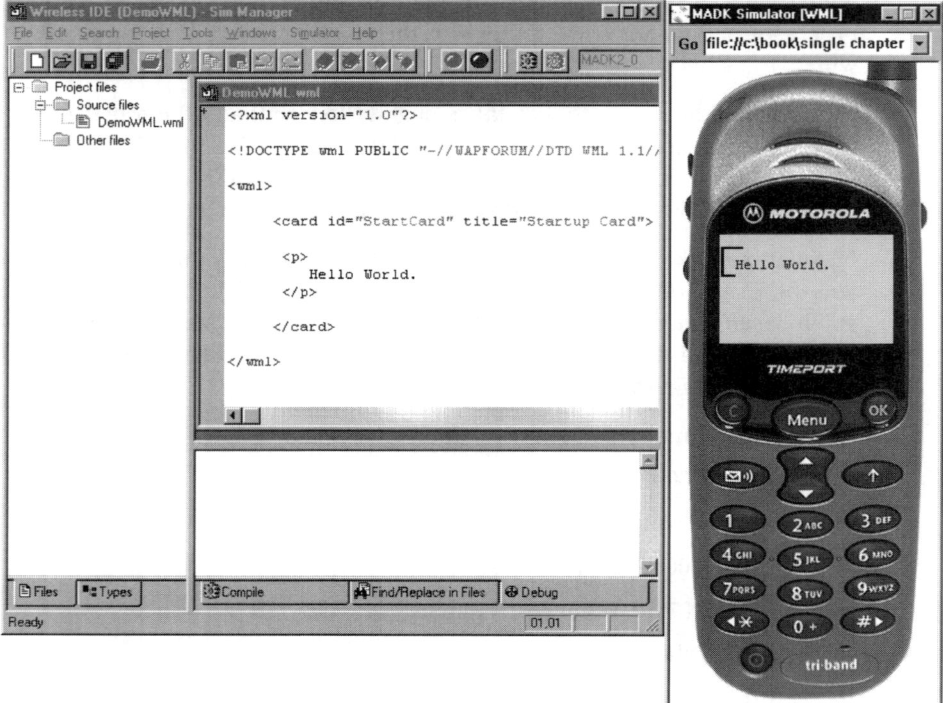

Figure 1.20 Motorola SDK.

This SDK is only installable on Windows NT 4.0, Windows 98, and Windows 2000. And in order to access your local WML files you'll also require Microsoft Internet Explorer 5 or newer. You'll also require the Java 2 Platform version 1.3.0 or later, available at http://java.sun.com. In order to perform correct simulations you will have to install the *Arial Narrow* font on your PC. Hardware requirements for this SDK are Pentium II class processor with 128-MB RAM and at least 20-MB available disk space.

In its basic installation this SDK supports WAP 1.2 standards and simulates two Web-enabled wireless phones, R520m and R320s. As with the majority of other toolkits, this one is also a two-window application: the device emulator and the status information window.

There are two ways to load content to this SDK browser:

- Load from a local WML file
- Load from a Web server via a WAP gateway

The nice point about this toolkit (see Figure 1.21) is that it has quite a bit of trace options. To view the trace messages, try the trace option under the emulator view option. Trace is divided into different multiple tabs: Console, Device, WAE, or Network, all available under the general *All* tab. Unfortunately, the downloadable Internet version does not include a WML editor, which would be a great addition if freely distributed.

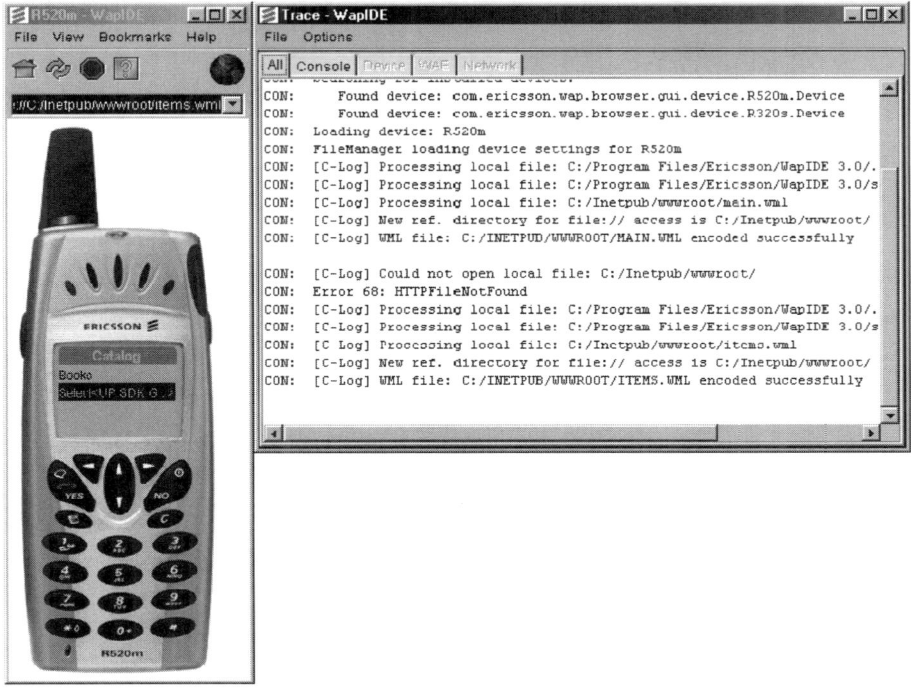

Figure 1.21 Ericsson SDK.

NOTE

Ericsson is one of the rare major manufacturers in the wireless field that provides a WAP microbrowser for PDAs such as PalmOS.

Microsoft Mobile Explorer 2.01

This emulator tool is a relative newcomer to the SDK toolkit arena. In order to run Mobile Explorer you will need Windows 2000 Professional or Windows NT 4 Workstation with Service Pack 3 or later. At the moment Mobile Explorer only displays monochrome or grayscale at any screen resolution.

Microsoft Mobile Explorer (MME) is an operating system-independent browser-based solution. It includes the world's first dual-mode microbrowser that can display both WAP 1.1 and HTML Internet content. This simulator supports cookies, bookmarks, and forms.

It is interesting to know that Microsoft's Mobile Explorer (see Figure 1.22) does not require *Real Time Operating System* (RTOS) on the wireless device hardware and it

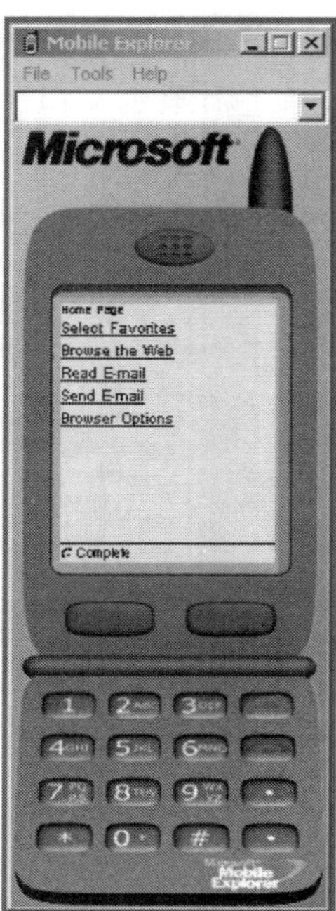

Figure 1.22 Microsoft MME.

supports all major wireless standards like GSM, GPRS, CDMA, 3G, TDMA, and PDC. At this time, it's the only tool that supports, with the same microbrowser, WAP 1.1, HTTP 1.1, HTML 3.2 (including support for cookies, bookmarks, and forms), GIF, and JPEG images. This feature or ability is extremely important to the wireless industry in that it allows the huge amount of existing Web developers with HTML knowledge to quickly wireless-enable their Web sites with very little transitional re-education. Imagine being able to develop wireless applications with tools like Visual Inter Dev, DreamWeaver, or DramBit. The concept is similar to what NTT DoCoMo did with their implementation of iMode and compact HTML for wireless devices.

Another nice feature of this toolkit is that it has one of the smallest installation footprints on the developer workstation and is extremely simple to install and configure.

Similar to the other toolkits and emulators that follow the strict WAPforum guidelines for WAP1.1, Microsoft Mobile Explorer will not support additional elements such as those introduced by Openwave. For example, in Up.Browser it is completely legitimate to use the Up.Browser <spawn> tag, but the MME WML compiler will not recognize this proprietary tag.

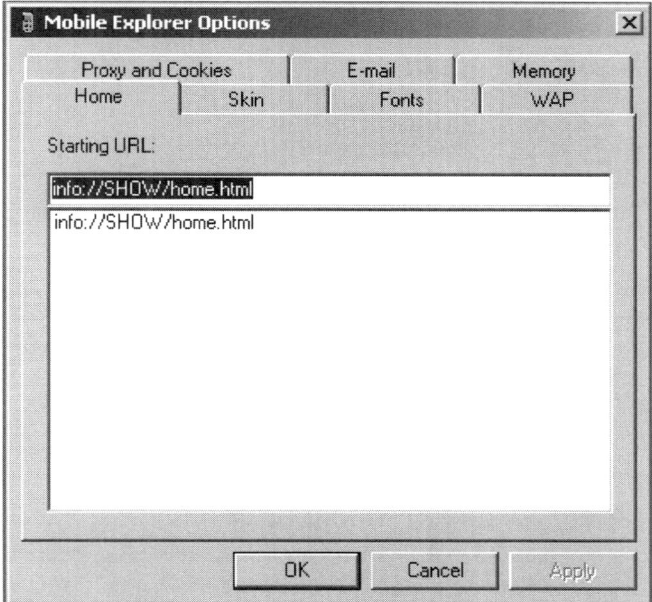

Figure 1.23 MME options.

Configuration and setting of the emulator is simple via Mobile Explorer options application (see Figure 1.23).

To learn more about Microsoft's Mobile Explorer emulator, visit the Microsoft Web site or www.benefon.com, which was an early development partner with Microsoft.

Introduction to Wireless Languages

All examples presented in this chapter have been developed and tested using Openwave's (formerly Phone.com) WAP toolkit version 4.1 and/or Nokia's WAP toolkit 2.0, unless stated otherwise. For more information on WAP toolkits, refer to the "Development Toolkits (SDK)" section of Chapter 1.

Every line of program code in this chapter is numbered for easy reference. Code on the CD is identical (but without the numbers), making it easy to simply copy and execute the code.

This chapter describes the basic components of the Wireless Markup Language—(WML). An introduction to the concept of tags and XML is followed by an introduction to HDML, which is very popular in the Americas. We'll then discuss the WML language, a subset of XML, in more depth since WML is quite popular worldwide. And within WML, we'll review WMLScript, which is becoming more widely used throughout the world.

We'll have a look at the basic languages, physical device screens, and structural uses of the language such as navigation, image usage, user interaction, variables, and parameters.

XML and DTDs

Extensible Markup Language (XML) is a tag-based language. If you are a programmer or have seen the HTML code behind Web pages, you're already familiar with the concept of tags. Tags are simply the idea of encapsulating specific information or data in a structured manner. Elements within documents, as they are called, begin with a start tag, <tag>, and finish with a corresponding end tag, </tag>. Tags are enclosed by less-than and greater-than symbols, < >. The ending tag contents usually begin with a forward slash / to differentiate it from the start tag. If a tag is not encapsulating information, data, or content then it's simply a one-time tag (no ending tag) and is denoted by its name and a forward slash after the tag contents, <tag/>; for instance a line break in WML is <br/>.

Think of XML as simply a method of identifying information through the use of subsets specific to different areas and/or topics. XML is based on how data is organized rather than the method in which it is displayed, which basically allows it to be platform, system, programming language, security, database or storage method, and transmission independent. If I missed any other "independents"— well, you get the picture. XML is purely the definition and method of structuring data.

Following the concept of structured data it stands to reason that XML tags can be organized into groups of related tags. These organizations are called *XML subsets*, which contain general and specific tags. These specific tags also have a second usage— descriptively defining the data content between the start and end tags. In these cases, the tags themselves are meta data to the data content and can be just as useful as the data itself. Imagine a document containing store and department tags as seen below. A program could count the number of <store> start tags to determine the number of stores being reported in the document.

```
<store>Branch1<department>Personnel</deparment></store>
<store>Branch2<department>Personnel</deparment></store>
```

There are many XML subsets such as WML, VoxML, VoiceXML, etc. By using XML subsets, programmers from different cultures and countries who speak different languages can merge their common knowledge by using the same standards and all share compatible and comprehendible applications. Think of all the programmers in the world all coding Web pages using the XML subset HTML.

Currently, in 2001, most WAP applications in North America use the HDML language while most other countries use the WML subset.

XML is an extensible markup language, which means as more subsets are required, individuals and organizations can create new subsets as they see fit. XML removes boundaries and hence allows individuals the opportunity to dynamically create subsets for their specific new concepts, applications, and usages. Anything not restricting the imagination offers freedom and hence advancement, which is why XML is becoming such an accepted standard.

XML tags have certain rules of order to ensure that standards are followed. First, a parser is used to ensure proper syntax is followed (similar to the first stage of a compiler). For instance, rules such as a begin tag must precede an end tag are checked. Another rule is that in certain instances, an end tag must be present before a corresponding open tag reappears and so forth. Of course there are more rules, but we'll leave it up to the reader to research the finer workings of XML as this is simply a brief introduction and not an in-depth look at the language.

Specific XML subsets have many tags and tag rules. These specific subset tags and rules are described in detail in an XML file called the Document Type Definitions

(DTD). Of course different groups can publish their own version of a specific XML subset DTD file. For the WML subset, two popular DTDs are available, the first from Openwave (formerly Phone.com) and the other from the Wireless Application Protocol Forum. Openwave offers http://phone.com/dtd/wml11.dtd, and http://wapforum.org/ DTD/wml_1.1.xml is from the WAP Forum, which is popular with Nokia applications.

You'll notice that every WML deck specifies which DTD is being used (notice the DTD entries in the wireless programs in this book). This is important since what is defined in one DTD may not exist in another. For this reason (among other reasons), it is very difficult to create WAP applications to function on all WAP devices. Cellular phone service providers may have one WAP gateway using a specific DTD while another cellular provider has a different gateway using another DTD. This is similar to creating a Web site with certain features that function on Netscape but not on Internet Explorer. So what can a programmer do, you ask? Well, we suggest programming your applications in their simplest form to ensure that they work with the top DTDs in the marketplace. Or write two distinct applications, one using Openwave and the other using the WAPForum DTD, which is what we do for complicated applications at WaveDev. Also note that DTD content may change as different versions of the file are released, so stay on top of what's being offered out there.

HDML and iMode (which is based on cHTML or compact HTML) do not use DTDs, which simplifies coding. So why not simply use HDML?—The reason is that WML is more advanced in that it has its own scripting language and many more extensions than HDML.

HDML Structure

Let's have a look at the popular North American wireless Internet XML tag-based language *Handheld Device Markup Language* (HDML). It will be several more years before U.S. carriers convert from HDML to WML. With the forecasted huge wireless Internet market developing within the next couple of years, if you want to tackle the U.S. market, you must know HDML.

HDML is an open language developed by Unwired Planed (renamed Openwave after being renamed to Phone.com). It is similar to HTML but with fewer features. The language was created to simply enable the display of information on a Web phone and interact with the phone holder. HDML was essentially the first step in mobile wireless Internet followed by WML.

Visit www.openwave.com for detailed HDML information and for the UP.SDK, Software Developers Kit, which is a must if you're developing applications in HDML. The following HDML information is a general view of the language but is by no means a full explanation of all HDML details. We've put together an overview in what we hope is an easy introduction to the general use and workings of the language.

Screen Layout

Most screen images used in this book are just that, screen images from the SDKs and not an image from an actual Web phone. Many Figures in Chapter 1 show an entire phone image as seen in the SDKs but for practical purposes in this chapter, we'll only show the phone's screen (or window) portion.

As shown in Figure 2.1, the typical HDML screen display is divided into three parts: Content Area, ACCEPT key, and Softkey. The Content Area contains all images and text. The ACCEPT key is used for navigation and acceptance of Content Area choices. The Softkey is usually used for navigation or as a secondary action to Content Area choices. The ACCEPT key label is usually on the bottom left side and the Softkey is usually on the bottom right. On some phones this may be reversed—beware when creating your applications. Also note that not all Web phones have the ability to show both ACCEPT and Softkey labels.

Each Web phone is different and so are the screen displays. They all follow the same standard layout as in Figure 2.1 but their size may differ. Many Web phones using HDML only have three or four lines visible in the display. To view the above screen, the user would have to scroll down. This limitation is very frustrating and hopefully the manufacturers will soon develop phones with larger screen displays.

Cards and Decks

To begin, an entire HDML program consists of one *deck* made up of one or more *cards*. The reasoning behind this terminology is that microbrowsers can hold multiple cards at once, hence the natural term *deck*. In the familiar HTML Web programming language,

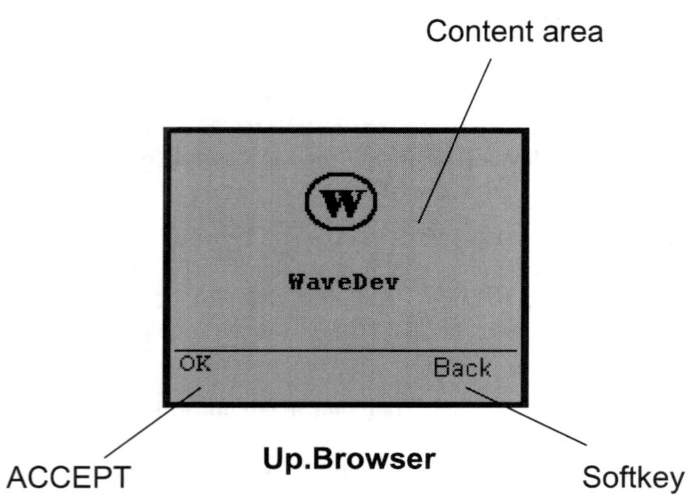

Figure 2.1 UP.Browser screen layout from UP.SDK 3.2 HDML.

only one page is returned to the browser but with HDML as well as WML, many pages are returned at once so the term *cards* is used rather than pages. While many cards are available to the microbrowser, only one card is visible at a time and the others are behind the scenes in memory of the physical device (called a *cache*). As mentioned in Chapter 1, physical device cache size is limited and therefore one must be aware of the deck size being sent to the device, which includes the image size. UP.Link server has a transmission limit to UP.Phones of roughly 1492 bytes but as a general rule, it's best to limit the maximum size to 1200 bytes.

The reason many cards are available to the WAP microbrowser at once is two fold. First, the cards are generally quite small and, second, since latency issues exist when fetching the cards from the WAP site, many cards are prefetched at the same time. Therefore, by sending multiple cards (a deck) per request, quick response times can be simulated. This sounds a bit odd, but it will make more sense as you read on. WML and HDML are similar to HTML in many areas. If you are not familiar with HTML Web programming, the following topics may be a little difficult to understand since we assume you have a minimal HTML foundation.

Figure 2.2 is an example of a simple HDML deck with one card.

Figure 2.3 illustrates the screen display, as seen from the UP.SDK 3.2 for HDML, that is the result of the simple HDML program in Figure 2.2.

Line 1 in Figure 2.2 pairs with Line 5 to define the language tag, which is required and interpreted by the UP.Link server. In HDML, these tags define the start and end of the deck.

Lines 2 and 4 define the start and end tags for the DISPLAY card.

Line 3 is the actual data to be displayed in the Content Area. Note that since an ampersand (&) is a special character on microbrowsers, special substitution must be used, which in this case is &. See Text Formatting later in this HDML section for more details.

The ACCEPT key defaults to OK if nothing is coded and the Softkey default is blank. We'll see how to code these keys later in this chapter.

HDML has four types of cards (as described in the HDML language reference from Openwave):

```
1. <HDML VERSION="3.0">
2.      <DISPLAY>
3.             Wiley &amp; Sons Inc.
4.      </DISPLAY>
5. </HDML>
```

Figure 2.2 Simple HDML deck with one card.

Figure 2.3 Screen display of simple HDML program.

- **DISPLAY cards.** These are used to display information in the Content Area.
- **CHOICE cards.** These display a list of options from which the user can choose a single option.
- **ENTRY cards.** These display a message or instruction and allow the user to enter text or a value.
- **NO-DISPLAY cards.** These are action or navigation cards and do not appear on the phone.

So what normally happens is that the phone receives a deck with one or more cards. By default, the first card in the deck is executed and if the card is not a NO-DISPLAY card, it is displayed on the phone. Depending on the type of card on the screen, the user can then either enter text, choose an option, or view the card and then continue the process by pressing a key corresponding to either the ACCEPT label or Softkey label, if it exists.

Display Cards

In DISPLAY cards, navigation is done via the ACCEPT key label or the Softkey; both are programmed via the ACTION command as shown in Figure 2.4.

This DISPLAY card will look identical to the original display card shown in Figure 2.3 but with the addition of the label *Cancel* in the Softkey area similar to the cancel label in Figure 2.6. Now when the button beneath the OK label is pressed, control is passed to the second card in this same deck.

To navigate to another card within the same deck, simply code the destination option with a number sign, #, followed by the name of the card where control is to be passed, as in line 4 in Figure 2.4. To navigate to a card in a completely new deck, specify the entire URL including the http:// portion as follows:

```
<ACTION TYPE=ACCEPT TASK="GO"
DEST="http://www.wiley.com/wireless/main.hdml">
```

To navigate to another card other than the first card in a new URL, simply add the number sign followed by the card name to the end of the URL as follows:

```
1.  <HDML VERSION="3.0">
2.      <ACTION TYPE=SOFT1 TASK="CANCEL" LABEL="Cancel" >
3.      <DISPLAY>
4.          <ACTION TYPE=ACCEPT TASK="GO" DEST="#card2">
5.          Wiley &amp; Sons Inc.
6.      </DISPLAY>
7.      <DISPLAY NAME="card2">
8.          Established in 1807.
9.      </DISPLAY>
10. </HDML>
```

Figure 2.4 Display card example.

```
<ACTION TYPE=ACCEPT TASK="GO"
DEST="http://www.wiley.com/wireless/main.hdml#card4">
```

Note quotation marks are optional in HDML for alphanumeric characters but are highly recommended. For dynamic HDML (HDML code generated by another program such as VB, ASP, PERL, or JAVA programs), it might be simpler to leave out the quotation marks since quotation marks are usually interpreted by most languages and hence may cause compile errors.

The ACTION command is used to assign a task to a phone function key. Actions are defined for individual cards and/or globally at the deck level. Of course, anything at the card level overrides definitions at the deck level. These are only a handful of possible actions which are ACCEPT (or OK), HELP, PREV, SOFT1, SOFT2, SEND, and DELETE. Types of tasks associated with these actions are GO, GOSUB, RETURN, CANCEL, PREV, CALL, and NOOP. The ACTION command has many more options. See Appendix A at the back of the book for more details.

Task types are key to the ACTION command:

- The GO task is primarily used to go to a URL or relative program or card.
- The GOSUB task is similar to calling a subroutine whereby the return or canceling of the subroutine passes control back to the calling program.
- PREV task simply passes control back to the previous card in the history.
- RETURN is just that; it returns from a subroutine with or without values, and CANCEL simply cancels the current activity.
- CALL is used to switch the phone into voice mode and automatically dials the programmed number.
- NOOP is a no-operation task, which is used to disable a default behavior of a specific action.

Again, see Appendix A for more details. We highly suggest downloading the HDML Language Reference from Openwave for the final word on HDML usage.

Even though the second card in the two-card deck in Figure 2.4 has no ACTION command specifically defined to it, the global ACTION command defined at the deck level will take effect for all cards unless another ACTION command with the same TYPE is defined at the card level. So, when the first or second card is displayed, both will have the *Cancel* label defined to the Softkey, which once invoked will cancel the current activity and return to the previous card.

Choice Cards

Web phones have limited display space, and it's quite difficult and frustrating to type information using the small numeric keypads. CHOICE cards are used to give the programmer the ability to associate numbered keys to specific actions, that is, press 1 to invoke some routine such as View Horoscope. From a user point of view, this dramatically simplifies the process since very little effort is required to navigate the application. We highly suggest building your applications with this type of navigation in mind.

Figure 2.5 shows a typical CHOICE card used to navigate a WAP site.

Note that a third card has been added to our initial program example. Lines 11 through 14 show a typical CHOICE card with two choices available, producing the screen display shown in Figure 2.6.

Notice the *Cancel* Softkey label produced from the ACTION command at the deck level and also that all Choice Entries (CE) are numbered, once displayed, to coincide with the keypad numbers. The first nine choices have default numbering from 1 through 9. If more than nine entries are created, entries after nine are not numbered and must be

```
1.  <HDML VERSION="3.0">
2.     <ACTION TYPE=SOFT1 TASK="CANCEL" LABEL="Cancel" >
3.     <DISPLAY>
4.        <ACTION TYPE=ACCEPT TASK="GO" DEST="#card2">
5.           Wiley &amp; Sons Inc.
6.     </DISPLAY>
7.     <DISPLAY NAME="card2">
8.        <ACTION TYPE=ACCEPT TASK="GO" DEST="#card3">
9.           Established in 1807.
10.    </DISPLAY>
11.    <CHOICE NAME="card3">
12.       <CE TASK=GOSUB
          DEST="http://www.wiley.com/wireless/books.hdml">Book Search
13.       <CE TASK=GOSUB
          DEST="http://www.wiley.com/wireless/info.hdml">Company Info
14.    </CHOICE>
15. </HDML>
```

Figure 2.5 Choice card example.

Figure 2.6 Choice screen display, card 3.

scrolled to and selected to be invoked. This is simply because there are only nine numbers (excluding zero) on the Web phone keypad.

Navigation for a CHOICE card is the essence of the card itself. This card type is used extensively in many applications to simplify user interaction and navigation. Think in terms of tree structures when designing an HDML site and program with choice cards as much as possible.

Choice Entries have many uses, which are described in Appendix A at the back of the book.

Entry Cards

For a user to enter text or a value to be accepted by the wireless application, ENTRY cards are used. ENTRY cards and variables can be discussed simultaneously since ENTRY cards cannot function without the use of variables. When the user enters information, that information is stored in a variable to be processed by the application. See Figure 2.7 for an ENTRY card example.

This program shows the use of the three card types explained so far. The first card, lines 3 to 8, is the CHOICE card, which results in the first screen display in Figure 2.8. Upon selecting option 1, search by title, control is passed to the second card in the deck, lines 9 to 12, the ENTRY card. The next two screen displays of Figure 2.8 are from this entry card. The first is the initial display and the second is once data has been entered. Once the ACTION command for the ENTRY card is invoked (by pressing the button under the OK label), control is passed to the third card in the deck, the DISPLAY card. Lines 13 to 16 of this card display the inputted title variable along with a text message as seen in the last screen display of Figure 2.8. If OK is pressed at this point, control is passed to the SearchTitle.asp program, which also uses the passed variable, VarTitle, from the second card.

Note the ACTION card at the deck level. It contains a CANCEL task, which appears on the first and last cards in the deck. Invoking this command from the third card (the DIS-

```
1.  <HDML VERSION="3.0">
2.     <ACTION TYPE=SOFT1 TASK="CANCEL" LABEL="Cancel" >
3.     <CHOICE>
4.        <CENTER>Wiley &amp; Sons<br>Book Search
5.        <CE TASK=GOSUB DEST=#card2>Search by Title
6.        <CE TASK=GOSUB
          DEST=http://www.wiley.com/wireless/author.hdml>Search by Author
7.        <CE TASK=GOSUB
          DEST=http://www.wiley.com/wireless/booklist.hdml>List of Books
8.     </CHOICE>
9.     <ENTRY NAME=card2 KEY=VarTitle>
10.        <ACTION TYPE=ACCEPT TASK=GO DEST=#card3>
11.        Title:
12.     </ENTRY>
13.     <DISPLAY NAME="card3">
14.        <ACTION TYPE=ACCEPT TASK=GO
   DEST=http://www.wiley.com/wireless/SearchTitle.asp? Title= $VarTitle>
15.        Searching for books with title:<BR> $(VarTitle)
16.     </DISPLAY>
17. </HDML>
```

Figure 2.7 ENTRY card example.

PLAY card) will send control back to the invoking task, which is the first card since the first card invoked the second card via a GOSUB command and the second card invoked the third via the GO command. So, the second and third cards are essentially within the same task level. Invoking the CANCEL command from the third card returns control to the higher level, which would be the first card in the deck. If we were to change the GO in the second card, line 10, to a GOSUB, then invoking the CANCEL task from the last card would return control to the second card.

We can also create subtasks using the GOSUB command that spans decks. If line 12 of the program (deck) in Figure 2.5 invoked the program in Figure 2.7, which was slightly changed, and the GOSUB was changed to a GO in line 5, then invoking the CANCEL command from the third card in Figure 2.7 would return control to the program in Figure 2.5.

Again, for more features and a description of the ENTRY card, see Appendix A.

NO-DISPLAY Cards

The NOOP card does not display on the physical device. When invoked, the card immediately triggers the ACCEPT or PREV action, depending on how the card was initiated. These cards are usually used to initialize variables and continue the processing with no user interaction.

Obviously these cards come in handy with certain types of processing that do not require any screen displaying or user interaction.

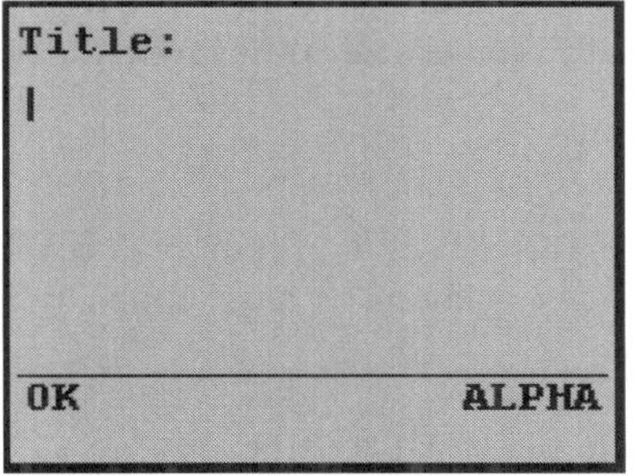

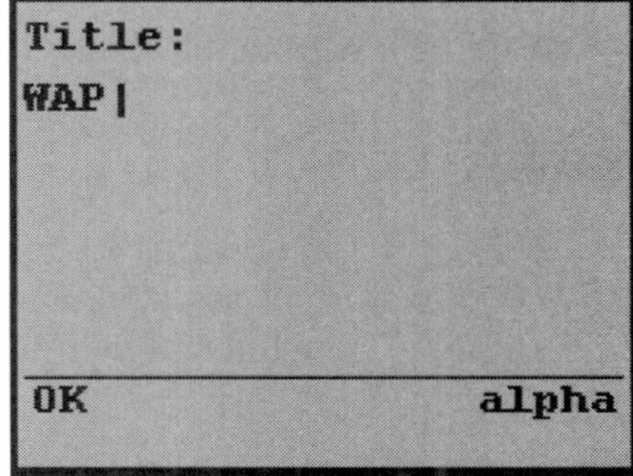

Figure 2.8 ENTRY card screen display.

Navigation

In instances where more than one card is required, navigation is used to jump from card to card within the same deck (forward or backward) or to another card in another deck altogether. Another deck could be another program in the same URL tree or a completely new URL. Remember the discussion under Cards and Decks? Typically, when a WAP gateway receives a deck, the first card is usually activated, though navigation can be directed to any card within the deck as follows: http://wavedev.com/wireless/deck1.hdml#card2.

History Stack

Every card displayed on the Web phone is kept in memory in an area called the *history stack*. As a card is invoked, its name is placed on top of the stack. The history stack is a Last-In-First-Out (LIFO) structure. When navigating backward using the PREV command, the last card entered into the stack is the next card to be displayed. If no more cards are in the stack, then nothing happens. Unlike Internet browsers, which have Back and Forward capabilities, WAP can only simulate the Back functionality via the PREV command.

Certain commands can wipe the stack clean. This is useful in certain events such as in security scenarios where we wouldn't want to return to a password entry card. Also if the user presses the Home key on the phone, control returns to the user's HOME card, which is the first card in the stack. This essentially removes all entries from the history stack.

Variables

As seen in the previous example, variables are a very important feature of the language since user input and dynamic data are the backbone to most applications. In HDML, variables have only a few rules such as:

- $, <, >, =, /, \, &, *, # are not allowed in the variable name.

- If using any of the these non alphanumeric characters in a variable's value, a noesc should be used, that is, $(Var:noesc). For instance if the $(Var) value was http://.wiley.com/wireless/books.hdml and noesc was not used, the resulting value of $(Var) would be http%3a%2f%2f.wiley.com%2fwireless%2fbooks.hdml.

- Variable names are case sensitive.

- Note that variable names are stored in the physical device's memory, which may impact overall deck size, so make the names short.

- Variables are level dependent—same idea as the CANCEL command description. A variable cannot be passed to another level unless the VARS option is used, that is, <CE TASK=GOSUB DEST=#card2> would have the extra VARS variables as follows, <CE TASK=GOSUB DEST=#card2 VARS=VarTitle>. (Of course this specific example does not apply to the program in Figure 2.7.)

- If an invoking level is expecting a value back from a variable in the lower level, use the RECEIVE option in the GOSUB statement. In the lower level, the RETVALS is used to return the values to the variables for the invoking level.

- To reference a variable, use the $(...) context with the variable name within parentheses.

Text Formatting

Of course where there is text, there is formatting. Formatting rules for HDML are as follows:

- There is no bold feature in HDML, which is the number one searched-for feature.

- For alignment use <RIGHT> and <CENTER>, which apply to the entire line only. There is no left alignment.

- Since white space is ignored in HDML, use   to include a horizontal space.

- To align columns, use the <TAB>. The device will automatically set tab stops. The phone treats the tab as a table column and thus uses the largest column width to define the width of all other columns. Don't use <TAB> with <CENTER>.

- As in HTML, a line break is <BR>.

- <LINE> will keep all text on one line. If the line is longer than the screen, the automatic wrapping mode is called "Times Square."

- <WRAP> will wrap all text within the viewable portion of the screen. Scrolling may be used to view all text beyond the screen display's visible area.

- Certain characters are interpretable by the microbrowser so their escape sequence must be used as shown in Table 2.1.

Images

Initial Web phones that had only HDML capabilities had limited image usage. Many of the phones and devices can handle images, but we recommend not using them since it is difficult to determine which phones will function correctly and which will not. More advanced Web phones that handle WML as well as HDML can more easily handle images compared to older phones.

Images can be used in the text portion of all cards except NO-DISPLAY cards. They can also be used for choice items on CHOICE cards and also as the Softkey label in an ACTION statement. Review the descriptions in Appendix A for further details.

Openwave has 175 predefined icons available to devices as described in the HDML Language Reference. These special icons are very handy to use and give applications a nice GUI look.

Table 2.1 Escape Sequences

<	<
>	>
"	"
&	&
$	&dol;
space	
Any ASCII character	&#nn; (nn is the ASCII code)

Figure 2.1 uses an image—the big W in a circle. The image is only 302 bytes, which is well within our 1200-byte total deck size maximum that we mentioned earlier. As in HTML, images have their own <img> tag. Figure 2.9 is the source code for Figure 2.1.

Voice Mode

A major feature of using the Internet via a Web phone is the WTA functions which, for example, has the ability to have the application auto-dial a telephone number with the press of a single button. The CALL option does just that—it allows the program to be coded in such a way that with the push of a button the phone switches from the Internet mode to regular phone mode. This is excellent when the user wants to call a company for goods or services, call for assistance with the application, or whatever.

The CALL option is coded wherever there is a task feature such as in the ANCHOR, ACTION, and CHOICE Entry. In Figure 2.10 we introduce the CALL task on the first card. Now the user can simply press the fourth button representing the fourth item on the CHOICE card to call our fictitious application's Wiley & Sons publishers, as seen on line 8.

The result of executing the program in Figure 2.10 is similar to Figure 2.7, except now we've added option 4 on the first card, line 8. When that number 4 is pressed, even though the program code specifies one number (212-555-1234), the microbrowser knows to display the three typical choices for the number. The programmer does not have to figure out if the user is within the same area code. Now the user simply selects the proper number to dial and the phone is switched to voice mode from Internet mode. The third screen display is created only from the SDK and since voice calls are not possible from the SDK, a screen display is invoked to simulate the voice mode. See Figure 2.11.

WML Structure

Wireless Markup Language (WML) is another subset of XML and is used specifically for the wireless Internet industry. The widely used current version of WML is 1.1 with ver-

```
1. <HDML VERSION="3.0">
2.     <DISPLAY>
3.        <ACTION TYPE=ACCEPT TASK=GO
          DEST=http://www.wavedev.com/wireless/default.asp>
4.        <BR><BR><CENTER><IMG SRC="wavebig.bmp" ALT="WaveDev"><BR>
5.        <BR><CENTER>WaveDev
6.     </DISPLAY>
7. </HDML>
```

Figure 2.9 Image example of Figure 2.1.

```
1.  <HDML VERSION="3.0">
2.     <ACTION TYPE=SOFT1 TASK="CANCEL" LABEL="Cancel" >
3.     <CHOICE>
4.        <CENTER>Wiley &amp; Sons
5.        <CE TASK=GOSUB DEST=#card2>Search by Title
6.        <CE TASK=GOSUB
           DEST=http://www.wiley.com/wireless/author.hdml>Search by Author
7.        <CE TASK=GOSUB
           DEST=http://www.wiley.com/wireless/booklist.hdml>List of Books
8.        <CE TASK=CALL NUMBER="212-555-1234">Call Wiley
9.     </CHOICE>
10.    <ENTRY NAME=card2 KEY=VarTitle>
11.       <ACTION TYPE=ACCEPT TASK=GO DEST=#card3>
12.       Title:
13.    </ENTRY>
14.    <DISPLAY NAME="card3">
15.       <ACTION TYPE=ACCEPT TASK=GO
          DEST=http://www.wiley.com/wireless/SearchTitle .asp?Title=$VarTitle
          >
16.       Searching for books with title:<BR> $(VarTitle)
17.    </DISPLAY>
18. </HDML>
```

Figure 2.10 CALL option example (also known as WTAI).

sion 1.2 available but not widely used since many gateways and microbrowsers are not fully up to par.

WML is an open structured language developed by the WAP Forum (www.wapforum.org) specifically to accommodate handheld devices such as Web phones and PDAs. WML is a tag-based language like HTML and HDML, and is a case-sensitive language where all tags must be written in lowercase.

As with HDML, detailed WML information can be found at the WAP Forum, and Openwave (www.openwave.com). Additional WML information can also be found at Nokia (www.nokia.com) as well as other major wireless Internet Web sites such as AnyWhereYouGo.com (www.anywhereyougo.com). In this chapter, we'll mostly be using Openwave's software development kit, UP.SDK 4.1, for our examples as well as the other popular software development kit, which is the Nokia WAP toolkit 2.0.

As with the HDML section, let's first look at the screen displays.

Screen Layout

A WML screen display for Up.Browser is virtually identical to an HDML screen display for Up.Browser even though the Up.Browser versions are different. The main differ-

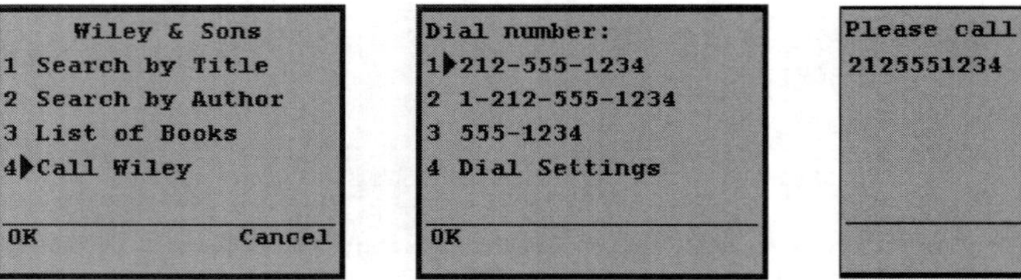

Figure 2.11 CALL option screen displays.

ence is that developers seem to refer to the two option labels and respective option keys as Softkey1 and Softkey2 as seen in Figure 2.12.

The typical screen display is divided into three parts: Content Area, Softkey1, and Softkey2. The Content Area contains all images and text. Softkey1 is used for navigation and acceptance of Content Area choices, and Softkey2 is usually used for navigation or as a secondary action to Content Area choices. Take note that these keys, depending on the Web phone models, may be reversed with Softkey1 on the bottom right side and Softkey2 on the bottom left side. This is mostly because Up.Browser is supplied on many different phones manufactured by many different manufacturers, each with their own specific settings.

Each Web phone is different and so are the screen displays. Although the screens all follow the same standard layout as in Figure 2.12, their sizes may differ. Many Web phones have only three or four visible lines in the display. To view the screen, the user must manually scroll down using the phone's scroll button. As we mentioned in the HDML

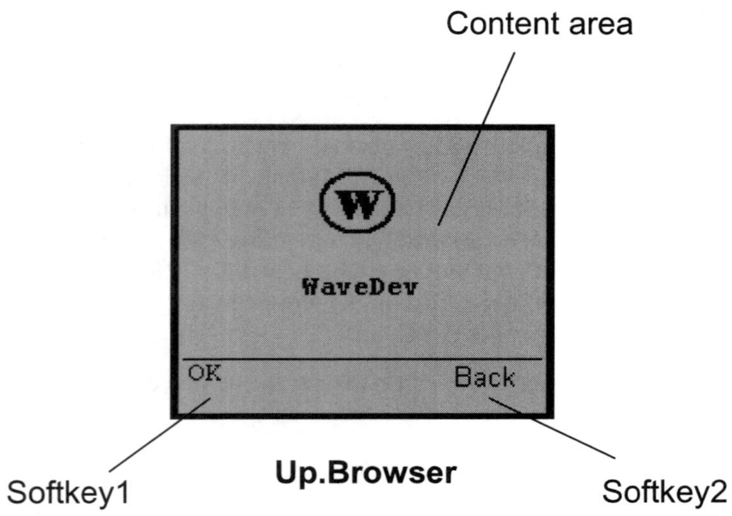

Figure 2.12 Up.Browser screen layout from UP.SDK 4.1.

section, this limitation is very frustrating and hopefully the manufacturers will soon develop phones with larger screen displays.

The second most popular Web phone microbrowser is from Nokia, which has its own screen display image as seen in Figure 2.13. Basically both the Up.Browser and Nokia screens generally look the same on the actual devices but the SDKs do have different appearances as seen in Chapter 1.

Even so, there are some operational differences, for example, the Softkey is placed on the lower right side and the Option key is placed on the lower left side of the display. This may look the same but is actually completely different behind the scenes as will be explained later on. Note that these keys are not reversed on any models other than Nokia since only Nokia uses the Nokia browser and therefore can ensure certain standards for all phones using the Nokia browser.

Cards and Decks

An entire WML program consists of one *deck* made up of one or more *cards*. The reasoning behind this terminology is that microbrowsers can hold multiple cards at once, hence the natural term *deck*. In the familiar HTML Web programming language, only one page is returned to the browser but with WML as well as HDML, many pages are returned at once so the term *cards* is used rather than pages. While many cards are available to the microbrowser, only one card is visible at a time and the others are behind the scenes in memory of the physical device (called a *cache*). As mentioned in Chapter 1, physical device cache size is limited and therefore one must be aware of the deck size being sent to the device, which includes the image size. UP.Link server has a transmission limit to UP.Phones of roughly 1492 bytes but as a general rule, it's best to limit the maximum size to 1200 bytes.

The reason many cards are available to the WAP microbrowser at once is twofold. First, the cards are generally quite small and, second, since latency issues exist when fetch-

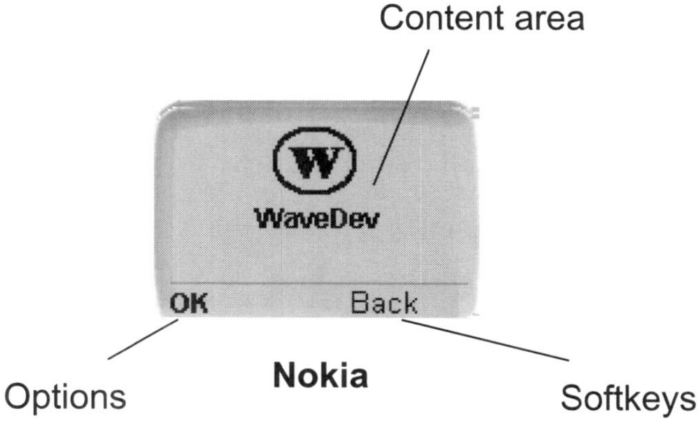

Figure 2.13 Nokia screen layout from Nokia WAP Toolkit 2.0.

ing the cards from the WAP site, many cards are prefetched at the same time. Therefore, by sending multiple cards (a deck) per request, quick response times can be simulated. This sounds a bit odd, but it will make more sense as you read on. WML and HDML are similar to HTML in many areas. If you are not familiar with HTML Web programming, the following topics may be more difficult to understand since we assume you have a minimal HTML foundation.

Figures 2.14 and 2.15 show examples of a simple WML program (deck) with one card. Notice that Figure 2.14 uses the Phone.com (Openwave) DTD, line 2.

Line 1 from Figure 2.14 defines the entire program as an XML document.

Line 2 specifies the DTD being used and the URL to that DTD. If using the DTD for Nokia (found at the www.wapforum.com), the following code would be used:

```
<!DOCTYPE wml PUBLIC "-//WAPFORUM//DTD WML 1.1//EN"
"http://www.wapforum.org/DTD/wml_1.1.xml">
```

Lines 3 and 9 represent the begin and end tags for a simple WML deck, <wml> and </wml>.

Lines 4 through 8 is one WML card that defines the actual data to be displayed in the Content Area. The begin card tag, <card id="card1">, contains the *id* attribute, which is used to define a specific card and is used in other cards or decks for navigational purposes. For more details on this attribute and a list of attributes for this and other tags, see Appendix B. Attributes may or may not exist, depending on which DTD profile is used. Again see Appendix B for a thorough list including which popular DTDs contain which tags and tag attributes.

Lines 5 and 7 contain the begin and end paragraph tags, <p> and </p>, identical to HTML paragraph tags. In WML all displayable text is put, by default, in paragraph mode.

Line 6 is the main attraction for our example since it contains the actual displayable data to be shown on the screen display. Note that since an ampersand (&) is a special character on microbrowsers, special substitution must be used, in this case &. See Text Formatting for more details.

```
1.  <?xml version="1.0"?>
2.  <!DOCTYPE wml PUBLIC "-//PHONE.COM//DTD WML 1.1//EN"
    "http://www.phone.com/dtd/wml11.dtd">
3.  <wml>
4.      <card id="card1">
5.          <p>
6.          Wiley &amp; Sons Inc.
7.          </p>
8.      </card>
9.  </wml>
```

Figure 2.14 Basic WML program with one card using Phone.com DTD.

Figure 2.15 Result of WML program ch02fig14.wml (Figure 2.14).

In this simple case, the exact same WML code can be used for Nokia with one small result difference; since no navigation features are used, the phone display will not show the OK Options label as it does for Up.Browser's Softkey1—on the SDKs.

Basic Components

WML is a full open source markup language. This means that by mixing and matching tags and their attributes, a programmer can create code to perform specific functions. From the Web phone's point of view, the individual functions are all interconnected by means of some sort of navigation, which all comes down to pressing buttons on the phone pad.

From this overly simplified description of WML, we can begin our introduction of the basic components and usage of the language. In this section we do not intend to teach the full usage of the WML language but to introduce the concept and elements of the language. By describing the basic tags and showing their usage in several programs, we hope to quickly educate the reader in understanding the language. Hopefully, after reading our examples, you will be able to modify the code to suit your own needs. And with the help of the vendor's development guides, language references, and our appendices, you'll be able to advance your programming knowledge to design and develop working usable WAP applications for yourself.

As with HTML Web programming, WAP applications have the same basic requirements. First is to simply display information on the screen. Enlarging or reducing the size of certain words, arranging the words, sentences, or topics in specific manners or, since a picture is worth a thousand words, simply displaying an image can enhance this information. Next is to allow the user to navigate. For Web phones, pressing buttons usually accomplishes this. Or, as with HTML, navigation is done by clicking on hyperlinks or choosing an item from a drop-down list box. In WAP, all values for drop-down boxes are immediately displayed, thus allowing the user to select from a list of items by either simply scrolling to the item and clicking the related button for its acceptance or by pressing a predefined related button that corresponds to that item. From a programmer's point of view, navigation can be back and forth between cards within the same deck or between cards in different decks.

In addition to the screen appearance and the ability to select a navigational action, users may want to enter data for use by the application to compute the next course of action, which in turn may be one of these functions all over again—and so on.

For users, this is about all that can happen on the physical device. From the programmer's perspective, there are many methods to achieve these tasks and different programmers may choose different methods. To make matters a bit more complex, programming for different browser types and physical phone models can be difficult since different browsers interpret the code in different manners as per the DTD definitions.

Screen Display

The end user may see a simple screen displayed on the Web phone but, as all programmers know, to arrive at even the most basic displays requires a certain fundamental knowledge of text formatting, image usage, and table definitions, which are explained below.

Text Formatting

Text formatting includes the use of white space, styles, paragraphing, line wrapping, line breaks, and special characters.

White Space. Both Nokia and Up.Browser limit white space usage by reducing recurring contiguous white space to a single occurrence. White space is defined as a newline, carriage return, space, or tab character.

Styles. Both popular microbrowsers also share the same style tags, which are similar to their corresponding HTML tags, shown in Table 2.2.

Paragraph, Line Wrapping, and Line Breaks. Paragraph tags, <p>..</p>, are similar to their HTML counterpart but unlike forgiving HTML browsers, for Up.Browser and Nokia browsers, the ending </p> must always be specified. Also, since WML is case-sensitive, the tags must always be written in lowercase. The paragraph tags will section text by forcing a line break at the beginning of the paragraph. A card displaying text must contain a paragraph tag—SDKs will add the tags if they are initially omitted. As in HTML, alignment can be specified by using the align attribute. Left, center, or right can be specified with the default being left, <p align="left">..</p>.

Line wrapping can be enforced via the same paragraph tags. Simply specify the mode attribute to either wrap or nowrap the line. Line wrapping always defaults to the last specified mode value or to nowrap if no previous mode has been specified, <p align="left" mode="wrap">..</p>. Line wrapping forces the text to appear within the size of the device's display window. Scrolling is then simply up and down via the scroll key. If nowrap is entered, text will span the width of the device, plus some, forcing the user to right/left scroll if the device allows it. Up.Browser automatically goes into the "marque" mode where each screen width of text will be displayed for a split second, kind of an automatic right and left screen scroll, which is very handy.

Table 2.2 Style Tags

Big	<big>..</big>	Change the relative size of text bigger.
Bold	<b>..</b>	Make text stand out in boldface.
Emphasis	<em>..</em>	Less popular but same as italic.
Italic	<i>..</i>	Make text stand out in italics.
Small	<small>..</small>	Change the relative size of text smaller.
Strong	<strong>..</strong>	Less popular but same as bold b.
Underline	<u>..</u>	Underline text.

The line break tag, <br/>, is also similar to HTML except a forward slash is included to identify it to the WML gateway. This takes effect no matter which paragraph mode is being used.

Special Characters. Certain characters are interpretable so their escape sequence (or ASCII number) must be used, if they are to be included as text. See Table 2.3.

Images

Other than text, the only other item that can show up on a WAP screen is an image. Remember the discussion on deck size limits? Well, the size of an image is also counted toward that limit restriction. Different devices have different limits but when coding your programs, we found it best to code for the least common denominator—1200 bytes. So, an image of 2K within a deck may allow the card to display on an SDK but will return an error on an actual phone, depending on phone cache size.

Images used on wireless devices must currently conform to specific rules due to the size limitations and lack of device processing power (used to decompress images). Images can only be black and white, and noncompressed. These images have their own type called *wireless bitmap* (WBMP).

WAP gateways convert images to WBMPs automatically; however, this may cause problems. We've used .bmp files for Up.Browser and .gif images for the Nokia browsers, and they seem to work fine. However, the correct thing to do would be to convert the image using a conversion tool, which can be found at www.anywhereyougo.com. A nice conversion tool is pic2wbmp, which gives really nice results.

Another problem with images is the size of the device window. Many devices still only allow four visible lines in the display window. If the image spans more lines, you'll have to scroll down. Even worse, some devices will crop the image if it doesn't completely fit in the viewable window.

Another sort of image used is called an *icon image*. These images are predefined and available on the gateway supplied by the vendor. These are generally used to denote a link, that is, a smiley face, a tiny picture of a car, a left hand or right hand icon, etc. For more details, see the vendor's WML language reference manual.

Table 2.3 Special Characters

NAME	CHAR	ASCII	ESCAPE SEQUENCE
Ampersand	&	&	&
Apostrophe	'	'	'
Dollar sign	$		&dol; or $$
Greater than	>	>	>
Less than	<	<	<
Nonbreaking space	space		
Quote	"	"	"
Soft hyphen	-		
Any ASCII character		&#nn;	(nn is the ASCII code)

Images are represented by the <img/> element tag. Remember, a single tag with a slash denotes that no end tag is required. The main attributes are the alt and src. Alt is the alternative text displayed in place of the image if the image doesn't exist, cannot be found, or simply cannot be displayed. The src attribute is used as the source location of the image. The Localsrc attribute is used to override the src attribute if an icon is being used. The localsrc name is the actual icon name such as lefthand or smileyface. See Figures 2.16 and 2.17.

With the proper images and wireless Internet device, animation is possible with the scrolling of multiple images. The comic strip in Figures 2.18 and 2.19 is simply three consecutive decks each with one card containing one image. In the examples, pressing the Next button will jump from one image to the next. The inclusion of a timer (explained in the Navigation section) could automate the Next button pressing.

Notice the <img> tag at lines 8, 18, and 28 in the three programs in Figure 2.18. Also notice the formatting on the same lines, which centers the image on the screen via the <p align="center">..</p> tags.

For these programs to function on the Nokia browser, the image source must be changed to either a .gif or better yet the .wbmp format.

Tables

Tables are a method of organizing the display. But be careful of wrapping column content and line breaks.

The table tags, <table>..</table>, are similar to the table tags in HTML but with limitations. Table tag attributes are align (left, center, right), title (to label the table), and columns (specific number of columns in the table, must be greater than zero). The column attribute must be specified, and we recommend always specifying the title attribute too. Tables have rows, <tr>..</tr>, and columns, <td>..</td>. None of these tags has any attributes. See Figures 2.20 and 2.21.

```
1.  <?xml version="1.0"?>
2.  <!DOCTYPE wml PUBLIC "-//PHONE.COM//DTD WML 1.1//EN"
       "http://www.phone.com/dtd/wml11.dtd">
3.  <wml>
4.     <card id="card1">
5.         <p align="center"><br/>
6.         <img src="http://www.wavedev.com/wireless/wavebig.bmp"
           alt="WaveDev"/>
7.         <br/><br/><b>WaveDev</b>
8.         </p>
9.     </card>
10. </wml>
```

Figure 2.16 Image tag usage.

Notice the paragraph tags: If they are left out or, more precisely, the table tags are not between them, the program will receive an error. The table tag must have the column attribute defined as well as be between the paragraph tags.

Navigation

From the physical device usage point of view, navigation is simple. Either press a button or scroll down to an item on the screen and then press a button. If all else fails, press another button. Someone has to understand the technical details behind all this button pressing, which involves knowing how to design and code the basic navigational tags. This section will explain to that someone, the common methods used to program those buttons.

Links, Menus, and Buttons

It all starts with the screen display. The screen is divided into two general areas: the Content Area and the key labels (Option and Softkey). The Content Area navigational

Figure 2.17 Screen using image.

```
Island1.wml
1.  <?xml version="1.0"?>
2.  <!DOCTYPE wml PUBLIC "-//PHONE.COM//DTD WML 1.1//EN"
       "http://www.phone.com/dtd/wml11.dtd">
3.  <wml>
4.     <card id="card1">
5.        <do  type="accept" label="Next">
6.           <go  href="http://www.wavedev.com/wireless/island2.wml"/>
7.        </do>
8.        <p align="center"><img src="Island1.bmp" alt="Panel1"/></p>
9.     </card>
10. </wml>


Island2.wml
11. <?xml version="1.0"?>
12. <!DOCTYPE wml PUBLIC "-//PHONE.COM//DTD WML 1.1//EN"
       "http://www.phone.com/dtd/wml11.dtd">
13. <wml>
14.    <card id="card1">
15.       <do  type="accept" label="Next">
16.          <go  href="http://www.wavedev.com/wireless/Island3.wml"/>
17.       </do>
18.       <p align="center"><img src="Island2.bmp" alt="Panel2"/></p>
19.    </card>
20. </wml>


Island3.wml
21. <?xml version="1.0"?>
22. <!DOCTYPE wml PUBLIC "-//PHONE.COM//DTD WML 1.1//EN"
      "http://www.phone.com/dtd/wml11.dtd">
23. <wml>
24.    <card id="card1">
25.       <do  type="accept" label="Next">
26.          <go  href="http://www.wavedev.com/wireless/Island1.wml"/>
27.       </do>
28.        <p align="center"><img src="Island3.bmp" alt="Panel3"/></p>
29.    </card>
30. </wml>
```

Figure 2.18 Island animation program

items are either numbered items or anchors. *Anchors* are called *links* or *hyperlinks* in HTML Web programming.

Openwave bases its content on numbered items while Nokia bases its content more on nonnumbered items or anchors. Anchors function on both microbrowsers, but on

Figure 2.19 Island animation strip.

Up.Browser they are represented by the item enclosed in square brackets—not too visually appealing.

By default, Openwave's first nine items (options) are numbered from one through nine. These numbers are directly related to the numbers on the phone keypads. Press any button 1 through 9 on the phone and it directly relates to the underlying link for the first numbered item on the screen display. Obviously, Openwave's design was initially designed for Web phones. Nokia, on the other hand, also allows numbered items but not by default. With Nokia's browser, the programmer must specifically set the accesskey on the GO or INPUT statements to correspond to the phone's keypad numbers. Some programmers enjoy the Openwave default; others prefer Nokia's open source. I don't think one way is necessarily better than the other; they are simply different methods of programming that one must consider when creating an application that incorporates both microbrowser types. Most phones only display a few lines so the

```
1.  <?xml version="1.0"?>
2.  <!DOCTYPE wml PUBLIC "-//PHONE.COM//DTD WML 1.1//EN"
      "http://www.phone.com/dtd/wml11.dtd">
3.  <wml>
4.      <card id="card1">
5.          <p>Basketball Score
6.          <table title="table1" columns="2">
7.              <tr>
8.                  <td>Bears</td>
9.                  <td>Tigers</td>
10.             </tr>
11.             <tr>
12.                 <td>82</td>
13.                 <td>110</td>
14.             </tr>
15.         </table>
16.         </p>
17.     </card>
18. </wml>
```

Figure 2.20 Table example code.

Up.Browser

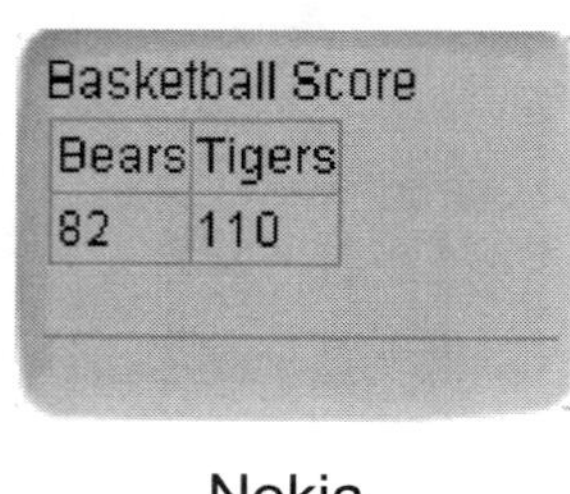

Nokia

Figure 2.21 Table screen results.

user must scroll down the list to find a desired item, numbered or not. Once an item is found, then the user can either press the Option or Softkey label relating to the item or press the related keypad button, if the items are numbered. I guess Nokia figures that since most users will probably be scrolling anyway, they'll use the Option label key rather than the keypad buttons.

Now since the whole concept behind Web phones is based on minimal input, maximum choices, and lots of scrolling, applications should be designed in a structural manner giving the users navigational options via choosing one item or another. The least amount of button pressing (*clicks* in Web terms) to obtain the desired result the better. In general, we find it best to use the nine items with two or three navigational choices per card method. This forces more attention on the application structure in the design phase.

Up.Browser: Select and Options. The Select/Options element is often used with Up.Browsers to create numbered menu items as seen in Figure 2.22. Nokia can use Select/Options for menus too, but we find the Select element is mostly used for selecting options for input, very much like drop-down list boxes in HTML Web programming.

As can be seen in the result, Figure 2.23, a nice numbered menu is easily generated and simple to use. For example, to select *Search by Title* simply press the 1 button on the phone's keypad.

Lines 6 through 10 of Figure 2.22 show the simple Select and Option code. There are more attributes to the Select statement but none are necessary for our example. See Appendix B at the back of this book for more details on other attributes.

Lines 7, 8, and 9 show the Option attributes, which also use the *onpick* attribute. An obvious usage here, when the item (option) is selected or picked, control is given to the full or relative URL in this attribute. Very easy and simple to maintain, which is one of the top requirements when building any application.

Nokia presents the same code from Figure 2.22 in a slightly different manner. Of course, the WAPForum DTD would be used here. Nokia displays the first select

```
1.  <?xml version="1.0"?>
2.  <!DOCTYPE wml PUBLIC "-//PHONE.COM//DTD WML 1.1//EN"
       "http://www.phone.com/dtd/wml11.dtd">
3.  <wml>
4.      <card id="card1">
5.          <p align="center"><b>Wiley &amp; Sons<br/>Book Search</b></p><p
            align="left">
6.          <select>
7.              <option onpick="title.wml">Search by Title</option>
8.              <option onpick="author.wml">Search by Author</option>
9.              <option onpick="booklist.wml">List of Books</option>
10.         </select>
11.         </p>
12.     </card>
13. </wml>
```

Figure 2.22 Up.Browser Select element usage.

option on the main screen and by pressing the options (Select) key, the entire selection appears at which point the user can scroll and select the desired choice, not a great use of the same technique and actually a bit of a hassle. See Figure 2.24. For this reason, when programming this same design on Nokia microbrowsers, we use the Anchor element as described next and only use the Select option for selecting data choices.

Nokia: Anchor and Go. We find a much more reasonable approach to creating Nokia menus is through the use of the Anchor and Go elements as seen in Figure 2.25.

As you can see, the resulting Figure 2.26 is more similar to Figure 2.23 as our initial design was intended. Here the user simply scrolls down to the desired item and presses the Option label key. The documentation does mention the accesskey attribute for the Anchor element with Nokia—but the SDK does not seem to accept it so we left it out. The difference on the screen is that each item is underlined and is very intuitive since we're all accustomed to this usage on regular Web pages.

Figure 2.23 Up.Browser Select element usage.

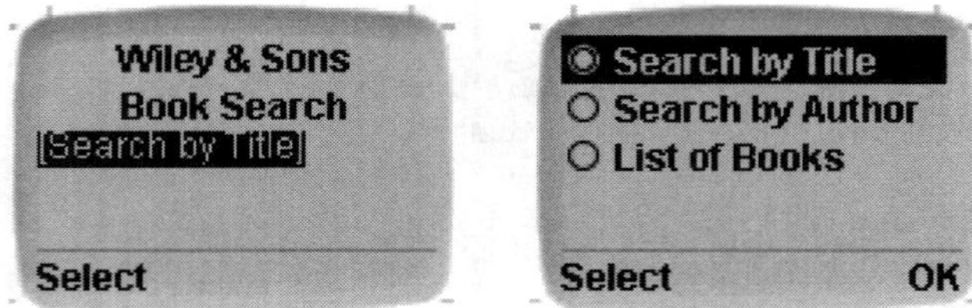

Figure 2.24 Nokia Select element usage.

Figure 2.25 shows the basic usage of the Anchor element only having the titles attribute. This attribute, which is available on both microbrowsers, sets the Option label, which adds a little more descriptive context to each item. As the user scrolls down the list of items, the Option label changes.

Following is the basic Go element. This element is used to specify the full or relative URL address. Once the user presses the Option label key for the selected item, control is passed to that URL.

Figure 2.27 is a result of the same code in Figure 2.25, but using phone.com's DTD. Notice here that the items are not numbered and instead of being underlined, each item is defined between square brackets, not a pretty picture, but still very usable. We suggest using the Anchor element for Nokia menus and the Select element for Up.Browser menus.

As you become more aware of different WAP sites, you'll notice other differences in appearance and now you'll know from just a simple glance how the code is set up, the potential dual usage considerations of the application, the potential primary program functionality considerations, and more.

```
1.  <?xml version="1.0"?>
2.  <!DOCTYPE wml PUBLIC "-//WAPFORUM//DTD WML 1.1//EN"
    "http://www.wapforum.org/DTD/wml_1.1.xml">
3.  <wml>
4.      <card id="card1">
5.          <p align="center"><b>Wiley &amp; Sons<br/> Book Search</b></p><p
            align="left">
6.          <anchor title="Titles"><go href="title.wml"/>Search by
            Title</anchor><br/>
7.          <anchor title="Authors"><go href="author.wml"/>Search by
            Author</anchor><br/>
8.          <anchor title="List"><go href="booklist.wml"/>List of
            Books</anchor><br/>
9.          </p>
10.     </card>
11. </wml>
```

Figure 2.25 Nokia Anchor element usage.

Figure 2.26 Nokia Anchor element usage.

Buttons. Let's not forget about the buttons. You've been reading about them and their usage. We've already seen the default usage of the keypad buttons in Up.Browser's Select and Options statements. In passing we mentioned the accesskey attribute to the Anchor element, which assigns an Anchor item to a keypad button—also used as an attribute to the Nokia's Input element as seen in the next section.

Let's simplify and reorganize the potential uses for buttons. First, there are the keypad buttons and then the Options/Softkey buttons.

Keypad Buttons. For Up.Browser, keypad buttons are programmed mainly by the use of the Select/Option statements as explained above.

For Nokia microbrowser, keypad buttons are programmed via the accesskey attribute of the Anchor and the Input elements, but we rarely use them. We prefer simple links (anchors), scrolling, and using the Options label key.

Options, Softkeys, and Back Buttons. Most navigation is done via the Option, Softkey, and Back buttons. Most selectable items on a screen have the Option button defined. And most Web phones have a Back button defined.

The Back button is used to navigate back through the history stack (refer to the section on History Stack in the HDML Structure section earlier in this chapter because it applies to WML also). Some phones don't have a defined Back button and so it's wise to always program for such an event along with the application's regular navigational commands. There are two ways to program a Back button. First is to include it in the

Figure 2.27 Up.Browser Anchor element usage.

menu selection list (Select/Option for Up.Browser or Anchor for Nokia). Second is to specify it as either the primary or secondary Softkey label. I call the Option label (for Nokia) or Softkey1 (for Up.Browser) the primary Softkey label. The secondary Softkey label is Softkey (for Nokia) and Softkey2 (for Up.Browser). See Figures 2.12 and 2.13.

Do Statement

A widely used navigational statement is the Do element. Do, as it implies, does an action based on some type of event.

```
<do  type="accept" label="Titles">
    <go  href="#titles"/>
</do>
<do  type="accept" label="Authors">
    <go  href="#authors"/>
</do>
```

Here, two Do statements are defined to the Softkeys. On Up.Browser, if the specific phone has the ability to show two Softkeys, one would show Titles and the other would show Authors. If another Do statement were defined, the microbrowser would jump into menu mode, which is similar to Figure 2.24 when Nokia uses the Select/Option statement. Up.Browser will display the first Do statement on one Softkey label and show the word Menu for the other. If the Menu label button is pressed, the next screen image will contain all but the first Do statement choices as in Figures 2.28 and 2.29.

Nokia is different here. The Nokia microbrowser only allows one Do statement per Accept type. The code in Figure 2.28 will not function and will return a compile error of multiple Do statement names. Beware that even though many of the commands look the same for Up.Browser and Nokia, they do not produce the same results.

There are many Do types but by far the most used are Accept, Prev, and Options. Accept is the normal result associated with OK for most applications, Prev is associated with the usual Back function, and Options is used as a general type each differentiated by the name attribute.

Instead of using the Accept type for the above example, the Options type would be better suited. Rather than <do type="accept" label="Titles"> use <do type="options" label="Titles" name="titles">. The Options type shows up better on the screen and is functional on both Up.Browser and Nokia with the same results. See Figures 2.30 and 2.31.

PROGRAMMING TIP

■■■■■■ We try to program as much as possible in structured menus as mentioned earlier. If there are many navigational choices, we include these at the end of the nine-item menu. In the case of Figures 2.28 and 2.30, we would have used a simple Select/Option statement for Up.Browser and Anchor/Go for Nokia. Yes, we prefer two distinct program source directories, one for each microbrowser, rather than using the Do/Options choice just presented—a pain but worth the effort.

```
1.  <?xml version="1.0"?>
2.  <!DOCTYPE wml PUBLIC "-//PHONE.COM//DTD WML 1.1//EN"
      "http://www.phone.com/dtd/wml11.dtd">
3.  <wml>
4.      <card id="card1">
5.          <do  type="accept" label="Titles">
6.              <go  href="#titles"/>
7.          </do>
8.          <do  type="accept" label="Authors">
9.              <go  href="#authors"/>
10.         </do>
11.         <do  type="accept" label="Books">
12.             <go  href="#booklist"/>
13.         </do>
14.         <p align="center"><b>Wiley &amp; Sons<br/>Book Search</b></p><p
            align="left">
15.         Choose the type of Search
16.         </p>
17.     </card>
18. </wml>
```

Figure 2.28 Many Do's.

Template

For a deck with many cards, there can be recurring identical DO statements. Rather than duplicating the same statement for every card in the deck, the Template option is used at the deck level. All statements within the Template would then apply to every card within the deck. Individual cards can override the deck level statements by simply specifying the same DO statement name and a different action at the card level.

In Figure 2.32, lines 4 through 14 show the use of the TEMPLATE statement. Every card in the deck will have these three DO statements unless an individual card is overridden by its own DO statement as on lines 21 to 23 in the Titles card. For every card, when the

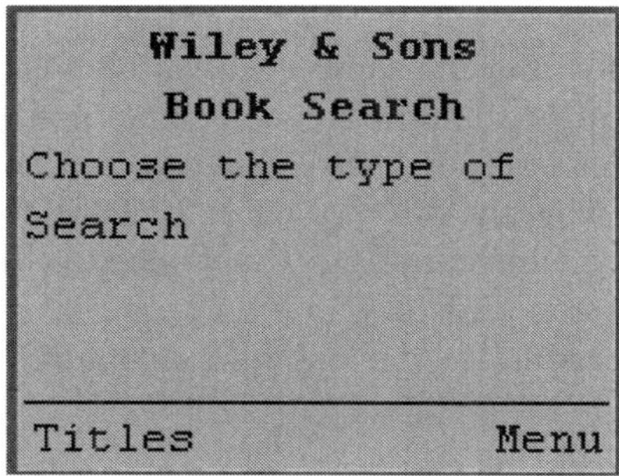

Figure 2.29 Many Do Results.

```
1.  <?xml version="1.0"?>
2.  <!DOCTYPE wml PUBLIC "-//PHONE.COM//DTD WML 1.1//EN"
     "http://www.phone.com/dtd/wml11.dtd">
3.  <wml>
4.      <card id="card1">
5.          <do type="options" label="Titles" name="titles">
6.             <go href="#titles"/>
7.          </do>
8.          <do type="options" label="Authors" name="authors">
9.             <go href="#authors"/>
10.         </do>
11.         <do type="options" label="Books" name="books">
12.            <go href="#booklist"/>
13.         </do>
14.         <p align="center"><b>Wiley &amp; Sons<br/>Book Search</b></p><p
            align="left">
15.         Choose the type of Search
16.         </p>
17.     </card>
18. </wml>
```

Figure 2.30 Many Do's with Options type.

Softkey labeled Titles is pressed, control is passed to the Titles card. On this card, if Titles is pressed, control is passed to the OldTitles card. Again, once on the OldTitles card, if Titles is pressed, control will be passed to the Titles card. For the Options type, if the DO statement name attribute is identical to another DO statement name attribute, it will be replaced. Try this example and change the name on line 21 from titles to oldtitles and see what happens. Result: When on the Titles card, there will be four options: OldTitles, Titles, Authors, and Books.

The Template statement is also valid for Nokia but with several different attributes. The usage is identical but only one Accept type is allowed.

Backward and Forward

We've seen how to jump to another card within the same deck via menus, links, and do's. Remember that to jump to another card within the same deck requires the # symbol followed by the card name where the URL is specified. We've also seen how to jump to a card in another deck by simply specifying the full or relative URL followed by the card name in the deck, i.e., <go href="titles.wml#card2"/>. This jumps to card2 in program titles.wml, which is located in the same directory as the current program. If no card is specified, the default is the first card in the deck. Jumping to another card or URL is mostly a forward navigation.

To jump backward to a previous URL or card, use either the Back button on the keypad or the Prev element. Both of these methods remove the current URL from the top of the

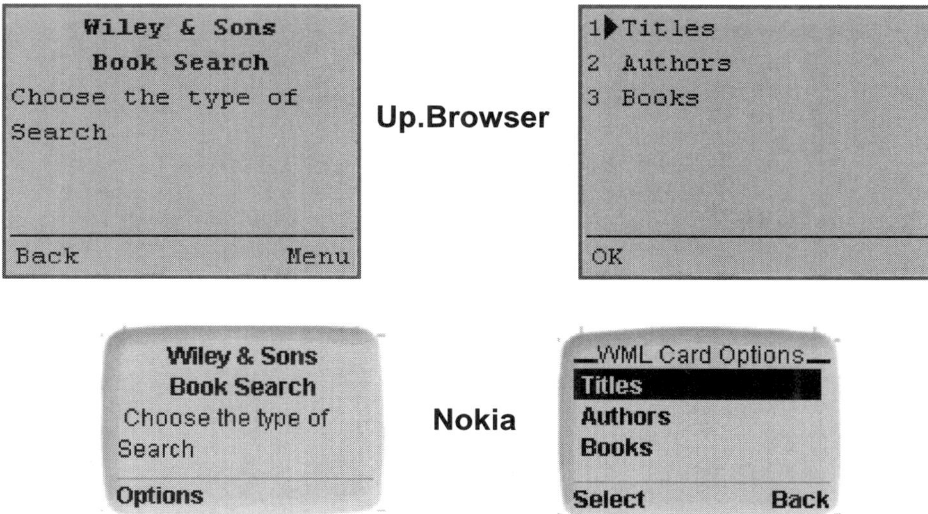

Figure 2.31 Many Do's Results.

history stack and pass control to the previous entry in the stack. If no more entries exist in the stack, then nothing happens.

The history stack is a one-way stack. Every time a new URL is encountered, it is placed on the history stack. To navigate backward, simply pass control to the previous entry in the stack. Once this is done, the top entry in the stack is removed and navigation cannot return to any removed items unless the URL is reentered. Note: To instantly clear the history stack, a newcontext=true attribute can be set at the <card> level. This will remove all context specific variables, and clear the stack history.

The Prev element can be used by itself, </prev>, or with content (only setvar elements), <prev>content</prev>, that is, <do type="accept" label="Prev"></prev></do>. This Do statement will display the Prev as one of the Softkeys or in a menu if more than two DO statements are encountered. Once the user presses the related button, control will pass back to the previous history stack entry.

Events

The most used form of programmable navigation is events. An *event* represents an action that is to take place such as onpick, onenterforward, onenterbackward, and ontimer.

- **Onpick.** A user selects an option.
- **Onenterforward.** A card has been invoked via a GO statement.
- **Onenterbackward.** Navigation to a card via the Prev statement.
- **Ontimer.** A timer element has expired thus invoking an action.

```
1.  <?xml version="1.0"?>
2.  <!DOCTYPE wml PUBLIC "-//PHONE.COM//DTD WML 1.1//EN"
    "http://www.phone.com/dtd/wml11.dtd">
3.  <wml>
4.      <template>
5.          <do type="options" label="Titles" name="titles">
6.              <go href="#titles"/>
7.          </do>
8.          <do type="options" label="Authors" name="authors">
9.              <go href="#authors"/>
10.         </do>
11.         <do type="options" label="Books" name="books">
12.             <go href="#booklist"/>
13.         </do>
14.     </template>
15.     <card id="card1">
16.         <p align="center"><b>Wiley &amp; Sons<br/>Book Search</b></p><p
            align="left">
17.         Choose the type of Search
18.         </p>
19.     </card>
20.     <card id="titles">
21.         <do type="options" label="OldTitles" name="titles">
22.             <go href="#oldtitles"/>
23.         </do>
24.         <p align="center"><b>Wiley &amp; Sons<br/>Titles</b></p><p
            align="left">
25.         Titles
26.         </p>
27.     </card>
28.     <card id="oldtitles">
29.         <p align="center"><b>Wiley &amp; Sons<br/>Old Titles</b></p><p
            align="left">
30.         Old Titles
31.         </p>
32.     </card>
33.     <card id="authors">
34.         <p align="center"><b>Wiley &amp; Sons<br/>Authors</b></p><p
            align="left">
35.         Authors
36.         </p>
37.     </card>
38.     <card id="booklist">
39.         <p align="center"><b>Wiley &amp; Sons<br/>Book List</b></p><p
            align="left">
40.         Book List
41.         </p>
42.     </card>
43. </wml>
```

Figure 2.32 Template example.

These events are invoked via an <onevent> element, an <option> element, or as part of a <template> or <card> element. Let's say navigation passes from a menu card to a card giving some sort of warning and then passes on to a signon card. If you were to back up one level once on the signon card, you'd want control to return to the menu card and not the warning card. This is done via the onenterbackward type of onevent as shown in Figure 2.33.

So, when control is passed to card1 of Figure 2.33 via a </prev> command, the <onevent> is invoked because of the onenterbackward type. Then the </prev> command within that <onevent> removes the current URL from the history stack, which is the current card, and returns control to the previous entry in the stack, which is the original menu card from our example.

The onenterforward type works in the same manner but is invoked if control is passed to the card via a GO statement from another card.

We could have put the onenterbackward type at the card level rather than include an <onevent> element on line 4 as shown in Figure 2.34.

On the card element, onenterbackward specifies a specific URL and not the last entry in the history stack. So, if control is to return to a specific URL, this method is quite useful.

Timers

Timers are useful for automatic navigation usually used to invoke another task after some period of time. The Timer element is used to count down in tenths of a second. <timer name="abc" value="30"> will count down 3 seconds.

Used with the ontimer type of an <onevent> element, the Timer element is primarily used to briefly display messages, logos, advertisements, or help screens. See Figure 2.35.

As seen on line 4, the ontimer attribute is used to invoke the relative URL, mainmenu.wml. This action is taken only after the timer on line 5 counts down from 3 seconds to 0 seconds in increments of 1/10th second. In the meantime, if the user wants to proceed without waiting for the timer, the Softkey label OK is programmed to go to the same URL and can be invoked at any time.

User Input

The last topic of the three wireless Web phone divisions is user input. We have already discussed screen display and navigation. Applications may have screen display and navigation but without user input, no dynamic interaction is possible. So we need some sort of user input statement to accept the data as well as a method to pass the input from one card, deck, or program to another.

Input Statement

Other than clever or strategic Select and/or Option elements, the best method to accept user input is via the <input> element. The concept is the same as the <input> element

```
1.  <?xml version="1.0"?>
2.  <!DOCTYPE wml PUBLIC "-//PHONE.COM//DTD WML 1.1//EN"
       "http://www.phone.com/dtd/wml11.dtd" >
3.  <wml>
4.      <card id="card1">
5.          <onevent type="onenterbackward">
6.              </prev>
7.          </onevent>
8.          <do type="accept" label="OK">
9.              <go href="signon.wml"/>
10.         </do>
11.         <do type="accept" label="Back">
12.              </prev>
13.         </do>
14.         <p align="center"><b>WorldJobMart</b>** Warning **</p><p
            align="left">
15.         Members Only<br/>beyond this point.
16.         </p>
17.     </card>
18. </wml>
```

Figure 2.33 Onevent and onenterbackward example.

for a FORM statement in HTML programming. This is a powerful element for WML. Input data formats can be used, default values can be set, and maxlength as well as emptyok can be specified. With all this, the programmer can place controls on the type of input data received.

There are only two types of input: text and password. Password will mask the input with asterisks. Note, however, that the password mask is not encrypted, and this may be a security problem area.

The format mask is a very powerful attribute. Specific values can be forced in specific locations of text or password types of input as explained in Table 2.4. The number of characters can be limited by specifying a single-digit number before the character tag—this repetition can only be specified at the end of the string. Oppositely, specifying an asterisk before a character tag allows any number of symbolic or lowercase alpha characters—again this repetition can only be specified at the end of the string, that is, format="AAA5N" will only allow three uppercase alpha characters (or symbols) followed by five numbers. But if format="5NAAA" were specified, the format would not take effect since the 5N is at the beginning of the string.

If an input field must have a value entered, use the emptyok=false attribute. If it's OK for no data to be entered, use emptyok=true.Let's have a look at a typical user input as seen on lines 41 and 43 of card 3 in Figure 2.36.

```
1. <?xml version="1.0"?>
2. <!DOCTYPE wml PUBLIC "-//PHONE.COM//DTD WML 1.1//EN"
   "http://www.phone.com/dtd/wml11.dtd">
3. <wml>
4.    <card id="card1" onenterbackward="mainmenu.wml">
5.       <do type="accept" label="OK">
6.          <go href="signon.wml"/>
7.       </do>
8.       <do type="accept" label="Back">
9.          </prev>
10.       </do>
11.       <p align="center"><b>WorldJobMart</b>** Warning **</p><p
          align="left">
12.       Members Only<br/>beyond this point.
13.       </p>
14.    </card>
15. </wml>
```

Figure 2.34 Onenterbackward in <card> element.

This example is a little more complicated than usual as many items are coming together. Since this deck involves userid and a password, it's a good idea to clear the history stack and variables every time the specific card is invoked. We use several methods; first is the newcontext="true" attribute of the Card element on line 12 and second is resetting the variables themselves. The only problem with the first method is that the history stack is cleared, so be sure to explicitly include any navigational choices, as we did on cards 2 and 3 since clearing the history stack will remove previous navigation information.

Table 2.4 Input Format Masks

TAG	DESCRIPTION
A	No numbers—any symbolic or uppercase alpha character
a	No numbers—any symbolic or lowercase alpha character
N	Any numbers—nothing else
X	Any symbolic, uppercase alpha character, or number
x	Any symbolic, lowercase alpha character, or number
M	Any symbolic, uppercase alpha character, or number. For multiple character input, default uppercase first character (DEFAULT)
m	Any symbolic, lowercase alpha character, or number. For multiple character input, default lowercase first character

```
1.  <?xml version="1.0"?>
2.  <!DOCTYPE wml PUBLIC "-//PHONE.COM//DTD WML 1.1//EN"
     "http://www.phone.com/dtd/wml11.dtd">
3.  <wml>
4.     <card id="card1"  ontimer="mainmenu.wml">
5.         <timer name="timer" value="30"/>
6.         <do  type="accept" label="OK">
7.            <go  href="mainmenu.wml"/>
8.         </do>
9.         <p align="center">
10.          <br/><b>powered<br/>by<br/>WaveDev, Inc.</b>
11.          </p>
12.      </card>
13.  </wml>
```

Figure 2.35 Timer example.

The newcontext attribute is included on card 2 rather than the expected card 3 for strategic purposes. By including it on card 2, the stack is cleared every time the card is invoked. If it were to be included on card 3, we'd be wiping out the card 2 variable settings on lines 15 and 16 every time card 3 is invoked. So once on card 4, if the back button is pressed, control goes to the original card 3 with the variables set from the first card 2 settings. Confused yet? Well, to simplify things, run this example on an SDK and at each step of the way, have a look at the history stack and variables to see exactly what's going on.

Lines 41 and 43 contain the input elements. Line 41 is a text type with a maximum length of 15 positions, which cannot be empty as specified by the emptyok="false." A format is also specified, which must be XXXNN*m. This means the first three positions can be any symbolic, numeric, or uppercase alpha character and the next two positions must be numeric (the device will not allow alphabetic characters to be entered). *m means all following positions (only 10 left out of the maxlength of 15) will all be of format mask type m, which means any lowercase character, number, or symbol.

Line 43 defines the password input variable. It is of type password, meaning it will be masked to the user by asterisks. Note that the underlying input data will not be encrypted and will be fully visible to network eyes. Try using an SDK and view the variables after entering data in a password type field. Again a format is used but this time it is XXX5N which means the first three positions are uppercase alphabetic characters or numbers and the last five positions of the maximum eight positions must be numeric. Also note that the recurring numeric in the format denoted by 5N is at the end of the string.

Variables and Parameters

As shown in Figure 2.36 on lines 15 and 16 and 29 and 30, variables can be used to hold and retain data. The <setvar> element is fairly simple: <setvar name="name"

```
1.  <?xml version = "1.0"?>
2.  <!DOCTYPE wml PUBLIC "-//PHONE.COM//DTD WML 1.1//EN"
      "http://www.phone.com/dtd/wml11.dtd">
3.  <wml>
4.  <card id="card1">
5.      <do type="accept" label="OK">
6.          <go href="#card2"/>
7.      </do>
8.      <p align="center"><b>Home<br/>card1</b></p>
9.      <p align="left">Invoke next card via a go<br/>
10.     Userid: $(User)<br/>Password: $(Pswd)</p>
11. </card>
12. <card id="card2" newcontext="true">
13.     <onevent type="onenterforward">
14.      <go href="#card3">
15.         <setvar name="User" value="ABC12abcdefghij"/>
16.         <setvar name="Pswd"  value=""/>
17.      </go>
18.     </onevent>
19.     <do type="accept" label="ReStart">
20.         <go href="#card1"/>
21.     </do>
22.     <p align="center"><b>card2</b></p>
23.     <p align="left">Only see this by pressing back button<br/>
24.     Userid: $(User)<br/>Password: $(Pswd)</p>
25. </card>
26. <card id="card3">
27.     <onevent type="onenterbackward">
28.      <prev>
29.         <setvar name="User" value="www00"/>
30.         <setvar name="Pswd"  value="abcdefgh"/>
31.      </prev>
32.     </onevent>
33.     <do type="accept" label="Login">
34.         <go href="#card4"/>
35.     </do>
36.     <do type="options" label="Home" name="home">
37.         <go href="#card1"/>
38.     </do>
39.     <p align="center"><b>card3<br/>Members Only</b></p><p align="left">
40.         <b>UserID:</b>
41.         <input name="User" maxlength="15" type="text" format="XXXNN*m"
             emptyok="false"/><br/>
42.         <b>Password:</b>
43.         <input name="Pswd" maxlength="8" type="password" format="XXX5N"
             emptyok="false"/><br/>
44.     </p>
45. </card>
46. <card id="card4">
47.     <do type="accept" label="OK">
48.         <go href="login.asp?U=$(User)&amp;P=$(Pswd)"/>
49.     </do>
50.     <do type="options" label="Back">
51.         <prev/>
52.     </do>
53.     <p align="center"><b>card4</b></p>
54.     <p align="left">Press Back button to see variables change.<br/>
55.     Userid: $(User)<br/>Password: $(Pswd)</p>
56. </card>
57. </wml>
```

Figure 2.36 Input element example.

value="value"/> where the name and value attributes are required and, *setVar* can be used in <go>, <prev>, or <refresh> elements. The variables themselves can be defined or used in many other elements as initially seen in the input statement on lines 41 and 43.

In the example, the User and Pswd variables are defined via the <input> elements and set via each <setvar> element. Or is it the other way around? We've included them on each card to show the values of the variables as the program jumps from card to card within the deck. To reference a variable, place the name within parentheses and begin the item with a dollar sign, i.e., $(User). Remember everything is case sensitive so $(user) and $(User) are two different variables.

Lines 16 and 30 each set the variable Pswd to a specific value. Notice the values do not coincide with the format definition on the <input> statement on line 43 (format="XXX5N") since the format attribute only applies to the <input> element.

A method to initialize variables is via the <go>, <prev>, and <refresh> elements. Variables are usually reset or initialized during navigational steps as in lines 14 to 17. These lines basically set the variables that follow to a set value before going to URL (card 3 in this case). Figure 2.36 was created to show the changes in the two variables under differing circumstances. If you execute the program yourself, you'll see how each variable changes. We also suggest playing a bit by adding, deleting, and/or moving specific attributes to see the overall results, that is, move the newcontext attribute from card 2 to card 3. Try moving the <onevent> statement from card 2 to card 3 and see the results.

Line 48 shows the usage of variables as parameters in an HTTP URL request:

```
<go href="login.asp?U=$(User)&amp;P=$(Pswd)"/>
```

As with regular HTTP requests, parameters are introduced by adding a question mark after the program name. An ampersand (&) is usually used to separate two or more parameters in a URL statement. However, an ampersand is a special character in WML (see Text Formatting in Screen Display section) and therefore must be replaced with &. If you've ever spent many hours trying to figure out why an HTTP URL request statement wasn't working and eventually figured out the "special characters" clause in a WML manual, believe me you'll never forget about special characters.

Postfield

Another method of passing variables to an HTTP server is via the postfield element, which operates in conjunction with the <go> statement.

Figure 2.37 shows only the code that replaces the entire fourth card in Figure 2.36, both beginning at line 46. The change is simple, just add the method="post" attribute to the <go> tag and include the postfield elements. The postfield name attributes are the variable names accessible to the asp program.

Figure 2.38 illustrates the login.asp program. In cooperation with both programs (Figures 2.36 and 2.37), login.asp will accept two variables and display them on the screen via line 14. Again note the password field is not encrypted and will be fully visible as the passing and displaying of variables demonstrates.

```
46. <card id="card4">
47.    <do type="accept" label="OK">
48.       <go method="post" href="login.asp">
49.          <postfield name="U" value="$(User)"/>
50.          <postfield name="P" value="$(Pswd)"/>
51.       </go>
52.    </do>
53.    <do type="options" label="Back">
54.       <prev/>
55.    </do>
56.    <p align="center"><b>card4</b></p>
57.    <p align="left">Press Back button to see variables change.<br/>
58.    Userid: $(User)<br/>Password: $(Pswd)</p>
59. </card>
```

Figure 2.37 New card 4 using postfield.

The <go> tag also allows the get method. If postfields are used but no method is specified, the Post method is the default. The difference between the two is that the Get method appends its variables to the end of the URL while the Post method will not show on the URL and is passed within the body of the message. Post is the best bet since URLs may be limited in length on some servers and so appending information to the URL may result in lost data. Also note that line 48 of Figure 2.36 requires special character coding since special characters in a Post method are interpretable but characters in the body of the message are not interpretable and hence do not require special character conversion.

```
1. <%
2. Response.Buffer= TRUE
3. Response.ContentType= "text/vnd.wap.wml"
4. strU = request("U")
5. strP = request("P")
6. %>
7. <?xml version="1.0"?>
8. <!DOCTYPE wml PUBLIC "-//PHONE.COM//DTD WML 1.1//EN"
     "http://www.phone.com/dtd/wml11.dtd">
9. <wml>
10.    <card>
11.       <do type="accept" label="ReStart">
12.          <go href="ch02fig37.wml"/>
13.       </do>
14.       <p>UserID: <%=strU%><br/>Password: <%=strP%></p>
15.    </card>
16. </wml>
```

Figure 2.38 Login.asp program.

WMLScript

While the WML language is nice, it lacks processing flexibility, which is where WMLScript enters the picture. If you are familiar with JavaScript or VBScript, WMLScript should not be difficult to learn. The only current problem with this scripting language is that it's not widely used by developers and therefore there is not as much support as there should be.

WMLScript is designed a bit differently than its cousin JavaScript. Because of device limitations, WMLScript is its own file rather than being appended to the WML program as JavaScript would be in HTML programs. So why use this language extension? The reason is that WML is lacking in functionality and the only scripting language available to WML on the client side (Web phone or PDA) is WMLScript. Client-side data manipulation is important because WAP currently has low bandwidth so that return trips from the device to the server and back again are very slow. The last thing you want is for your users to use someone else's application because yours doesn't function well.

WMLScript files have the .wmls extension and the programs are invoked from the WML cards just as a URL link would be called via an <anchor> tag. The #func1($(DD)) is the function within the file ch02fig40.wmls, which is the same idea as invoking a card within a deck.

```
<a href="ch02fig40.wmls#func1($(DD))>Call Function</a>
```

To get this going, your Web server must be set up with the proper MIME types to allow WMLScript to function. These MIME types are .wmls and .wmlsc (for compiled WMLScript). Also be sure the microbrowser as well as the WAP gateway that are being used support WMLScript.

Basics

Let's look at the basics to this scripting language. We've jotted down in point form many items that you're most likely already familiar with since they form the basis of other scripting languages:

- Commands end with semicolon (;) just as in JavaScript.

- WMLScript is case sensitive.

- Single-line comments begin with // and end at the end of the line.

- Multiple-line comments begin with /* and end with */ (can also only be a single line).

- Define a variable with var (Boolean, Float, Integer, Invalid, or String) all based on the value within the variable, that is, var abc; or var abc, def, xyz; or var cnt = 0; Variable must be defined before being used.

- Arithmetic operations can be done: +, -, *, /, or div. Refer to the vendor's documentation for more details. Shorthand is also available, for example, x++, ++x, or x +=1 all mean the same: x = x + 1.

- Logical operators are &&, ||, and !, and they represent AND, OR, and NOT, respectively.

- Comparison operators are ==, !=, >, >=, <, and <=, and they represent equal, not equal, greater than, greater than or equal to, less than, and less than or equal to, respectively.

- Typeof operators are 0, 1, 2, 3, 4 for integer, float, string, boolean, and invalid. For example, x = typeof y (where y = 2) gives a value in x equal to 0 since y contains an integer.

- Isvalid operator: x = isvalid y gives true if the value is valid or false if invalid as when y = 5/0. (cannot divide by zero).

- If statement: if (condition) statement1 else statement2;
  Don't forget to end the line with a semicolon.
  Can also have if (condition) { statement; }, that is, if (a=b) {x=y;} or if (a=b) x=y;.

Loops: For and While

For (x=1; x<4; x++) { y++; }: The x variable must first be defined, var x;. This for loop will begin with variable x set to 1 and continue the for loop until x reaches a minimum of 4. The loop's variable, x, is incremented by 1 on each re-iterance via the x++ setting. For each loop, the variable y will be incremented by 1 via the y++ command.

While (x<4) { x++; }: Again, the x variable must be defined and now initialized before the while loop. These two functions can be done in one go, i.e, var x = 1;. In the while example, variable x starts at 1 and while it's less than 4, the loop contents will be processed. And the content, x++, will simply add 1 to x on each iteration.

Each type of loop can be stopped at any time via the *break* command, with execution continuing at the command immediately following the loop command.

```
While (x<4)
{
   if (x == 2) break;   // if x is equal to 2 break out of the while loop
   x ++;   // increment the x variable by 1
};
```

Ok, so now we know the basics to the scripting language. If you're a curious sort, then you've probably downloaded and set up Openwave's WML SDK by now. And in doing so, you've seen their WML examples section and quickly viewed the WMLScript examples. To save time, the examples have all been downloaded onto your PC as you installed the SDK. If you had a look, you'd notice much more in the code than just the basics previously described. You'll see the words *function, extern, WMLBrowser, dot* whatever, *Dialog dot* whatever, and so on. These form the second level of WMLScript—the advanced level. A discussion of each follows, but we do recommend that you view each vendor's own documentation.

Functions

Functions are invoked via URL invokable commands such as <anchor> and <go> tags as follows:

```
<a href="ch02fig40.wmls#func1($(DD))>Call Function</a>
```

The file ch02fig40.wmls will contain a function called func1 and will be passed a variable called DD. Functions with the optional keyword extern before the function word itself within the wmls file can be called from outside that file as in our example. Other functions lacking this keyword in the file can only be called from within the file itself. Functions cannot be embedded within another function, but one function can call another.

The WML program ch02fig39.wml has two cards. See Figure 2.39. The first, card0, is to stay in compliance with the onenterforward element in card1, which must be invoked via a GO command. Removing card0 will still allow card1 onenterforward to be invoked, but we decided to stay in compliance with the syntax for the sake of syntax rules.

This program will show the value of a variable initially blank since it's not yet set. Then, on entry to card1, the value is set to 99. With a click on the anchor, line 17, the WMLScript code listed in Figure 2.40 is invoked.

```
1.  <?xml version="1.0"?>
2.  <!DOCTYPE wml PUBLIC "-//PHONE.COM//DTD WML 1.1//EN"
    "http://www.phone.com/dtd/wml11.dtd">
3.  <wml>
4.     <card id="card0">
5.         <do type="accept" label="OK">
6.             <go href="#card1"/>
7.         </do>
8.         <p>a: $(DD)</p>
9.     </card>
10.    <card id="card1">
11.        <onevent type="onenterforward">
12.            <refresh>
13.                <setvar name="DD" value="99"/>
14.            </refresh>
15.        </onevent>
16.        <p>
17.        <a href="ch02fig40.wmls#func1($(DD))">call function</a><br/>
18.        Value: $(DD)
19.        </p>
20.    </card>
21. </wml>
```

Figure 2.39 Invoking WML program, ch02fig39.wml.

```
1. extern function func1(aa)
2. {
3.    var bb = 55;
4.    if (aa < bb)  bb = aa;
5.    func2(bb);
6. }
7. function func2(cc)
8. {
9.    Dialogs.alert("DD value: " + cc + " has been set.");
10.    WMLBrowser.setVar("DD", cc);
11.    WMLBrowser.refresh();
12. }
```

Figure 2.40 WMLScript file, ch02fig40.wmls.

The WMLScript program, ch02fig40.wmls contains two functions, func1 and func2. Func1 can be called from outside the file, and func2 can only be invoked from within the file.

When func1 is externally called, variable DD is passed from ch02fig39.wml, which is locally renamed, to aa on entry to func1. This renaming automatically defines the variable and therefore no var is required. Line 3 defines variable bb and sets it to 55. Depending on the value of variable aa, variable bb remains the same or is changed as per the if statement on line 4. Then function func2 is called on line 5, passing variable bb, which is renamed to cc once in func2. Here in func2, line 9, an alert is sent to the device with some information for the end user. Once the alert is confirmed, the WML variable DD back in ch02fig39.wml is set to the value of cc and upon control being returned to the calling wml program, the current card is refreshed via the command on line 11 of ch02fig40.wmls.

Note, when a return is not specified in a function, an empty string is returned. We could have included a return statement in each function and specified a return value for DD but we chose to use the WMLBrowser.setVar statement instead.

Also notice that each statement in the WMLScript file ends with a semicolon.

Libraries

WMLScript libraries are logically grouped, prebuilt functions that are actually stored on the physical device. To call a function within a library, simply specify the library name followed by a dot and the function name, that is, WMLBrowser.getVar("WMLvariable"). Before writing a complicated script, check to see if it is already written or partly written in one of the libraries. It is always a good idea to refer to existing scripts to see how the other person programmed a particular process.

The available libraries are:

- **WMLBrowser.** Access to WML browser content
- **Dialogs.** Set of functions of typical user-interface abilities (alert, confirm, prompt)
- **URL.** Functions used for handling absolute and relative URLs
- **String.** String functions used on arrays. Arrays are accessed via the index (begins at 0) or via separated entries (in which the separator can be defined)
- **Float.** Floating-point functions—not always available on all devices
- **Lang.** Useful functions closely related to the WML language
- **Console.** Functions used for printing debug information to the SDK info window

Many of the individual library functions are defined in Appendix E, but let's look at the more popular functions being used.

Web Browser

It is very useful to set or get WML variables from within a function, to refresh a card, invoke the prev or newcontext commands, or to simply reroute control to another card, depending on the outcome of some WMLScript calculation or condition. These are done via the WMLBrowser library.

Similar to the examples in Figures 2.39 and 2.40, these figures show the invoking program, ch02fig41.wml, which calls a WMLScript function, ch02fig42.wmls.

```
1.  <?xml version="1.0"?>
2.  <!DOCTYPE wml PUBLIC "-//PHONE.COM//DTD WML 1.1//EN"
      "http://www.phone.com/dtd/wml11.dtd">
3.  <wml>
4.     <card id="card1">
5.        <onevent type="onenterforward">
6.           <refresh>
7.              <setvar name="DD" value="99"/>
8.           </refresh>
9.        </onevent>
10.       <do type="accept" label="OK">
11.          <go href="ch02fig42.wmls#func1()"/>
12.       </do>
13.       <p>
14.       Value: $(DD)
15.       </p>
16.    </card>
17.    <card id="card2">
18.       <p>card2<br/>Value: $(DD)</p>
19.    </card>
20. </wml>
```

Figure 2.41 Invoking WML program, ch02fig41.wml.

Figure 2.42 shows an external callable function called func1, which has no parameters, ( ). We've included alerts (lines 3, 7, and 14) to show the flow of control when executing the scripts.

Line 4 defines and sets variable bb to the value of WML variable DD. Variable DD is actually in the calling WML program, ch02fig42.wml.

Lines 7 through 10 are invoked if the local variable bb is greater than 0.

Line 7 displays an alert on the device and simply displays 222.

Line 8 has the same effect on the current WML card as if the card were invoked with a newcontext="true" attribute. It essentially clears the history stack and all variables.

Line 9 sets the WML variable DD, back in ch02fig41.wml, to 0.

Line 10 will redirect control from the current WML card to card2 in ch02fig41.wml. This command will take effect after the WMLScript function finishes and control returns to the invoking program.

Lines 14, 15, and 16 will be processed if the local variable bb is not greater than 0.

Line 14 displays the message 333 on the device.

Line 15 sets the WML variable DD, back in ch02fig41.wml, to 2.

Line 16 simply refreshes the current WML card once control is returned to the browser showing the new value of DD.

```
1.  extern function func1()
2.  {
3.     Dialogs.alert("111");
4.     var bb = WMLBrowser.getVar("DD");
5.     if (bb > 1)
6.         {
7.             Dialogs.alert("222");
8.             WMLBrowser.newContext();
9.             WMLBrowser.setVar("DD",0);
10.            WMLBrowser.go("ch02fig41.wml#card2");
11.        }
12.    else
13.        {
14.            Dialogs.alert("333");
15.            WMLBrowser.setVar("DD",2);
16.              WMLBrowser.refresh();
17.        }
18. }
```

Figure 2.42 WMLScript file, ch02fig42.wmls.

Dialogs

The most useful dialog library function is the Dialog.alert("message") command. This acts the same as a JavaScript alert command whereby the message in the alert clause is displayed on the device screen, execution then awaits the users confirmation, and then control is returned to the next command with an empty result string.

Figure 2.43 is similar to Figure 2.42 with several enhancements. Here, if the local bb variable is greater than 0, an alert is displayed to the user with a message. Once the user confirms the alert, a confirm message is displayed on the screen asking whether to continue on or not. If the user chooses Yes, the if statement becomes true and another alert is shown, followed by several WMLBrowser commands, and a redirect to card2 of ch02fig41. If the resale is false, control is sent to the same card but a different alert is first displayed.

These are the WMLScript basics. For more details see the WMLScript in Appendix E at the end of this book and read the vendor's documentation as well.

```
1. extern function fund1()
2. {
3.     Dialogs.alert("111");
4.     var bb = WMLBrowser.getVar("DD");
5.     if (bb > 1)
6.     {
7.         Dialogs.alert("222");
8.         if (Dialogs.confirm("Continue on?","Yes","No")) //if true continue
9.         {
10.             Dialogs.alert("333");
11.             WMLBrowser.newContext();
12.             WMLBrowser.setVar("DD",0);
13.             WMLBrowser.go("ch02fig41.wml#card2");
14.         }
15.         else
16.         {
17.             Dialogs.alert("444");
18.             WMLBrowser.go("ch02fig41.wml#card2");
19.         }
20.     }
21.     else
22.     {
23.         Dialogs.alert("555");
24.         WMLBrowser.setVar("DD",2);
25.         WMLBrowser.refresh();
26.     }
27. }
```

Figure 2.43 WMLScript dialog example, ch02fig43.wmls.

Programming Hints

Here are a few programming hints:

- Don't put anything before the <?xml version="1.0"?>.
- Test your programs with both WAPForum and Up.Browser DTDs.
- Try to use the most basic programming for compatibility between the two DTD types but be ready to create two distinct applications specific to each.
- Convert images to WBMP format by using a free conversion tools.

Web to WAP Integration (HTML Web Scraping)

A ll WML examples presented in this chapter have been developed and tested using Nokia's WAP toolkit version 2.0, unless stated otherwise. For more information on WAP toolkits, refer to the Development Toolkits (SDK) section of Chapter 1.

Every line of program code in this chapter is numbered for easy reference. Code on the CD is identical but without the numbers.

What Is HTML Web Scraping?

New technology inevitably creates new business opportunities. With wireless Internet gaining visibility, businesses are looking to jump into this new technology as quickly as possible. Many firms who already have a Web site for visibility or e-commerce reasons are the first to want to open this new doorway to their products and services, in hopes of attracting new revenue opportunities. Many ventures simply wish to establish a presence with the latest technology since the first to arrive at the party will most likely have a higher market visibility, which hopefully translates to sales.

The first step in establishing this presence is to implement the new technology in its simplest form and in the most cost-effective manner. By far, HTML Web scraping is the simplest method other than a static wireless application.

The idea behind HTML Web scraping is to create an application that is basically 100 percent nonintrusive (or 99.9 percent nonintrusive, as you'll see) that will handle dynamic changes on the Web page. Don't touch the existing business and don't touch the existing Web application; just create a new independent WAP application that has no impact on the existing systems, hence, nonintrusive. Businesses just want to get something going with the new technology—essentially just create a presence with the least possible impact. In simple terms, get a presence on Web phones and other WAP-enabled devices to attract attention and customers.

This chapter introduces the concept of HTML scraping of Web pages to create a WAP application. In simple technical terms, the end user will press a button on the Web phone invoking a Perl program that will read a regular Internet HTML Web page, capture the required text on the Web page, and return the produced WML WAP code and captured text to the Web phone. The end user will never know if he or she is invoking a true WAP application or simply HTML scraping a Web page.

The Perl programming language is used as the programming language of choice for our examples simply because it's efficient and easy to learn quickly. Perl uses sophisticated pattern-matching techniques to scan large amounts of data very quickly and is optimized for scanning text. Perl considers the Web page HTML code as one long string of text and hence can parse the page fairly quickly.

You don't have to be a Perl programmer to understand the examples since most lines of code are explained in detail. You can easily copy the code onto your Web server and it will function as is. ASP and Visual Basic could have been used but we found that for HTML Web scraping, Perl was much simpler to use. We'll also give examples of how and what to change in the programs to generate HDML and iMode code for people who are using these languages.

Don't worry about not being a Web programmer either. The concept of HTML Web scraping is fairly straightforward and, as mentioned, all code is fully explained. The idea is simple: Write a program, which will search the text in the HTML code of a Web page looking for specific tags—no Web programming is required at all. Only Perl programming here, but we've already written the code so you can easily use all our examples as templates of your own.

Although we call this process *HTML Web scraping*, most firms still use the term *screen scraping*, which is an older, more familiar term based on legacy systems integration of mainframe applications. This term is used quite often but you should know the modern term and why it is called HTML Web scraping.

So what is HTML Web scraping? Well, basically Web pages are created with HyperText Markup Language (HTML). HTML is a tag-based language, that is, <b>bold word</b>. Tags usually come in sets with a start tag <b> and an end tag </b>. With HTML Web scraping, we simply create a program to read the Web page and search the underlying HTML code for the desired tags, skipping any tags, text, or images that don't interest us. Once the required start tag is found, we proceed to capture all text immediately after the tag up to but not including the end tag. Our Perl program then creates WAP code—WML format in our examples—and sends the WAP code and captured text to the Web phone for display, at which point our HTML Web scraping is complete.

HTML Web Scraping Process Flow

Let's look at how HTML Web scraping works from a high-level network view and from a programmer's point of view.

Figure 3.1 shows the technical high-level process flow behind HTML Web scraping. Starting at the Web phone, the request is invoked by the end user from the WAP device and sent to the WAP gateway over the wireless network. The WAP gateway is normally owned and operated by the wireless service provider, who bought the gateway from one of the major gateway vendors. The wireless network is the regular cellular phone network used for regular cellular phones.

The WAP request is then converted to an HTTP request by the gateway. Now the request is traveling on the Internet.

The initial request from the Web phone is really a WAP program (WML format in our case), which issues a call to another program (Perl in our examples). The HTTP request executes this Perl program from our Web server. The program is coded to retrieve a

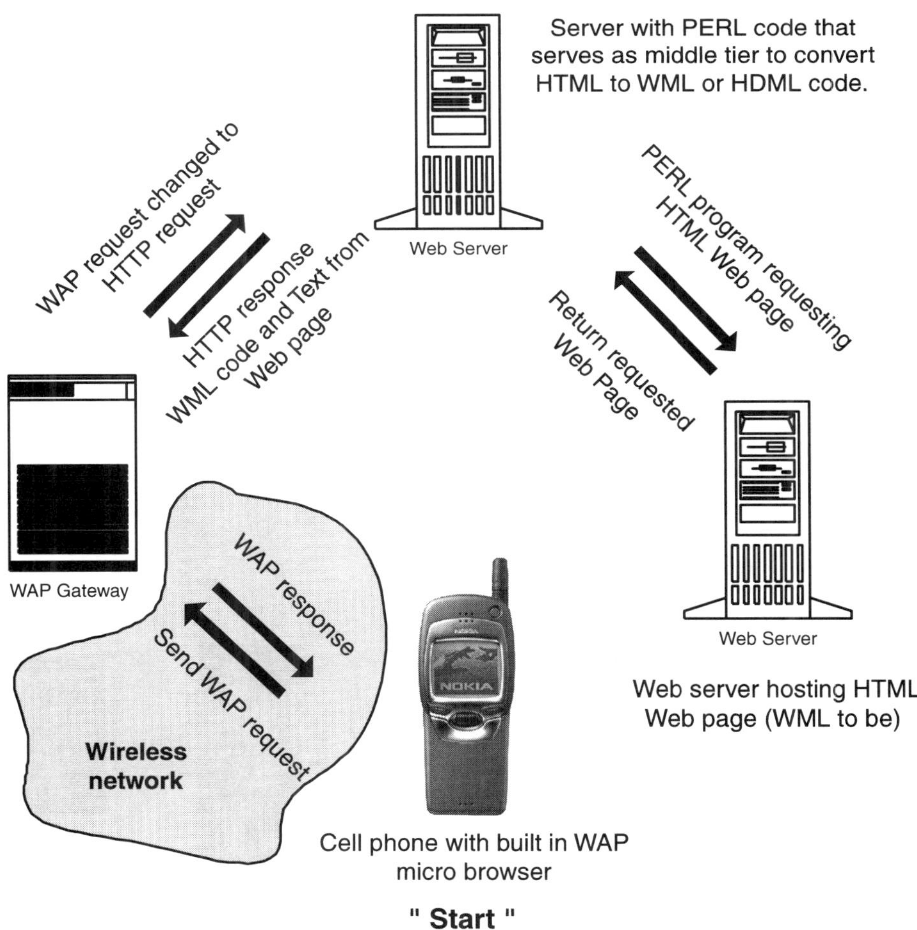

Figure 3.1 High-level process flow behind HTML Web scraping.

specific HTML Web page (URL is http://wavedev.com/book/ch03 /Ch03Ex1.htm in our example), which normally resides on another Web server somewhere out there in the Internet world. In our case, the Perl program and requested Web page are both on the same server.

The requested Web page is returned to the Perl program, which parses the HTML code looking for specific tags as specified in the Perl program. Once the tags are found, the desired text is captured and WML code is created, all still executing on our Web server.

The code and reformatted text are then returned as the HTTP response (to the initial HTTP request) to the WAP gateway. The WAP gateway will convert the HTTP request into its corresponding WAP response to the originating WAP request. The WAP response then travels via the wireless network to the Web phone for display to the end user, completing the journey.

From a programmer's point of view, Figure 3.2 shows the process flow of a simple Web page containing the text "Hi Mom," that is being invoked by an initial request. Then the text on the Web page is HTML Web scraped to reproduce the text on the Web phone.

Of course, this example is extremely simple but it does show the complete concept of HTML Web scraping.

The process from start to finish is as follows:

1. End user invokes Web scraping by pressing OK on Web phone.

2. Web page (HTML source code) is read using a Perl program.

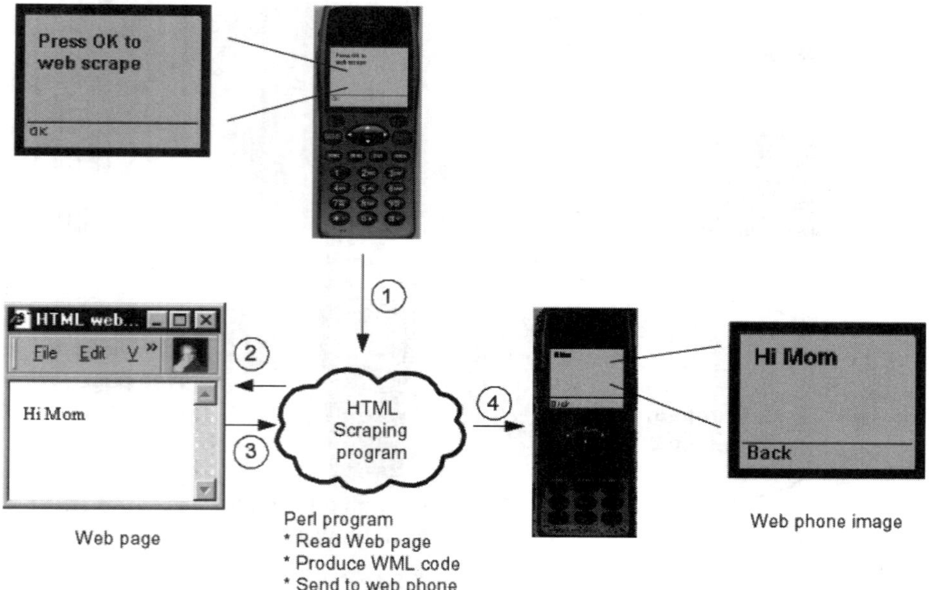

Web page

Perl program
* Read Web page
* Produce WML code
* Send to web phone

Web phone image

Figure 3.2 Process flow of a simple Web page.

3. Perl program scans for one or more specific tags and captures all text between the start and end tags.

4. WML (or HDML or iMode) code is created and, along with the captured text, is sent to the Web phone for display to the end user.

The concept is rather simple and easy to follow. Click the Web phone button and receive information from a Web site. In writing the Perl program, care must be given to the analysis of the Web page being HTML scraped. One must review the HTML code looking for specific tags that uniquely identify the desired text area.

Figure 3.3 illustrates all the code for the preceding example: Web page HTML code; Perl program code; the resulting WML code from the Perl program, which is eventually displayed as the result on the Web phone; and the originating Web phone WML code.

The HTML Web scraping for this example is very easy. We simply look for the paragraph HTML tags (<p> and </p>) in the Web page HTML code. Once we find the start tag <p> (line 6), we know the following text up to the end tag </p> (line 8) is all we want. So we can skip everything before the start tag and anything after the end tag inclusive.

Figure 3.4 shows the Perl program code used to HTML Web scrape the preceding Web page and to create the required WML code to be displayed on the Web phone.

Line 1 defines the location of where Perl is to run on the server.

Line 2 is simply Perl initiation code.

Line 3 is another comment, and so are lines 5, 21, 22, 25, and 27.

Line 4 is how Perl fetches the required Web page:

```
4.    $WebPage=get("http://www.wavedev.com/book/ch03/Ch03Ex1.htm");
```

Here we have our URL hardcoded, which is fetched via the GET command and placed in variable "WebPage."

Beginning at lines 5 through 20 is the start of our WML code. This portion is static so we've lumped it all together in a variable called "deck_start." The WML code includes the XML version definition, DTD declaration, and the start of the WML deck and card.

```
1.    <html>
2.    <head>
3.       <title>HTML web scraping</title>
4.    </head>
5.    <body>
6.       <p>
7.       Hi Mom
8.       </p>
9.    </body>
10.   </html>
```

Figure 3.3 Ch03Ex1.htm, Web page HTML source code.

```
1.  #!/usr/local/bin/perl
2.  use LWP::Simple;
3.  # Read into memory web page to be scraped (parsed)
4.  $WebPage=get("http://www.wavedev.com/book/ch03/Ch03Ex1.htm");
5.  # Create static portion of WML code
6.  $deck_start = '
7.  <?xml version="1.0"?>
8.  <!DOCTYPE wml PUBLIC "-//WAPFORUM//DTD WML 1.1//EN"
    "http://www.wapforum.org/DTD/wml_1.1.xml">
9.  <wml>
10. <card  id="card1">
11. <do  type="accept" label="Back">
12. <go  href="http://www.wavedev.com/book/ch03/Ch03Ex1I.wml"/>
13. </do>
14. <p>
15. ';
16. $deck_end = '
17. </p>
18. </card>
19. </wml>
20. ';
21. # HTML web scraping
22. # Get rid of everything before <p> and after </p> tags
23. $WebPage =~ s/.*<p>//s;
24. $WebPage =~ s/<\/p>+.*//s;
25. # Parsing done, now set content-type for WAP gateway
26. print "Content-type: text/vnd.wap.wml\n\n";
27. # Send results to web phone
28. print $deck_start;
29. print $WebPage;
30. print $deck_end;
31. exit;
```

Figure 3.4 Ch03Ex1.pl, "Hi Mom" Perl program.

The Web phone display will show Back as the only Softkey for navigation. You can see that if Back is pressed, http://wavedev.com/book/ch03/Ch03Ex1I.wml will be invoked (line 12). The same action would occur if the phone's Back button were pressed, since the previous card is the last card in the history deck.

Line 16 is another variable ("deck_end") containing more static WML code. This portion of the WML code is simply end tags of opened WML code tags from lines 17 to 19. Line 20 is the closing quote for the definition of the variable on line 16.

Lines 23 and 24 are the most important lines in this Perl program:

```
23.    $WebPage =~ s/.*<p>//s;
24.    $WebPage =~ s/<\/p>+.*//s;
```

These lines actually do the HTML Web scraping.

Line 23 says, remove everything before the start tag (including the start tag itself) from data in variable "WebPage" and replace it with nulls.

Line 24 says, remove everything after , our end tag (including the end tag itself), and replace that with nulls too. This will leave only the desired text "Hi Mom" in variable "WebPage." This is why we selected Perl as our programming language. Only two simple lines can parse an entire Web page. This is a very simple example, yet you can see that Perl is a very efficient language.

Line 23 (=~ s/.* //s;) decrypts as follows: =~ means to match a pattern within a string. For s/.* //; the s means search and replace as follows: s/a/b/, search for a and replace with b. The .* means any character (the dot portion) and the * means zero or more of the previous characters. So, .* means to search for zero or more characters up to the first and replace with // nulls since nothing is between the forward slashes (or called *wacks* in Seattle!!). The last s is an option meaning treat the string as a single line. The ending semicolon signifies the end of a command in Perl.

Line 24 (=~ s/<\/p>+.*//s;) is as follows: =~ again means to match a pattern within a string, followed by the search and replace function s/ /. Again it ends with //;, which means replace whatever with nulls. The <\/p>+* means starting at the next which has an extra back slash, which means take the next character as is. This is done for special characters that have their own interpretive meaning in Perl. Then the + is one or more of the previous pattern followed by the .* again, which means any character and * for zero or more of the previous pattern which is the dot interpreted. The last s and semicolon are the same as explained earlier. Done.

Line 25 is a comment.

Line 26 is setting the content-type for the WAP gateway (see Chapter 1 for more details):

```
26. print "Content-type: text/vnd.wap.wml\n\n";
```

Content-Type tells the WAP gateway to expect WML code to follow, in this example. Notice this is a PRINT command. PRINT is the command used in Perl to write the output, in this case to the requesting device, which is a Web phone. The two \n commands are simply line breaks for the PRINT command for formatting purposes in the output.

Lines, 28 to 30 print the variables we created to hold the beginning static WML code, the remains of the Web page (WebPage variable), which is the desired text from that page (line 29), followed by the closing static WML code:

```
28. print $deck_start;
29. print $WebPage;
30. print $deck_end;
```

The Perl program ends with the standard EXIT command on line 31.

```
31. exit;
```

Done. The Perl program is simple and yet very efficient in parsing the Web page HTML code.

The WML code produced from the Perl program is shown in Figure 3.5. The code was created line by line from the Perl code given previously with absolutely no differences. You can see that lines 7 to 14 from the Perl program exactly match lines 1 to 8 of the WML code. Lines 23 and 24 in the Perl program created line 9 in Figure 3.5. And lines 10, 11, and 12 in Figure 3.5 were created by the "deck_end" variable from lines 17 to 19 in the Perl program.

To initiate the middle-tier Perl program that does the actual HTML Web scraping and produces the resulting WML code, an initial WML program on the WAP device (Web phone in our example) must be invoked by the end user. As shown in Figure 3.2, the initiating WML code is invoked by the end user pressing the button beneath the OK on the Web phone display. By doing so, the program in Figure 3.6 is invoked. This program then calls the Perl program (Ch03Ex1.pl in Figure 3.4), which in turn does the entire HTML Web scraping and produces the WML code which is returned to the invoking Web phone.

The initiating WML program code and phone display are shown in Figures 3.6 and 3.7:

How to Web Scrape HTML

Let's look at an example where a News Web page is parsed for its specific news headlines and news stories to be displayed in WML code format on a Web phone.

News Example (Reading the Web Page)

The Web site shown in Figure 3.8 will be HTML Web scraped to produce a WAP application as follows.

Starting from a preexisting WAP application on a Web phone (Figure 3.9A), the end user will select the News category as shown. This action will invoke a Perl program, which will HTML Web scrape a specific Web page (Figure 3.8) looking for news headlines. The

```
1.  <?xml version="1.0"?>
2.  <!DOCTYPE wml PUBLIC "-//WAPFORUM//DTD WML 1.1//EN"
      "http://www.wapforum.org/DTD/wml_1.1.xml">
3.  <wml>
4.  <card  id="card1">
5.     <do  type="accept" label="Back">
6.         <go  href="http://www.wavedev.com/book/ch03/Ch03Ex1I.wml"/>
7.     </do>
8.     <p>
9.     Hi Mom
10.    </p>
11. </card>
12. </wml>
```

Figure 3.5 Ch03Ex1R.wml, "Hi Mom" WML code.

```
1.  <?xml version="1.0"?>
2.  <!DOCTYPE wml PUBLIC "-//WAPFORUM//DTD WML 1.1//EN"
       "http://www.wapforum.org/DTD/wml_1.1.xml">
3.  <wml>
4.  <card  id="card1">
5.    <do  type="accept" label="OK">
6.       <go  href="http://www.wavedev.com/cgi-bin/Ch03Ex1.pl"/>
7.    </do>
8.    <p>
9.    Press OK to web scrape
10.   </p>
11. </card>
12. </wml>
```

Figure 3.6 Ch03Ex1I.wml, initiating WML program.

Web phone image as seen by Figure 3.9B will be produced. Again the end user will select one of two news headlines which will invoke a second Perl program. This second Perl program will again HTML Web scrape the same Web page but this time searching for the specific news story for the selected news headline. The resulting WML code will produce the final image as seen in Figure 3.9C.

Static Portion (The Web Page)

For this example, the parsing program will be doing straightforward parsing of the Web page (Figure 3.8), looking for all news headlines and stories. For the sake of simplicity, our news site will only contain two news stories and so we will program accordingly. See the enlarged version of the two news stories in Figure 3.10. If there were a varying number of stories on the Web page, the HTML Web scraping program would be modified to include a loop to run through each news headline and story. This modification portion is left to the reader.

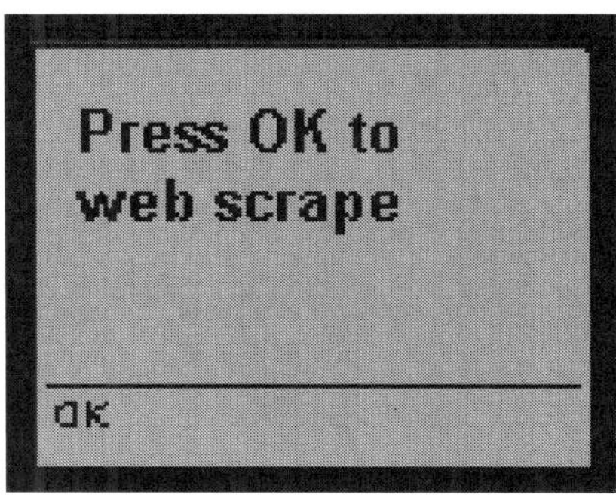

Figure 3.7 Resulting WAP device screen.

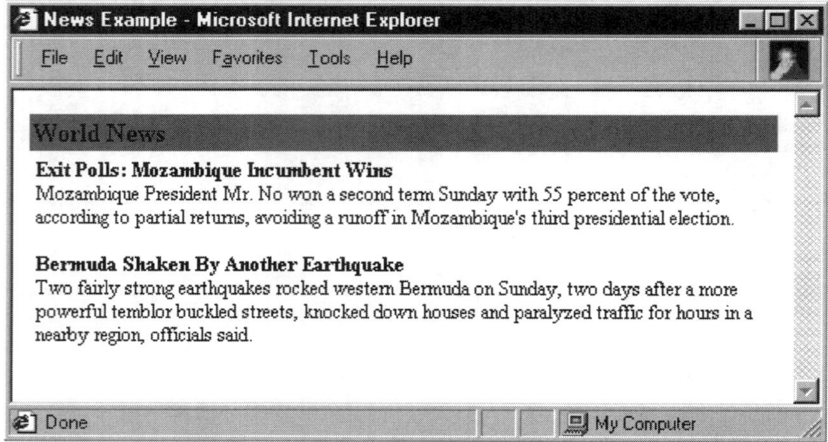

Figure 3.8 Web page with news headlines and stories.

Figure 3.11 shows the Web page HTML source code.

As seen in the HTML source code in Figure 3.11, each news headline will have start tags of <td><b> (lines 13 and 19) and end tags of </b>
 (lines 13 and 19). Each news story itself will have a start tag of <font size="-1"> (lines 14 and 20) and end tags of </font>
</td> (lines 16 and 22). You will notice that all these groups of tags selected are unique on the page and hence will correctly identify our headlines and stories. All else on the Web page will be ignored.

To distinguish the first news story from the second news story, when parsing we'll use the headline start tag plus the first 10 characters of each news story's headline. Instead of using <font size="-1"> to identify each news story, we'll use, for example, <td><b> Bermuda sh. This should be enough to uniquely identify each news headline. If you are not totally convinced that the first 10 characters will be unique, simply add more but take into account the length of the smallest possible news headline, if this is known.

Although the Web page content can be dynamic and may change on a daily basis, the tags should always remain the same and represent the same items on the Web page.

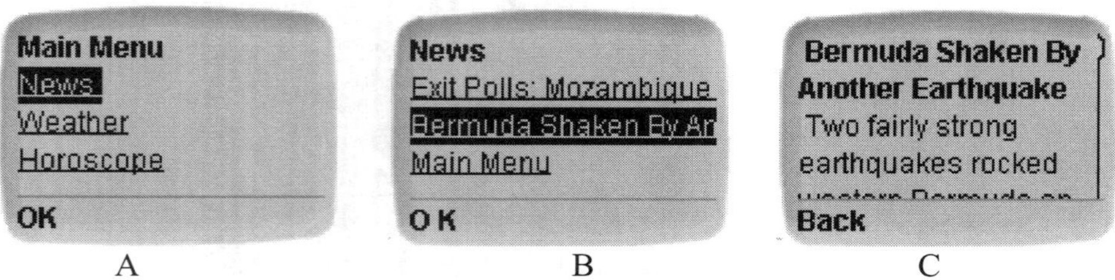

Figure 3.9 (A) Main Menu, (B) News Headlines, (C) News Story.

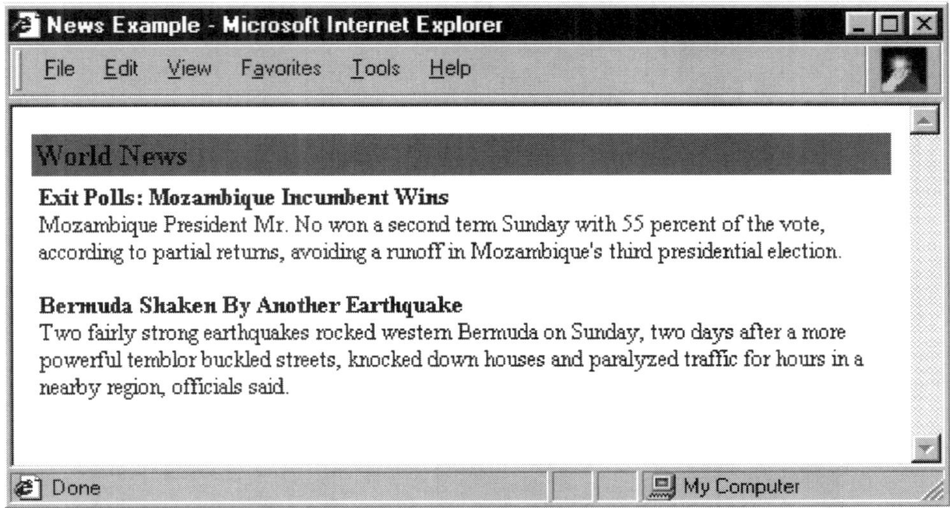

Figure 3.10 (3.8 Enlarged) Web page HTML source code.

However, this may not always be true. There will be more on this pessimism in the Pros and Cons of HTML Web scraping section at the end of this chapter. Basically, we're just looking for specific tags in the Web page's HTML code and grabbing whatever is between the tags to display on the Web phone.

Web Phone Initiation

The entire HTML Web scraping process is invoked by the end user selecting a category on the Web phone screen as shown in Figure 3.12.

The end user selects <u>News</u> on the display and presses the OK button. The underlying WML code, shown in Figure 3.13, is invoked and as seen on line 9, control goes to Perl program Ch03Ex2.pl. Remembering the process flow discussion at the start of this chapter, the Perl program invoked is executed on the Web server that contains the Web site http://wavedev.com/cgi-bin/.

The actual WML code that produces this Main Menu display can be written in many different methods. Two of them are presented here. Both will produce the same results but may appear differently depending on the Web phone device, the WML version, and the DTD being used. See Chapter 1 for more details on devices, WML versions, and DTDs.

The first WML code is written with the <anchor> and <go> tags. The second WML program is written with the <select> and <option> tags. Both methods are valid in WML for the primary browser types (Microsoft Mobile Explorer, UpBrowser, Nokia, and Ericsson).

Figure 3.13 shows the WML code using <anchor> and <go> tags.

We'll use this first method, program Ch03Ex2A.wml, in our examples since it shows up nicely on the Web phone. Note that in this example, we could change each anchor title

```
1. <html>
2. <head>
3. <title>News Example</title>
4. </head>
5. <body>
6. <table cellspacing="0" cellpadding="2" border="0" width="100%">
7. <tr>
8. <td bgcolor="green"><font size="+1"><b>World News</b></font></td>
9. </tr>
10. </table>
11. <table cellspacing="0" cellpadding="4" width="100%">
12. <tr>
13. <td><b>Exit Polls: Mozambique Incumbent Wins</b><br>
14. <font size="-1">Mozambique President Mr. No won a second term
    Sunday with 55
15. percent of the vote, according to partial returns, avoiding a
    runoff in Mozambique's
16. third presidential election.</font><br></td>
17. </tr>
18. <tr>
19. <td><b>Bermuda Shaken By Another Earthquake</b><br>
20. <font size="-1">Two fairly strong earthquakes rocked western
    Bermuda on Sunday, two
21. days after a more powerful temblor buckled streets, knocked down
    houses and paralyzed
22. traffic for hours in a nearby region, officials
    said.</font><br></td>
23. </tr>
24. </table>
25. </body>
26. </html>
```

Figure 3.11 Ch03Ex2.htm, news Web page source code.

parameter with something more appropriate per category link instead of always using OK. In other words, line 8 in Figure 3.13 could be <anchor title="News">, line 12 could begin with <anchor title="Weather">, and line 13 could start with <anchor title="Horoscope">. So when the Web phone user scrolls down the categories, the Softkey name would change. The more dynamic an application, the more captivating and hence usually a higher return usage. On the other hand, standardizing your application to always show an OK is less confusing and will also attract a following. The style is completely up to you.

The next programming method shows the first menu link on Nokia's WAP toolkit version 2.0, and the word *options* is displayed where the OK should be. We must invoke the "options" choice and then select either another menu category or OK to proceed, which is very cumbersome. The last thing we want when developing a WAP application

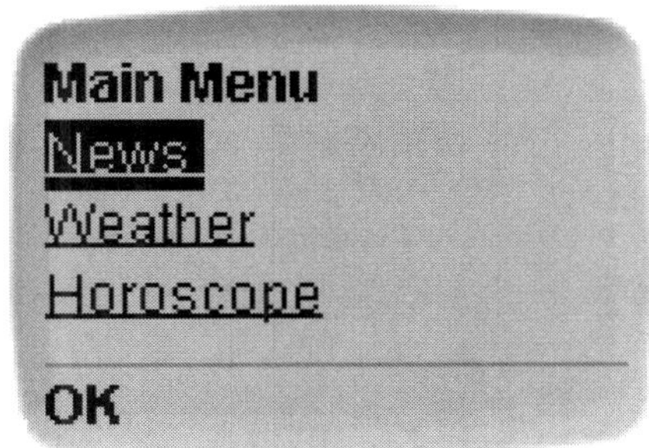

Figure 3.12 (from Figure 3.9A): Main Menu.

is for the end user to have to press more buttons than absolutely necessary. Scrolling is fine since the card is already in cache and most users are familiar with scrolling from desktop file usage. But moving on to more decks and/or cards just to select OK is cumbersome and frankly annoying to many. When building a WAP application, remember, the fewer clicks the better. Smart design is also a big factor since simplicity and ease of use makes for great applications and keeps users coming back for more.

```
1.  <?xml version="1.0"?>
2.  <!DOCTYPE wml PUBLIC "-//WAPFORUM//DTD WML 1.1//EN"
      http://www.wapforum.org/DTD/wml_1.1.xml">
3.  <wml>
4.  <card  id="card1">
5.  <p>
6.  <b>Main Menu</b>
7.  <br/>
8.  <anchor title="OK">
9.  <go href="http://www.wavedev.com/cgi-bin/Ch03Ex2.pl"/>News
10. </anchor>
11. <br/>
12. <anchor title="OK"><go href="#card2"/>Weather</anchor><br/>
13. <anchor title="OK"><go href="#card2"/>Horoscope</anchor><br/>
14. </p>
15. </card>
16. <card  id="card2">
17. <do type="accept" label="Back">
18. <prev/>
19. </do>
20. <p>
21. <b>Under Construction</b>
22. </p>
23. </card>
24. </wml>
```

Figure 3.13 Ch03Ex2A.wml, Anchor and Go example.

Figure 3.14 (from Figure 3.9A): Main Menu using WML <anchor> and <go> tags.

The <option> tag in WML assumes code in the Softkey area but can be used within the phone screen display as in our Select usage given in Figure 3.15. If more than two option entries are specified for a card, for most phones as in our case, the OK is replaced by the word *option* and once invoked, another screen is displayed with all options available to the application, including the OK option. This is a common feature for many phones and browsers, but in our opinion it is very annoying.

Figure 3.15 shows WML code using <select> and <option> tags.

Figure 3.16 shows Web phone images with the <select> and <option> tags. So, to select the first category, News, press the Softkey, which displays screen B. Then scroll down to OK and press the Select Softkey to view the news headlines. If the user wished to view Weather, the Softkey on screen A would be pressed. Then keeping the cursor on "Select Item," the Softkey for Select would be pressed. On Screen C, the user would scroll to Weather, and press Select, which would return to screen A with Weather instead of News. Then, again, the Options Softkey would be pressed showing the user screen B, where finally the user could scroll down to OK and press the Select key, which would, in our example, invoke the "Under Construction" screen. Not our recommended programming approach.

You'll notice in these examples that if a category other than News is selected, control will be passed to card2. As seen on lines 16 through 23 in the first WML code or lines 17 to 24 of the <select> and <options> example, card2 is simply an "Under Construction" display with only one control selection. See Figure 3.17. The only selection is back to the previous card in the history deck, as coded on line 17, which is the "Main Menu" card.

Middle Tier (First Perl Program)

The Perl programming language is an excellent choice to use in parsing Web pages. It is a powerful language. With only a handful of code, it can parse the HTML code very quickly and efficiently.

Practical Extracting and Reporting Language (Perl) is maintained as open source (free to everyone) at ActiveState (www.activestate.com). ActiveState provides binary builds for Linux, Windows, and Solaris platforms. The latest stable version available for download is Perl version 5.6 or 5.22 available on CD.

Perl is an interpreted scripting language and, as such, it can be used on a variety of Web platforms such as O'Reilly WebSite professional 2.0, Microsoft Internet Information Server v2.0 or later, Netscape FastTrack, or Enterprise servers v2.0 or later.

Over the Web, Perl can be invoked by simply executing the script via the address bar of an HTML Web browser, i.e., http://wavedev.com/cgi-bin/Ch03Ex1.pl. Or Perl can be called from within another program as we often do in our examples in this chapter. Another method is to call it from the command line. A great way to test individual Perl scripts is by invoking the script from a command window prompt as follows:

```
C:\inetput\wwwroot\cgi-bin>Perl Ch03Ex1.pl
```

```
1.  <?xml version="1.0"?>
2.  <!DOCTYPE wml PUBLIC "-//WAPFORUM//DTD WML 1.1//EN"
     "http://www.wapforum.org/DTD/wml_1.1.xml">
3.  <wml>
4.  <card  id="card1">
5.  <do type="accept" label="OK">
6.  <go href="$(cat1:noesc)"/>
7.  </do>
8.  <p>
9.  <b>Main Menu</b><br/>
10. <select name="cat1">
11. <option value="http://www.wavedev.com/cgi-bin/Ch03Ex2.pl">News
     </option>
12. <option value="#card2">Weather</option>
13. <option value="#card2">Horoscope</option>
14. </select>
15. </p>
16. </card>
17. <card  id="card2">
18. <do type="accept" label="Back">
19. <prev/>
20. </do>
21. <p>
22. <b>Under Construction</b>
23. </p>
24. </card>
25. </wml>
```

Figure 3.15 Ch03Ex2A.wml, Select and Option example.

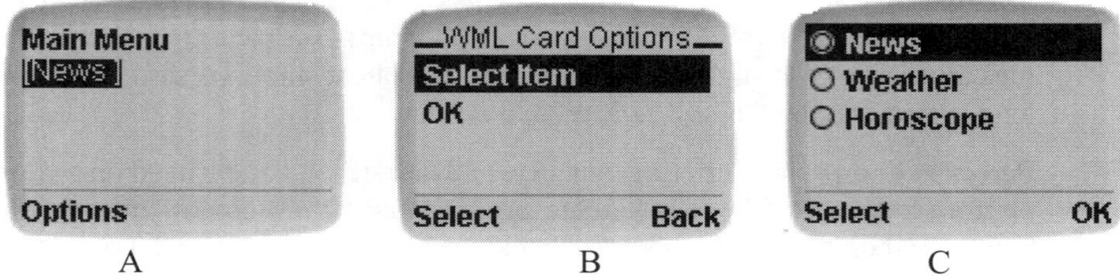

Figure 3.16 Web phone images using <select> and <option> tags.

In our example, the news stories are straightforward with no tags embedded within the text, making our parsing quite simple. However, if there were unwanted tags, only a few lines of Perl code would be required to remove them.

To continue our discussion, when the Web phone user selects the News category from the Main Menu screen, a Perl program is invoked to HTML Web scrape the Web page and to produce WML code for the next Web phone screen display. The new screen display will show both news headlines from the Web page and a Main Menu link, which is navigation back to the Main Menu. The end user then simply selects the required news headline and presses OK to continue. The final screen will be the individual news story itself.

The Perl program in Figure 3.18 will parse the News Web page HTML code, searching only for the news headlines by searching for the headline start tags. The HTML code for each news headline in Figure 3.10 will have start tags of <td><b> and end tags of </b>
.

Invoked from the Main Menu, the Perl program in Figure 3.18 will HTML Web scrape the News Web page, searching for the specific tags and producing WML code.

The resulting News Headline Web phone display is shown in Figure 3.19.

Let's review this Perl program code, Ch03Ex2A.pl:

Figure 3.17 Under construction.

```
1.  #!/usr/local/bin/perl
2.  use LWP::Simple;
3.  # Lets get the web page to be parsed
4.  $WebPage=get('http://www.wavedev.com/book/ch03/Ch03Ex2.htm');
5.  # Create WML page start and page end
6.  $deck_start = '
7.  <?xml version="1.0"?>
8.  <!DOCTYPE wml PUBLIC "-//WAPFORUM//DTD WML 1.1//EN"
    "http://www.wapforum.org/DTD/wml_1.1.xml">
9.  <!--  Wavedev News Parser  Ch03Ex2A  -->
10. <wml>
11. <card  id="card1">
12. <p mode="nowrap">
13. <b>News</b><br/>
14. ';
15. $deck_end = '
16. <anchor title="OK"><go
    href="http://www.wavedev.com/book/ch03/Ch03Ex2A.wml"/>Main
    Menu</anchor><br/>
17. </p></card></wml>';
18. # Begin HTML web scraping (parsing)
19. # Find the first News headline which is tagged by <td><b> and ends
    with </b><br>
20. $FirstTitle = $WebPage;
21. $FirstTitle =~ s/<\/b><br>+.*//s;
22. $FirstTitle =~ s/.*<td><b>//s;
23. # Set the WML code for the title
24. $FirstTitle = '<anchor title="OK"><go
    href="http://www.wavedev.com/cgi-bin/Ch03Ex2B.pl?headline='.
    substr($FirstTitle,0,10) .
    '"/>' . $FirstTitle . '</anchor><br/>';
25. # Get second News headline. Remove first news headline start tag
    then continue parsing
26. $SecondTitle = $WebPage;
27. $SecondTitle =~ s/.*<td><b>//s;   # position to second headline
    since first headline start tags are gone now
28. $SecondTitle =~ s/<\/b><br>+.*//s;
29. # Set the WML code for the second title
30. $SecondTitle =  '<anchor title="OK"><go
    href="http://www.wavedev.com/cgi-bin/Ch03Ex2B.pl?headline='.
    substr($SecondTitle,0,10) . '"/>' . $SecondTitle .
    '</anchor><br/>';
31. # All done so send proper Content type
32. print "Content-type: text/vnd.wap.wml\n\n";
33. # Send WML code to NOKIA microbrowser
34. print $deck_start;
35. print $FirstTitle;
36. print $SecondTitle;
37. print $deck_end;
38. exit;
```

Figure 3.18 Ch03Ex2A.pl, first Perl program.

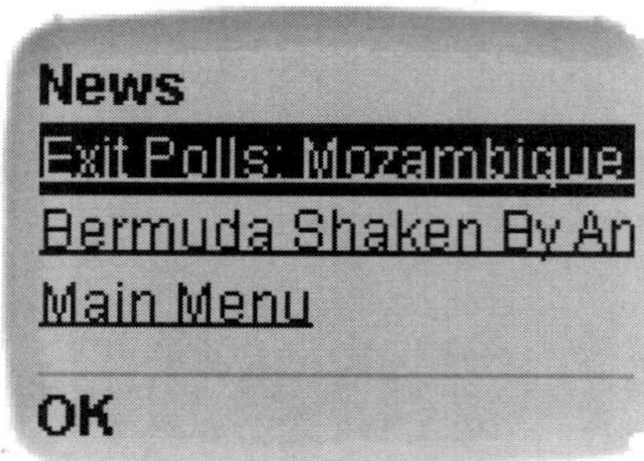

Figure 3.19 (from Figure 3.9B): News Headlines.

All lines beginning with # are comments, except for the very first line which is defining the Perl program directory on the Web server.

Lines 1 to 2 are specific to Perl.

Line 4 is how Perl fetches the required Web page.

```
4.  $WebPage=get("http://www.wavedev.com/book/ch03/Ch03Ex2.htm");
```

Here we have our URL hardcoded, which is fetched via the GET command and placed in variable "WebPage."

Beginning at lines 6 through 17 is the start of our WML code creation. Lines 7 to 13 form the beginning of the static portion of the WML code and are stored in variable "deck_start" on line 6. Lines 15 to 17 contain the end of the WML deck consisting of a navigation link and closing tags. These tags are stored in variable "deck_end."

We've added the navigation link at the end of the other links rather than as a Softkey display. This is because we would have had only two options: OK and Main Menu. Some phones do not have access to a second Softkey and would put the application into the Options mode as explained earlier. Remember that the Options mode is frustrating since it adds extra clicks to the application, making the process quite annoying.

Lines 20 to 30 form the main HTML Web scraping portion. As seen here, the first portion, Lines 20 to 24 parse for the first News headline.

```
20. $FirstTitle = $WebPage;
21. $FirstTitle =~ s/<\/b><br>+.*//s;
22. $FirstTitle =~ s/.*<td><b>//s;
23. # Set the WML code for the title
24. $FirstTitle = '<anchor title="OK"><go href="http://www.wavedev.com/
        cgi-bin/Ch03Ex2B.pl?headline=' . substr($FirstTitle,0,10) . '"/>' .
        $FirstTitle . '</anchor><br/>';
```

Line 20 sets a variable called "FirstTitle" to the entire Web page, which is simply an HTML code stream.

Line 21 from the end tag </b>
 replaces the rest of the page with nulls leaving only the first news headline in the "FirstTitle" variable. Note the backslash in line 20 <Vb> is for Perl to take the / as is and not as a Perl command.

Line 22 replaces anything up to and including the start tag <td><b> with nulls in variable "FirstTitle."

Line 24 then prepares the first headline for display on the Web phone. It sets the Softkey anchor to OK and as in HTML hyperlinks, sets the first link to the first headline found and the underlying hyperlink to our second Perl program with a parm (headline) to the first ten characters of the headline itself, Substr($FirstTitle,0,10).

The second News headline is retrieved from lines 26 to 30 as follows:

```
26. $SecondTitle = $WebPage;
27. $SecondTitle =~ s/.*<td><b>//s;  # position to second headline since
      first headline start tags are gone now
28. $SecondTitle =~ s/<\/b><br>+.*//s;
29. # Set the WML code for the second title
30. $SecondTitle =  '<anchor title="OK"><go href="http://www
      .wavedev.com/cgi-bin/Ch03Ex2B.pl?headline=' .
      substr($SecondTitle,0,10) . '"/>' . $SecondTitle . '</anchor><br/>';
```

Line 26 sets a variable called "SecondTitle" to the entire Web page.

Line 27 searches and replaces anything up to and including the news headline start tag <td><b> with nulls and places the remainder of the HTML code in variable "SecondTitle."

This positions us on the second news headline.

Line 28 says, starting at the news headline end tag, remove everything else on the page, including the end tag and replace it with nulls. This essentially leaves only the second news headline in variable "$SecondTitle."

Line 30 is nearly identical to line 24 given earlier, except for the obvious variable name. This line prepares the second news headline for display on the Web phone.

Line 32 is setting the content-type for the WAP gateway (see Chapter 1 for more details). Again, two formatting commands end the content-type. \n is used to create a new line.

```
31. # All done so send proper Content type
32. print "Content-type: text/vnd.wap.wml\n\n";
```

Content-Type tells the WAP gateway to expect WML code to follow. Notice this is a PRINT command. PRINT is the command used in Perl to write our output, in this case to the requesting device, which is a Web phone.

Lines 34 to 37 print the variables we created to hold the static WML code, creating the WML deck and cards, the first and second news headlines followed by the closing static WML code, "$deck_end."

```
34. print $deck_start;
35. print $FirstTitle;
```

```
36. print $SecondTitle;
37. print $deck_end;
```

After the program exists, it's done and the second Web phone display is created in our News HTML Web scraping example.

We could have simplified this process by looping through the news headline parsing logic. The routine could then handle any number of news headlines on the same Web page. The only concern with a loop would be if too many news headlines caused a problem for the Web phone since devices are limited to specific memory cache sizes (refer to Chapter 1). This, too, can be handled in the Perl program, but this is getting ahead of ourselves at this point.

The result of the first middle-tier HTML Web scraping program is the WML code and Web phone display as shown in Figure 3.20.

The Perl program added a paragraph tag with a nowrap option for all news headline and title of the display (News). It also ensured the display title would be in bold by using the bold tags <b>..</b>. See Figure 3.21.

Note that there is a difference here between WML versions and DTDs. Phone.com's UP.Browser allows for the "Times Square" feature but Nokia does not. Times Square is an automatic feature whereby once positioned on a line having the nowrap mode, the line will seem to automatically scroll right to left a screen's width at a time, allowing the viewer to read the entire line without scrolling to the right. Within the Nokia context, the user must manually scroll to the right using the arrow keys to read the entire line display if larger than the screen width.

```
1.  <?xml version="1.0"?>
2.  <!DOCTYPE wml PUBLIC "-//WAPFORUM//DTD WML 1.1//EN"
       "http://www.wapforum.org/DTD/wml_1.1.xml">
3.  <!--  Wavedev News Parser  Ch03Ex2  -->
4.  <wml>
5.  <card  id="card1">
6.     <p mode="nowrap">
7.     <b>News</b><br/>
8.     <anchor title="OK"><go href="http://www.wavedev.com/cgi-
          bin/Ch03Ex2B.pl?headline=Exit Polls"/>Exit Polls: Mozambique
          Incumbent Wins</anchor><br/>
9.     <anchor title="OK"><go href="http://www.wavedev.com/cgi-
          bin/Ch03Ex2B.pl?headline=Bermuda Sh"/>Bermuda Shaken By Another
          Earthquake</anchor><br/>
10.    <anchor title="OK"><go
          href="http://www.wavedev.com/book/ch03/Ch03Ex2A.wml"/>Main
          Menu</anchor><br/>
11.    </p>
12. </card>
13. </wml>
```

Figure 3.20 Ch03Ex2B.wml, news headline WML code.

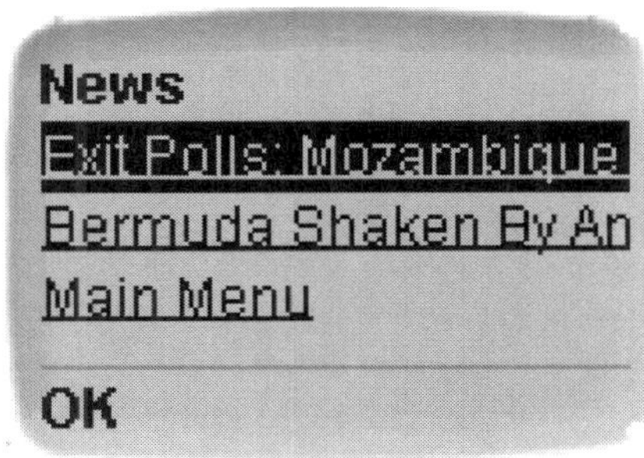

Figure 3.21 (from Figure 3.9B): News Headlines.

Middle Tier (Second Perl Program)

Part two of the middle-tier process is to finish our News example by allowing the end user to select either of the news headlines to arrive at the actual news story itself. By selecting either news headline and pressing OK, the second Perl program is invoked. This second program will HTML Web scrape the same HTML Web page as before, but now it will search for a specific news story based on the news headline selected. The result will be WML code containing the news story itself to be displayed on the Web phone. From a navigation point of view, there will be only one option, which is displayed as "Back" as the left Softkey and will basically return to the previous history stack card, in this example, the news headline card.

We will use the first news headline in our example. The end user would scroll to the first news headline and press OK (Figure 3.9B: news headlines), which invokes the Perl program shown in Figure 3.22.

Since much of the code is similar to the first Perl program, let's just look at the differences.

Line 8 reads the input parameter (headline) created by the previous program and passed in the URL call.

Lines 10 to 20, the static initial WML code, include a <do> tag defining the "Back" option button (line 16). This will be the only navigation possible on the Web phone display for News stories.

Lines 29 to 34 may look tricky but are very simple.

```
29. $Body = $WebPage;
30. $HeadlineStart = ".*<td><b>" . $InputParm;
31. $StoryEnd = "<\/font><br><\/td>";
32. $Body =~ s/$HeadlineStart//s;
33. $Body =~ s/$StoryEnd+.*//s;
34. $Body = $InputParm . $Body;
```

```perl
1. #!/usr/local/bin/perl
2. use CGI;
3. $q = new CGI;
4. use LWP::Simple;
5. # Lets get the web page to be parsed
6. $WebPage=get('http://www.wavedev.com/book/ch03/Ch03Ex2.htm');
7. # Read in Parm
8. $InputParm = $q->param('headline');
9. # Create WML page start and page end
10. $deck_start = '
11. <?xml version="1.0"?>
12. <!DOCTYPE wml PUBLIC "-//WAPFORUM//DTD WML 1.1//EN"
      "http://www.wapforum.org/DTD/wml_1.1.xml">
13. <!--  Wavedev Perl News Parser  -->
14. <wml>
15. <card  id="card1">
16. <do  type="accept" label="Back" name="return">
17. <prev/>
18. </do>
19. <p mode="wrap">
20. <b>
21. ';
22. $deck_end = '
23. </p>
24. </card>
25. </wml>
26. ';
27. # HTML page parsing
28. # Find proper News heading and story
29. $Body = $WebPage;
30. $HeadlineStart = ".*<td><b>" . $InputParm;
31. $StoryEnd = "<\/font><br><\/td>";
32. $Body =~ s/$HeadlineStart//s;
33. $Body =~ s/$StoryEnd+.*//s;
34. $Body = $InputParm . $Body;
35. # Format headline and story
36. $Body =~ s/<br>/<br\/><\/p><p mode=\"wrap\">/s;
37. $Body =~ s/<font size=\"\-1\">//s;
38. # Send proper Content type to WAP gateway
39. print "Content-type: text/vnd.wap.wml\n\n";
40. # Send WML code to Nokia microbrowser
41. print $deck_start;
42. print $Body;
43. print $deck_end;
44. exit;
```

Figure 3.22 Ch03Ex2B.pl, second Perl program.

Line 29 sets variable "$Body" to the entire Web page.

Line 30 sets variable "$HeadlineStart" to the entire Web page.

Line 31 sets variable "$StoryEnd" to the entire Web page.

Line 32 searches for the "HeadlineStart" variable containing any and all characters on the Web page up to and including <td><b> and the first ten characters of the news headline and will replace all this with nulls.

Line 33 then searches for the "StoryEnd" variable content, being </font>
</td>, and replaces everything from that point (inclusive) and anything remaining on the Web page with nulls. This leaves just the news headline (minus the first ten characters), some tags, and the news story itself.

Line 34 then re-adds the first 10 characters to the news headline, which was passed as the parameter to this program on initiation.

Now everything we need for the news story is in place. The last programming effort is to replace several tags for formatting purposes as follows:

```
35. # Format headline and story
36. $Body =~ s/<br>/<br\/><\/p><p mode=\"wrap\">/s;
37. $Body =~ s/<font size=\"\-1\">//s;
```

Line 36 replaces

 tags with </p><p mode="wrap">. This allows the news story body itself to wrap so the viewer can easily read the contents on the Web phone screen. Up and down scrolling is required at this point.

Line 37 searches and replaces <font size="-1"> with nulls, which completely removes it from the body.

Along with the printing of all variables and exiting Perl, this is the final portion of our News example.

The produced WML code and screen image is as shown in Figures 3.23 and 3.24.

WAP Results (Web Phone Displays)

The entire WAP application from the Web phones' point of view is as follows.

Figure 3.25 shows three simple Web phone displays with simple navigation in a tightly controlled programmed architecture. With the basics found in this application, anyone with a little programming experience can create a WAP application based on an existing Web page. This method is 100 percent nonintrusive.

The number of lines that appear on the Web phone will differ from device to device but the underlying programs are the same across devices. Simple scrolling up and down is the only complication, which is minimal effort.

```
1. <?xml version="1.0"?>
2. <!DOCTYPE wml PUBLIC "-//WAPFORUM//DTD WML 1.1//EN"
    "http://www.wapforum.org/DTD/wml_1.1.xml">
3. <!-- Wavedev Perl News Parser -->
4. <wml>
5. <card id="card1">
6. <do type="accept" label="Back" name="return">
7. <prev/>
8. </do>
9. <p mode="wrap">
10. <b>
11. Bermuda Shaken By Another Earthquake</b><br/></p><p mode="wrap">
12. Two fairly strong earthquakes rocked western Bermuda on Sunday,
    two days
13. after a more powerful temblor buckled streets, knocked
    down houses and
14. paralyzed traffic for hours in a nearby region, officials said.
15. </p>
16. </card>
17. </wml>
```

Figure 3.23 Ch03Ex2R.wml code.

HDML Version

For those coding in HDML (used mostly in the United States), we've included this section to show how to change our first example in this chapter to produce HDML version 3.0 code. The first example is the HiMom example.

Figure 3.24 (from Figure 3.9C): News Story.

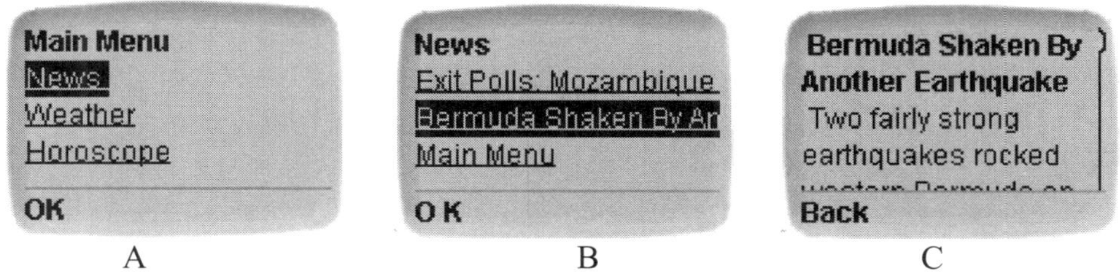

Figure 3.25 (A) Main Menu, (B) News Headlines, (C) News Story.

HDML is the predecessor of WML and only runs on Phone.com's Up.Browsers. Nokia microbrowser devices cannot interpret HDML and hence cannot execute or display HDML applications.

The Web page HTML will remain the same but the Web phone display will change from WML to HDML code.

The initiating WML program code is shown in Figure 3.26.

And its equivalent HDML code is shown in Figure 3.27.

The HTML Web scraping Perl program (Ch03Ex1.pl of Figure 3.4) code would change too. Lines 6 to 20 in the WML code would be replaced with the code in Figure 3.28.

Since this language is HDML, the content-type must be changed. As explained earlier, the content-type statement tells the WAP gateway to interpret the upcoming code in a specific language type, in this case, HDML rather than WML.

So, the statement:

```
print "Content-type: text/vnd.wap.wml\n\n";
```

```
1.  <?xml version="1.0"?>
2.  <!DOCTYPE wml PUBLIC "-//WAPFORUM//DTD WML 1.1//EN"
      "http://www.wapforum.org/DTD/wml_1.1.xml">
3.  <wml>
4.  <card  id="card1">
5.  <do  type="accept" label="OK">
6.  <go  href="http://www.wavedev.com/cgi-bin/Ch03Ex1.pl"/>
7.  </do>
8.  <p>
9.  Press OK to web scrape
10. </p>
11. </card>
12. </wml>
```

Figure 3.26 WML code copied from Figure 3.6.

```
1.  <HDML VERSION="3.0">
2.  <DISPLAY>
3.  <ACTION TYPE=ACCEPT TASK="GO" LABEL= OK
      DEST="http://www.wavedev.com/cgi-bin/Ch03Ex1.pl">
4.  Press OK to web scrape
5.  </DISPLAY>
6.  </HDML>
```

Figure 3.27 HDML code version of Figure 3.26 (CH03Ex1I.hdml).

Changes to:

```
Print "Content-type: text/x-hdml\n\n";
```

The resulting HDML code from the Perl program is shown in Figure 3.29.

The resulting display on the Web phone (in this case, Phone.com's HDML emulator version 3.2) is shown in Figure 3.30.

Most applications will be coding for WML-enabled microbrowsers. However, HDML is still popular in North America, and many firms are still planning to use HDML, so programming in both HDML and WML would be a good idea.

iMode Version

And for those programming in Japan or wherever iMode is in use, the coding shown in Figure 3.31 is the same "HiMom" example in iMode code.

The end result "Hi Mom" screen in iMode (or cHTML) code produced by the Perl HTML Web scraping program would be as shown in Figure 3.32.

```
6.  $deck_start = '
7.  <HDML VERSION="3.0">
8.  <DISPLAY>
9.  <ACTION TYPE=ACCEPT TASK="GO" LABEL= Back
      DEST="http://www.wavedev.com/book/ch03/Ch03Ex1I.hdml">
10. ';
11. deck_end = '
12. </DISPLAY>
13. </HDML>
14. ';
```

Figure 3.28 HDML code replacement for Ch03Ex1.pl lines 6-20.

```
1. <HDML VERSION="3.0">
2. <DISPLAY>
3. <ACTION TYPE=ACCEPT TASK="GO" LABEL= Back
     DEST="http://www.wavedev.com/book/ch03/Ch03Ex1I.hdml">
4. Hi Mom
5. </DISPLAY>
6. </HDML>
```

Figure 3.29 Resulting HDML code from Ch03Ex1.pl (program CH03Ex1R.hdml).

And the Perl HTML Web scraping program would follow all the same rules as described in the WML code-generating program in this chapter. You can see from lines 7 through 23 that the iMode code differs from HDML and WML. The reading of the Web page is identical, the Web scraping logic remains the same, and the content-type and printing are identical to the Perl program that produces the WML code.

So, iMode is similar in Web scraping logic and basics, just the iMode code changes. See Figure 3.33.

Pros and Cons of HTML Web Scraping

HTML Web scraping is a useful method to create a WAP site without worrying too much about intruding on the existing Web site. A WAP application can be completely built on HTML Web scraping and hence can be a remote system on a completely different platform or server, in a completely different country, for that matter.

However, there are some drawbacks. Modifications to the specific Web page can be done but anything affecting the tags or anything within the required text area may cause

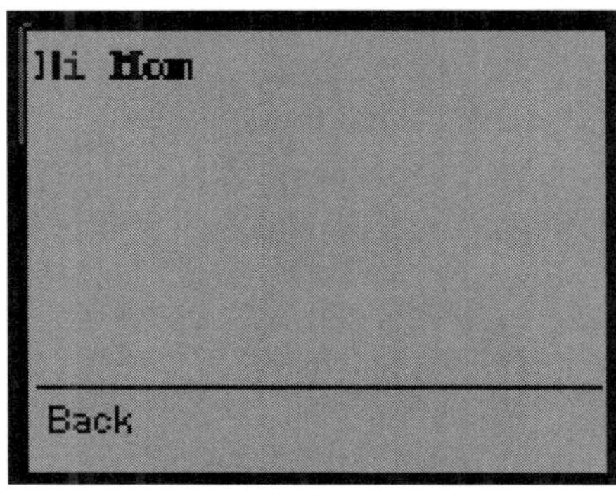

Figure 3.30 Resulting WAP device screen display.

```
1. <!DOCTYPE HTML PUBLIC "-//W3C//DTD HTML 3.2//EN">
2. <HTML>
3. <HEAD>
4. <META HTTP-EQUIV="Content-Type" CONTENT="text/html;
   charset=Shift_JIS">
5. <TITLE>iMODE Start</TITLE>
6. </HEAD>
7. <BODY>
8. <CENTER>
9. <A HREF=" http://www.wavedev.com/cgi-bin/Ch03Ex1.pl"
   accesskey="1">1 Press 1 to web scrape</A>
10. </CENTER>
11. </BODY>
12. </HTML>
```

Figure 3.31 iMode code for "Hi Mom" example.

the WAP application to stop functioning. If the Web page is not yours, you are at the mercy of that site's Webmaster. You will simply have to regularly check your application to make sure it still functions.

If you have control over the Web page, there is a simple addition you can do to better stabilize your WAP application. Instead of searching for a specific tag set, add a com-

```
1. <!DOCTYPE HTML PUBLIC "-//W3C//DTD HTML 3.2//EN">
2. <HTML>
3. <HEAD>
4. <META HTTP-EQUIV="Content-Type" CONTENT="text/html;
   charset=Shift_JIS">
5. <TITLE>iMODE results</TITLE>
6. </HEAD>
7. <BODY>
8. <CENTER>
9. <A HREF="http://www.wavedev.com/book/ch03/Ch03Ex1.wml "
   accesskey="1">1 Press 1 to return</A>
10. <BR>
11. <P>
12. Hi Mom
13. </P>
14. </CENTER>
15. </BODY>
16. </HTML>
```

Figure 3.32 Resulting iMode code from Ch03Ex1.pl.

```perl
1.  #!/usr/local/bin/perl
2.  use LWP::Simple;
3.  # Read into memory web page to be scraped (parsed)
4.  $WebPage=get("http://www.wavedev.com/book/ch03/Ch03Ex1.htm");
5.  # Create static portion of iMode code
6.  $deck_start = '
7.  <!DOCTYPE HTML PUBLIC "-//W3C//DTD HTML 3.2//EN">
8.  <HTML>
9.  <HEAD>
10. <META HTTP-EQUIV="Content-Type" CONTENT="text/html;
    charset=Shift_JIS">
11. <TITLE>iMODE results</TITLE>
12. </HEAD>
13. <BODY>
14. <CENTER>
15. <A HREF="http://www.wavedev.com/book/ch03/Ch3Ex1.htm"
    accesskey="1">1 Press 1 to return</A>
16. <BR>
17. <P>
18. ';
19. deck_end = '
20. </P>
21. </CENTER>
22. </BODY>
23. </HTML>
24. ';
25. # HTML web scraping
26. # Get rid of everything before <p> and after </p> tags
27. $WebPage =~ s/.*<p>//s;
28. $WebPage =~ s/<\/p>+.*//s;
29. # Parsing done, now set content-type for WAP gateway
30. print "Content-type: text/vnd.wap.wml\n\n";
31. # Send results to web phone
32. print $deck_start;
33. print $WebPage;
34. print $deck_end;
35. exit;
```

Figure 3.33 Ch03Ex1.pl updated to generate iMode code.

ment line and search for that comment line. For example, in the earlier examples, simply include <//—Title —//> before the required text portion and <//—EndTitle—//> after the required text portion. Now the parsing program searches for these specific comment tags, which is much easier for you and the Web application programmer to recognize.

```
12. <tr>
13. <td><b>Exit Polls: Mozambique Incumbent Wins</b><br>
14. <font size="-1">Mozambique President Mr. No won a second term
    Sunday with 55
15. percent of the vote, according to partial returns, avoiding a
    runoff in Mozambique's
16. third presidential election.</font><br></td>
17. </tr>
```

Figure 3.34 Ch03Ex2.htm (from Figure 3.11).

For instance, in the News HTML code, we would add specific start and end tags for ease of parsing. In this case our original code (see Figure 3.34) would become the code in Figure 3.35.

This technique will also help your Webmaster to insert refreshed data into HTML code with more accuracy. This is the 99.9 percent nonintrusive approach mentioned at the beginning of the chapter.

HTML Web scraping has minimal impact on existing systems and nearly always guarantees finding only the required portion of the Web page that is being sought after.

Another potential problem with HTML Web scraping is poor Web site programming. It is not uncommon for Web pages to have errors such as a start tags without end tags. Many Web browsers will accept such code while others will not. For example, if you are coding for an open paragraph tag, <p>, and expect to find an end paragraph tag, </p>, but do not, your Perl program may not function correctly. Take note of this potential scenario in your preliminary analysis of the Web page. If the page is dynamic (changes regularly), the problem may not show up today but might in the future, so take note, program accordingly, and check your WAP application regularly to ensure that everything is functioning as planned.

HTML Web scraping is a quick and easy method to "wireless enable" an existing Web site. Many firms have spent large amounts of money to obtain this sort of WAP application and yet Web scraping is fairly easy to accomplish once you know the proper techniques.

```
12. <tr>
13. <td><b><//—Title—//>Exit Polls: Mozambique Incumbent Wins<//—End
    Title—//></b><br>
14. <font size="-1"><//—Body—//>Mozambique President Mr. No won a
    second term Sunday with 55
15. percent of the vote, according to partial returns, avoiding a
    runoff in Mozambique's
16. third presidential election. <//—End Body—//></font><br></td>
17. </tr>
```

Figure 3.35 Upgraded Ch03Ex2.htm source code.

Dynamic WAP

All examples presented in this chapter have been developed and tested using Phone.com's UP.SDK 4.0 for WML code, UP.SDK 3.2 for HDML programs, ASP 3.0, VBScript 5.0, IIS 5.0, Microsoft Access 2000, and with some minor modifications Microsoft SQLServer 7.0 and 2000, unless stated otherwise. For more information on WAP toolkits, refer to the Development Toolkits (SDK) section in Chapter 1.

Most lines of program code in the examples are numbered for easy reference. Code on the CD is identical but without the numbers.

This chapter describes dynamic WAP in detail with examples. First is an introduction of the topic and architecture followed by an introduction to the technology used in our examples: ASP, methods of database connectivity, and ADO. Then we take a quick look at how to handle large result sets from database queries along text file queries. As with other chapters, we end with a working program example. Our example, Kid Care, describes in detail a wireless WML application that queries, updates, and inserts into a back-end database. Again, this example uses all the techniques and technology discussed in this chapter.

What Is Dynamic WAP?

Information is knowledge. With access to more data, individuals have more information, giving them the opportunity and, hopefully, the ability to enhance their decision making. With more information, we can quickly determine which route to take, which stocks to trade, whether to travel or not to travel due to weather conditions, whether to change business and/or personal plans based on reservation schedules, or whatever.

Remember that it has only been half a decade or so that we've been regularly using dynamic real-time information via the Internet. Even so, there are still many firms around the world that are not up to speed with Internet technology. Many of those who have undertaken to merge their businesses with the Internet have, for the most part, been quite successful. Firms that supply, for example, stock quotes, weather, and news in real time were hugely profitable in the late 1990s (or so it seemed). These Internet firms supply information in real time so that users can browse their information for up-to-the minute changes. Other successful ventures supply searchable information such as Internet portals and e-commerce bookstores where customers can search for specific books by name, author, and topic.

Thanks to a fast and reliable method to deliver the latest information in a timely manner, a whole new generation of market and information delivery specialists has developed. All this would not have been possible without the dynamic generation of Web content.

The latest technological leap is called *dynamic WAP* for the wireless Internet. A whole new world of mobile technologies, infrastructures, and devices like personal communicators is providing new unlimited possibilities for delivering information to end users. The Internet brought the world's information together and opened opportunities to the masses. Now wireless technology will bring that Internet ability to more people, anytime, anywhere. In underdeveloped countries, a cellular phone is more prevalent than a personal computer simply because the physical device costs less than a personal computer. Also, many countries do not have the underlying wired infrastructure for telephones, so wireless Internet access is the perfect solution. As predicted in Chapter 1, there will be more individuals accessing the Internet from mobile devices than from PCs in the near future. With the wireless Internet available on mobile devices and dynamic WAP available to applications, Internet access and information of all kinds will be available to more people around the world than ever before in human history. The world is advancing technologically, and dynamic WAP is helping to lead the way.

We define *dynamic WAP* as the ability to view or inquire about changing data from a mobile wireless Internet-capable device. Think of dynamic WAP as a program that creates a WML (or HDML) page with changing content that is most likely dependent on a back-end database or some other data source. Several major advantages of providing dynamic WAP content are

- Delivery of time-sensitive information directly to customers, anytime, anywhere
- Personalization of services based on customer requirements
- Personalization of services based on the type of wireless devices used
- Ability to perform dynamic searches of back-end databases
- Ability to create different views of the same result sets dynamically
- Ability to provide large data sets to the customers by implementing dynamic drill-down menus
- Advancements in overall Internet and mobile device technology owing to increased usage, wider audience participation, and improved device usability and features

It has been said that the Internet is still in its initial stages, but this is hard to believe since the Internet seems to be quite a huge complicated entanglement of worldwide networked data. Now, with the arrival of mobile wireless Internet capabilities and possibilities, it's becoming easier to imagine the unlimited potential of all these technologies and how these technologies affect world communications. Dynamic WAP is the cornerstone of this new technology and the second step in the overall Internet evolution. Now that dynamic WAP is becoming more and more available, it becomes easier to see where we are and how much more is still out there. What great times we live in!

The only disadvantage to dynamic WAP is in this current initial wireless Internet stage. Many devices are too small with too little memory and restrict the amount of information visible onscreen. This current drawback will only last another year or so as the industry fumbles in the development stage. However, proper application design and programming should allow end users to intuitively scan through large amounts of data with just a few clicks. Designs such as drill-down menus, cursors, and paging will help in this evolution.

Dynamic WAP Architecture

The architecture for dynamic WAP is very similar to HTML Web Scraping architecture (see Chapter 3) with the addition of back-end databases that supply the dynamic information.

To begin, access to the data is initiated from the wireless Internet device (see the Web phone shown in Figure 4.1), which connects via the cellular airwaves to the wireless network and onto the WAP gateway. The WAP gateway translates the request to the Internet protocol, which is then directed to the requested Web site. The specifically designed Web application at the Web site will query the required information on the back-end database. The results are then returned to the end user for viewing on his or her wireless device.

This architecture flow shows how connectivity to the database comes about. The data contained in the database can be added to, updated, or removed by some other back-end application whenever required so that this entire process occurs in real time. For integration of the wireless Internet availability to legacy corporate systems, this approach works wonderfully. This is the same approach used in designing and architecting access to data marts in a data warehouse scenario. Applications could also be created on the Web site to dynamically connect to legacy systems on differing platforms. These programs could then, either directly or through the legacy system, access data currently being used to run the business. The advantage of the integration with legacy systems is that sales staff, field engineers, remote employees, and the general public (including clients) can all view your data now available on wireless Internet-enabled mobile devices. This will open a new window to businesses for clients or employees to access information and possibly bring about an opportunity of increased awareness of the current business and, hopefully, new business.

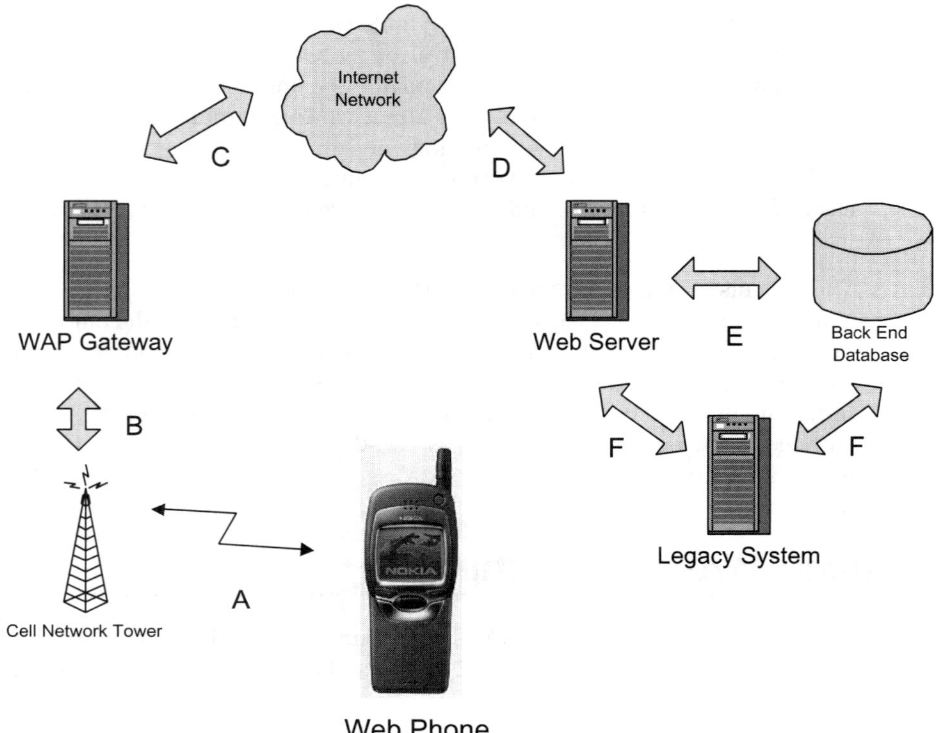

Figure 4.1 Dynamic wireless content architecture.

Figure 4.1 shows the overall steps in the WAP architecture. The flow of information request in this case is initiated by the end user clicking on a WAP application option on the cellular phone. Dynamic wireless content can also be initiated from the Web side. Scheduled messages can be sent directly to a specific Web phone with up-to-date information such as stock quote alerts or news flashes. I predict that, in the future, as wireless devices increase in capacity, individuals will be able to set timers so that specific information is refreshed regularly, once they have accessed a specific application. This sort of dynamic ability is typical of streaming video, which is the ability to receive dynamic data, be it images, text, or sound. Streaming video will enhance our daily lives with the ability to see, hear, and interpret information at will—anytime, anywhere.

Figure 4.1 illustrates a request from the Web phone to the back-end database for dynamic content:

A. The wireless device user initiates a call to the wireless network. This is automatic via Web phones since they have an Internet function-option built directly into the device. The user simply types in the required URL or selects an option or hyperlink and is directly connected to the underlying URL.

B. The call, now a WAP request, is directed via the airwaves to the WAP gateway.

C. The request is translated by the gateway to an Internet-understandable format (HTTP request).

D. The HTTP request is received by the specific URL from the WAP request, which is on a specific Web server.

E. The Web application is initiated by the HTTP request and executes a query on the back-end database via some type of scripting language (PERL, VB, ASP, ...).

F. Also, the HTTP request could initiate a request to a legacy system application that would perform a query on its back-end data system.

The return trip with the dynamic data from the back-end system to the wireless device would take the same route in reverse:

E. Rows of data (or a single row, depending on the type of query) are returned to the Web server.

D. The application program on the Web server reformats the result set into nicely formatted rows ready for display on a WAP device.

C. The result is then transferred across the Internet to the WAP gateway, which will convert the information into a wireless stream.

B. The wireless stream is transmitted over the cellular networks to the particular wireless device.

A. The call request is now complete with the results being displayed on the device.

To build an application that will perform the preceding requests requires special consideration, along with some basic programming skills, database connectivity knowledge, and the ability to manipulate the data once it's retrieved. The rest of this chapter will introduce certain aspects of Active Server Pages (ASP), different methods to access a back-end database, ActiveX Data Objects, and will discuss large result sets for databases and text files. Finally, we will show an entire dynamic WAP application. This application, even though it lacks many features, is a working system, demonstrating all the features and options mentioned in this chapter, including several more interesting points that will be discussed in upcoming chapters. Of course, all examples can be found on the CD that accompanies the book.

Active Server Pages

We're using ASP, along with VBScript, as the programming language. Many other languages can be used but VBScript is by far the most commonly used programming language with ASP. If you haven't noticed yet, Active Server Pages files have an extension of .asp rather than .htm or .html. ASP runs on the server side rather than on the individual's personal computer unlike HTML programs, which run on the client side.

ASP is Microsoft's alternative to using Common Gateway Interface (CGI) scripts and usually runs on Internet Information Server (IIS). If you have Windows 2000, you'll also have IIS version 5.0 since they are shipped together. If you have Windows NT 4.0, then IIS can be installed from Option Pack 4 for NT. A downside to using CGI is that each time a CGI script is executed, a new process is started. Just imagine what will happen when thousands of users are simultaneously accessing the same sites using CGI scripts (on the other hand, process isolation is much higher in the CGI case).

Let's talk a little about the basic components of ASP that you'll see in the program examples in this chapter. ASP 3.0 is composed of many different objects such as Application, ASPError, Request, Response, Server, and Session objects. But we'll only be looking at the *Request*, *Response*, and *Session Objects*. This quick introduction is by no means a thorough, in-depth description of ASP or of its fundamentals. We simply give a brief overview to the components and features that we'll be using in our examples.

In brief, ASP is interpreted by the asp.dll on the server. The first thing ASP looks for when interpreting code is the delimiter tags, <% and %>. These tags delimit all ASP code and will be included in all our coding.

Request Objects

Request Objects deal with reading information from the client-requested Web page or submitted form. For example, you'll see *Request.ServerVariables* and *Request("variable")* in many of our examples.

When invoking a program via an HTTP address line of a browser such as http://wavedev.com/wireless/default.asp?Iname=abc, the variable is called Iname and its value is abc. To access this variable in ASP, we'd simply write Request("Iname"). This method is called an HTTP get. The other method is called HTTP Post, which means to post the variable's values to a form and have the form variable passed to the program. The Post method does not show the variables or its values in the URL on the HTTP address line. In both cases, the requesting method is the same.

Here is a method of querying the value of an HTTP variable, called *requesting*:

```
<%
if InStr(Ucase(Request.ServerVariables("HTTP_REFERER"),"ABC")) > 0
then
     response.redirect ("NextPGM.asp")
end if
%>
```

The read-only HTTP variable ServerVariables is a collection of all HTTP header values from the client. The value we're querying here is HTTP_REFERER, which basically contains the invoking URL string. In this example, we're checking to see if the word ABC appears in the header variable ServerVariables ("HTTP_REFERER"). We first convert the contents of ServerVariables to uppercase (Ucase), which is just a programming method to bypass checking for lowercase, uppercase, or a combination of either. Then we use the InStr command to parse the string for a specific value, which is ABC. If the word ABC is found (> 0) then program flow is redirected to the program NextPGM.asp. If the word ABC is not found, we simply continue processing.

The object request ("variable") is really a global request that searches several collections. A *collection* is the grouping of specific variable types. The search of the collections occurs in the following order: QueryString, Form, Cookies, ClientCertificate, and ServerVariables until the search finds the first occurrence of the variable being requested. It is much more efficient to access the required collection directly. For example, if accessing a variable from an HTTP Post request, it would be best to qualify the request by specifying the form collection as follows: <% request.Form("variable") %>. In our example (http://wavedev.com/wireless/default.asp?Iname=abc), we could request the Iname variable value as follows: <% request.QueryString("Iname") %>.

Response Objects

Response Objects deal with output or flow control used when sending information and variables back to the client. The accessible variables include HTTP variables that identify the server, program variables, and cookie information.

In the previous example, we saw how we can redirect control of processing logic to another program via the *Response.Redirect* command. This is extremely useful, and we use it often in our programming to direct flow to another program, which could be another ASP program, an HTML program, or a Perl CGI program, etc. Actually, the redirect option tricks the client browser by sending a *302 Object Moved* message in the HTTP response header that tells the browser to load a new page as specified in the URL parameter of the redirect command, that is, response.redirect("url").

Note that when doing a response.redirect, it is always best to perform a response.clear first. This will erase any buffered page content from the IIS response buffer. Mind you, this only works if the Response.Buffer is set to True. Also note that the HTTP response headers will not be erased.

Using the redirect command is basically the same as using the meta refresh command both of which operate on the client's browser. The META usage is HTML-based and the response.redirect usage is pure ASP. The following will redirect control to NextPGM.asp after a refresh of 0 seconds:

```
<META HTTP-EQUIV="REFRESH" CONTENT="0;URL=NextPGM.asp">
```

If using ASP 3.0 and IIS 5.0, look into using the Server.Transfer object. This new option executes on the server side and is therefore more efficient since it doesn't have to return control to the client browser. With a redirect, control passes from the ASP server to the client browser, then back to the ASP server for redirection to the new program. A good point here about Server.Transfer is that control and all variables are still in effect and the Back, Forward, and Refresh buttons all function as expected. The Server.Execute command is also available, but this command functions like a subroutine that returns control to the next statement in the calling program when the subroutine is completed.

Another very common Response Object is the *Write* option, which is used to write to output. This option is often used in our programming since this is how we output all code to the browser.

```
<% response.write "<b>WAP Integration</b>" %>
```

For a dynamic approach to this example, we could include a variable from input to be displayed as follows:

```
<% response.write "<b>WAP Integration</b> by " &
Request.QueryString("lname") %>
```

The ampersand in this example (or we could have used a + sign) is required to concatenate the literal and the variable. Note, when sending an ampersand for concatenation in WML, we must specify its ASCII definition, which is &. We will discuss this later in the chapter. To follow our example from the Request Objects, the output of this write command would be:

```
WAP Integration by abc
```

Session Objects

Session variables are used to pass information from one program to another or to ensure that information is available throughout the browser session (while still within the default time-out period). Session variables are extremely useful in our programming efforts since we can easily store specific information in a variable and have it available for the duration of our application usage. The only problem with using Session Objects is that they are directly related to cookies. If the client browser does not accept cookies, then the Session objects won't work on that client, which could seriously affect your application (some WAP gateways support so called principle of "cookie proxy" in which case the WAP gateway acts as the cookie agent for the WAP subscriber).

In the following example, when an end user signs into the application, we retain his or her name (lname) in a specific session variable called UserName, which would be available to all ASP pages accessed in the same session.

```
<% Session("UserName") = Request("lname") %>
```

Of course there's a lot more to Session Objects, but we only need to understand the basic usage of this type of object for our programming examples. If you are already knowledgeable about ASP, then you understand that there are many more intricacies to these objects than what we've explained here. But if you don't know the language, hopefully this very quick introduction will have helped you understand the coding in this chapter and why we use specific ASP objects.

Connectivity and Database Access

Let's talk about database connectivity. Accessing the database from a dynamic WAP application is very similar to accessing the database from a dynamic Web application since the back-end database code is identical in both cases. Looking at the entire process, we see that the application is a three-tier process, as shown in Figure 4.2.

Each tier in the process has its own specific requirements. The first tier is the client's Internet browser, such as Netscape or Microsoft Internet Explorer for the Web (Up.Browser or Nokia for WML). Without a browser, we can't really see the results of our work, so it's kind of important. The second tier is our Web server containing ASP and VBScript. The server on this tier will take the hits when a user connects to our system. Once on the Web server, our application will request access and information from the database, which is usually on a completely different box—hence the third tier in our system. This back-end database will do the entire query processing, which is why it's a good idea to have it on its own machine. In our example, we'll be using Microsoft Access and Microsoft's SQL Server 2000. If using Microsoft Access, there is no need for the third tier since the Access database could easily be supported on the Web Server box along with the application.

For access to the third-tier database server, our application on the second tier must somehow connect to the database on the third tier. Connectivity to the database can be done by several methods. Open DataBase Connectivity Data Source Name (ODBC DSN) is the old-timer and is still heavily used in the industry. Then there is ODBC DSN-less connectivity, which is the same as ODBC DSN but the administration is controlled by the programmer rather than by the NT administrator (no ODBC Data Source Administrator usage). Then there is ADO and OLE DB, which is much more popular in the development circles these days. There are more choices, but let's stick to these common methods.

ODBC

ODBC is an application programming interface (API) from Microsoft that provides a common method for applications to access databases or other data sources. Microsoft initially developed ODBC, but now an international consortium controls its standards since many more products than just those developed by Microsoft use it.

An ODBC driver and ODBC DSN are required for connecting directly to a specific database or data source, in our case MS Access and SQL Server. To see if an ODBC driver has been set up on your server (or PC), click on Start, then Settings, and then

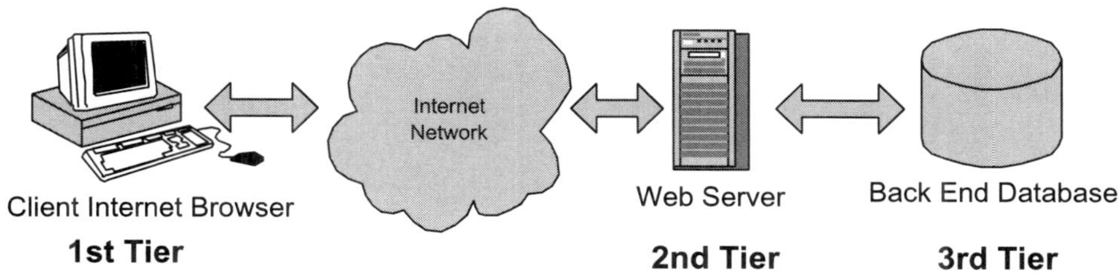

Figure 4.2 Three-tier Web application.

Control Panel. You should see an icon for 32-bit ODBC. Click on this icon to get the ODBC Data Source Administrator panel and look in the Drivers tab for Microsoft Access Driver (*.mdb) and SQL Server. There are many versions so be sure you have the proper ones: version 4.00 for MS Access and version 3.70 for SQL Server 7 as seen in Figure 4.3.

For the ODBC DSN, click on the System DSN tab and look for an appropriate System Data Source Name that has the proper Driver name, depending on the required database. If you can't find a DSN entry, one must be created.

Step 1 in using the administration program is to set up the Data Source Name (DSN). From the Systems DSN tab on the ODBC Data Source Administrator panel, click on the Add button. Then select the appropriate driver name, then click on Finish. This will bring up either ODBC Microsoft Access Setup or Create a New Data Source to SQL Server, depending on which one you select.

For MS Access, fill in the DSN source name to be used in your program—any name will do but you should make it easy to identify. Then click on the Select button in the Database section and enter the database name after selecting its location on the server. Click on OK, and all is ready for an ODBC DSN connection to your MS Access data-

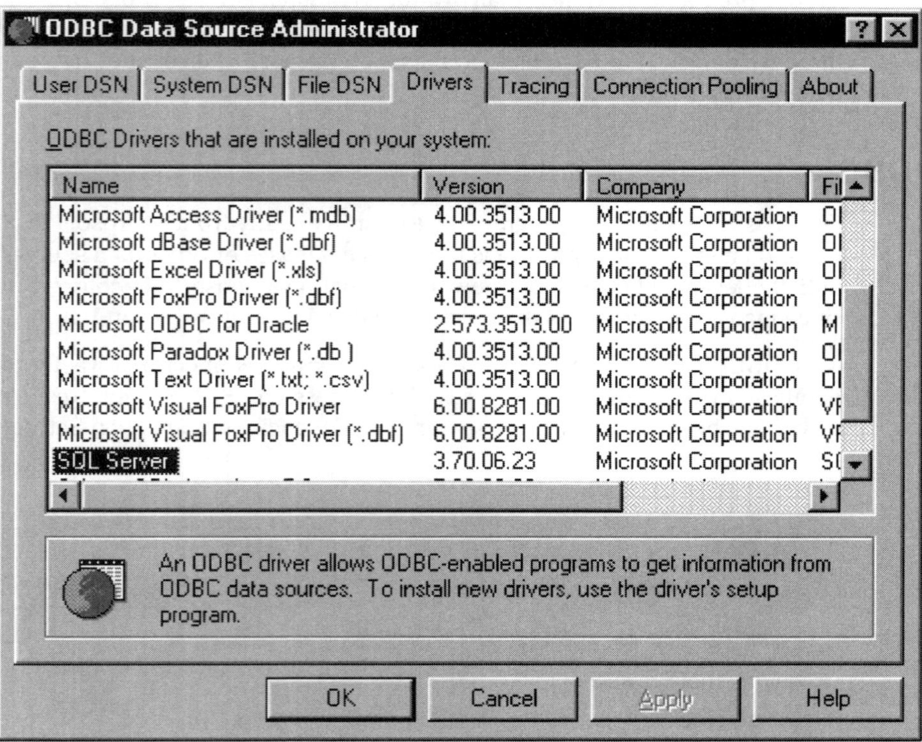

Figure 4.3 ODBC Drivers.

base. This is the simplest setup possible for MS Access. Figure 4.4 shows an example of the completed panel.

For an SQL Server, once on the Create a New Data Source to SQL Server window, proceed as follows:

- Fill in the data source name; again, any name will do but it's helpful to make it descriptive and easy to recognize.
- Fill in the SQL Server name containing the required database.
- Click on Finish if all other connection information (database, userID, and Password) is handled in the program itself.

Then click on Next and continue as follows, and as shown in Figure 4.5:

- If the Login ID and Password are to be authenticated at the SQL Server, then click on With SQL Server authentication using a login ID and Password entered by the user.
- If the Login ID and Password are to be hardcoded here in the ODBC DSN, then enter the Login ID and Password.
- Click on Next, which authenticates the parameters immediately against the SQL Server Logins and moves on to the next window.
- Once on Next, select the default database required (MyDB for our example).

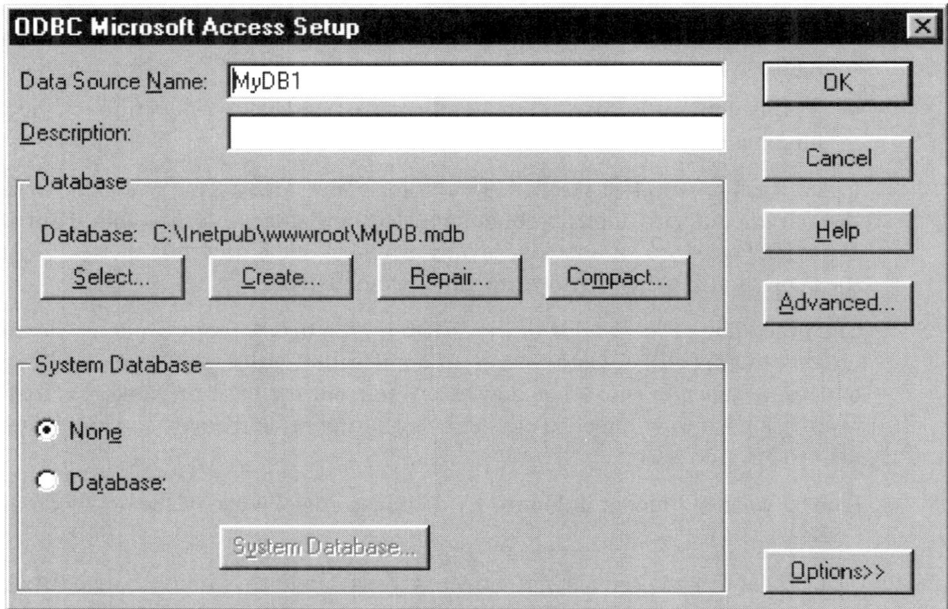

Figure 4.4 ODBC MS Access Setup.

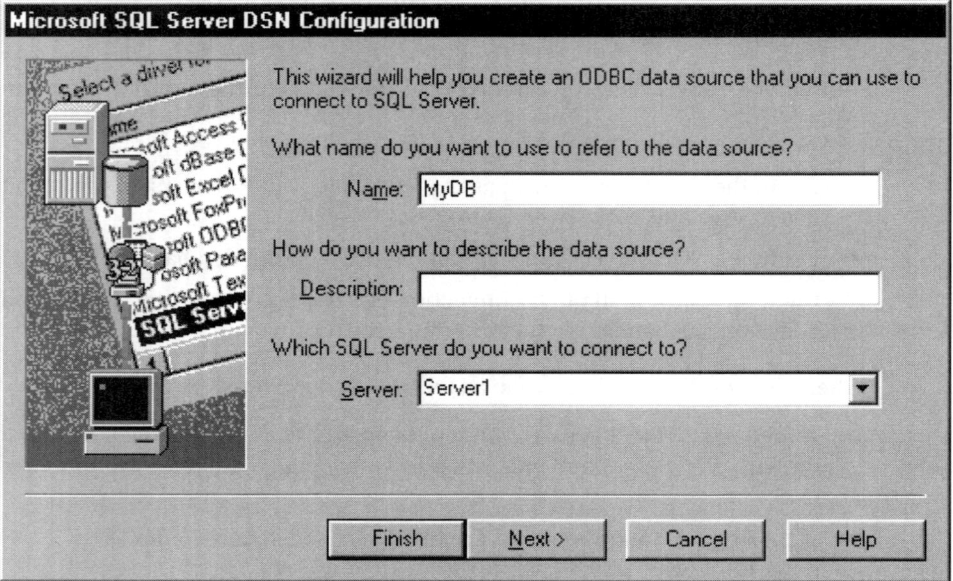

Figure 4.5 SQL Server DSN setup.

- Leave all the other defaults as is (unless you have reason to change them) and click on Next.

- On this last window, keep all defaults as is (unless there is reason not to) and click on Finish.

- At this point, it is possible to test the actual database connection or finish up by clicking on OK.

It is always best to test the data source for connectivity. This will ensure that with all the parameters provided, a connection to the database is possible. However, if the Login ID, Password, or database is only available in the program, then you'll have to run the program to test authentication and connectivity.

The preceding process adds to the ODBC.ini file that will now hold all the information created by this ODBC Data Source Administration process. Figure 4.6 shows only the entries in question. All other entries are left out for ease of viewing. The first entry, MyDB, is used to connect to SQL Server and the second entry, MyDB1, is used to connect to MS Access.

Line 5's open statement in Figure 4.7 demonstrates the use of the newly created ODBC DSN entry.

Now if this were to run against the MS Access database, simply change the Open statement to "MyDB1" instead of "MyDB". This is simple connectivity with low maintenance, but is it efficient?

```
[ODBC 32 bit Data Sources]
MyDB=SQL Server (32 bit)
MyDB1=Microsoft Access Driver (*.mdb) (32 bit)

[ODBC Data Sources]
[MyDB]
Driver32=C:\WINNT\System32\sqlsrv32.dll
[MyDB1]
Driver32=C:\WINNT\System32\odbcjt32.dll
```

Figure 4.6 ODBC.ini file.

DSN-Less

Another method of database connectivity is the ODBC DSN-less connection. This method allows for all required parameters to be under the programmer's control rather than, for example, your Internet Service Provider's (ISP) database administrator. It's not the most efficient method of database connectivity, but it is fairly simple.

For those people not wanting to pay an ODBC set-up fee for each database connection to their ISP, the DSN-less database connection is an alternative. Even though the initial set-up fee for ODBC is minimal, many people prefer to forgo the fee by using their own DSN-less connections.

This method relates only to MS Access database connections. It consists of a file having all the DSN parameters hardcoded and available to the program. Figure 4.8 is a copy of the DSN-less file we created instead of using the generated ODBC DSN from the Advanced Options screen of the ODBC DSN Administrator utility as explained as follows.

```
1. <%
2. Dim SQL, Conn, RS
3. SQL = "insert into audit (username) values ('Bob')"
4. Set Conn = Server.CreateObject("ADODB.Connection")
5. Conn.Open "MyDB"
6. Set RS = Conn.Execute(SQL)
7. Conn.Close
8. Set RS = nothing
9. Set Conn = nothing
10. %>
```

Figure 4.7 Program Ch04Ex01.asp, SQL Server connectivity.

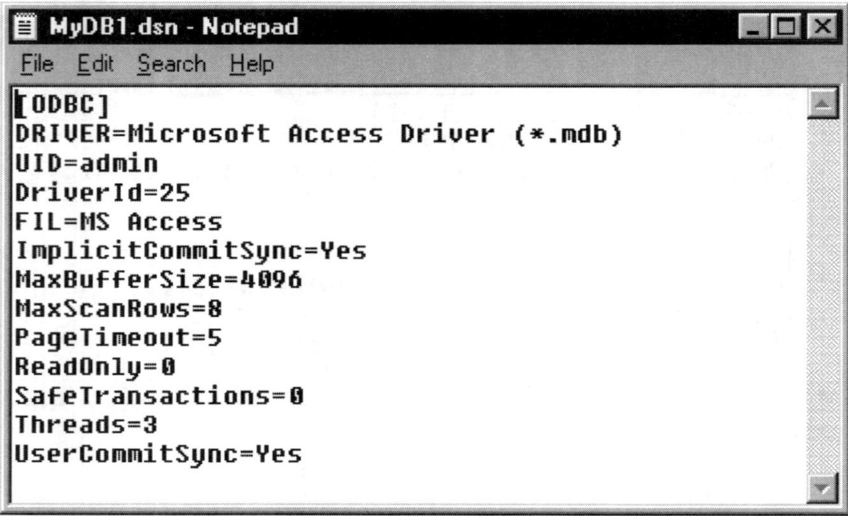

Figure 4.8 DSN-less file.

Figure 4.9 illustrates the ODBC administration panel. Again, click on Start, Settings, and Control panel. Then click on the ODBC 32 icon that brings up the ODBC Data Source Administrator. Find a data source name using the Microsoft Access Driver, under System DSN or User DSN, and double-click on the name. Clicking on the Advanced button will result in a screen similar to Figure 4.9.

Comparing Figures 4.8 and 4.9, you'll notice that the parameters are very similar. This is how a programmer can bypass the ODBC administration and use his or her own ODBC DSN-less file.

To complete our example, the code in Figure 4.10 shows how the DSN-less file is used for database connectivity in an ASP and VBScript program.

The program in Figure 4.10 does a simple insert into an existing database table. It defines the database file, the DSN file, and their relative paths on the Web server. Then, after defining the variables and SQL statement, it connects to the database via the DSN-less parameters and executes the SQL statement. It finishes by closing the connection and resetting the variables.

Let's look at each line of code. Remember, we are connecting to an MS Access database, which is on the same server and in the same directory structure as the application program. This scenario uses a two-tier rather than a three-tier system, since the database sits on the Web server with the application programs so there is no need for the third-tier database server. For our example, we'll be using URL address: http://wavedev.com/test/Ch04Ex02.asp.

Note that the URL address is simply the Uniform Resource Locator that is translated by a Domain Name Service (DNS) server to an Internet Protocol (IP) identifier,

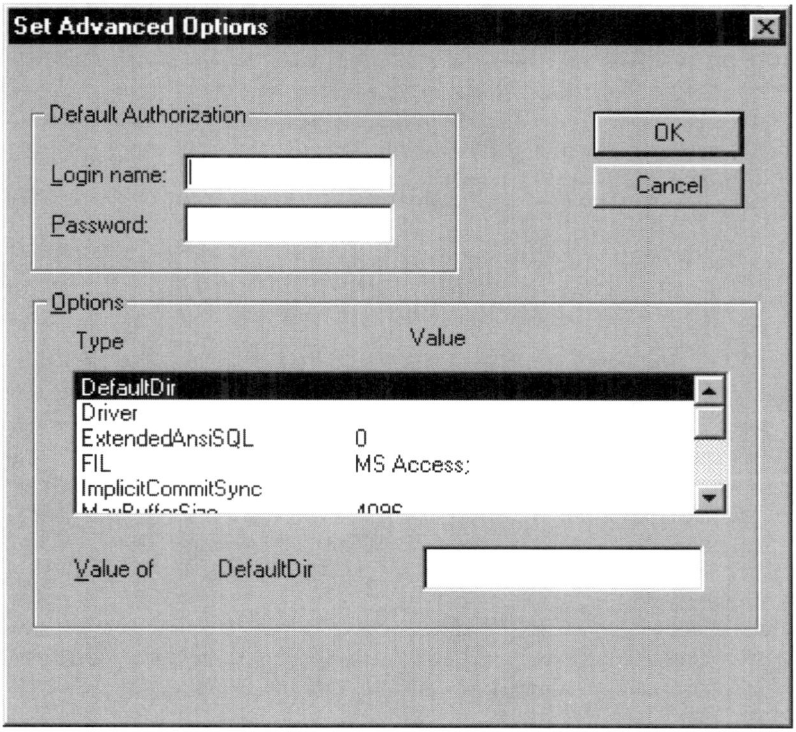

Figure 4.9 Advanced options of ODBC DSN.

which is 216.149.171.218 for our domain name, www.wavedev.com. This IP number is basically an address to our physical Web server machine that holds the specified directory (/test/) and application program (Ch04Ex02.asp). The IP address is really a specific path to the network card on the Web server. The Web server actually determines the physical path on the box. In our case, the specific path is D:\home\wavedev\ (which is not exactly true since we don't want hackers to know too much about our Web server, so we specified something a little different). Line 8 shows Server.MapPath, an ADO variable that maps to the physical location on the server itself. If you do a Response.write Path immediately after line 8, you'd see the server's actual physical path. Try it on your own server. Hopefully this quick technical note on URL to Web server path translation helps with the explanations of the program code.

Let's look at the program code line by line. The first half of the program determines, from the URL address line, the path being used on the server, which is important to know so the database and DSN files can be accessed on the Web server.

Lines 1 and 25 are begin and end tags, <% and %> required by ASP.

Line 2 is a comment.

```
1.  <%
2.  '---- Define DSN-less connection to database
3.  DB      = "database\MyDB1.mdb"
4.  File    = "database\MyDB1.DSN"
5.  Dir     = Request.ServerVariables("SCRIPT_NAME")
6.  Dir     = StrReverse(Dir)
7.  Dir     = Mid(Dir, InStr(1, Dir, "/"))
8.  Dir     = StrReverse(Dir)
9.  Dir     = replace(Dir,"/","\")
10. Path    = Server.MapPath("xyz")
11. Path    = replace(Path,"xyz","")
12. DPath   = Path
13. if Dir <> "\" then
14.    Path = replace(Path,Dir,"\")
15. end if
16. DSNa = "fileDSN=" & Path & File & ";DefaultDir=" & DPath &
       ";DBQ=" & Path & DB & ";"
17. Dim SQL, Conn, RS
18. SQL       = "insert into audit (username) values ('Bob')"
19. Set Conn  = Server.CreateObject("ADODB.Connection")
20. Conn.Open DSNa
21. Set RS    = Conn.Execute(SQL)
22. Conn.Close
23. Set RS    = nothing
24. Set Conn  = nothing
25. %>
```

Figure 4.10 Program Ch04Ex02.asp, DSN-less example.

Lines 3 and 4 define variables DB and File that specify the relative path on the Web server to the database and DSN files, respectively, from the default path, D:\home\wavedev\.

```
3. DB  = "database\MyDB1.mdb"
4. File= "database\MyDB1.DSN"
```

Line 5 defines variable Dir, which holds the SCRIPT_NAME value from the ADO ServerVariables collection (same as PATH_INFO value). For the sake of simplicity, we repeated the individual steps that create the value in the Dir variable. This is the part of the URL address specified after the http://wavedev.com, which is /test/Ch04Ex02.asp for this example.

Lines 6 through 9 manipulate the SCRIPT_NAME portion to remove the program name as follows:

Line 6 reverses the contents of variable Dir resulting in psa.20xE40hC/tset/. Notice the forward slashes remain the same.

Line 7 removes everything before the first forward slash. This essentially removes the program name, leaving only the path information in reverse.

Line 8 reverses the contents of variable Dir back again, resulting in /test/.

Line 9 replaces all forward slashes with backward slashes giving \test\.

Line 10 places the full current server path into variable Path, excluding the invoking program but with xyz at the end. We append xyz at the end because Server.MapPath requires a parameter.

```
10. Path = Server.MapPath("xyz")
```

The resulting value of Path is:

```
D:\home\wavedev\test\xyz
```

Line 11 replaces the xyz with nothing, which essentially removes the xyz but keeps the full current server path—our default path, D:\home\wavedev\test\ (There's an easier way to do this, but this method shows the basics quite well.)

Line 12 copies the value of Path into DPath since the variable Path will change in the upcoming code.

Lines 13 to 15 determine the server default path by removing the SCRIPT_NAME portion and adding a backslash. The backslash is required if anything is to be appended to this variable.

Line 16 contains the DSN-less parameters in variable DSNa.

```
16. DSNa = "fileDSN=" & Path & File & ";DefaultDir=" & DPath &
    ";DBQ=" & Path & DB & ";"
```

This is where it all comes together. All the required parameters to access the database via the DSNa variable are created here. fileDSN is the physical path on the Web server where the DSN file can be found (fileDSN=D:\home\wavedev\database\MyDB1.DSN). DefaultDir is the basic default path on the Web server (DefaultDir= D:\home\wavedev\test\). DBQ the physical path on the Web server where the MS Access database is found (DBQ=D:\home\wavedev\database\MyDB1.mdb).

```
fileDSN=D:\home\wavedev\test\database\MyDB1.DSN;
DefaultDir=D:\home\wavedev\test\;
DBQ=D:\home\wavedev\test\database\MyDB1.mdb;
```

The remaining code in program Ch04Ex02.asp is used to connect to the database, run an SQL statement, and then close the connection. The connection is made using the derived variable from line 16, DSNa.

```
17. Dim SQL, Conn, RS
18. SQL = "insert into audit (username) values ('Bob')"
19. Set Conn = Server.CreateObject("ADODB.Connection")
20. Conn.Open DSNa
21. Set RS = Conn.Execute(SQL)
22. Conn.Close
23. Set RS = nothing
24. Set Conn = nothing
```

Line 17 defines variables to be used.

Line 18 defines the SQL statement to be used, which is a simple insert of one row into a table.

Line 19 creates the ADO connection object.

Line 20 makes the connection to the database using the DSNa variable containing all the required DSN-less parameters created in the first half of the program.

Line 21 executes the SQL statement and stores the result in variable RS.

Lines 22 through 24 simply close the database connection and reset the variables.

There you have it: two methods of connectivity to a database. The first is through an ODBC DSN setup via the ODBC administration tool good for SQL Server and other data sources including MS Access. The second is the manual setup of an ODBC DSN-less file for use directly in your program without having to go through the ODBC administration setup.

And yet a third popular method of database connectivity exists.

OLE DB

Open Linking and Embedding DataBases (OLE DB) is a set of interfaces that allows uniform access from programs to data stored in or on different data sources, as seen in Figure 4.11.

OLE DB is the native connection method to SQL Server and is more efficient in connecting to MS Access than an ODBC connection. This direct connection is called *native* because as seen on the left side of the diagram, there is no need to use an ODBC driver to connect to the data source.

The lower right side of the diagram shows how a connection could be made through OLE DB and then through ODBC to connect to a database. This would be called the nonnative connection. Note the top right side of the diagram shows that scripting languages cannot access OLE DB directly and therefore use ADO, which provides the interface.

OLE DB uses the term *Provider* in its documentation and as a keyword, as seen in the ConnectionString that follows. Providers are used to connect to data stores (anything holding data). There are a variety of Providers, some of which are listed in Figure 4.12.

An example of a manually entered native connection to SQL Server through an OLE DB Provider using the ADO ConnectionString is as follows. This is explained in more detail in the ADO 2.5 section.

```
Conn.ConnectionString = "Provider=SQLOLEDB; Data Source=MyServer; Initial
Catalog=MyDB; User Id=bob;Password=test"
```

Similar to ODBC, OLE DB administration can be configured via a utility called the Data Link API. Setting up an entry is called *setting up a link server*, which is similar in concept to creating an ODBC DSN entry. It consists of registering the connection information for a specific data source so a query program knows how to connect and query the underlying database.

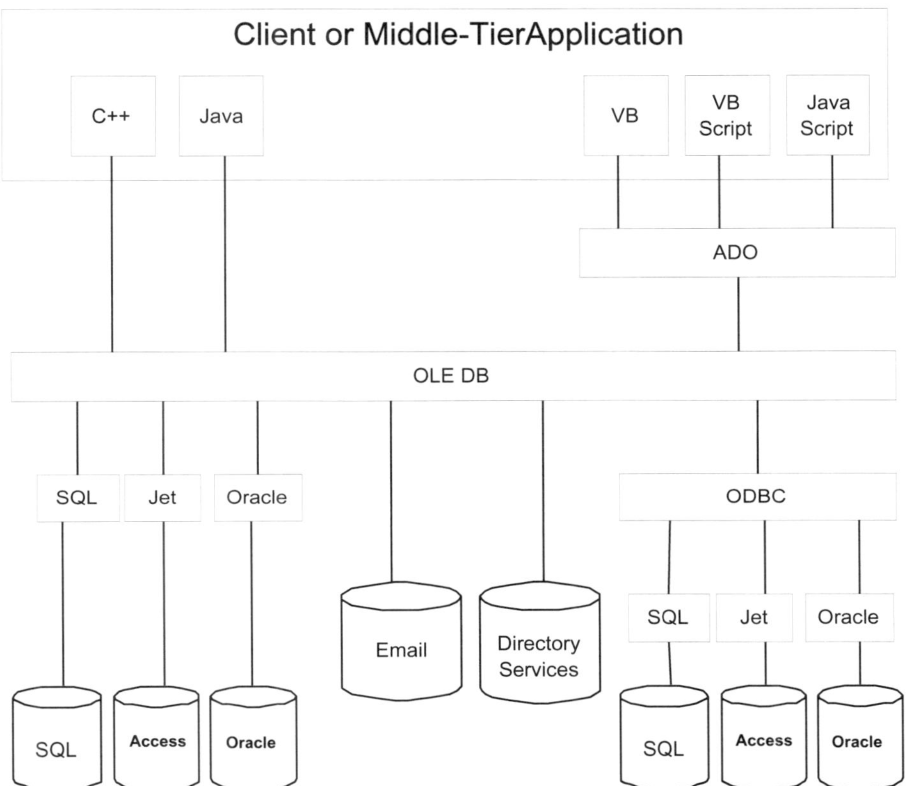

Figure 4.11 ADO and OLE DB diagram.

To set up a Data Link server, place your cursor on the right side of an Exploring window (on the Windows NT Server) and click on New, then Microsoft Data Link. This will create a new .udl file, which can be named whatever you wish. Then simply double-click on the filename and the Data Link utility will pop up. The Provider tab shows all the OLE DB providers installed on the system. To configure a connection, select an OLE DB provider and click on Next.

Depending on the Provider selected, the Connection screen will look different and have different configuration connection attributes. In our case, we'll use SQL Server as seen in Figure 4.13.

After clicking on the OK button (Figure 4.14), the .udl file is created (myUDL.uld) (see Figure 4.15).

If you use the .udl file in the ConnectionString rather than hardcoding, it would turn out as:

```
Conn.ConnectionString = "File Name=D:\home\wavedev\database\myUDL.udl"
```

Microsoft Jet 3.51 OLE DB Provider—For Microsoft Access databases

Microsoft Jet 4.0 OLE DB—For Microsoft Access databases

Microsoft OLE DB Provider for DTS Packages—For the SQL Server Data Transmission Services

Microsoft OLE DB Provider for ODBC Drivers—For ODBC Data Sources

Microsoft OLE DB Provider for OLAP Services—For the Microsoft OLAP server

Microsoft OLE DB Provider for Oracle—For Oracle databases

Microsoft OLE DB Provider for SQL Server—For Microsoft SQL Server database

Microsoft OLE DB Simple Provider—For simple text files

MSDataShape—For hierarchical data

SQL Server DTS Flat File OLE DB Provider—For the SQL Server Data Transformation Services flat file manager.

Microsoft Directory Services—For the Windows 2000 Directory Services

Internet Publishing—For access to Web servers

Indexing Service—For Index Catalogs

Site Server Search—For the Site Server search catalog

Figure 4.12 Providers.

Or directly in an ADO connection object's Open method such as:

```
Conn.Open = "File Name= D:\home\wavedev\database\myUDL.udl"
```

Of course, for this technique to function, the .udl file must be placed in a location that the ADO application can access.

ADO 2.5

We have used ActiveX Data Objects (ADO) in several of our examples so far, now let's look into it a bit more. ADO is the object model provided by Microsoft and sits on top of OLE DB (see Figure 4.11). Its purpose is to provide a common approach to accessing data regardless of the data source.

ADO contains objects. Again, the purpose here is not to explain all the details of ADO but to introduce the major objects being used in our program examples. Our goal is to explain enough so that you, the technical reader, can move ahead and actually do some coding using the presented components.

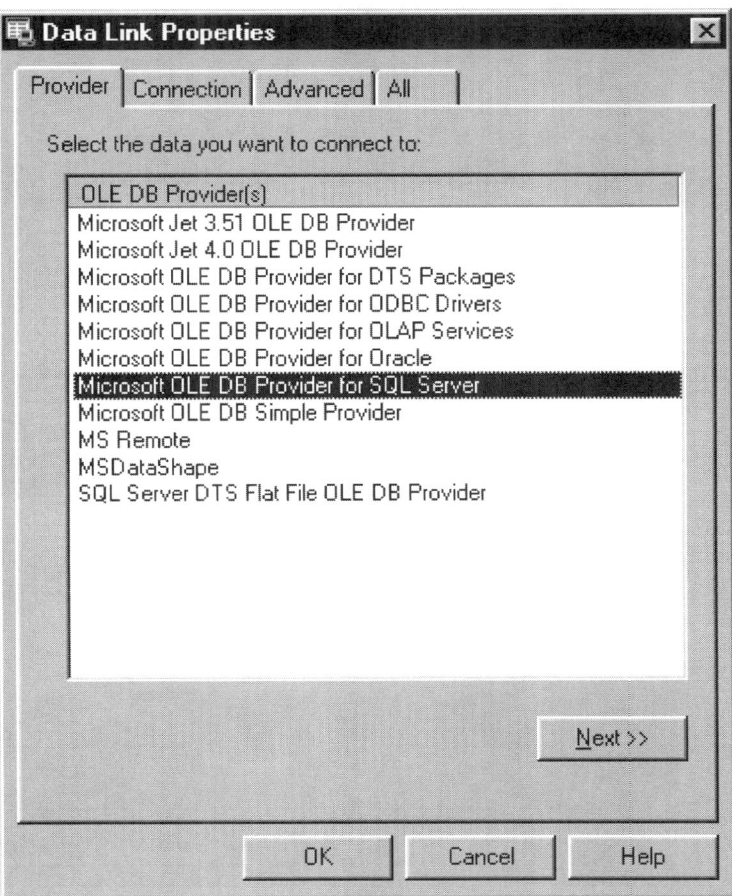

Figure 4.13 Data Link Utility.

ADO is a generic approach to accessing data—in our case, a database. The first thing to do is to define the database and connect to it with the Connection object. Once connected, we'll retrieve data via the ADO RecordSet object. Think of the RecordSet object as one big result set that contains all the data from a database query. A program can retrieve specific columns by simply scrolling through the data and predefining the result set parameters. In our examples, we predefine the number of rows per displayable page and scroll through the pages, which gives the end user the feeling of paging. There will be more on this shortly.

Connecting to the Database

Step 1 in connecting to the database is to define the properties of the data source using the Server.CreateObject, which creates an instance of the object:

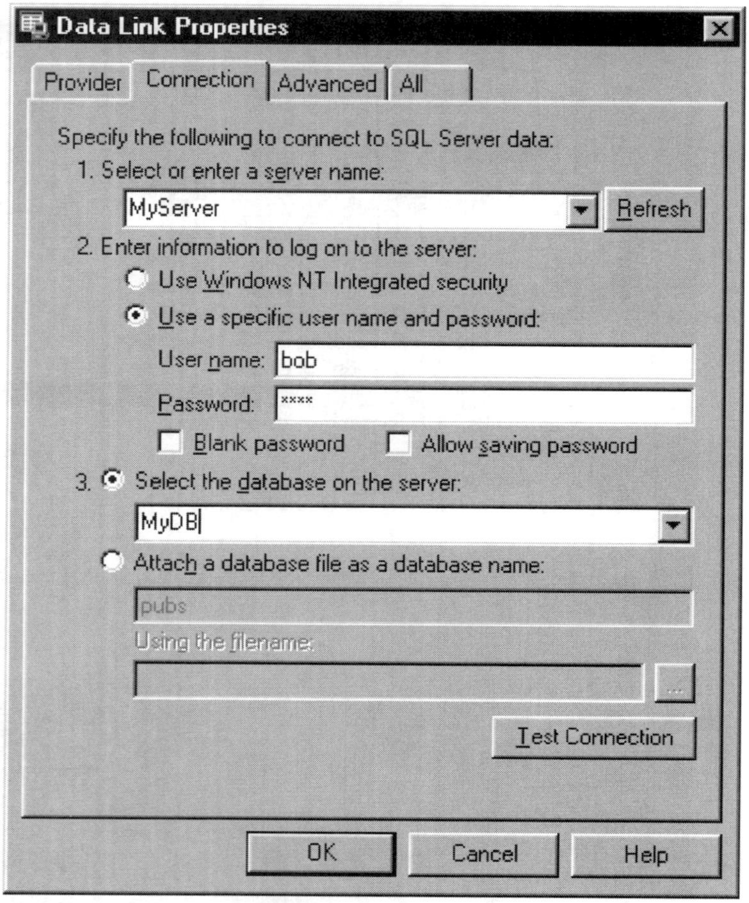

Figure 4.14 Data Link Connection screen.

```
Dim conn
Set conn = Server.CreateObject("ADODB.Connection")
```

Step 2 is to create the ConnectionString, which supplies all the required parameters for connection to the specific database (as described in the OLE DB section) and define it to the object instance as follows:

```
Conn.ConnectionString = "Provider=SQLOLEDB;Data Source = MyServer; Initial
Catalog=MyDB; User Id=bob;Password=test"
```

With the object and all parameters defined, we're ready to open the database, which is done as follows:

```
Conn.open
```

That's it. If you wish to change the underlying database or server, simply change the parameters in the ConnectionString.

Figure 4.15 myUDL.uld file.

Accessing the Data

Now that we know how to connect and access the database, we're ready to do some data manipulation. We can insert rows, update columns, or query the data. All data activity has a result, whether it's a result set or a simple result code, so we must define a result variable to contain the result. Then we can specify the query and finally access the database with results going into the Defined Result variable.

```
Dim rs  '--Define result set variable rs
Set rs = Server.CreateObject("ADODB.RecordSet")
Dim sql
sql = "select username from audit"
rs.Open sql, conn
```

Now the result of username from the audit table in our database is returned into variable rs. To display the result, the ASP Response Object Write (as described earlier in the chapter) can be used.

```
Dim UserCount
UserCount = 0
Do While Not (rs.EOF or rs.BOF)
  UserCount = UserCount + 1
  Response.Write UserCount & rs("username") & "<br/>"
  Rs.MoveNext
Loop
```

A counter called UserCount has been included to show how to add a line count per output line. We scroll through the results using a *While* loop, which checks to ensure there is data by testing the predefined ADO variables EOF (End-Of-File) or BOF (Beginning-Of-File). If results exist, we increment the counter, write the counter, username, and a line break (for a wireless device), fetch the next row and go back to the loop condition test.

To finish up, the RecordSet object is closed, the Connection to the database is closed, and the objects are released as follows:

```
rs.Close                    'close the RecordSet object
conn.Close                  'close the database Connection
Set rs = Nothing            'release the RecordSet object
Set conn = Nothing          'release the Connection object
```

Since WAP and Web applications can allow access to hundreds if not thousands of users, we highly suggest connecting to the database and creating the RecordSet as late as possible in your program. And in the same respect, close the connections and release the objects as soon as possible.

The following code can be used for database commands that do not return a scrollable result set but simply a single return code, as inserts and updates do. Here a row is inserted into our audit table example:

```
Dim sql
sql = "insert into audit (username) values ('Bob')"
Set rs = Conn.Execute(sql)
conn.Close                     'close the database Connection
Set rs = Nothing               'release the RecordSet object
Set conn = Nothing             'release the Connection object
```

No RecordSet is required. We simply use the Execute command, which executes the SQL statement. This is basically all we require to connect, query, and disconnect from a database. Other than the ConnectionString, the same code can be used to access an MS Access, SQL Server, or Oracle database. This code can easily be used for either Web or WAP applications with the exception of the line break, which is different for HTML and WAP.

Dynamic Data Retrieval

We've seen the components used to access a back-end database using ASP, VBScript, ADO, and OLE DB. Now let's look at how to retrieve large data result sets. We'll also look at another data source type: text files.

Large Result Sets

With regular HTML Web programming, large amounts of data can be displayed in a single window. With WAP programming, we must take into account the small screens and cache size of the wireless devices. Many wireless devices can display only a few lines of information and hold only 1024 bytes (1K) in memory. In the near future, these devices will evolve into sophisticated machines with the ability to cache a large number of lines all viewable from memory with the flick of a thumb mouse or roller button. Until then, we must carefully architect our screens and results.

Since wireless devices deal primarily with informational data, such as text rather than visual images, and since we're dealing with small displays and cache sizes, drill-down architecture should be used. However even with drill-down, there may still be large amounts of data to display from the result sets. We deal primarily with two types of result sets. First there is the basic large result set of text such as description and instruction-type text (or whatever), but basically it is a large amount of data from one database column. The second type is from multiple database entries where each line on the display represents a row in the database.

A simple technique to use when displaying one large column is to simply restrict the output size to less than 1024 bytes. Taking into account any overhead used for transmission of a device screen and whatever else, we restrict the large column of data to the first 800 bytes as follows:

```
<%response.write left(RS("Description"), 800) + " ... " + chr(13) +
chr(10)%>
```

VBScript's left feature is used to take the first 800 bytes. To expand on this idea, we could create logic that would page through 800 bytes at a time, thus allowing the end user to view the entire document. This would be useful when displaying job descriptions, instructions, and so on.

Note, in VBScript we often end write statements with the code chr(13)+chr(10) which adds line break characters to the source code, and which is only viewable on a wireless device emulator. We could leave this code out but then the underlying source code would be all strung together and difficult to read and debug. The display on the wireless device would not be affected either way. Most code on the CD contains these statements. Try taking the line break code out of one program and see what happens when you view the source code—for example, press F5 on Up.Browser SDK 4.0.

The second type of large result set deals with presenting multiple rows of data to the screen a little at a time by means of programming and the use of scrolling (paging). The idea behind paging is the ability to transmit only one page to the device rather than all the data. We can then page through the result set efficiently and, along with some programming logic, can turn a complicated WAP application into a very flexible query tool for the user.

In the following example we use the PageSize, PageCount, and AbsolutePage properties of the ADO RecordSet object. PageSize is the number of records on a page (default is 10), PageCount is the total number of pages in the RecordSet (based on PageSize), and AbsolutePage is the current page number.

The example in Figure 4.16 shows the paging logic.

Line 2 sets up the upcoming text to be in nowrap format since the data to be presented will be individual entries unrelated to the next line and would be more easily viewed on one line.

Lines 3 and 26 establish the select tags.

Line 4 sets the size of the rows on the page to 9. We're using 9 simply because if we wish to access any of the displayed rows, we can simply press a corresponding number on the device keypad as well as scroll to the specific line and press OK. This number can be set to whatever you wish; just keep in mind the 1024K generic cache limit.

Line 5 reads in the PgNo variable from the URL request and sets the variable ScrollAction with its numeric value. If there is no PgNo variable on the URL request, then ScrollAction will be set to 0.

```
1.  <%
2.  response.write "<p mode="+chr(34)+"nowrap"+chr(34)+">" +
    chr(13)+chr(10)
3.  response.write "<select>" + chr(13)+chr(10)
4.  RS.PageSize     = 9        '--Number of rows per page
5.  ScrollAction    = Cint(Request.QueryString("PgNo"))   '--Read in page
    number
6.  if ScrollAction < 1 then
7.  PageNo = 1
8.  elseif ScrollAction > RS.PageCount then
9.  PageNo = RS.PageCount
10. else
11. PageNo = ScrollAction
12. end if

13. RS.AbsolutePage = PageNo  '--Set current page number
14. MaxNum = 1
15. do while MaxNum < 10
16. response.write "<option onpick="+chr(34)+"getInfo.asp?ID=" +
    RS("UserID") +  chr(34)+">" + RS("Name") + "</option>" +
    chr(13)+chr(10)
17. RS.MoveNext             '--Move cursor up and get next row
18. If RS.EOF then
19. Exit do
20. End If
21. MaxNum = MaxNum + 1
22. Loop

23. if MaxNum = 10 then
24. response.write "<option onpick="+chr(34)+"Ch04Ex03.asp?PgNo=" &
    PageNo+1 & chr(34)+">More...</option>" + chr(13)+chr(10)
25. end if
26. response.write "</select></p>" + chr(13)+chr(10)
27. %>
```

Figure 4.16 Program Ch04Ex03.asp, paging example.

Lines 6 through 12 determine the page number to use. If ScrollAction is less than 1, the PageNo variable will be set to 1. If the value is larger than PageCount, which is the total number of pages in the result set based on line 4's setting, then PageNo will be set to PageCount. Otherwise, PageNo is set to the input value in ScrollAction.

Line 13 is another important variable. Here we set the AbsolutePage value to the current page. This will allow us to quickly reposition our cursor to the proper entry on the next iteration of the result set.

Line 14 initializes the loop counter variable MaxNum to 1.

Lines 15 to 22 contain the logic to display the retrieved data to the device. As long as the counter variable is less than 10, the process will continue to write output to the device as seen from line 16. Line 17 fetches the next database row; lines 18, 19, and 20 check to see if we have reached the end of our data. If so, then exit the loop or increment the loop counter on line 21 and reiterate through the loop if MaxNum is less than 10.

The If statement on line 23 checks the loop counter variable. If MaxNum is not 10, it means that the loop exited via line 19, meaning there was no more data to be displayed. If this is the case, then there is no need to continue with the If statement. However, if the value is 10, then there is more data, and we should display *More...* on the WAP device to notify the user that there is indeed more data available. To do this, line 24 shows that the same program is reinvoked but with an increased page number. This new page number will be used as the absolute page number the next time the program is invoked. This will then position the cursor at the beginning of the next page for the next loop iteration.

Note: When a Database Select statement is executed, all possible rows of data are retrieved from the database. Our program uses the RecordSet paging properties and the loop logic to scan the result set and only returns the nine rows of data we require. This process of sending to the physical device only what is required saves on transmission time and cache space, which is lacking on the currently available devices. There are other ways to do this paging (that is, through ASP and SQL Server), but the presented method shows the basic fundamentals, which are always nice to know.

Text Files

Not all data sources are databases. These days data can be found in emails, spreadsheets, and many other sources, including text files. To perform the same query type operation as in the previously mentioned program (Ch04Ex03.asp) but to a text file, the code in Figure 4.17 can be used. The difference is that instead of accessing a database and using ASP's paging features, we'll have to manually determine the current record and manually loop through all the entries.

Line 2 sets up the upcoming text to be in nowrap format since the data to be presented will be individual entries unrelated to the next line and would be more easily viewed on one line.

Lines 3 and 23 establish the select tags.

Lines 4, 5, and 6 define the text file to be used. Line 4 determines the absolute path on the server to the file. Line 5 defines a FileSystemObject, and line 6 opens the file in reading mode, which is the default open mode.

Line 7 reads in the LnNo variable from the URL request and sets the variable ScrollAction with its numeric value.

Lines 8 through 10 will loop through all the lines in the text file until line value LnNo is found. This basically positions us on the proper line as a cursor would in a database query.

```
1.  <%
2.  response.write "<p mode="+chr(34)+"nowrap"+chr(34)+">" +
      chr(13)+chr(10)
3.  response.write "<select>" + chr(13)+chr(10)

4.  set textfile    = Server.MapPath("Ch04Ex04.txt")
5.  set filesys     = CreateObject("Scripting.FileSystemObject")
6.  set openfile    = filesys.OpenTextFile(textfile)

7.  ScrollAction    = Cint(Request.QueryString("LnNo"))    '--Read in line
      number
8.  Do While openfile.Line <= ScrollAction and not
      openfile.AtEndOfStream
9.  openfile.SkipLine
10. Loop

11. strLineNumber = 0
12. MaxNum = 1
13. Do While MaxNum < 10 and not openfile.AtEndOfStream
14. MaxNum = MaxNum + 1
15. strLineNumber = openfile.Line      '-- Read in current line
      number
16. strEntireLine = openfile.ReadLine  '-- Read in entire line
17. response.write "<option onpick="+chr(34)+"getInfo.asp?ID=" +
      strLineNumber +   chr(34)+">" + strEntireLine + "</option>" +
      chr(13)+chr(10)
18. Loop
19. openfile.Close
20. if MaxNum = 10 then
21. response.write "<option onpick="+chr(34)+"Ch04Ex04.asp?LnNo=" &
      strLineNumber+1 & chr(34)+">More...</option>" + chr(13)+chr(10)
22. end if
23. response.write "</select></p>" + chr(13)+chr(10)
24. %>
```

Figure 4.17 Program Ch04Ex04.asp, paging example using a text file.

Line 11 sets strLineNumber to 0. This variable is used as the holding variable for the line number being read in from the file. If the file is empty, having this variable defined will allow the program not to abend later on in the code.

Line 12 sets our loop counter variable MaxNum to 1.

Lines 13 to 18 contain the logic to read the file and to display the retrieved data to the device. As long as the counter variable is less than 10, the process will continue to write output to the device as seen from line 17. Line 14 increments the counter, and line 16 gets the current line number generated by TextStream Object.

Line 19 closes the text file.

Line 20's If statement checks the loop counter. If the maximum amount of 10 has not been reached, it means that we found 9 entries to display and probably have more still. In this event, we will display a *More...* on the device to notify the user that there is probably more data. Notice on line 21 that to do this, we simply increase the strLineNumber variable value by 1. If this option is selected, the same program is reinvoked, and we'll loop through all lines until we reach this particular one.

Now, let's look at an entire example using all the tools, features, and techniques presented to date in this chapter.

Kid Care—Dynamic WAP Example

In the little town of El Fertilo, the wireless Internet has become available through the local cellular provider. Well, everyone was just abuzz with the freedom of accessing the Internet from his or her Web-enabled cellular phone. News, weather, wine crop reports, and so on were available to all in this cozy little village, anytime and anywhere.

Now El Fertilo has an unusually high number of youngsters for such a small village, which along with this newfound technology, inspired Martha to open a high-tech babysitting company. It soon became a huge success not only for Martha but also for all her clients. The service was quite clever; it matched available babysitters with needy parents. Most of her friends continuously complained about the lack of babysitters available on specific evenings only to discover the following day that Mrs. Noenfant was available or teenagers like young Nina or Alex were actually available at the time. So with a bit of inspiration and a knack for technology, Martha put together a wireless babysitting matchmaking service. Since most people in the town had a Web phone, the service filled a need.

Here's how the whole thing works. Babysitters and parents register with Martha directly via telephone, personal computer (Web), or email. Martha does her duty by investigating the person and then enters him or her into her database via her Web site application that captures the basic but essential details for the service such as name, Web phone number, and address.

Once registered, both client types (babysitters and parents) can query the system to find a match. For the purpose of simplicity in our example, the only rule when using the application is that all entries are for the current day. More information and rules could be added but for our purposes, this is all we need.

As mentioned, new clients are investigated and registered by Martha at her office, Kid Care Inc. The clients can use her system via the Web from a PC or from a Web phone. The funny thing about the town of El Fertilo is that more people own and use Web phones than PCs.

Let's have a look at the Kid Care application to see how Martha set up the process. First thing she did was to develop a simple WAP application, easy to use for both types of clients. Of course this example parallels our chapter and deals with dynamic WAP using a central database to hold all the information. The programming language is ASP and VBScript, the back-end database is SQL Server with connectivity being ADO and OLE DB.

Even though this application can easily exist as a PC-based Web application and Web phone WAP application, we'll only show the WAP side in our examples. The Web portion can easily contain the exact same window layouts and since the Web is more of a visual medium, the windows could contain much more information. Also, all the administration would be Web-based since the WAP side is geared more toward browsing and simple input. If you haven't guessed by now, Kid Care is a fictitious application created specifically as an example for this chapter. Any relation to any existing Web site is purely coincidental—yet all rights are proprietary. Of course the example is in its simplest form. Much more could be done to enhance this application. I say *application* because rather than simply showing several simple excerpts from a program, we've included an entire working application, which is also included on the CD. Let me say there are many ways to perform many portions of the code, and I'm sure many of you can whip up a much more efficient batch of programs. But as I said, these programs are presented in their simplest form.

Figure 4.18 is an overview of the entire application flow. Everything starts with a title page followed by a user sign-on. For this application, the individual users must manually sign into the application each and every time, which is a hassle from a Web phone since it involves typing a userID and Password. We could enhance the application by using cookies, which would automatically sign on the user when he or she used the Kid Care WAP site.

Then, depending on how Martha defined the user, either a Parent or BabySitter menu will appear. Both user types have a minimal set of features. Sitters can browse babysitting openings (jobs), post their availability, and check out their own personal information to ensure that Martha was on her toes when she entered it. Parents have essentially the same type of feature from a parent's perspective. They can browse available sitters, post their sitter needs, and check their personal information. When either type of user browses the availabilities, the individual can place a call simply by pressing a single button. This is simple and yet effective but, most of all, a functional application filling a need in the small community of El Fertilo.

Before we continue, this is a good place to have a look at the back-end database structure. As mentioned earlier, the database server being used is Microsoft SQLServer 7.0, which we ran on an NT server. The database is extremely simple but does the job as seen in Figure 4.19.

The Client table holds the userID, Password, and type defining if the user is a babysitter or a parent. Then the two main tables are BabySitter and Parent, each holding their appropriate information. All data definition language (DDL) for the database layout is included on the attached CD. The two transactional tables are SittersNeeded and AvailableSitters. These two tables are straightforward. Parents and Babysitters can each plug in their respective requests, hoping for the other to view their posting. If a parent needs a sitter, the parent posts the request into SittersNeeded, which sitters can

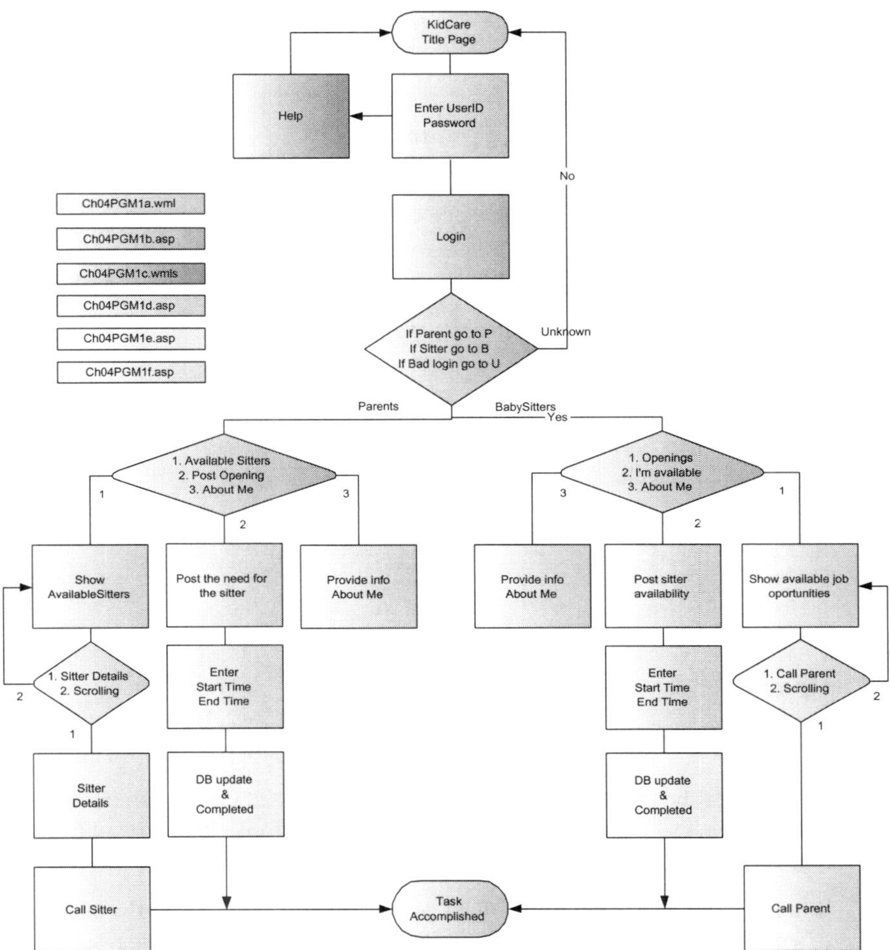

Figure 4.18 Kid Care overview.

view. Oppositely, if a sitter is available to babysit, that person could post his or her availability in AvailableSitters, which is viewable by the parents. Hopefully, one will call the other via Web phone and fill the need. So each has two options. First, post the opening and/or availability and wait for the other to call or browse the availablities and/or openings and call the other person. It works both ways. Of course there are many features and functionalities we could add but we'll leave the possibilities to your imagination.

Both SittersNeeded and AvailableSitters have extra columns called BookedBy, which are not used in our application. They were included to show the possibility of expanding the application to booking the job or sitter once both parties have come to an agreement.

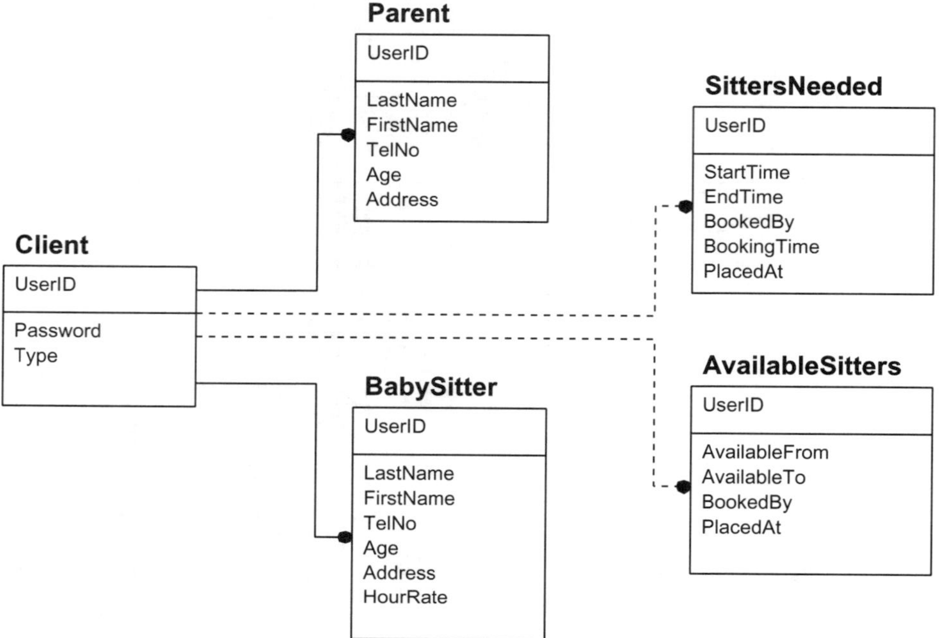

Figure 4.19 Kid Care database, MyDB.

Figure 4.20 shows the main WAP screens for the Kid Care application. The first screen is the title page "Kid Care" with an appropriate simple image displayed. Remember, as a general compatibility note: Image, text, and overhead should exceed 1024 bytes.

When the left Softkey (under OK) is pressed, control moves to the security screen (sign-in screen) requesting a UserID and Password. Note that if OK is not pressed on the title page, after 5 seconds a timer will automatically jump the viewer to the sign-in screen. This underlying sign-in security logic is our first dynamic input and initial database access routine.

Martha gave each person a UserID and Password when he or she registered and classified each person as either a babysitter or a parent. So once the user signs in, the inputted information will be validated against its respective database entry, and, if all is fine, the system will display the appropriate window on the Web phone. If the person is registered as a babysitter, then the Sitters screen is displayed. If the person is a registered parent, then the Parents screen is displayed. The Sitters screen options are shown in Figure 4.24 and the Parents screen options are shown in Figure 4.26.

Figure 4.21 shows the programs that produce the screens in Figure 4.20. Not all lines will be explained since many are repeated and the basics should be known by now after reading Chapter 2.

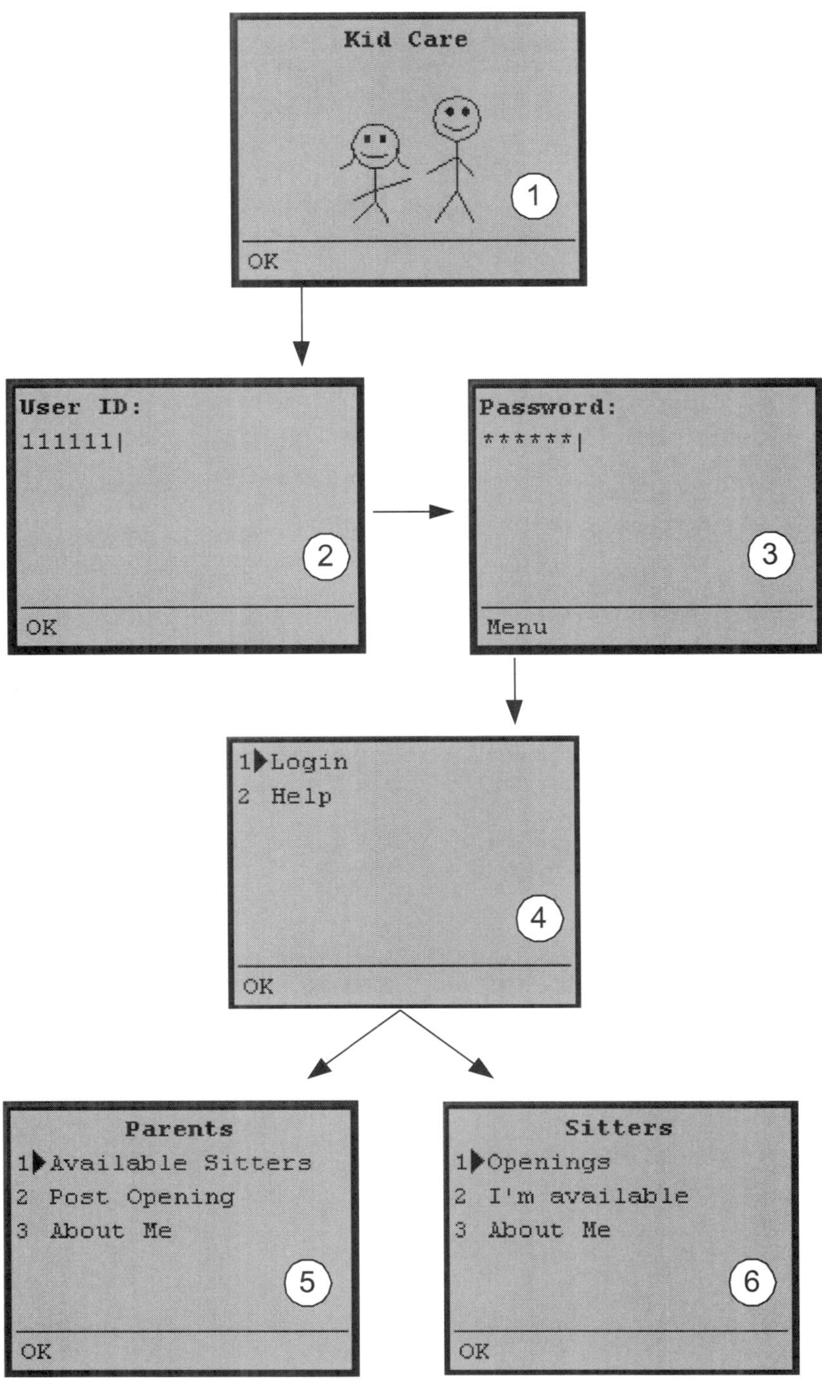

Figure 4.20 Kid Care main application.

```
1.  <?xml version="1.0"?>
2.  <!DOCTYPE wml PUBLIC "-//PHONE.COM//DTD WML 1.1//EN"
      "http://www.phone.com/dtd/wml11.dtd">
3.  <wml>

4.  <card id="KC1" ontimer="#UIDPWD" newcontext="true">
5.  <timer name="time" value="50"/>
6.  <do name="OK" type="accept" label="OK">
7.  <go href="#UIDPWD"/>
8.  </do>
9.  <p align="center">
10. <b>Kid Care</b><br/>
11. <img src="KidCare.bmp" alt="KidCare"/>
12. </p>
13. </card>

14. <card id="UIDPWD">
15. <onevent type="onenterbackward">
16. <go href="#KC1"/>
17. </onevent>
18. <onevent type="onenterforward">
19. <refresh>
20. <setvar name="HelpNeed" value="UIDPWD"/>
21. </refresh>
22. </onevent>
23. <do name="Login" type="accept" label="Login">
24. <go href="Ch04PGM1b.asp?UID=$(UID)&amp;PWD=$(PWD)"/>
25. </do>
26. <do name="Help" type="accept" label="Help">
27. <go href="Ch04PGM1c.wmls#helpme()"/>
28. </do>
29. <p>
30. <b>User ID:</b> <input name="UID" type="text" format="6N"
      emptyok="false" size="6" maxlength="6"/><br/>
31. <b>Password:</b> <input name="PWD" type="password" format="6N"
      emptyok="false" size="6" maxlength="6"/><br/>
32. </p>
33. </card>

34. <card id="HelpCard">
35. <do name="Back" type="accept" label="Back">
36. <go href="#KC1"/>
37. </do>
38. <p mode="wrap">$(WrText)</p>
39. </card>
40. </wml>
```

Figure 4.21 Program Ch04PGM1a.wml, title, and security WML pages.

This first program is pure WML and this deck has three cards used to produce the main title screen (Figure 4.20[1]), the sign-on screens (Figure 4.20[2], [3], and [4]), and the Help screen (not shown in our diagrams).

In keeping with our Phone.com (OpenWave) Up.Browser theme for this chapter, Ch04PGM1a.wml uses the Phone.com DTD as seen on line 2.

Lines 4 through 13 create the title page and set the newcontext to true on line 4. Newcontext will initialize all variables and clear the history stack—definitely something to use just before any sign-on screen.

Lines 4 and 5 show the use of a timer. Basically, if the timer has ticked through 50 milliseconds, control is passed from this card to card UIDPWD, as also seen on line 4.

The second card on lines 14 through 33 is used to capture the UserID and Password. Here we use the onenterbackward and onenterforward onevents. If this card is entered from the main title page, card KC1 (onenterforward), then the HelpNeed variable on line 20 is refreshed. If the card is invoked from card HelpCard on lines 34 through 39 (onenterbackward) or any other card in the history deck, then control is redirected to the main title page to ensure all variables and the history stack are cleared by means of the newcontext option.

Once the User ID from line 30 is entered, control is passed to line 31 to enter the Password. Once this is done, lines 23 to 25 and lines 26 to 28 take over, as seen in Figure 4.20(4). If Login is selected, control is passed to program Ch04PGM1b.asp as seen on line 24. If Help is selected, control is passed to Ch04PGM1c.wmls as seen on line 27. Program Ch04PGM1c.wmls (seen as follows in alphabetical order) will display a Help screen and return control to the last card in Ch04PGM1a.wml, card HelpCard.

HelpCard will display text from Ch04PGM1c.wmls and directs control to the first card in the deck (KC1) once the Back key is pressed as seen on line 36.

Program Ch04PGM1b.asp is invoked from Ch04PGM1a.wml, line 24. This program connects and queries the back-end database to verify the userID and Password. If found in the database, the type column is checked and the appropriate menu screen is built and displayed to the user. If the information is not found in the database, an error message is displayed on the screen and control is returned back to the previous program once the Login button is pressed.

The first thing you'll notice about Ch04PGM1b.asp in Figure 4.22 is that there are a lot of +chr(34) s. You may remember this from Chapter 3; it's the ASCII character for a quote. When writing an output line in VBScript, the output must be enclosed in quotation marks. However, the WML code also has quotation marks, which would be interpreted incorrectly by VBScript so to avoid this problem, we simply specify the quotes in an ASCII representation.

Line 2 sets the ASP buffer to TRUE. This allows all output to be first cached on the ASP server before being written to the WAP device.

```
1.  <%
2.  Response.Buffer = TRUE
3.  Response.ContentType = "text/vnd.wap.wml"

4.  '-- Open connection to database.
5.  Dim Conn
6.  Set Conn = Server.CreateObject("ADODB.Connection")
7.  Conn.ConnectionString = "Provider=SQLOLEDB;Data
      Source=MyServer;Initial Catalog=MyDB;User Id=bob;Password=test;"

8.  '-- Check for the existence of the user id and password.
9.  Dim rs
10. Set rs = Server.CreateObject("ADODB.Recordset")
11. Dim sql
12. sql = "select type from client where UserID=" +
      CStr(Request("UID")) + " and Password=" + CStr(Request("PWD"))
13. rs.Open sql, Conn

14. '-- Determine which type of person logged in. (P=parent,
      B=babysitter, U=unknown)
15. Dim UserType
16. if rs.EOF or rs.BOF then
17. UserType = "U"
18. Session("UserId") = ""
19. elseif rs("type") = "P" then
20. UserType = "P"
21. Session("UserId") = Request("UID")
22. else
23. UserType = "B"
24. Session("UserId") = Request("UID")
25. end if

26. rs.Close
27. Conn.Close
28. Set rs  = Nothing
29. Set Conn = Nothing

30. '-- Setup deck headers.
31. response.write "<?xml version="+chr(34)+"1.0"+chr(34)+"?>"
32. response.write "<!DOCTYPE wml PUBLIC "+chr(34)+"-//PHONE.COM//DTD
      WML 1.1//EN"+chr(34)+" "+chr(34)+
      "http://www.phone.com/dtd/wml11.dtd"+chr(34)+">"
33. response.write "<wml>"

34. '-- Setup card headers and softkeys.
35. if UserType = "P" then
```

Figure 4.22 Program Ch04PGM1b.asp, security and menu pages.

```
36. response.write "<card id="+chr(34)+"Parents"+chr(34)+">"
37. response.write "<do type="+chr(34)+"accept"+chr(34)+"
    label="+chr(34)+"OK"+chr(34)+">"
38. response.write "<go
    href="+chr(34)+"Ch04PGM1d.asp?Action=$(Parents)" + chr(34)+"/>"
39. response.write "</do>"
40. response.write "<p
    align="+chr(34)+"center"+chr(34)+"><b>Parents</b></p><p
    align="+chr(34)+"left"+chr(34)+"
    mode="+chr(34)+"nowrap"+chr(34)+">"
41. response.write "<select name="+chr(34)+"Parents"+chr(34)+">"
42. response.write "<option value="+chr(34)+"RS"+chr(34)+">Available
    Sitters</option>"
43. response.write "<option value="+chr(34)+"PO"+chr(34)+">Post
    Opening</option>"
44. response.write "<option value="+chr(34)+"AMP"+chr(34)+">About
    Me</option>"
45. response.write "</select>"
46. elseif UserType = "B" then
47. response.write "<card id="+chr(34)+"Sitters"+chr(34)+">"
48. response.write "<do type="+chr(34)+"accept"+chr(34)+"
    label="+chr(34)+"OK"+chr(34)+">"
49. response.write "<go
    href="+chr(34)+"Ch04PGM1d.asp?Action=$(Sitters)" + chr(34)+"/>"
50. response.write "</do>"
51. response.write "<p
    align="+chr(34)+"center"+chr(34)+"><b>Sitters</b></p><p
    align="+chr(34)+"left"+chr(34)+"
    mode="+chr(34)+"nowrap"+chr(34)+">"
52. response.write "<select name="+chr(34)+"Sitters"+chr(34)+">"
53. response.write "<option
    value="+chr(34)+"OP"+chr(34)+">Openings</option>"
54. response.write "<option value="+chr(34)+"IA"+chr(34)+">I'm avail
    able</option>"
55. response.write "<option value="+chr(34)+"AMS"+chr(34)+">About
    Me</option>"
56. response.write "</select>"
57. else
58. response.write "<card id="+chr(34)+"NoGo"+chr(34)+">"
59. response.write "<do type="+chr(34)+"accept"+chr(34)+"
    label="+chr(34)+"Login"+chr(34)+">"
60. response.write "<go href="+chr(34)+"Ch04PGM1a.wml" + chr(34)+"/>"
61. response.write "</do>"
62. response.write "<p><b>Invalid Login</b><br/><b>Try Again</b>"
63. end if
64. response.write "</p></card></wml>"
65. %>
```

Figure 4.22 Continued Program Ch04PGM1b.asp, security and menu pages.

Line 3 defines the ContentType for the ASP server. This tells ASP that the following code will be in the text/vnd.wap.wml MIME type and therefore should be properly interpreted.

Lines 4 through 7 define the database instance and the connection string using OLE DB parameters as seen in the OLE DB section earlier.

Lines 9 through 13 set up the result set variable (rs), defines the RecordSet object, and the SQL database query using the UID and PWD variables from the sign-in screens in Figure 4.20(1), (2), and (3).

Lines 15 through 25 set up the ASP session object userID to be used in later programs while the user is still in the current browser session.

Now the database connection and result set can be closed since we no longer require any more database access.

The remainder of the program is building the WML code for the proper user menu (Parents, Figure 4.20[5] or Sitters, Figure 4.20[6]) based on the user type from the database. Again if for some reason there is no type for that particular user in the database, an error message is displayed on the screen and control is returned back to the previous program once the Login button is pressed.

Notice that lines 38 and 49 use substituted variables in the "go href" statement. The names of the variables used (Parents or Sitters) are the names defined on the respective select statements, lines 41 and 52. Depending on the option selected by the user, the option value name is the select name, which is substituted in the 'go href' statement variable. This is a useful method to pass parameters from selection lists.

The first program, Ch04PGM1a.wml, invokes the following help program if the user selects Help from the log-in screen (Figure 4.20[4]). Basically, the WMLScript routine will read in a variable (line 3), check which card invoked the script (line 4), prepare an error message (line 6) based on the invoking card, and direct program control back to a particular card within a particular program (line 7).

We included the quick WMLScript program example in Figure 4.23 to show a hardcoded Help subroutine. Many more Help statements could be added by repeating lines 4 through 8 as needed.

In Figure 4.24, all screens have been numbered for easy reference and the program names, which created the screens, have been included. Also, since much of the main logic is in one program, Ch04PGM1d.asp, and the logic (case statement) is dependent on the option selected from the users' main menu, the case statement value has also been added for easy reference.

Figures 4.24(2a) and 4.26(2a) are only seen on the emulators. These screens would not appear on the actual Web phones since the call feature actually calls the number but the emulator does not—hence the visual screen.

```
1. extern function helpme()
2. {
3. var validIn = WMLBrowser.getVar("HelpNeed");
4. if (validIn == "UIDPWD")
5. {
6. WMLBrowser.setVar("WrText", "Please enter your six digit User ID
    and Password");
7. WMLBrowser.go("Ch04PGM1a.wml#HelpCard");
8. }
9. }
```

Figure 4.23 Program Ch04PGM1c.wmls, HELP WMLScript.

Figures 4.24(3b) and 4.26(3b) are both created from program Ch04PGM1e.asp, which updates the database with the new posting and returns the completed screen.

Ch04PGM1d.asp, shown in Figure 4.25, is the main program in our application example. The reason why it's so big is because we choose to use a "case" statement for each option on the main menu (Parents or Sitters menus). As mentioned earlier, we've decided to include all program code for the entire application.. This is to show a working example of a dynamic WAP application with back-end database connectivity and data retrieval via OLE DB, paging logic, ASP object variables, and VBScript write statements for the creation of the WAP screens.

Again, much of the logic has already been explained, so only specific code will be pointed out and explained.

Line 8 in Ch04PGM1d.asp reads in the ASP Session variable userID, which was created once the user sign-in was validated against the database in Ch04PGM1b.asp.

Line 9 reads in the Action variable from the URL command issued by program Ch04PGM1b.asp lines 38 and 49. The request could have been written as request.QueryString("Action").

Lines 11 through 13 set up the database connection and connection string.

Lines 17 to 18 are the start of the Select Case statement. Based on the value in strAction (from line 9), specific logic will be performed. If the value is not defined in a Case statement, logic beginning at Line 175 will handle unknown values.

Lines 18 through 57 are the largest portion of this program. They are used to create the screen in Figure 4.26(2), the Available Sitters paging logic. The logic will select available sitters from the database and display nine rows at a time on the WAP screen.

Line 21 opens the database using a result set variable. In this occurrence of the statement, the default cursor features are included. The 1,1 portion represents the default values, AdOpenKeyset for CursorTypeEnum and adLockReadOnly for LockTypeEnum.

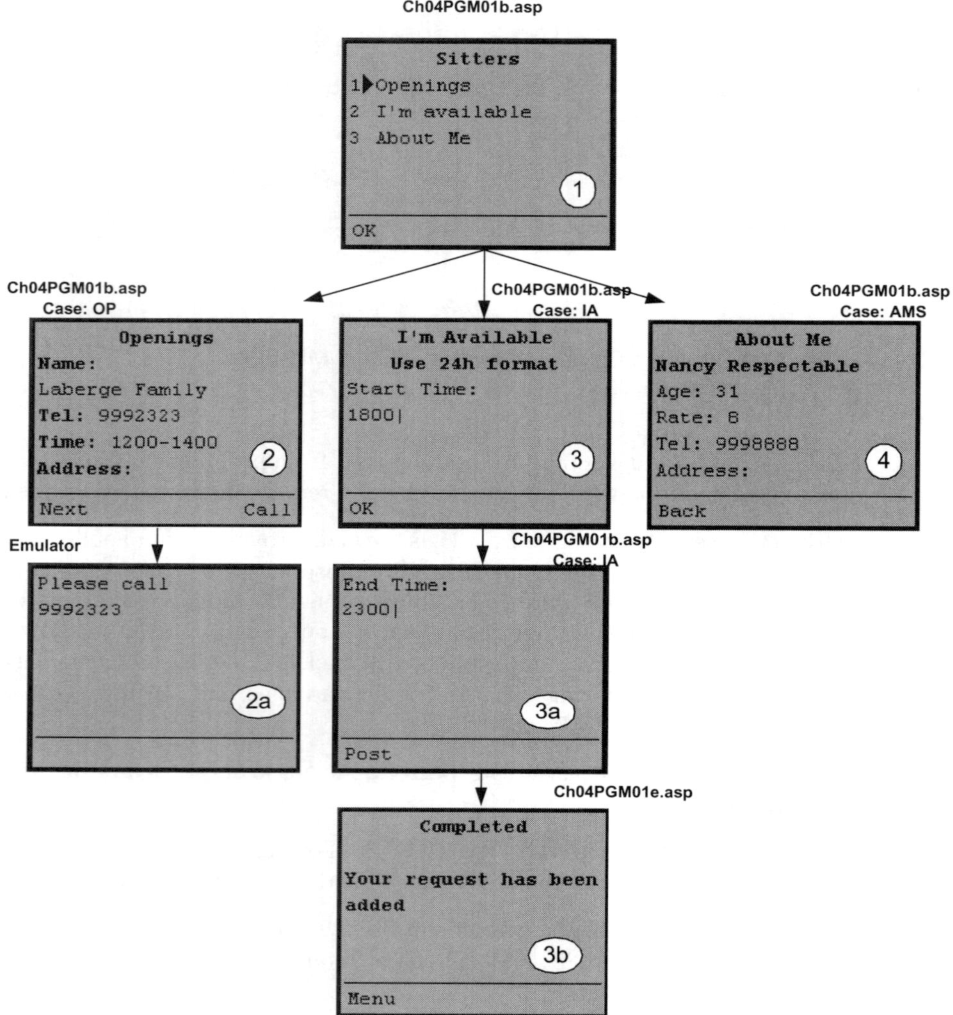

Figure 4.24 Kid Care application's BabySitter section.

Lines 22 through 31 set up the paging environment as explained earlier in this chapter under Large Result Sets.

Lines 36 through 44 are used to loop through nine database entries to be displayed as separate lines on the screen.

Lines 45 through 52 are used to set up scrolling. The first section is to scroll forward (Next) and the second part is used to scroll backward (Back). This uses simple logic based on adding or subtracting one from the current page number—very useful.

```
1.  <%
2.  Response.Buffer = TRUE
3.  Response.ContentType = "text/vnd.wap.wml"

4.  Dim rs
5.  Dim sql
6.  Dim strAction
7.  Dim strUID

8.  strUID  = Session("UserID")
9.  strAction = Request("Action")

10. '-- Open connection to database.
11. Dim Conn
12. Set Conn = Server.CreateObject("ADODB.Connection")
13. Conn.ConnectionString = "Provider=SQLOLEDB;Data
    Source=MyServer;Initial Catalog=MyDB;User Id=bob;Password=test;"

14. response.write "<?xml version="+chr(34)+"1.0"+chr(34)+"?>"
15. response.write "<!DOCTYPE wml PUBLIC "+chr(34)+"-//PHONE.COM//DTD
    WML 1.1//EN"+chr(34)+" "+chr(34)+
     "http://www.phone.com/dtd/wml11.dtd"+chr(34)+">"
16. response.write "<wml>"

17. Select Case strAction
18. Case "RS"  '-- Parent: Available Sitters.
19.    Set rs = Server.CreateObject("ADODB.Recordset")
20.    sql  = "select BabySitter.UserId,LastName,FirstName from
    BabySitter, AvailableSitters where BabySitter.UserId =
    AvailableSitters.UserId and BookedBy = 0 order by PlacedAt asc"
21.    rs.Open sql, Conn, 1,1
22.    rs.PageSize = 9      '-- Number of rows per page.
23.    ScrollAction = Cint(Request.QueryString("PgNo"))       '-- Read
    in page number.
24.    if ScrollAction < 1 then
25.       PageNo = 1
26.    elseif ScrollAction > rs.PageCount then
27.       PageNo = rs.PageCount
28.    else
29.       PageNo = ScrollAction
30.    end if
31.    rs.AbsolutePage = PageNo       '— Set current page number.
32.    response.write "<card id="+chr(34)+"Parents"+chr(34)+">"
33.    response.write "<p
    align="+chr(34)+"center"+chr(34)+"><b>Available Sitters</b></p>"
34.    response.write "<p align="+chr(34)+"left"+chr(34)+"
    mode="+chr(34)+"nowrap"+chr(34)+">"
```

Figure 4.25 Program Ch04PGM1d.asp, main application logic.

```
35.   response.write "<select>"
36.   MaxNum = 1
37.   do While MaxNum < 10
38.      response.write "<option
   onpick="+chr(34)+"Ch04PGM1f.asp?UID="+CStr(rs("UserID"))+chr(34)+"
   >"+rs("FirstName")+
      " "+rs("LastName")+"("+CStr(rs("UserID"))+")</option>"
39.       rs.MoveNext '-- Move cursor up to next row in DB.
40.       if rs.EOF then
41.          exit do
42.       end if
43.       MaxNum = MaxNum + 1
44.    Loop
45.    if MaxNum = 10 then
46.        '-- More rows ahead.
47.        response.write "<option
   onpick="+chr(34)+"Ch04PGM1d.asp?Action=RS&amp;PgNo=" & PageNo+1
   &">Next</option>"
48.    end if
49.    if PageNo > 1 then
50.        '-- More rows behind.
51.        response.write "<option
   onpick="+chr(34)+"Ch04PGM1d.asp?Action=RS&amp;PgNo=" & PageNo-1
   &">Back</option>"
52.    end if
53.    response.write "</select>"
54.    rs.Close
55.    Conn.Close
56.    set rs  = Nothing
57.    set Conn = Nothing

58. Case "PO"  '-- Parent: Post Opening.
59.     Conn.Close
60.     set Conn = Nothing
61.     response.write "<card id="+chr(34)+"Parents"+chr(34)+">"
62.     response.write "<do name="+chr(34)+"Post"+chr(34)+"
   type="+chr(34)+"accept"+chr(34)+"
   label="+chr(34)+"Post"+chr(34)+">"
63.     response.write "<go
   href="+chr(34)+"Ch04PGM1e.asp?Action=PO&amp;StartTime=$(StartTime)
   &amp;EndTime=$(EndTime)"
   + chr(34) + "/>"
64.     response.write "</do>"
65.     response.write "<p align="+chr(34)+"center"+chr(34)+"><b>Post
   Opening</b><br/>"
```

Figure 4.25 Continued Program Ch04PGM1d.asp, main application logic.

```
66.     response.write "<b>Use 24h format</b></p>"
67.     response.write "<p align="+chr(34)+"left"+chr(34)+"
   mode="+chr(34)+"nowrap"+chr(34)+">"
68.     response.write "Start Time: <input
   name="+chr(34)+"StartTime"+chr(34)+"
   type="+chr(34)+"text"+chr(34)+
   " format="+chr(34)+"4N"+chr(34)+"
   emptyok="+chr(34)+"false"+chr(34)+" size="+chr(34)+"4"+chr(34)+
   " maxlength="+chr(34)+"4"+chr(34)+"/><br/>"
69.     response.write "End Time: <input
   name="+chr(34)+"EndTime"+chr(34)+" type="+chr(34)+"text"+chr(34)+
   " format="+chr(34)+"4N"+chr(34)+"
   emptyok="+chr(34)+"false"+chr(34)+" size="+chr(34)+"4"+chr(34)+
   " maxlength="+chr(34)+"4"+chr(34)+"/><br/>"

70. Case "AMP"  '-- Parent: About Me.
71.     Set rs = Server.CreateObject("ADODB.Recordset")
72.     sql  = "select LastName, FirstName, TelNo, Age, Address from
   Parent where UserId=" + strUID
73.     rs.Open sql, Conn
74.     response.write "<card id="+chr(34)+"Parents"+chr(34)+">"
75.     response.write "<do name="+chr(34)+"Return"+chr(34)+"
   type="+chr(34)+"accept"+chr(34)+" label="+chr(34)+"Back"+chr(34)
   + ">"
76.     response.write "<prev/>"
77.     response.write "</do>"
78.     response.write "<p align="+chr(34)+"center"+chr(34)+"><b>About
   Me</b></p>"
79.     response.write "<p align="+chr(34)+"left"+chr(34)+"
   mode="+chr(34)+"wrap"+chr(34)+">"
80.     response.write "<b>"+ rs("FirstName") +" "+ rs("LastName")
   +"</b><br/>"
81.     response.write "Age: " + CStr(rs("Age")) +"<br/>"
82.     response.write "Tel: " + CStr(rs("TelNo")) +"<br/>"
83.     response.write "Address:<br/>"+ rs("Address")
84.     rs.Close
85.     Conn.Close
86.     set rs  = Nothing
87.     set Conn = Nothing

88. Case "OP"  '-- Sitters Needed.
89.     Set rs = Server.CreateObject("ADODB.Recordset")
90.     sql  = "select SittersNeeded.UserId, SittersNeeded.StartTime,
   SittersNeeded.EndTime, Parent.LastName, Parent.TelNo,
   Parent.Address from SittersNeeded, Parent where
   SittersNeeded.BookedBy = 0 and SittersNeeded.UserId =
   Parent.UserId order
   by PlacedAt asc"
91.     rs.Open sql, Conn, 1, 1
```

Figure 4.25 Continued Program Ch04PGM1d.asp, main application logic.

```
92.        '-- Set up paging but beware of one row per page.
93.        rs.PageSize = 1  '-- Number of rows per page.
94.        ScrollAction = Cint(Request.QueryString("PgNo"))        '-- Read
   in page number.
95.    if ScrollAction < 1 then
96.          PageNo = 1
97.    elseif ScrollAction > rs.PageCount then
98.          PageNo = rs.PageCount
99.    else
100.         PageNo = ScrollAction
101.    end if
102.    rs.AbsolutePage = PageNo       '-- Set current page number.
103.    MaxNum = 1
104.    do While MaxNum < 2
105.          strLastName = rs("LastName")
106.          strTelNo    = CStr(rs("TelNo"))
107.          strStartTime = CStr(rs("StartTime"))
108.          strEndTime  = CStr(rs("EndTime"))
109.          strAddress  = rs("Address")
110.          rs.MoveNext         '-- Move cursor up to next row in DB.
111.          if rs.EOF then
112.             exit do
113.          end if
114.          MaxNum = MaxNum + 1
115.    Loop
116.    response.write "<card id="+chr(34)+"Sitters"+chr(34)+">"
117.    if MaxNum = 2 then
118.          '-- More rows ahead.
119.          response.write "<do name="+chr(34)+"Next"+chr(34)+"
   type="+chr(34)+"accept"+chr(34)+" label="+chr(34)+"Next"+chr(34)
      + ">"
120.          response.write "<go
   href="+chr(34)+"Ch04PGM1d.asp?Action=OP&amp;PgNo=" & PageNo+1 &
   chr(34)+"/>"
121.          response.write "</do>"
122.    end if
123.    if PageNo > 1 then
124.          '-- More rows behind.
125.          response.write "<do name="+chr(34)+"Prev"+chr(34)+"
   type="+chr(34)+"accept"+chr(34)+
      " label="+chr(34)+"Prev"+chr(34)+">"
126.          response.write "<go
   href="+chr(34)+"Ch04PGM1d.asp?Action=OP&amp;PgNo=" & PageNo-1 &
   chr(34)+"/>"
```

Figure 4.25 Continued Program Ch04PGM1d.asp, main application logic.

```
127.          response.write "</do>"
128.     end if
129.     response.write "<do type="+chr(34)+"options"+chr(34)+"
   label="+chr(34)+"Call"+chr(34)+">"
130.      response.write "<go href="+chr(34)+"wtai://wp/mc;" + strTelNo
   + chr(34)+"/>"
131.      response.write "</do>"
132.      response.write "<p
   align="+chr(34)+"center"+chr(34)+"><b>Openings</b></p>"
133.      response.write "<p align="+chr(34)+"left"+chr(34)+"
   mode="+chr(34)+"wrap"+chr(34)+">"
134.      response.write "<b>Name:</b><br/>"
135.      response.write strLastName + " Family<br/>"
136.      response.write "<b>Tel:</b> " + strTelNo +"<br/>"
137.      response.write "<b>Time:</b> "+strStartTime+"-
   "+strEndTime+"<br/>"
138.      response.write "<b>Address:</b><br/>"
139.      response.write strAddress + "<br/>"
140.      rs.Close
141.      Conn.Close
142.      set rs  = Nothing
143.      set Conn = Nothing

144. Case "IA"  '-- Sitter: Im available.
145.      Conn.Close
146.      set Conn = Nothing
147.      response.write "<card id="+chr(34)+"Sitters"+chr(34)+">"
148.      response.write "<do name="+chr(34)+"Post"+chr(34)+"
   type="+chr(34)+"accept"+chr(34)+"
   label="+chr(34)+"Post"+chr(34)+">"
149.      response.write "<go
   href="+chr(34)+"Ch04PGM1e.asp?Action=IA&amp;StartTime=$(StartTime)
   &amp;EndTime=$(EndTime)"
   + chr(34)+"/>"
150.      response.write "</do>"
151.      response.write "<p align="+chr(34)+"center"+chr(34)+"><b>I'm
   Available</b><br/>"
152.      response.write "<b>Use 24h format</b></p>"
153.      response.write "<p align="+chr(34)+"left"+chr(34)+"
   mode="+chr(34)+"nowrap"+chr(34)+">"
154.      response.write "Start Time: <input
   name="+chr(34)+"StartTime"+chr(34)+" type="+chr(34)+"text"+chr(34)+
   " format="+chr(34)+"4N"+chr(34)+"
   emptyok="+chr(34)+"false"+chr(34)+" size="+chr(34)+"4"+chr(34)+
```

Figure 4.25 Continued Program Ch04PGM1d.asp, main application logic.

```
        " maxlength="+chr(34)+"4"+chr(34)+"/><br/>"
155.    response.write "End Time: <input
    name="+chr(34)+"EndTime"+chr(34)+" type="+chr(34)+"text"+chr(34)+
    " format="+chr(34)+"4N"+chr(34)+"
    emptyok="+chr(34)+"false"+chr(34)+" size="+chr(34)+"4"+chr(34)+
    " maxlength="+chr(34)+"4"+chr(34)+"/><br/>"

156. Case "AMS"          '-- Sitter: About Me.
157.    Set rs = Server.CreateObject("ADODB.Recordset")
158.    sql = "select LastName, FirstName, TelNo, Age, Address,
    HourRate from BabySitter where UserId=" + strUID
159.    rs.Open sql, Conn,1,1
160.    response.write "<card id="+chr(34)+"Sitters"+chr(34)+">"
161.    response.write "<do name="+chr(34)+"Return"+chr(34)+"
    type="+chr(34)+"accept"+chr(34)+" label="+chr(34)+"Back"+chr(34)
    + ">"
162.    response.write "<prev/>"
163.    response.write "</do>"
164.    response.write "<p align="+chr(34)+"center"+chr(34)+"><b>About
    Me</b></p>"
165.    response.write "<p align="+chr(34)+"left"+chr(34)+"
    mode="+chr(34)+"wrap"+chr(34)+">"
166.    response.write "<b>"+ rs("FirstName") +" "+ rs("LastName")
    +"</b><br/>"
167.    response.write "Age: " + CStr(rs("Age")) +"<br/>"
168.    response.write "Rate: " + CStr(rs("HourRate")) +"<br/>"
169.    response.write "Tel: " + CStr(rs("TelNo")) +"<br/>"
170.    response.write "Address:<br/>"+ rs("Address")
171.    rs.Close
172.    Conn.Close
173.    set rs  = Nothing
174.    set Conn = Nothing

175. Case Else          '--anything else
176.    Conn.Close
177.    set Conn = Nothing
178.    Session.Abandon
179.    Response.Clear
180.    Response.Redirect "Ch04PGM1a.wml"
181. End Select
182. response.write "</p></card></wml>"
183. %>
```

Figure 4.25 Continued Program Ch04PGM1d.asp, main application logic.

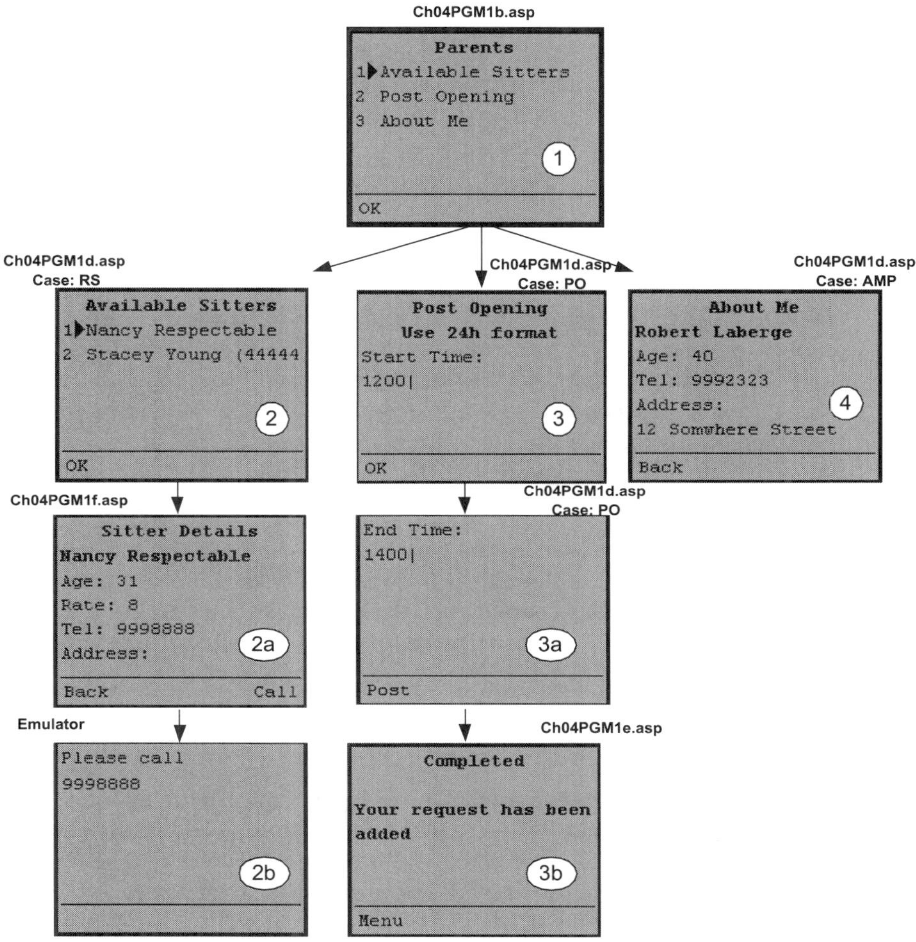

Figure 4.26 Kid Care application's parent section.

Notice that line 47 has & This represents a single ampersand, which must be represented this way for the WAP microbrowser. Variables in URLs for regular Web browsers concatenate with &, but WAP microbrowsers cannot and hence must have the ampersand spelled out as &

```
47. response.write "<option
onpick="+chr(34)+"Ch04PGM1d.asp?Action=RS&amp;PgNo=" & PageNo+1
&">Next</option>"
```

Lines 58 through 69 (Case PO) are used for the Parents to post their openings. Start and end times are required for the program logic in Ch04PGM1e.asp that will add the entry to the database and return the "Completed" screen. This logic will create two screens on the Up.Browser microbrowser as seen in Figure 4.24(3) and (3a) and Figure 4.26(3) and (3a).

Lines 70 through 87 (Case AMP) are used to create the Parents "About Me" screen. The logic will query the database for Parents details to be displayed. The session userID is used from line 8 to populate strUID, which is the current signed-in user. We do not take into account the possibility of the user being removed from the database—this is an optimistic program that assumes that all is where it should be! Notice on all the database accesses that the database is closed as soon as the case statement is done—this is for efficiency.

Lines 88 through 143 (Case OP) represent the second largest portion of this program. This logic is used to page through all the Parents openings posted for the day (Figure 4.24[2]). The individual Sitters can easily scroll through each and every Parent and see the times a Sitter is required. If the Sitter decides to sit for the Parent, then he or she simply presses the Call button Softkey created by line 130. We will explain more about this WTAI feature in Chapter 5. For testing purposes, when the Call button is pressed, the "Please call" screen is displayed since we're using an emulator and not an actual Web phone. This logic is similar to lines 18 through 57 that are used to produce the Available Sitters screen (Figure 4.26[2]). The difference here is that we're displaying only one entry per screen and we're displaying more than one column.

Lines 144 through 155 (Case IA) are very similar to Lines 58 through 69 (Case PO). This portion is specifically for the Sitters to register the start and end times they are available to babysit. With these parameters, the next underlying program, Ch04PGM1e.asp, will add the entry to the database and return the "Completed" screen.

Lines 156 through 174 (Case AMS) are the last case statement entry. Nearly identical to the Parents About Me logic in lines 70 through 87, these lines simply display, for the individual Sitter, their information to be sure all is correct.

Lines 175 through 180 are the catchall error logic. If the case value is unknown for some reason, the logic will close the database connection, abandon the session variables, clear the ASP buffer, and redirect the program flow back to the first title page, Ch04PGM1a.wml, where the user will have to start all over again.

That's it. It looks long and complicated but considering that the majority of all this application's logic is in this one program, it's not bad. Having all the logic basically in one place makes everything quite easy to manage. This program only runs on the ASP server and therefore does not impact the wireless device cache size. Most logic is repeated as both user types have similar requirements.

Both the Parents and Sitters routines use the program in Figure 4.27, Ch04PGM1e.asp, when either enters their need or availability, respectively. This program will simply insert a new row into one of the transactional tables.

The program starts off with setting the ASP buffer to TRUE, setting the ContentType value, and defining the variables to be used, as well as reading in the Action variable from the URL.

After setting up the database connection string and creating the WML code defining the deck and card, a select case statement is initiated. This statement will only have two valid case values, PO and IA. As seen in the logic, both insert rows into the required

```
1. <%
2. Response.Buffer = TRUE
3. Response.ContentType = "text/vnd.wap.wml"

4. Dim rs
5. Dim sql
6. Dim strAction

7. strAction = Request("Action")

8. '-- Open connection to database.
9. Dim Conn
10. Set Conn = Server.CreateObject("ADODB.Connection")
11. Conn.ConnectionString = "Provider=SQLOLEDB;Data
    Source=MyServer;Initial Catalog=MyDB;User Id=bob;Password=test;"

12. response.write "<?xml version="+chr(34)+"1.0"+chr(34)+"?>"
13. response.write "<!DOCTYPE wml PUBLIC "+chr(34)+"-//PHONE.COM//DTD
    WML 1.1//EN"+chr(34)+" "+chr(34)+
    "http://www.phone.com/dtd/wml11.dtd"+chr(34)+">"
14. response.write "<wml>" + chr(13)+chr(10)
15. response.write "<card id="+chr(34)+"Complete"+chr(34)+">" +
    chr(13)+chr(10)
16. response.write "<do name="+chr(34)+"Post"+chr(34)+"
    type="+chr(34)+"accept"+chr(34)+"
    label="+chr(34)+"Menu"+chr(34)+">"
17. response.write "<go href="+chr(34)+"Ch04PGM1d.asp" + chr(34)+"/>"
18. response.write "</do>"
19. response.write "<p align="+chr(34)+"center"+chr(34)+"><b>Completed</b></p>"
20. response.write "<p align="+chr(34)+"left"+chr(34)+"
    mode="+chr(34)+"wrap"+chr(34)+">"

21. Select Case strAction
22. Case "PO"     '— Parent Post Opening.
23.    sql = "insert into SittersNeeded (UserId, StartTime, EndTime, BookedBy,
    BookingTime, PlacedAt) values ("+Session("UserId")+
    ", "+Request("StartTime")+
    ", "+Request("EndTime")+",0,'01/01/00',getdate())"
24.       Set rs = Conn.Execute(sql)
25.       Conn.Close
26.       set rs  = Nothing
27.       set Conn = Nothing

28. Case "IA"     '— Sitter Im Available.
29.    sql  = "insert into AvailableSitters (UserId, AvailableFrom,
    AvailableTo, BookedBy, PlacedAt) values ("+Session("UserId")+
    ", "+Request("StartTime")+ ", "+Request("EndTime")+",0,getdate())"
30.       Set rs = Conn.Execute(sql)
31.       Conn.Close
32.       set rs  = Nothing
33.       set Conn = Nothing
34. Case Else     '— Anything else
35.       Conn.Close
36.       set rs  = Nothing
37.       set Conn = Nothing
38.       Session.Abandon
39.       Response.clear
40.       Response.Redirect "Ch04PGM1a.wml"
41. End Select

42. response.write "<br/><b>Your request has been added</b>" + chr(13)+chr(10)
43. response.write "</p></card></wml>"
44. %>
```

Figure 4.27 Program Ch04PGM1e.asp, completed, database inserts.

```
1.  <%
2.  Response.Buffer = TRUE
3.  Response.ContentType = "text/vnd.wap.wml"

4.  Dim rs
5.  Dim sql
6.  Dim strAction

7.  '— Open connection to database.
8.  Dim Conn
9.  Set Conn = Server.CreateObject("ADODB.Connection")
10. Conn.ConnectionString = "Provider=SQLOLEDB;Data
    Source=MyServer;Initial Catalog=MyDB;User Id=bob;Password=test;"

11. response.write "<?xml version="+chr(34)+"1.0"+chr(34)+"?>" +
    chr(13)+chr(10)
12. response.write "<!DOCTYPE wml PUBLIC "+chr(34)+"-//PHONE.COM//DTD
    WML 1.1//EN"+chr(34)+"
    "+chr(34)+"http://www.phone.com/dtd/wml11.dtd"+chr(34)+">" +
    chr(13)+chr(10)
13. response.write "<wml>" + chr(13)+chr(10)
14. response.write "<card id="+chr(34)+"Details"+chr(34)+">" +
    chr(13)+chr(10)
15. response.write "<do name="+chr(34)+"Return"+chr(34)+"
    type="+chr(34)+"accept"+chr(34)+"
    label="+chr(34)+"Back"+chr(34)+">" + chr(13)+chr(10)
16. response.write "<prev/>" + chr(13)+chr(10)
17. response.write "</do>" + chr(13)+chr(10)

18. Set rs = Server.CreateObject("ADODB.Recordset")
19. sql  = "select LastName, FirstName, TelNo, Age, Address, HourRate
    from BabySitter where UserId=" + request("UID")
20. rs.Open sql, Conn, 1, 1

21. response.write "<do type="+chr(34)+"options"+chr(34)+"
    label="+chr(34)+"Call"+chr(34)+">" + chr(13)+chr(10)
22. response.write "<go href="+chr(34)+"wtai://wp/mc;" +
    Cstr(rs("TelNo")) + chr(34)+"/>" + chr(13)+chr(10)
23. response.write "</do>" + chr(13)+chr(10)

24. response.write "<p align="+chr(34)+"center"+chr(34)+"><b>Sitter
    Details</b></p>" + chr(13)+chr(10)
25. response.write "<p align="+chr(34)+"left"+chr(34)+"
    mode="+chr(34)+"wrap"+chr(34)+">" + chr(13)+chr(10)

26. response.write "<b>"+ rs("FirstName") +" "+ rs("LastName")
    +"</b><br/>" + chr(13)+chr(10)
27. response.write "Age: " + CStr(rs("Age")) +"<br/>" +
    chr(13)+chr(10)
28. response.write "Rate: " + CStr(rs("HourRate")) + "<br/>" +
    chr(13)+chr(10)
29. response.write "Tel: " + CStr(rs("TelNo") ) +"<br/>" + chr(13)+chr(10)
30. response.write "Address:<br/>"+ rs("Address") + chr(13)+chr(10)

31. rs.Close
32. Conn.Close
33. set rs  = Nothing
34. set Conn = Nothing

35. response.write "</p></card></wml>"
36. %>
```

Figure 4.28 Program Ch04PGM1f.asp, BabySitter details.

tables and then immediately exit by closing the database connection and Result Set variables. As in our previous programs, if another case value is used, the program will close the database connection, abandon the session variables, clear the ASP buffer, and redirect the program flow back to the first title page, Ch04PGM1a.wml, where the user will have to start all over again.

The last program in this application, Ch04PGM1f.asp, deals with displaying the Sitter details after a Parent has selected a specific sitter from the Available Sitters screen. This display (shown in Figure 4.28) is very similar to the About Me for a Sitter and has the same functionality as the Openings screen for Sitters, Figure 4.24(2). Here the Parent will view all the Sitter details and have the ability to call him or her directly.

All these programs are available on the CD, including the database data definition language to set up the database structure. The database structure could easily be ported to MS Access too, but remember that whatever database you use, be sure to use the proper Provider information.

CHAPTER 5

Advanced WAPing

All examples presented in this chapter have been developed and tested using Openwave's (Phone.com) WAP toolkit version 4.1 unless stated otherwise. For more information on WAP toolkits, refer to the Development Toolkits (SDK) section of Chapter 1.

Lines of program code in this chapter are numbered for easy reference. Code on the CD is identical but without the numbers, making it easy to simply copy and execute.

This chapter describes many interesting wireless topics such as browser detection and redirection, sending and receiving emails, location-based services, and Short Message Service (SMS). We'll show multiple mini-applications, which you can easily use in your own development efforts. All program code in this chapter is 100 percent functional and can also be found on the CD.

Programming Tips

Before we begin, let's look at a couple of simple WML programming tips.

Content Type

The first tip is for ASP and VBScript programs. Since many WML decks are dynamically generated, make sure the ContentType header variable is explicitly set. See Chapter 1, the section on Server Environment Setup, for an explanation of MIME types and content-types. Basically, set the ContentType variable within VBScript as follows, for WML programs:

```
<%Response.ContentType = "text/vnd.wap.wml"%>
```

As it stands, when you dynamically generate the WML code, VBScript in our case, the generating program's file extension will be dynamically mapped on the Web server and a corresponding ContentType header variable will be generated. Since the generated variable is not a WAP-specific MIME type, the WAP gateway won't know what it is and will send an "Invalid Content Type" error message to the WAP device. But if you explicitly set (send) the ContentType variable within the data file, the WAP gateway will find it and correctly accept all following code as WAP code, thus allowing the dynamically generated deck to function properly.

Buffer

Another tip for the ASP and VBScript is the buffer variable. If the buffer variable is set to TRUE, the entire contents of the dynamically generated WML deck will remain in cache until completely generated. Only then will the deck be transmitted. If this variable is not set (default is FALSE), each line of code will be sent to the WAP gateway as it is created. When this happens, it'll hit the content-type problem explained previously. Add the following lines to your VBScript code before anything else (for WML programs):

```
<%Response.Buffer = TRUE%>
<%Response.ContentType = "text/vnd.wap.wml"%>
```

Line Feed

Software Development Kits (SDKs) are great tools for testing your application code. The problem is that for dynamically generated code, all lines in the deck area are strung together, making it very unreadable and difficult to debug. Try adding + chr(13) + chr(10) to the end of each line of code. This will simulate a line feed, making the code very readable in the SDK. These line feed characters will be interpreted by ASP and therefore will not take up any extra deck cache.

```
<%Response.Buffer = TRUE%>
<%Response.ContentType = "text/vnd.wap.wml"%>
<%response.write "<?xml version="+chr(34)+"1.0"+chr(34)+"?>" + chr(13) +
chr(10)%>
```

Viewing Source Code

A great hint in designing and developing is to run the WML-generating programs on Microsoft Internet Explorer 5.0. Because Internet Explorer 5.0+ has a built-in XML parser that can interpret and present XML code, a generated WML deck can be displayed on the browser unlike IE4. This method will allow you to review the code immediately, and it can also be copied to an offline browser for testing. Older versions of the Web browser will hide XML tags and will not show your code.

Testing Variable Content

When testing the value of input variables, we suggest setting the entire variable to either lowercase or uppercase. This ensures that no combination of uppercase and lowercase strings are missed. Instead of checking for Docomo, docomo, or DOCOMO, setting the variable to uppercase would result in one simple test for DOCOMO.

```
if InStr(Ucase(request.ServerVariables("HTTP_USER_AGENT")), "DOCCMO") > 0
then
```

Browser Detection

Do not confuse the visitor with multiple Web site addresses. Having a number of URL addresses to connect to your site can be confusing and may just drive the viewer away. I personally don't want to have to remember that www.xxx.com is for the Web site, www.xxx.com/upbrowser is for the WAP Up.Browser site, and that www.xxx.com /nokia is for the WAP Nokia microbrowser. This is much too confusing and much more prone to typing errors if using a Web phone, which is very frustrating. The best course of action is to have every user use the same generic Web site address no matter which client browser is invoked. One program behind the initial URL on the Web server can detect the client browser type based on the page header (HTTP header) and redirect the visitor to the appropriate application for his or her particular client browser type.

There are two methods of doing redirection. First, if possible, is to change the default Web page address on the Web server, as just mentioned, and the second is to use a specific Web address with several go-arounds, depending on the application.

Normally, a Web address is set to a specific default page on the Web server. When a visitor selects a specific URL, for example, www.worldjobmart.com, control is passed to the proper Web server somewhere out there in the Internet world. How the Web site name (URL address) finds its way to the proper Web server is a completely different, complicated topic dealing with Internet redirection based on DNS servers that we will not discuss in this book. For our purposes, once the URL is entered, the site is found on the Web and that specific site on its Web server has an initial kick-off program. The typical default Web server program is index.html. This means that when www.worldjobmart.com is entered as a URL on the client browser, the Web server containing the site really substitutes www.worldjobmart.com/index.html as the final destination. Of course, this is a very general description of how this whole thing works, but the point is made.

Many Web sites can share the same Web server as seen in Figure 5.1. One site may be directed to their index.html page while another is directed to their redirect.asp page or, if not available, to the secondary page for that site, index.html, if one exists as it does in the diagram.

When a client browser wants to view or execute a program on the Web server, it does a request for that program. Requests are really HTTP protocol messages, which have

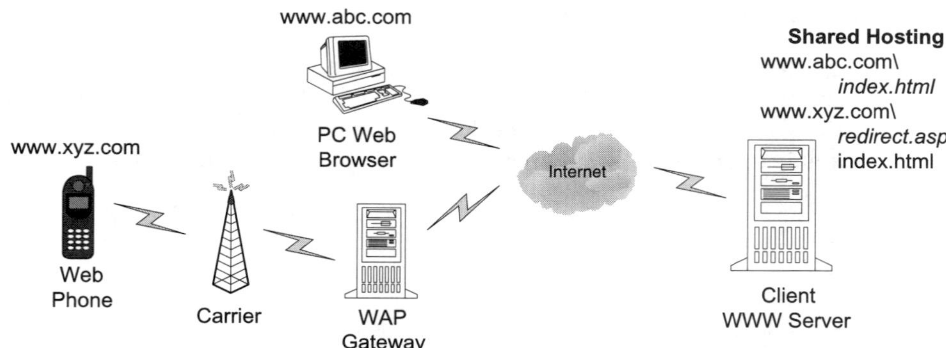

Figure 5.1 Default Web server page.

certain headers and parameters. Most HTTP requests include the invoking browser type as one of the header variables. Without getting too involved here, let's keep it simple and say that when a request to a specific Web site, for example, www.worldjobmart.com, is issued, a program could be written to read the headers of the HTTP request. This method would allow a very high probability of determining the type of browser the client is using in the request, that is, pertaining to a personal computer, Web phone, or something else.

For more details on HyperText Transfer Protocols (HTTP) headers, visit http://w3.org/Protocols/rfc2616/rfc2616-sec14.html#sec14.

Program Redirection

The simplest approach to recognizing the browser type that is accessing your Web site is to change your default Web server page from an HTML program, which is not too flexible, to another type of program, which can easily be used to test the header variables. We use VBScript in an active server page program named redirect.asp. By the way, if you don't own or administer your own Web server, you'll have to request that the server administrator change the default Web page.

With this new program set as your default Web page, you can easily check header information of the incoming request to determine the client browser. Then, based on the discovered invoking browser type, you can easily redirect the incoming application flow to the appropriate directory of programs. Requests from Web browsers such as Netscape or Microsoft Internet Explorer would be directed to the regular Web programs in the regular Web directory. Requests from UP.Browser microbrowsers using HDML can be directed to the HDML program directory while WML requests from the same microbrowser vendor can be routed to special Openwave WML programs in their own directory. Similarly, requests from devices having the Nokia microbrowser would go to their own special grouping of programs. As you see, this allows specific coding and features for specific requesting devices. I'm sure you can imagine the possibilities here and, if not, the remaining portion of this section will spell it out in more detail.

The program in Figure 5.2 shows how to read and interpret the specific HTTP header variables. Our examples use active server pages (ASP), but you can use any number of other programming languages that would suit your own needs.

The redirect.asp program is quite basic. It first checks the HTTP_USER_AGENT header variable for some sort of recognizable word specifically relating to a particular type of browser. As seen on lines 2, 4, 12, 14, and 16 of Figure 5.2, we are mostly interested in the top five types of browsers: Mozilla, which denotes Web browsers such as Microsoft Internet Explorer or Netscape; the letters UP which are for Openwave's Up.Browser; Nokia from and for itself; DOCOMO from NTT DOCOMO used specifically from iMode devices; and MME which is Microsoft's Mobile Explorer. We set the default for everything else to a regular Web browser just as Mozilla requests. When testing the header variables, the server variable is set to uppercase with the Ucase command. This is to ensure that we test the results only once rather than having to test for different variations, such as Docomo, docomo, or DOCOMO—just a simple programming tip. Another tip to take note of is that the examples presented in this section, while valid and functional, are still quite generic.

Since Openwave's Up.Browser may refer to either the HDML or WML languages, we check the HTTP_ACCEPT header variable for either HDML or WML. Depending on the result, execution is directed to the appropriate directory of programs. In many instances, the HTTP_ACCEPT variable will contain both the HDML and WML words and so control should be directed to the WML programs since WML takes precedence over HDML. If only the word *HDML* appears, execution would use the HDML programs. For this reason when coding the redirect.asp program, we find it best to first check for WML and then HDML and if neither is found, we assume the first if the HTTP_USER_AGENT variable contains the letters UP.

The last portion of the program, lines 19–25, exists for cases when we cannot determine the HTTP_USER_AGENT variable contents. We would then proceed to check the HTTP_ACCEPT header variable for either WML or HDML and if neither is found we assume the referring browser type is Web-based (meaning not from a wireless device and probably from a personal computer). We then redirect execution flow to the first program in the Web-based application. If WML or HDML is found, we assume the invoking device is using Openwave's Up.Browser microbrowser, since it's by far the most popular wireless microbrowser worldwide, and execution is directed to that application's initial program.

The second redirection method depends on several issues. If the default Web page, for some reason, cannot be changed, then only specific URL names can be used for WAP site addresses. Many Web sites may want to change their default Web page to the redirect.asp concept but still want to use their old index.html default page. This is easily accomplished by simply having the index.html page as the secondary default page set on the Web server itself.

```
1.  <%
2.  if InStr(Ucase(request.ServerVariables("HTTP_USER_AGENT")),
    "MOZILLA") > 0 then
3.      response.redirect ("http://www.worldjobmart.com/wjm000.htm")
4.  elseif InStr(Ucase(request.ServerVariables("HTTP_USER_AGENT")),
    "UP") > 0 then
5.    if InStr(Ucase(request.ServerVariables("HTTP_ACCEPT")), "WML") >
      0 then
6.        response.redirect
          ("http://www.worldjobmart.com/wireless/UpBrowser/index.wml")
7.      elseif InStr(Ucase(request.ServerVariables("HTTP_ACCEPT")),
        "HDML") > 0 then
8.        response.redirect
          ("http://www.worldjobmart.com/wireless/HDML/index.wml")
9.      else
10.        response.redirect
           ("http://www.worldjobmart.com/wireless/UpBrowser/index.wml")
11.    end if
12. elseif InStr(Ucase(request.ServerVariables("HTTP_USER_AGENT")),
    "NOKIA") > 0 then
13.     response.redirect
         ("http://www.worldjobmart.com/wireless/nokia/index.wml")
14. elseif InStr(Ucase(request.ServerVariables("HTTP_USER_AGENT")),
    "DOCOMO") > 0 then
15.     response.redirect
         ("http://www.worldjobmart.com/wireless/imode/home.htm")
16. elseif InStr(Ucase(request.ServerVariables("HTTP_USER_AGENT")),
    "MME") > 0 then
17.     response.redirect
         ("http://www.worldjobmart.com/wireless/mme/home.htm")
18. else
19.    if InStr(Ucase(request.ServerVariables("HTTP_ACCEPT")), "WML")
       > 0 then
20.        response.redirect
           ("http://www.worldjobmart.com/wireless/UpBrowser/index.wml")
21.     elseif InStr(Ucase(request.ServerVariables("HTTP_ACCEPT")),
        "HDML") > 0 then
22.        response.redirect
           ("http://www.worldjobmart.com/wireless/HDML/index.wml")
23.     else
24.        response.redirect ("http://www.worldjobmart.com/wjm000.htm")
25.    end if
26. end if
27. %>
```

Figure 5.2 Redirect.asp program.

Many firms have their initial Web page registered with popular Web search engines and over time that registration has reached a high search priority position. I certainly wouldn't want to change my Web site name after achieving this difficult task. There is an alternative. For these scenarios, keep the shortened version of the index.html program with only the basic tags but include a META tag command with the REFRESH attribute. This will redirect control to another program where continued processing can occur. When someone selects your site, qualifying it with the index.html program, he or she will now be redirected to your new front-end program, redirect.asp. This, of course, only functions if the receiving browser can support HTML commands. If not, then the client browser will have to explicitly specify the required program's name.

Line 10 of Figure 5.3 shows the REFRESH attribute of the META tag. Because it is an HTML program, it's executed on the client browser. The refresh keyword tells the browser to redirect control to the value in the associated content variable value. After 0 seconds, this could be set to any value but we want the redirection to the specified URL to be immediate, which happens to be our redirect.asp program. This means that for any Web browser accessing the www.worldjobmart.com Web site, control will be automatically redirected to www.worldjobmart.com/redirect.asp instead of being directed to index.html.

The inefficiency with this method is that control is initially sent from the server to the client machine. The client browser executes the META tag statement and the refresh attribute immediately redirects control back to the server to initiate the new ASP program. If the redirection occurred entirely on the server, it would be much less time consuming and hence more efficient.

```
1.  <html>
2.  <head>
3.  <title>WorldJobMart.com Redirect</title>
4.  <meta http-equiv="content-type" content="text/html; charset=iso-
    8859-1">
5.  <meta name="author" content="WorldJobMart.com">
6.  <meta Name="keywords" content="job, jobs, contract, employment,
    resume">
7.  <meta Name="classification" content="jobs, employment, career,
    technology, business">
8.  <meta Name="description" content="WorldJobMart.com - A free global
    job and resume search engine.">
9.  <meta Name="copyright" content="Copyright 2001, WorldJobMart.com">
10. <meta http-equiv="REFRESH" content="0;
    URL=http://www.worldjobmart.com/redirect.asp">
11. </head>
12. <body>
13. </body>
14. </html>
```

Figure 5.3 Index.htm program.

Hit Statistics

Because the redirect.asp program is very detailed and can determine which browser is invoking the Web site, it gives us an excellent opportunity to gather hit- and browser-type access statistics. We can gather our own statistics from every request accessing the Web site via the redirect.asp program by simply adding hit-counter logic.

The idea is to register a hit for each type of browser accessing the Web site. For each browser type being checked, a regular flat text file is created. A specific file is created for sites using Mozilla browsers, another for UP.Browser microbrowsers, and so on. Then each time a person invokes the site from whatever browser, the value in the text file is incremented by 1. At any time the number in the particular text file is the number of hits manually recorded for that particular browser type.

By setting several variables after each browser determination, a generic hit record routine can be accomplished. The redirect.asp program has been modified in Figure 5.4 to include the strHitsFile and strURL variables. The first is set to the specific text filename for the invoking browser and the second variable, strURL, is set to the program that control will be redirected to.

Lines 39 to 45 open the specific text file, depending on which value has been set in the strHitsFile variable. Line 42 reads the value in the file, and line 43 adds 1 to that value. Then line 45 rewrites the file with the new value. This process is repeated for every user who accesses the site from any browser being checked in the program.

Line 47 will then redirect control to the site and program specified in the strURL variable.

To view all the new statistics or to reset them, a Web side application can be built. We've included a quick sample on the CD called Webhits.asp. This will make a complete system whereby statistics can be accumulated, viewed, and reset.

Display Header Information

If you'd like to know the specific values for certain browser header variables such as HTTP_USER_AGENT and HTTP_ACCEPT, use the same program logic as the original redirect.asp from Figure 5.2 with a twist. This time, again depending on browser type, invoke a specific program that reads and displays the variables directly on the client device.

For wireless SDKs, the variables are visible on the SDK emulator, but it is always best to look at the source for easier viewing. On the Openwave SDK, press F5 (view source) to get all variables to appear in the phone information window, which is much simpler to view than on the small simulator window. See Figure 5.5.

Different programs are invoked for different browser types. However the MME and regular Web browser types invoke the same program, hvweb.asp, since the underlying code is identical.

As an example, if the program in Figure 5.5 is invoked from a Web browser, HTTP_USER_AGENT being equal to MOZILLA, the program hvweb.asp in Figure 5.6

```
1. <%
2. dim strHitsFile, strURL

3. if InStr(Ucase(request.ServerVariables("HTTP_USER_AGENT")),
   "MOZILLA") > 0 then
4.    strHitsFile = "\HitsWeb.txt"
5.    strURL = "http://www.worldjobmart.com/wjm000.htm"
6. elseif InStr(Ucase(request.ServerVariables("HTTP_USER_AGENT")),
   "UP") > 0 then
7.    if InStr(Ucase(request.ServerVariables("HTTP_ACCEPT")), "WML") >
      0 then
8.       strHitsFile = "\HitsUPWML.txt"
9.       strURL =
         "http://www.worldjobmart.com/wireless/UpBrowser/index.wml"
10. elseif
      InStr(Ucase(request.ServerVariables("HTTP_ACCEPT")),"HDML") > 0
      then
11.       strHitsFile = "\HitsUPHDML.txt"
12.       strURL ="http://www.worldjobmart.com/wireless/HDML/index.wml"
13.   else
14.       strHitsFile = "\HitsUPWML.txt"
15.       strURL =
         "http://www.worldjobmart.com/wireless/UpBrowser/index.wml"
16.   end if
17. elseif InStr(Ucase(request.ServerVariables("HTTP_USER_AGENT")),
   "NOKIA") > 0 then
18.   strHitsFile = "\HitsNokia.txt"
19.   strURL = "http://www.worldjobmart.com/wireless/nokia/index.wml"
20. elseif InStr(Ucase(request.ServerVariables("HTTP_USER_AGENT")),
   "DOCOMO") > 0 then
21.   strHitsFile = "\HitsDOCOMO.txt"
22.   strURL = "http://www.worldjobmart.com/wireless/imode/home.htm"
23. elseif InStr(Ucase(request.ServerVariables("HTTP_USER_AGENT")),
   "MME") > 0 then

24.   strHitsFile = "\HitsMME.txt"
25.   strURL = "http://www.worldjobmart.com/wireless/mme/home.htm"
26. else
27.   if InStr(Ucase(request.ServerVariables("HTTP_ACCEPT")), "WML") >
      0 then
28.       strHitsFile = "\HitsUPWML.txt"
29.       strURL =
         "http://www.worldjobmart.com/wireless/UpBrowser/index.wml"
30.   elseif InStr(Ucase(request.ServerVariables("HTTP_ACCEPT")),
      "HDML") > 0 then
31.       strHitsFile = "\HitsUPHDML.txt"
```

Figure 5.4 StatRedirect.asp with statistics.

```
32.      strURL = "http://www.worldjobmart.com/wireless/HDML/index.wml"
33.   else
34.      strHitsFile = "\HitsWeb.txt"
35.      strURL = "http://www.worldjobmart.com/wjm000.htm"
36.   end if
37. end if


38. '--Record a hit
39. Set FileObject = Server.CreateObject("Scripting.FileSystemObject")
40. HitsFile = Server.MapPath ("/") & strHitsFile
41. Set InStream = FileObject.OpenTextFile (HitsFile, 1, false)
42. OldHits = Trim(InStream.ReadLine)
43. NewHits = OldHits + 1
44. Set OutStream = FileObject.CreateTextFile (HitsFile, True)
45. OutStream.WriteLine(NewHits)


46. '--Redirect flow
47. response.redirect (strURL)
48. %>
```

Figure 5.4 Continued StatRedirect.asp with statistics.

will execute. Try it on either Netscape or Microsoft Internet Explorer if you're using IIS Active Server Pages.

The results of this program running on a Microsoft Internet Explorer browser are shown in Figure 5.7.

The code in Figure 5.8 will be executed if the site is being accessed from an Up.Browser WML microbrowser.

The resulting header values on the Openwave UP.SDK 4.1, using direct mode rather than going through an UP.Link Server is shown in Figure 5.9.

Since the screen is small and does not accommodate the entire results, for Openwave it would be best to press the F5 key to view the source directly in the associated information window on your PC.

If you run the same program—hvweb.asp on the Nokia WAP toolkit 2.0—the results in Figure 5.10 would appear. Notice how the values all change.

We've included two more programs on the CD: hvweball.asp and hvwmlall.asp. These programs will show more than just the two header variables we've mentioned so far. The hvweball.asp program will loop through all header variables and nicely display them on your Web browser. It's the same idea with the hvwmlall.asp program. This program will show all the header variables pertaining to the WAP programs. Unfortunately, the WAP device cache cannot contain all the generated information. So, we've commented out the header values, and the program currently only displays the header vari-

```
1.  <%
2.  if InStr(Ucase(request.ServerVariables("HTTP_USER_AGENT")),
    "MOZILLA") > 0 then
3.      response.redirect ("http://www.wavedev.com/hvweb.asp")
4.  elseif InStr(Ucase(request.ServerVariables("HTTP_USER_AGENT")),
    "UP") > 0 then
5.      if InStr(Ucase(request.ServerVariables("HTTP_ACCEPT")),-"WML") >
        0 then
6.          response.redirect ("http://www.wavedev.com/hvwml.asp")
7.        elseif InStr(Ucase(request.ServerVariables("HTTP_ACCEPT")),
          "HDML") > 0 then
8.          response.redirect ("http://www.wavedev.com/hvhdml.asp")
9.      else
10.         response.redirect ("http://www.wavedev.com/hvwml.asp")
11.     end if
12. elseif InStr(Ucase(request.ServerVariables("HTTP_USER_AGENT")),
    "NOKIA") > 0 then
13.     response.redirect ("http://www.wavedev.com/hvwml.asp")
14. elseif InStr(Ucase(request.ServerVariables("HTTP_USER_AGENT")),
    "DOCOMO") > 0 then
15.     response.redirect ("http://www.wavedev.com/hvimode.asp")
16. elseif InStr(Ucase(request.ServerVariables("HTTP_USER_AGENT")),
    "MME") > 0 then
17.     response.redirect ("http://www.wavedev.com/hvweb.asp")
18. else
19.     if InStr(Ucase(request.ServerVariables("HTTP_ACCEPT")), "WML")
        > 0 then
20.         response.redirect ("http://www.wavedev.com/hvwml.asp")
21.       elseif InStr(Ucase(request.ServerVariables("HTTP_ACCEPT")),
          "HDML") > 0 then
22.         response.redirect ("http://www.wavedev.com/hvhdml.asp")
23.     else
24.         response.redirect ("http://www.wavedev.com/hvweb.asp")
25.     end if
26. end if
27. %>
```

Figure 5.5 Header variable display program, hvredirect.asp.

able names themselves. Once you determine which variables you wish to see, simply hardcode them into the program and reexecute it for the results. These programs can be very useful tools in determining header variable values such as cookie content, and especially if you are trying to determine the value of a particular variable whose exact name you can't determine or remember.

```
1. <%
2. response.write "<html><head><title></title></head><body>"
3. response.write "<b>Start</b>"
4. response.write "<br><b>HTTP_USER_AGENT:</b><br>" &
   request.ServerVariables("HTTP_USER_AGENT")
5. response.write "<br><b>HTTP_ACCEPT:</b><br>" &
   request.ServerVariables("HTTP_ACCEPT")
6. response.write "<br><b>End</b>"
7. response.write "</body></html>"
8. %>
```

Figure 5.6 Hvweb.asp program.

Device Recognition

To go a bit further with the HTTP header information, an application could be created to evaluate the HTTP_USER_AGENT information and to act accordingly. If, for example, it is determined that a Nokia phone is accessing the Web site, certain specific action could be taken. Not only can redirection of program execution to the proper bunch of programs based on the agent string occur but other events could also be involved such as advertising splash screens. If it's determined that Microsoft's Pocket PC is querying your site, a special advertisement or offer could be sent to the client browser. The possibilities are enormous.

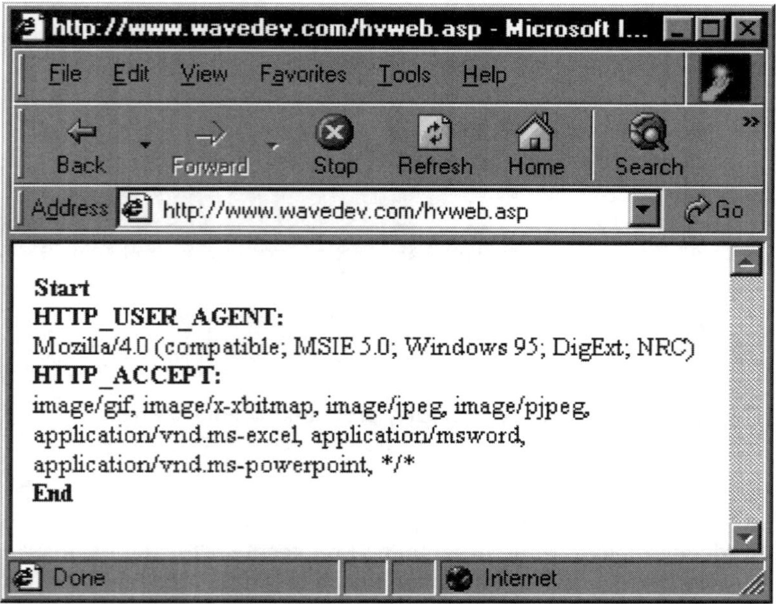

Figure 5.7 WEB header results for hvweb.asp.

```
1. <%Response.Buffer = TRUE%>
2. <%Response.ContentType = "text/vnd.wap.wml"%>
3. <%response.write "<?xml version="+chr(34)+"1.0"+chr(34)+"?>" +
   chr(13) + chr(10)%>
4. <%response.write "<!DOCTYPE wml PUBLIC "+chr(34)+"-//WAPFORUM//DTD
   WML 1.1//EN"+chr(34)+"
   "+chr(34)+"http://www.wapforum.org/DTD/wml_1.1.xml"+chr(34)+">" +
   chr(13) + chr(10)%>
5. <%response.write "<wml><card><p>" + chr(13) + chr(10)%>
6. <%response.write "<b>Start</b>" + chr(13) + chr(10)%>
7. <%response.write "<br/><b>HTTP_USER_AGENT:</b><br/>" + chr(13) +
   chr(10)%>
8. <%response.write request.ServerVariables("HTTP_USER_AGENT") +
   chr(13) + chr(10)%>
9. <%response.write "<br/><b>HTTP_ACCEPT:</b><br/>" + chr(13) +
   chr(10)%>
10. <%response.write request.ServerVariables("HTTP_ACCEPT") + chr(13)
    + chr(10)%>
11. <%response.write "<br/><b>End</b></p></card></wml>" + chr(13) +
    chr(10)%>
```

Figure 5.8 WAP WML header display program, hvwml.asp.

The program in Figure 5.11 is a simple back-end database retrieval application with a database table that contains many different agent strings and if one forms part of the queried agent header variable, then a match is found. Once this happens, the associated text value in the database for that particular agent string is sent to a routing program

Figure 5.9 WML header results on Openwave UP.SDK 4.1.

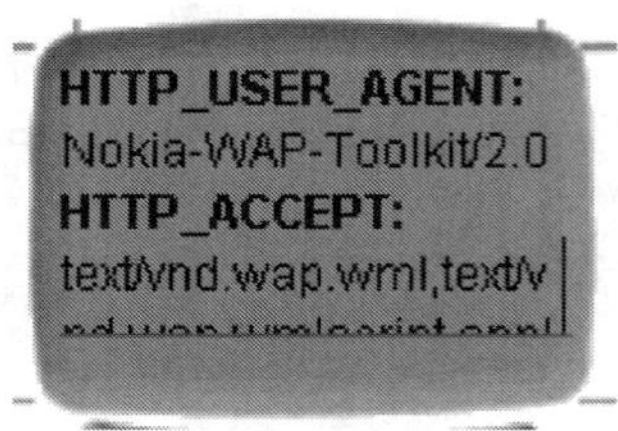

Figure 5.10 WML header results on Nokia WAP toolkit 2.0.

that will determine, based on the text value, where to proceed next. This is where an advertisement or specific event can be included.

An Access database called AgentString.mdb was created with one table named ASTable. It has three columns as shown in Figure 5.12.

The table is populated with many different agent strings but is by no means complete. The associated Text column, for the sake of this example, is initially populated with the same data as the AString column, and the Enabled column is set to true.

Since the program in Figure 5.13 is self-populating, just having it invoked in a production mode will fill the AString values as users access your Web site.

Line 23 loops through all rows in the database, which are presented in ascending sorted order by the AString column.

Line 24 tests to see whether the agent string value stored in the database is in the HTTP_USER_AGENT variable. Since the header variable can contain many strings, it is best to compare the database values to the header variable and not the other way around. If the database string does not show up in the header string, the loop continues with a comparison of the next row until all values are done.

If there is a match, line 26 will set the strEOR variable to 1, the strText variable to the value of the Text column associated with the agent string in the database, and the loop is then exited via line 31.

If the loop ended without a match, strEOR=0, then the database is checked to ensure the agent string doesn't already exist but is disabled, lines 33 to 35. This logic is to ensure all new strings are stored in the database but are not active until manually

ASTable : Table	
Field Name	Data Type
AString	Text
Text	Text
Enabled	Yes/No

Figure 5.11 ASTable row definitions.

⊞ ASTable : Table		
AString	**Text**	**Enabled**
UP.Browser/3	UP.Browser/3	☑
UP.Browser/4	UP.Browser/4	☑
UP.Link/4.1.HTTP-DIRECT	UP.Link/4.1.HTTP-DIRECT	☑

Figure 5.12 ASTable data.

reviewed since we don't really know what to expect as the value of the string. If a new string appears, lines 35 to 38 store it in the database but only once and set it to disabled. Close the database and redirect control to the HTTPmatch.asp program with a txtResult value of 0 as shown on line 42.

If there was a match in the original loop, then close the database and send the associated Text value from the database as a parameter to the HTTPmatch.asp program, line 47.

Email

Access to applications connecting to the Internet from a mobile wireless device is a technological breakthrough. And the ability to send and receive email from almost anywhere at any time remotely from one's wireless mobile device is definitely a huge asset. It may be just the edge that salespeople require to stay one step ahead of the competition. As more people go wireless, the demand for wireless email will grow and portals without this ability will surely suffer.

The beauty of email is that it's a very simple application. Millions of people use it everyday without really knowing the intricacies behind the scenes. Email is a great example of the ultimate user experience. By just knowing a person's email address, a user can send an email around the globe in a matter of seconds without knowing where that person is located. The less complicated an application and the less effort it takes to use it, the more likely it is to become a successful and widely accepted system just like the typical email application.

An email is initially created on some device and sent via a transport mechanism to a mail server. The mail server queues up the message along with all other email messages ready to send it out over the Internet or Intranet. Without going into the journey details, let's just say that the email eventually finds its way to the receiver's inbound mail server. For the receiver to retrieve her personal emails, she logs on to the server and extracts her messages. And, depending on the client application used to get the email, the message is delivered to the client's computer.

If using Microsoft's Outlook (or Outlook Express or another similar pulling email application), the email is eventually pulled to the receiver's own personal computer from the

```
1.  <% @LANGUAGE="VBSCRIPT" %>
2.  <% Response.Buffer = True %>
3.  <% Response.Expires = 0 %>
4.  <%
5.  '-- Open DSNless connection to database
6.  DB    = "database/agentstring.mdb"
7.  Dir   = Request.ServerVariables("SCRIPT_NAME")
8.  Dir   = StrReverse(Dir)
9.  Dir   = Mid(Dir, InStr(1, Dir, "/"))
10. Dir   = StrReverse(Dir)
11. Path  = Server.MapPath(Dir) & "\"
12. file  = "database/agentstring.dsn"
13. DSNa = "filedsn=" & Path & file & ";DefaultDir=" & Path & ";DBQ="
    & Path & DB & ";"

14. dim Conn, RS, sql
15. dim strAgentString, strEOR, strText
16. strEOR=0
17. strAgentString=request("HTTP_USER_AGENT")

18. Set Conn = Server.CreateObject("ADODB.Connection")
19. Set RS   = Server.CreateObject("ADODB.RecordSet")
20. Conn.Open DSNa
21. sql = "select Text from ASTable where Enabled=true order by
    AString asc"
22. RS.Open sql, Conn, 1,1

23. do while not (RS.EOF or RS.BOF)
24.   if InStr(Ucase(strAgentString),Ucase(RS(0)) > 0 then
25.       '--DB text value is in http string
26.       strEOR=1
27.       strText=RS(0)
28.       exit do
29.   end if
30.   RS.MoveNext
31. loop

32. if strEOR=0 then
33.   sql="select count(*) from ASTable where Enabled=false and
      AString='"& strAgentString
34.   Set RS = Conn.Execute(sql)
35.   if RS(0)= 0 then
36.       sql="insert into ASTable (AString,Text,Enabled)
          values('"& strAgentString &"','',false)"
37.       Set RS = Conn.Execute(sql)
38.   end if
```

Figure 5.13 AgentString.asp program.

```
39.    Conn.Close
40.    set RS = nothing
41.    set Conn = nothing
42.    response.redirect
          ("http://www.worldjobmart.com/HTTPmatch.asp?txtResult=0")
43. else
44.    Conn.Close
45.    set RS = nothing
46.    set Conn = nothing
47.    response.redirect
          ("http://www.worldjobmart.com/HTTPmatch.asp?txtResult="& strText)
48. end if
49. %>
```

Figure 5.13 Continued AgentString.asp program.

mail server. If using the popular Hotmail service, the email remains on the server. Since the server keeps all messages, people can retrieve their emails from anywhere in the world and from nearly any computer with access to the Internet and to Hotmail. No need to worry about connectivity details, POP3 or SMTP servers, or transport protocols. Hotmail made emailing easy, and this made Hotmail very popular very quickly and the owners very rich.

Before creating an email application, one must understand the basics of how emails are sent and received and how they move around. Emails travel over the Internet or Intranets (for internal company email systems). The applications used to create and receive emails are called *Mail User Agents* (MUA). The means by which the email is transferred from server to server across the Internet is called *Mail Transfer Agents* (MTA). And the application that delivers the email to the receiver's mailbox is called *Mail Delivery Agent* (MDA). See Figure 5.14.

As mentioned in Chapter 1, Multipurpose Internet Mail Extensions (MIME) was originally created for electronic mail. Usually, emails are sent from the MUAs in MIME format to the MTAs. MIME types set the Content-Type for a header, which details the character set and the basic encoding type, that is, text/plain meaning plain text.

When messages travel the Internet from MTA to MTA, they use a transfer protocol. Think of this as the vehicle that transports its occupants. The vehicle knows everything about where the message came from and where it's going. The most popular protocol for this is Simple Mail Transport Protocol (SMTP).

When the message arrives at its final mailbox destination, the most common retrieval protocol is POP3 or IMAP4. Post Office Protocol (POP3) allows users to get emails from a remote mailbox via their MUA and store the email on their personal devices. Interactive Mail Access Protocol (IMAP4) is POP3's alternative and is becoming very popular. Think of this as the advanced and more flexible version of POP3.

Figure 5.14 Email system.

This is email basics in a nutshell. There's a whole lot more to every part of electronic mail, but for our purposes we only need to have a rudimentary understanding.

Sending Emails

Figure 5.15 illustrates a simple sending email application using WML and ASP. Some mail servers will not allow sending emails if the *from* email address is not from the same domain as the sending mail server. Mind you, if the server does allow this, then you can send emails with any from address you like and the receiver will think it's from that sender rather than from your true email address.

The following program will gather the required input parameters to send an email. Since we're using the *input* command, each input field will be presented on its own screen as seen in Figure 5.16. The program is fairly straightforward in that it initializes the input field values to null, gathers the field values one by one, and then sends them to the next program via the postfield method. We're using this method to send the fields rather than append them directly to the URL address because the URL address has a limit of 127 bytes. The postfield can handle much more input and since an email can have a larger message than just 127 bytes, the postfield method was used.

Lines 7 through 15 are used to reset all the input fields to null if the program is invoked rather than return to the Back button.

Lines 18 through 22 declare the input fields as postfields.

Lines 26 through 35 are used to gather each required email field. The Cc (copy to) field is not required but has been added as well. Notice that the individual input fields have preset lengths and are all of type text. The format allows for all characters.

As you can see in Figure 5.16, each input field is processed individually on its own screen even though only one program is executing. When the last input field is gathered, control is passed to the program, sendmail.asp, on line 17. Note again that the from email address field must exist on the server that is executing the program. This is usually a restriction that the administrator enforces; otherwise, the application could be used to spam others since the from address wouldn't be legitimate.

```
1. <% @LANGUAGE="VBSCRIPT" %>
2. <wml>
3.     <head>
4.         <meta http-equiv="Cache-Control" content="max-age=0"/>
5.     </head>
6.     <card>
7.         <onevent type="onenterforward">
8.           <refresh>
9.                 <setvar name="to"       value=""/>
10.                <setvar name="from"     value=""/>
11.                          <setvar name="cc"        value=""/>
12.                <setvar name="subject" value=""/>
13.                <setvar name="body"     value=""/>
14.           </refresh>
15.        </onevent>
16.       <do  type="accept" label="OK">
17.         <go href="SendEmail.asp">
18.             <postfield name="T" value="$(to)"/>
19.             <postfield name="F" value="$(from)"/>
20.             <postfield name="C" value="$(cc)"/>
21.             <postfield name="S" value="$(subject)"/>
22.             <postfield name="B" value="$(body)"/>
23.          </go>
24.        </do>
25.      <p align="center"><b>WaveDev<br/>E-Mail</b></p><p
         align="left">
26.       <b>To:</b>
27.           <input name="to" maxlength="30" type="text"
              format="*M"/><br/>
28.       <b>From:</b>
29.           <input name="from" maxlength="30" type="text"
              format="*M"/><br/>
30.       <b>Cc:</b>
31.           <input name="cc" maxlength="30" type="text"
              format="*M"/><br/>
32.       <b>Subject:</b>
33.           <input name="subject" maxlength="15" type="text"
              format="*M"/><br/>
34.       <b>Body:</b>
35.           <input name="body" maxlength="300" type="text"
              format="*M"/><br/>
36.          </p>
37.      </card>
38. </wml>
```

Figure 5.15 SendEmail.wml program.

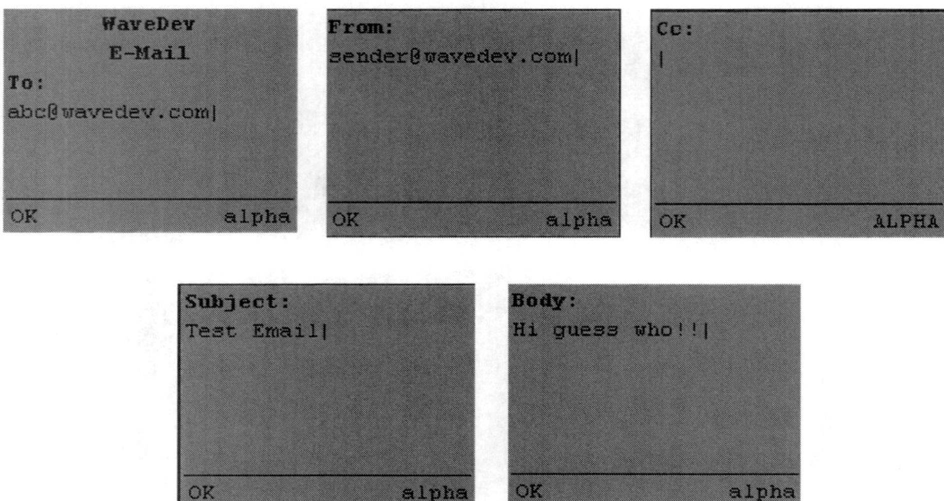

Figure 5.16 Email input screens.

The second program in the application (Figure 5.17) has just the basics to send an email. No special checks, just read in the passed parameters, set up the email variables, and perform a send, line 14. The last portion, line 16, redirects control to the last program in our application. This program will simply display a screen, Figure 5.19, saying the email has been sent.

```
1.  <% @LANGUAGE="VBSCRIPT" %>
2.  <% Response.Buffer = True %>
3.  <%
4.  dim objEMail
5.  '--send the email
6.  set objEMail        = Server.CreateObject("CDONTS.NewMail")
7.  objEMail.To         = request("T")
8.  objEMail.From       = request("F")
9.  objEMail.Cc         = request("C")
10. objEMail.Subject    = request("S")
11. objEMail.Body       = request("B")
12. objEMail.BodyFormat    = 0
13. objEMail.MailFormat    = 0
14. objEMail.Send
15. Response.clear
16. Response.redirect("http://www.wavedev.com/EmailSent.wml")
17. set objEMail = nothing
18. %>
```

Figure 5.17 SendEmail.asp program.

Figure 5.18 shows a basic send email application. What good would mobile wireless devices be without the ability to send an email?

The program in Figure 5.18 will display the screen in Figure 5.19 for 30 seconds, lines 4 and 5, and then return to the original input screen, program SendEmail.wml. Since the first program is specifically initiated, the onenterforward command, line 7, is invoked, and all the input parameters are reset to null.

Reading Emails

Compared to sending emails, reading them is much more complicated. We must ensure that our program will function on the popular mail servers holding the email messages. At the moment, two popular mail servers are Microsoft's IIS 4.0 SMTP server and Exchange Server. Also, remember that WAP devices have smaller cache sizes so the body of the email must be limited, and attachments are definitely out of the question. Another concern is the number of messages. If too many emails exist on the server that is displaying all the messages, even if on a selection list with only the limited sender or subject fields, the volume may still overflow the device's cache size.

Our application will use the Collaboration Data Objects for NT Server (CDONTS) method to retrieve emails from the server. The program requires a user display name and an email address. We'll be using the LogonSMTP method, but this will not validate the user's identity; it will merely get into the mail server. So, any friendly name and email address can be supplied to this method and CDO for NTS will not complain. If the SMTP email address is incorrect, the message will not be delivered. Once a session has been established, the Inbox and Outbox folders for that session can be accessed. When finished, simply log off and set the Session Object to nothing.

In Figure 5.20 the WML program in our email fetching application simply gathers the two input fields: User Name and User Email.

```
1. <?xml version="1.0"?>
2. <!DOCTYPE wml PUBLIC "-//PHONE.COM//DTD WML 1.1//EN"
   "http://www.phone.com/dtd/wml11.dtd">
3. <wml>
4.    <card id="card1" ontimer="SendEmail.wml">
5.       <timer name="time" value="30"/>
6.         <do  type="accept" label="OK">
7.             <go href="SendEmail.wml"/>
8.         </do>
9.         <p align="center">Your email has been sent</p>
10.    </card>
11. </wml>
```

Figure 5.18 EmailSent.wml program.

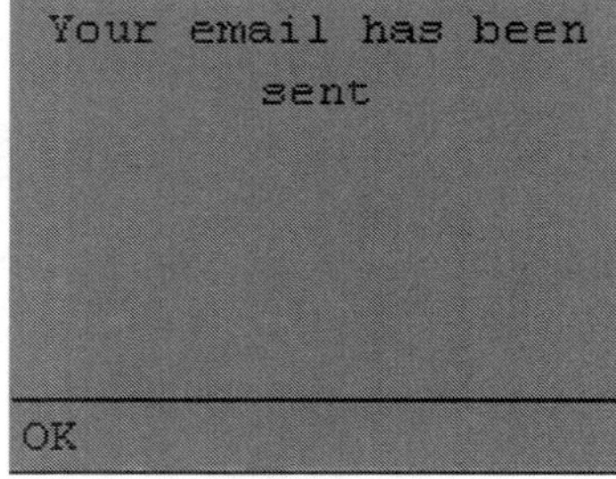

Figure 5.19 Email has been sent.

The GetEmail.wml program is very similar to the SendEmail.wml program. It gathers input fields and then passes them via the postfield method to a second program, lines 13 through 16. If the program is explicitly initiated, its input fields are reset to null, lines 6 through 11. The result is shown in Figure 5.21.

```
1.  <wml>
2.      <head>
3.          <meta http-equiv="Cache-Control" content="max-age=0"/>
4.      </head>
5.      <card>
6.      <onevent type="onenterforward">
7.         <refresh>
8.              <setvar name="UserName"  value=""/>
9.              <setvar name="UserEmail" value=""/>
10.        </refresh>
11.     </onevent>
12.     <do  type="accept" label="OK">
13.      <go href="getemail2.asp">
14.             <postfield name="N" value="$(UserName)"/>
15.             <postfield name="E" value="$(UserEmail)"/>
16.      </go>
17.     </do>
18.     <p align="center"><b>WaveDev<br/>E-Mail</b></p><p align="left">
19.         <b>User Name:</b>
20.         <input name="UserName" maxlength="30" type="text"
            format="*M"/><br/>
21.         <b>User Email:</b>
22.         <input name="UserEmail" maxlength="50" type="text"
            format="*M"/><br/>
23.     </p>
24.      </card>
25.  </wml>
```

Figure 5.20 GetEmail.wml program.

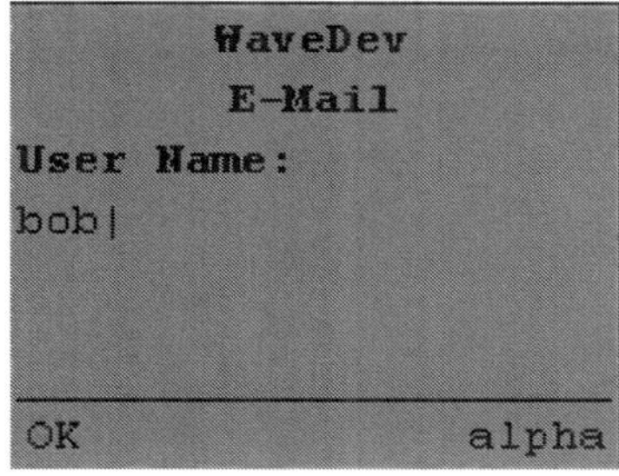

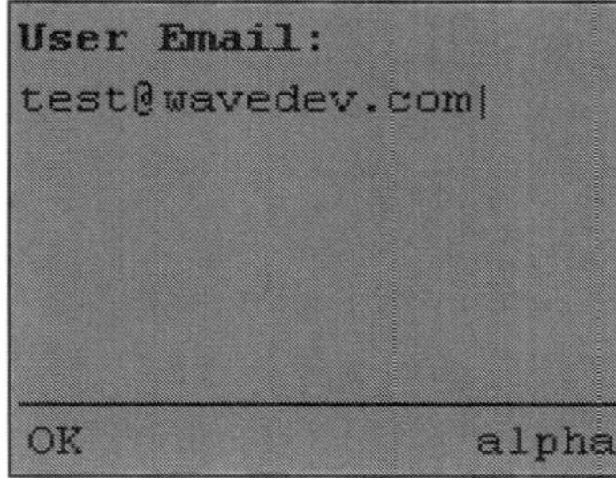

Figure 5.21 GetEmail.wml screens.

To make life real easy, the second program, getemail2.asp (Figure 5.22), simply reads all emails on the mail server for the specific recipient after a session has been correctly established. It will then display the number of available emails followed by a link to each message. The title for each email will be the subject line of the email itself. This program is very simple, and no extra checks are performed. So, hopefully, there aren't many emails on the server for the user, as too many emails would quickly fill up the WAP device's memory.

Lines 8 and 9 show the parameters passed from the previous input program being read in and stored in two local program variables.

Line 11 sets up the CDONTS Session Object and line 12 initializes it, using the two local variables containing the name and email address captured from the first program.

With a successful session established, we now look at the user's Inbox folder. Once we have the Inbox variable, line 13, we're ready to access the collection of messages within it. Once a session is established, the default folder will depend on whether the CDO for NTS is being run against the SMTP service of IIS 4.0 or Exchange Server. If it's Exchange Server, the Inbox property will return the user's regular mailbox. If it's IIS 4.0, the Inbox property will return the Drop directory.

Now, using the Count property on the message collection of the Inbox, we can check to see whether there are any messages in the Inbox, line 14. If not, a simple message is sent to the user's device.

We could also set the message collection on line 17 and write the total number of existing messages to the device, line 18.

Lines 19 through 21 loop through each message writing a WML anchor tag with a link to each message. The link contains the next program in our application with the original name and email parameters from the first input screen, along with a new variable—the index of the message from the Inbox. This is not a foolproof method because if another message arrives from this point on, it could certainly mix up our counter loop efforts. Each message's Subject is used as the links text as shown in Figure 5.23.

```
1. <%
2. Response.Buffer = TRUE
3. Response.ContentType = "text/vnd.wap.wml"
4. response.write "<?xml version="+chr(34)+"1.0"+chr(34)+"?>"
5. response.write "<!DOCTYPE wml PUBLIC "+chr(34)+"-//WAPFORUM//DTD
   WML 1.1//EN"+chr(34)+"
   "+chr(34)+"http://www.wapforum.org/DTD/wml_1.1.xml"+chr(34)+">"
6. response.write "<wml><card><p
   align="+chr(34)+"center"+chr(34)+"><b>WaveDev<br/>E-Mail</b><br/>"

7. dim strName, strEmail, objSession, objInbox, colMessages
8. strName = Request.QueryString("N")
9. strEmail = Request.QueryString("E")
10.
11. Set objSession = CreateObject("CDONTS.Session")
12. objSession.LogonSMTP strName, strEmail

13. Set objInbox = objSession.Inbox
14. If objInbox.Messages.Count = 0 Then
15.     response.write "No messages in the Inbox"
16. Else
17.     Set colMessages = objInbox.Messages
18.     response.write Cstr(colMessages.Count) & " Messages<br/>"
19.     For i = 1 to colMessages.Count
20.         response.write "<anchor><go href="+ chr(34)
            +"getemail3.asp?N="+ strName +"&amp;E="+ strEmail
            +"&amp;Mi="+ Cstr(i) +chr(34)+"/>"+ colMessages(i).Subject
            +"</anchor><br/>"
21.     Next
22. End If

23. Set colMessages = Nothing
24. Set objInbox = Nothing
25. objSession.Logoff
26. Set objSession = Nothing

27. response.write "</p></card></wml>"
28. %>
```

Figure 5.22 GetEmail2.asp program.

Once done, the variables and objects are set to nothing, and the Session is logged off, line 25.

The final program in Figure 5.24 shows how to view the body (text) of the individual email message. Simply select any link on the previous screen and its body is displayed, see Figure 5.25. Again, there are no checks, so, hopefully, the body is not too big and

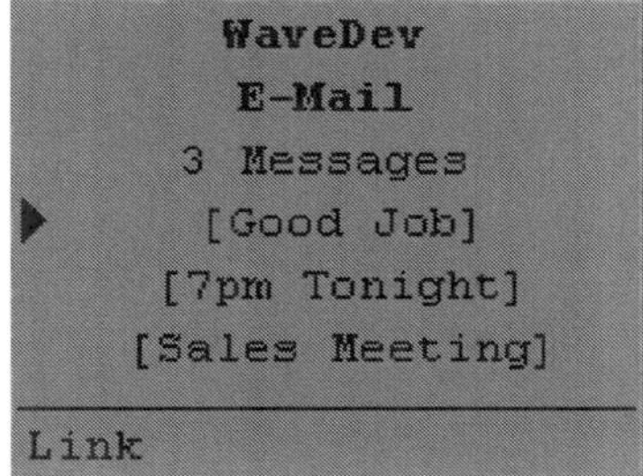

Figure 5.23 List of emails.

there are no troublesome characters in the message. And let's hope that no new messages appear as we're invoking this routine. Do add your own checks for these programs if you are going to use them as templates.

Lines 8, 9, and 10 read in the variables passed from the GetEmail2.asp program.

Again, a Session is established via LogonSMTP using the user name and email address. Then we check for messages in the Inbox. If none exist, we simply display a message saying so and proceed to the end of the program.

If messages do exist, using the index parameter passed from the previous program, the proper email message is retrieved and its Subject text is displayed as part of the screen title as seen with the code on line 18. Then the message body, line 19, is retrieved to display on the WAP device screen as seen in Figure 5.25.

This reading email application is very basic and requires many tests and checks to be added to make sure it runs smoothly in a real production environment.

An HTML version of this application, GetEmailHTML.asp, has been included on the CD. Transfer it to your Web site, supply the user name and email address parameters, and it will show you all email messages in your Inbox, depending on your mail server and the manner in which it is setup.

Location-Based Services

The future of the mobile wireless industry will have much to do with location-based services (LBS). This process grants access of the geographic location of an individual's wireless device to the content or service provider. In other words, LBS will allow the content providers to provide specific information or services to the WAP phone user based on the registered location of his or her wireless device. One day it may also allow emergency operators to pinpoint the specific location of the device, give or take a few meters. Imagine using your cellular phone to call for medical assistance, and the emergency system would be able to recognize your exact location automatically.

```
1.  <%
2.  Response.Buffer = TRUE
3.  Response.ContentType = "text/vnd.wap.wml"
4.  response.write "<?xml version="+chr(34)+"1.0"+chr(34)+"?>"
5.  response.write "<!DOCTYPE wml PUBLIC "+chr(34)+"-//WAPFORUM//DTD
    WML 1.1//EN"+chr(34)+"
    "+chr(34)+"http://www.wapforum.org/DTD/wml_1.1.xml"+chr(34)+">"
6.  response.write "<wml><card><p
    align="+chr(34)+"center"+chr(34)+"><b>Email Body<br/>"

7.  dim strName, strEmail, strMsgIndex, objSession, objInbox,
    colMessages
8.  strName = Request.QueryString("N")
9.  strEmail = Request.QueryString("E")
10. strMsgIndex = Request.QueryString("Mi")

11. Set objSession = CreateObject("CDONTS.Session")
12. objSession.LogonSMTP strName, strEmail

13. Set objInbox = objSession.Inbox
14. If objInbox.Messages.Count = 0 Then
15.    response.write "Error, no messages found"
16. Else
17.    Set colMessages = objInbox.Messages
18.    response.write colMessages(strMsgIndex).Subject & "</b></p><p>"
19.    response.write colMessages(strMsgIndex).Text
20. End If

21. Set colMessages = Nothing
22. Set objInbox = Nothing
23. objSession.Logoff
24. Set objSession = Nothing

25. response.write "</p></card></wml>"
26. %>
```

Figure 5.24 GetEmail3.asp program.

Subscribers of the service could receive information about nearby movie theater offerings or restaurant advertisements from surrounding city areas. Internet job sites can add job search categories that are specific to the user's registered location, among other features. If the person is detected as being registered in the New York area when viewing a specific site, the content provider could supply specific New York categories making the entire user experience much more convenient. There are many possibilities.

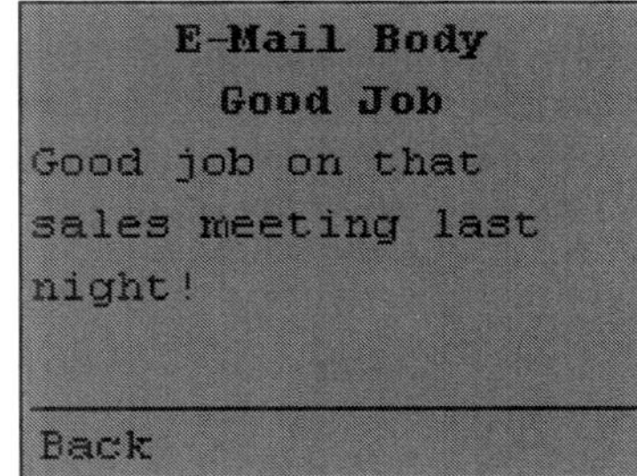

Figure 5.25 Email message.

Although this technology is new and still considered to be an advanced topic, several firms such as Openwave have designed and implemented working models. But even so, for this type of service to really become widely used, a high level of participation among network carriers, wireless equipment and/or device manufacturers, and content providers must be achieved. Recognizing this, Motorola, Ericsson, and Nokia have established a special forum, www.locationforum.org, to centralize efforts and concerns for location-based service technology. Through this forum, individuals and organizations will be able to raise issues at many different levels to eventually create industry standardization in technological areas and for uses of location-based services.

Issues to be addressed by the forum include:

- Equipment and application interoperability

- Subscriber privacy and information (about subscriber's location) security

- Methods that will provide location-based service to roaming subscribers

- Third-party- and in-house-developed applications interoperability

- Models for multilocation billing and revenue sharing

These are only a few of the current issues that must be resolved in order for location-based services to gain momentum. As with any new product or service, the main issue includes usage. The service is just now becoming more widely known, available, and therefore used by clients. Operators in the United Kingdom, such as Orange, are well ahead of the game with their own LBS availability. And as mentioned earlier, governments in many countries are adopting new laws that will, to a certain extent, promote location-based services. For example, the FCC in the United States is seriously looking into LBS for emergency purposes. They would like for all new mobile wireless devices to have the ability to pinpoint the user (or caller) to within 100 meters.

Components

Location-based services are mostly based on two general types of geographic location information. First, the user's location can be based on his or her address, city, zip code, and/or country. Second, the person could register his or her longitude and latitude coordinates. Now we're really getting closer to a *Star Trek* like scenario. Remember when Captain Kirk would say, "*Scotty, beam it to my coordinates*"? Well, with longitude and latitude information, location-based recognition from mobile devices is a very real futuristic scenario used now only in GPS systems.

So what's involved in setting up a location-based service? We could build an application that asks the user his or her specific location. If in Chicago, press 1 or if in Paris, press 2. Or we could simply present a list of geographic locations to click on as many Web sites currently do. But by far the best method is to have the device registered to a particular area and have the content providers offer the choice of selecting content in that specific location or anywhere else. This also depends on the type of content or service being offered. I certainly wouldn't want a list of all pizza delivery restaurants in Geneva when I live in Singapore, but I may want all course schedules starting with my current location followed by the next closest location, and so on. I may want to know if a course is offered in London even though I live in Montreal, since I may be traveling there next month. Having my location as the first choice in a list of offerings is very helpful and will definitely encourage the reuse of the service. But content from other locations must also be available.

The following LBS set-up requirements are based on Openwave's location-based service architecture and are illustrated in Figure 5.26. This service includes all the regular setup requirements for UP.Link Server and UP.Browser.

- The content provider's application must also be designed in such a way as to be able to take advantage of the location-based services.

- Mobile Location Server (MLS) installed as part of the wireless operator offerings (this connects to the UP.Link Server)

- Location Enabled Services (LES) enabled on the UP.Link Server

- Geographic Markup Language (GML) enabled on the content provider's Web server and Web application

- Registration of content provider's URL with MLS and UP.Link Server (LES)

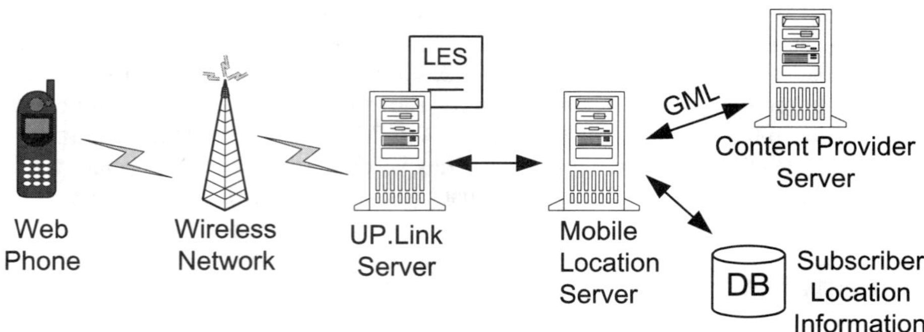

Figure 5.26 LBS infrastructure.

Geographic Markup Language (GML) is yet another XML subset. It's a formatted set of XML tags structured specifically to send location-based messages. This is the only format currently available via Openwave's architecture. A complete set of details and documentation can be found at www.opengis.org/techno/specs.htm. Since the subset uses longitude and latitude, another interesting site for location-based services and the mobile location server is www.bcca.org/misc/qiblih/latlong.html. This site will map almost any location to a longitude and latitude.

The overall concept requires the participation of several factors. First the carrier must have the UP.Link Server. Then the carrier must include a Mobile Location Server, which will handle the security, subscriber information, and special GML headers. Once in place, a content provider can register his or her URL or specific URL extension (for example, www.wavedev.com/wireless/upbrowser/pizzadelivery.asp). The URL is registered against the UP.Link Server where the URL name is put into the location-enabled services (LES) file for quick reference. The URL is also registered on the MLS server. Now the subscriber must register with the service, supplying as much or as little information as he or she desires. This information is stored on the MLS system and is only sent to the content provider with the permission of the subscriber. The subscriber may wish to authorize the sharing of this information on each separate connection to the content provider or may choose to allow it under all circumstances. Once the subscriber authorizes the sending of location information for a specific site, the MLS creates two HTTP headers to send to the content provider. The content provider must then parse the header information to obtain the location information to be used in location-based programs. The location-specific content or service is then sent back to the subscriber to complete the transaction.

The first HTTP header sent by the MLS server is HTTP_X_UP_LOCDOCTYPE. This header is used to tell the receiver of the location document what format is to be found in the second header. Currently, only GML format is available. The second HTTP header, HTTP_X_UP_LOCDOC, contains all the subscriber's location information. This information is XML-based as seen in Figure 5.31.

Client Setup

In actual usage, individuals will subscribe to the location-based service and register their location information from their wireless devices. For development purposes, settings must be specified in the UP.SDK toolkit.

First of all, you will have to set your current or testing location. This process can be achieved by selecting the Set Location option from the Location menu item on your Openwave UP.SDK simulator. See Figure 5.27.

The next screen that pops up is the Location Settings window (see Figure 5.28). Enter as much information as required to perform your development tests under the Current Phone Location tab.

All the fields can be set or just the address fields, or just the latitude and longitude.

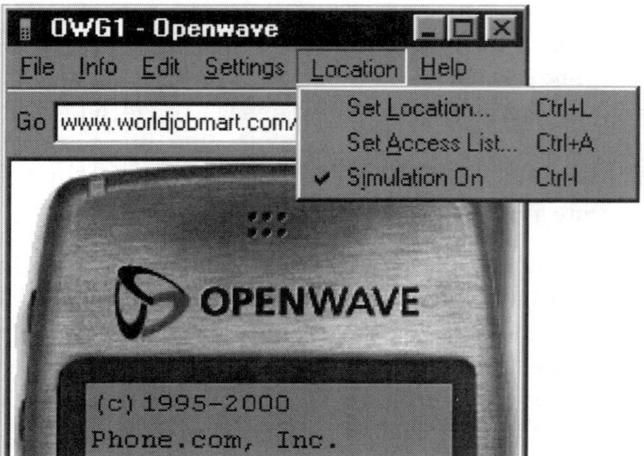

Figure 5.27 UP.SDK Settings.

More than one current phone location can be set. By selecting the Location Address Book tab, you can test your application for multiple locations without ever leaving the comfort of your chair. Set up multiple locations, change or delete specific address entries, or choose another address as the current device location; but only one address can be set at any given time.

Figure 5.28 Location Settings.

Content Provider Setup

Again, in real life the content provider would have to contact the carrier to register the URL or URL extension with the UP.Link Server and on the Mobile Location Server. For development purposes, the UP.SDK also provides for an area to register your test URL. This is important since the UP.Simulator will provide the test GML HTTP headers for your application to interpret. Registration of the URL is done with the second item in the drop-down menu shown in Figure 5.27, Set Access List. Figure 5.29 shows the details.

By selecting the Add button, the developer can add a new URL or URL extension and specify which HTTP header entries are to be received from the UP.Simulator. This will simulate the header information sent out by the MLS server to the content provider. The header information is the subscriber location data, which would normally be entered by the client at registration or when subscribing to the service.

Once the developer accesses a specific URL using the UP.Simulator, if the URL is registered in the Location Access List, as shown in Figure 5.30, an HTTP header, HTTP_X_UP_LOCDOCTYPE, will be set to a value of GML. In a live environment, this would be set by the MLS server but for development purposes it will be set by the Location Access List.

As mentioned, a second HTTP header is also created, HTTP_X_UP_LOCDOC (see Figure 5.31). This header will contain the location information from the subscriber. The information in this header will be parsed and used by the content provider to determine what content to supply back to the subscriber.

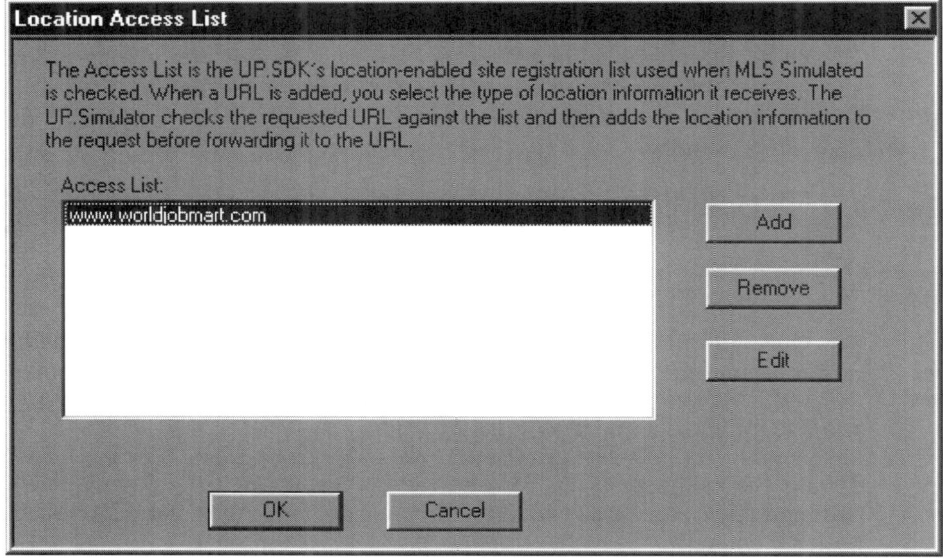

Figure 5.29 Location Access List (content provider URL).

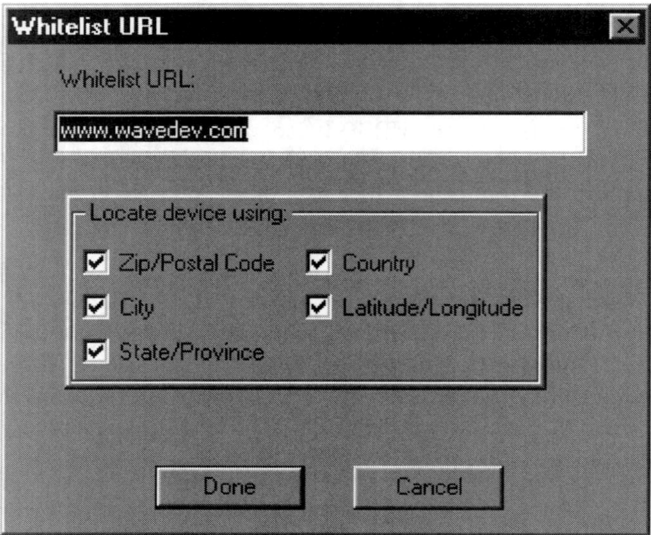

Figure 5.30 MLS GML HTTP header settings.

The header format is an XML document with multiple tags, each describing the specific fields as entered in Figure 5.28. Here all fields have been entered, but normally either the address or longitude and latitude information would be entered.

Content Provider Header Parsing

Having all the header information and knowing the location information document type—GML—as noted on the first header, we can proceed to parse the data and determine where the location-based subscriber is located so we may provide the targeted content or service.

The first program that we will use to determine if there is any location-based information by checking for the GML value is LBS1stHeader.asp. See Figure 5.32. If the value is not found, control is passed to the NoGML.wml program, which displays a WML screen with a simple message. Both of these programs are included on the CD.

Any type of desired parsing language can be used for the parsing of the XML document in the second header: PERL, ASP, JAVA, Microsoft's XMLDOM, or whatever. In our examples, we use ASP. We'll parse the second HTTP header to extract the city information and then build a WML deck containing that data.

The program in Figure 5.33, GML.asp, will execute on the content provider's server. It'll be found in the registered URL directory as specified in the location Access list (Figure 5.29).

Line 2, as always, sets the buffer setting to TRUE.

```
<?xml version="1.0" encoding="UTF-8"?>
<!DOCTYPE Feature SYSTEM "gmlfeature.dtd">
<Feature typeName="Location">
    <property typeName="city">New York</property>
    <property typeName="state">NY</property>
    <property typeName="country">United States</property>
    <property typeName="errorShape">ellipse</property>
    <property typeName="errorUnit">kilometers</property>
    <property typeName="errorMajor">2</property>
    <property typeName="errorMinor">1</property>
    <geometricProperty typeName="position">
        <Point srsName="EPSG:4326">
            <coordinates>40_ 47' N,73_ 58' W</coordinates>
        </Point>
    </geometricProperty>
</Feature>
```

Figure 5.31 HTTP_X_UP_LOCDOC header.

Lines 5 through 8 set up the content type and the initial XML, DTD, and WML requirements.

Line 9 once again tests for the GML format in the first HTTP header; if not found, lines 18 through 20 are executed. These simply set the <card> tag and center a simple message on the screen.

Lines 10 through 15 are the main portions of the program. These lines will parse the XML document passed in the HTTP header. First, it sets the second HTTP header to a working variable. Then it looks for the starting position of the <property typeName="city"> tag within that variable, line 11. After adding the length of the tag to the starting position of the tag to obtain the end of the starting tag, line 12, everything before and including the tag is removed, line 13. Then the position of the ending tag is found on line 14, and everything after that position is removed, leaving only the city name contained within the tag, line 15.

```
<%
if InStr(Ucase(request.ServerVariables("HTTP_X_UP_LOCDOCTYPE")),
"GML") > 0 then
      response.redirect ("http://www.wavedev.com/GML.WML")
else
      response.redirect ("http://www.wavedev.com/NOGML.WML")
end if
%>
```

Figure 5.32 First header parsing program, LBS1stHeader.asp.

```
1.  <% @LANGUAGE="VBSCRIPT" %>
2.  <% Response.Buffer = True %>
3.  <% Response.Expires = 0 %>
4.  <%
5.  response.ContentType = "text/vnd.wap.wml"
6.  response.write "<?xml version="+chr(34)+"1.0"+chr(34)+"?>"
7.  response.write "<!DOCTYPE wml PUBLIC "+chr(34)+"-//PHONE.COM//DTD
    WML 1.1//EN"+chr(34)+" "+chr(34)+
    "http://www.phone.com/dtd/wml11.dtd"+chr(34)+">"
8.  response.write "<wml>"

9.  if Ucase(request.ServerVariables("HTTP_X_UP_LOCDOCTYPE")) = "GML"
    then
10.     MyGML = request.ServerVariables("HTTP_X_UP_LOCDOC")
11.     StartLocation = InStr(MyGML, "<property typeName=" + chr(34) +
        "city" + chr(34) + ">")
12.     StartLocation = StartLocation +25
13.     MyGML = Right(MyGML, Len(Trim(MyGML)) - StartLocation)
14.     StopLocation = InStr(MyGML, "</property>")
15.     PrintOut = left(MyGML, StopLocation - 1)
16.     response.write "<card id="+chr(34)+"GML"+chr(34)+">"
17.     response.write "<p align="+chr(34)+"center"+chr(34)+"><b>Your
        Location is:<br/>" + Trim(PrintOut) + "</b></p>"
18. else
19.     response.write "<card id="+chr(34)+"NOGML"+chr(34)+">"
20.     response.write "<p align="+chr(34)+"center"+chr(34)+">No
        location set</p>"
21. end if
22. response.write "</card>"
23. response.write "</wml>"
24. %>
```

Figure 5.33 Parsing program, GML.asp.

Line 16 sets the <card> tag.

Line 17 creates the message to appear in the client WAP device window with the city name.

This program shows how the content provider would parse for specific values to then be used in another program to supply targeted content back to the client microbrowser as seen in Figure 5.34.

The security and privacy of the subscriber's geographical location should be protected. However, each carrier is responsible for deciding whether or not the subscriber location data is delivered using HTTP or the secured HTTPS protocol. Privacy negotiation between the subscriber's information and the content provider is also an important part of location-based services. Fortunately, developers are spared the extra coding since the security features are built into the mobile location server. Each subscriber can define whether or not each item is to be secured, private, or neither.

Short Message Service (SMS)

Imagine yourself in a large auditorium with hundreds of other attendees listening to a very boring presentation scheduled for the next 3 hours. Somewhere on the other side of the room is your good friend from out east who is here at the same conference, and you know he's probably half asleep by now. No worries—SMS to the rescue! Since talking on your cell phone would disturb others in the room, you tap in a quick message and with SMS it quickly arrives on your friend's cell phone: *Let's get out of here—Bob.* Next thing you know, you're both reminiscing over coffees about those college years way back when.

Believe it or not, SMS has really become quite popular, with over 10 billion SMS messages being sent every month worldwide. And it hasn't even taken off in the United States yet!

Short message service is a quick and inexpensive method of sending short messages to another person's SMS-enabled cellular phone or device. SMS is inexpensive because a typical SMS message is about the same as a 1-second voice conversation. Quick because messages are usually delivered almost immediately.

SMS messages are mostly 160 characters long, but there are ways to string multiple messages together to form larger messages. Depending on the network, traffic, SMS gateway usage, and message type, most messages are delivered immediately, if the receiving device is turned on. If the phone is in use, an SMS message can still appear on the screen, since the two abilities are distinct.

Messages can be set to "delayed," meaning they can arrive within several hours but mostly they are immediate. Messages can also have replies sent back to the sender. In many business areas, such as Singapore, the reply messages were overwhelming servers to the point that the reply message was being returned to the sender as much as 24 hours later.

Figure 5.34 Resulting screen from GML.asp.

Messages can be replied to, intercepted, and used to transport data to devices. Ring tones, logos, and device configuration are currently the most popular types of SMS messaging other than the regular personal messaging. Soon URLs will be popular SMS messages where the receiver can click on the URL and be transported to its underlying Web (WAP) site. This feature is still in the works but if it can be imagined, it can be done, and probably will be within the next several years.

SMS messages are based on two modes: point-to-point and cell-broadcast mode (or point-to-omnipoint). Point-to-point refers to one user sending a message to another subscriber, as in the auditorium example mentioned previously. Cell-broadcast mode deals with messages being sent to specific subscribers in a certain region like batch SMS or multiple recipients. Imagine the new spamming potential with cell-broadcast!

Even though typing on cellular phones and devices is difficult and frustrating, people are finding ways to speed up the process. Small icons like happy faces are becoming more popular, and old tricks once used to reduce the cost of sending telegrams are being revived. This type of shorthand changes I LOVE YOU to ILVU or instead of BY THE WAY you could use BTW. Who knows, this 160-character restriction and tough typing could evolve into a generation of children with short names!

One of the reasons why SMS hasn't truly taken off yet in the United States is because, for the most part, digital wireless interface standards such as GSM are in their early stages. GSM is a requirement for SMS to function. The United States uses mostly CDMA and TDMA standards over GSM, which are very limited in SMS capabilities.

GSM

Global Systems for Mobile communications (GSM) was introduced and discussed in Chapter 1. GSM is a digital network, which can encode, transmit, and decode information in a fraction of the time required to produce sound—it's fast. Up to eight subscribers can share the same channel at the same time, or so it seems, because it's so fast compared to regular analog transmissions. GSM transmits data at speeds up to 9600 bytes per second.

Most GSM phones have removable Subscriber Identity Module (SIM or smart card) cards containing the device's telephone number, subscriber account information, and other interesting tidbits. One of the reasons GSM phones can store SMS messages is because of the SIM card, which is where the messages are stored. Another area where messages are stored is on the SMS Center.

Short Message Service Center (SMSC)

Just like emails, SMS messages do have a *store and forward* ability. This is mainly due to the SMS Center or server. As messages are sent, they pass into the SMSC. One of SMSC's tasks is to transfer messages to the correct mobile subscribers. To do so, the following processes are performed.

First, the Home Location Register (HLR) is queried and that gives the status of the target subscriber. HLR will respond with either an inactive or active reply. If the subscriber is temporarily inactive, that is, the phone is shut off, SMSC will store the message for a predetermined amount of time. Once the subscriber becomes active, HLR notifies SMSC of the status change, and SMSC will deliver the message. When the message has been delivered, SMSC *marks* the message as delivered and will not resend the same message.

Sending Messages

The following three methods show how to develop SMS messaging applications. The first method uses a homegrown VB6 (Visual Basic) application with Nokia's PC connectivity SDK 2.0, which is simply a batch of DLLs and permissions on Nokia's development system. In this method, the developer's application sends an SMS message via an SMS-enabled cellular phone connected to the developer's PC via a serial or infrared communication link. The message is sent over Nokia's developer network with the reply returning to the application.

The second method also uses a homegrown VB6 application, sending an SMS message via a serial or infrared connected SMS-enabled cellular device. This time, straight AT (modem) commands are used to send the message via a direct dial-in service.

The last example uses the SMTP protocol and a carrier relaying the message to the proper receiver.

Nokia PC Connectivity SDK 2.0

One method to send SMS messages is to use specific vendor-provided software development kits such as Nokia's PC Connectivity SDK 2.0. This is a free toolkit downloadable from www.nokia.com. This is a great toolkit and has only a few requirements before the developer can start building applications:

- The SDK's only supported operating systems are Windows 95, 98, 98SE, NT4.0, or 2000.
- The developer must have a Nokia wireless device, which supports this SDK.
- There must be an available serial or infrared port on the developer's workstation.
- The developer must register with NOKIA as an SMS developer, which is free.
- The SDK must be downloaded and installed on the PC.

Documentation for this SDK is provided in the form of 400 pages of a well-written document in PDF format. It will help you to understand the requirements and intricacies in developing your applications with Nokia's PC Connectivity SDK 2.0.

Only certain types of devices are available to connect to your PC via either the serial or infrared link. Nokia serial link device models are 5110, 5130, 5190, 6110, 6130, 6150, and

6190. Infrared-supported devices are 8210, 8290, 8810, 8850, and 8890. And device models that support both link types are 6210, 6250, 7110, and 7190.

Our example consists of a Visual Basic 6 program, but any other language compatible with the Windows development environment like VC++ or Delphi can be used. Before beginning the development process, Nokia's SDK libraries must be added in your Visual Basic 6 IDE. See Figure 5.35.

In order to demonstrate how easy it is to create SMS-enabled applications, the program in Figure 5.36 will send an SMS message and query the response code to confirm that the message was successfully sent.

The VB6 application code is given in Figure 5.36. This VB program is quite simple, but let's go through its general functionality. The code on line 10 is basically the core statement. It executes an API call to the Nokia SMS ToolKit. Lines 5 to 9 serve as the collection point for the GUI-entered variables such as SMSC number, Subscriber Number, and the message itself. Once the message has been created and sent to the SMS Center, lines 17 through 34 check for a successful transmission in the response code from the SMS API. Then an associated message text from the interpreted response code will be sent to the application and displayed in the System Responses area.

If the program was successfully invoked, a window similar to the one in Figure 5.37 will appear. The way the application works is that the developer enters a message in the

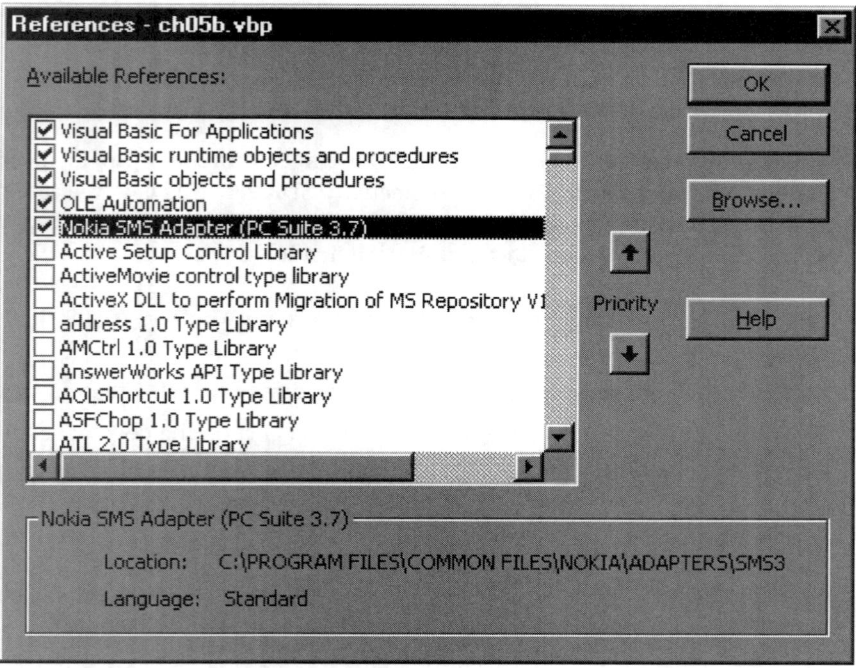

Figure 5.35 Nokia SMS Adapter DLLs.

```
1. Private SendSMSMsg As SMS3ASuiteLib.SMS_SuiteAdapter

2. Private Sub Command1_Click()
3.    Dim MyMessage As SMS3ASuiteLib.ShortMessage
4.    On Error GoTo MessageError

5.    Set SendSMSMsg = New SMS3ASuiteLib.SMS_SuiteAdapter
6.    Set MyMessage = SendSMSMsg.CreateShortMsg
7.    MyMessage.UserDataText = Trim(Text1.Text)
8.    MyMessage.OtherEndAddress = Trim(tex3.Text)
9.    MyMessage.SCAddress = Trim(Text2.Text)

10.    Call SendSMSMsg.Send(MyMessage)

11.    SendSMSMsg.Terminate
12.    Set SendSMSMsg = Nothing
13.    Exit Sub

14.    MessageError:
15.    Dim MsgError As NmpAdapterError
16.    MsgError = SendSMSMsg.GetLastError

17.    Select Case MsgError
18.       Case errPhoneNotConnected
19.          Text4.Text = Text4.Text + "Error: Device is not
              connected" + Chr(13) + Chr(10)
20.       Case errSmsCreateFailed
21.          Text4.Text = Text4.Text + "Error: SMS component failed to
              create" + Chr(13) + Chr(10)
22.       Case errSmsInvalidUserDataLength
23.          Text4.Text = Text4.Text + "Error: SMS message to long" +
              Chr(13) + Chr(10)
24.       Case errSmsTooLongSCAddress
25.          Text4.Text = Text4.Text + "Error: SMS Service Center
              number too long " + Chr(13) + Chr(10)
26.       Case errSmsNoSCAddress
27.          Text4.Text = Text4.Text + "Error: SMS Service Center
              number is missing" + Chr(13) + Chr(10)
28.       Case errCommunicationError
29.          Text4.Text = Text4.Text + "Error: Communication error
              PC<->terminal" + Chr(13) + Chr(10)
30.       Case errNoError
31.          Text4.Text = Text4.Text + "Success: SMS operation
              succeeded" + Chr(13) + Chr(10)
32.       Case Else
33.          Text4.Text = Text4.Text + "Error: some other error " +
              CStr(MsgError) + " " + Chr(13) + Chr(10)
34.    End Select
35. End Sub

36. Private Sub Command2_Click()
37.    Unload Me
38. End Sub
```

Figure 5.36 Ch05b.vbp VB program code.

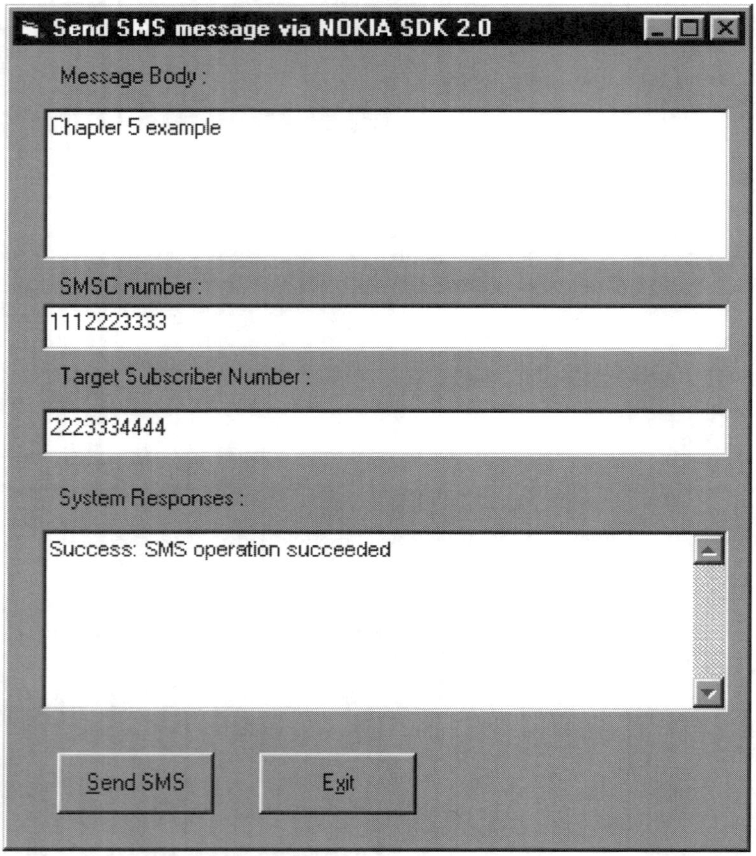

Figure 5.37 Ch05b.vbp resulting application.

Message body area, the SMSC number, as well as the target subscriber telephone number. After pressing the Send SMS button, the message is sent via the SDK 2.0 DLLs to the serial or infrared port to the SMS-enabled Nokia cellular phone. The phone relays the message to the Nokia development SMSC server to send the message to the target subscriber. A reply is then returned to the invoking application and seen in the System Responses area.

The SMSC and Target Subscriber numbers are fictitious. You'll have to use real numbers in your development efforts if you want a successful SMS message sent.

Direct Dial-In Service

This method uses another developed VB program, which uses a dial-in service via the terminal equipment connected to the PC. Similar results as the first method can be achieved by issuing a series of AT commands directed to the wireless device connected to your PC. The connection is the same as in the Nokia method earlier. *AT* is an abbreviation for the Attention commands, which were initially used for modem connections.

SMS text messages can be sent to the cell phone but manual port configuration, along with basic AT commands, must be sent to the device. The following command is used to set the phone to accept text messages:

```
AT+CMFG=1
```

If the device is connected correctly, the PC reply will be an OK. The AT command is required to terminate with a carriage return and a line feed string, as we'll see in the program in Figure 5.40. These termination strings are nothing more than Enter key simulations to counter the OK reply from the AT command.

The next important step will be to initiate the sending of the message by issuing the following AT command:

```
AT+CMGS="+XXXXXXXXXX", 129
```

This AT command must also terminate with a simulated Enter. The XXXXXXXXXX value represents the target subscriber's number. The required 129 parameter is the default value for SMS text mode.

The wireless device will reply with a prompt sign and wait until the text message is entered. As usual, the text message must also be terminated by the simulated Enter, which is the carriage return and a line feed string. To mark the end of the message body a Ctrl+Z [in Visual Basic use chr(26)] keystroke combination is added.

This completes the message creation and sending phase. The wireless device will then reply with the +CMGS value followed by the message reference number.

The diagram in Figure 5.38 shows the overall process flow.

To create the VB application, you'll need to add Microsoft's Comm Component to your list of available controls. That is the only additional component required from the default start-up components. After the successful addition of this control, you should see a window similar to that shown in Figure 5.39.

The code in Figure 5.40 is our second SMS application.

This example uses the enhanced set of AT commands sent via the serial interface of your PC, one of the COM ports to the SMS-enabled cell phone. Connection preparatory work is done in the Form_Load subroutine, lines 19 through 27, where the port number, link speed, and link parity are set, just as when connecting to a modem.

The sequence of AT commands, seen in the *response from device* area in Figure 5.41, starts at line 3 in Figure 5.40. Once the command is sent, if everything is fine, the system will respond with an OK message.

The command on line 6, AT+CMGF=1, sets the type of message to follow as being text.

Line 7 sets the receiver's telephone number.

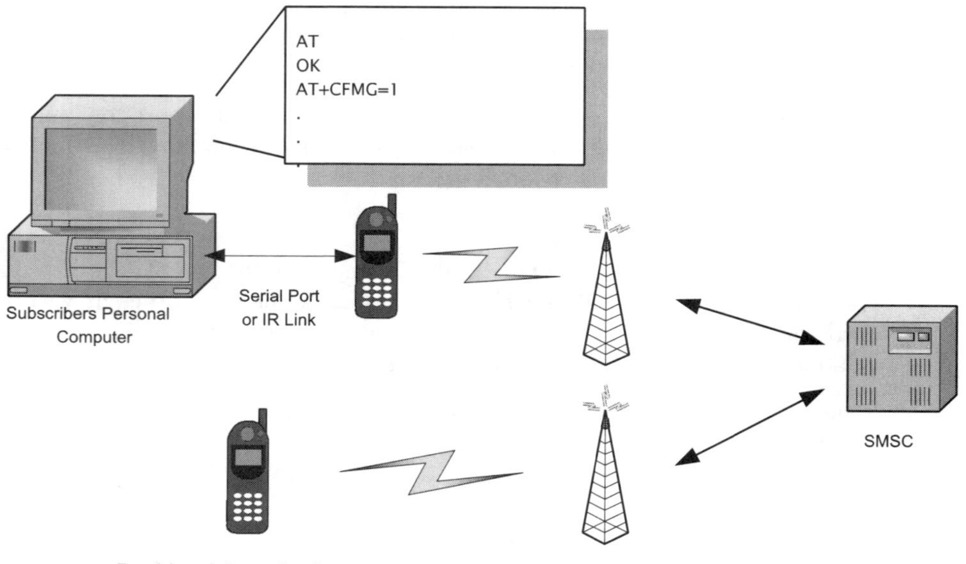

Figure 5.38 Direct dial service.

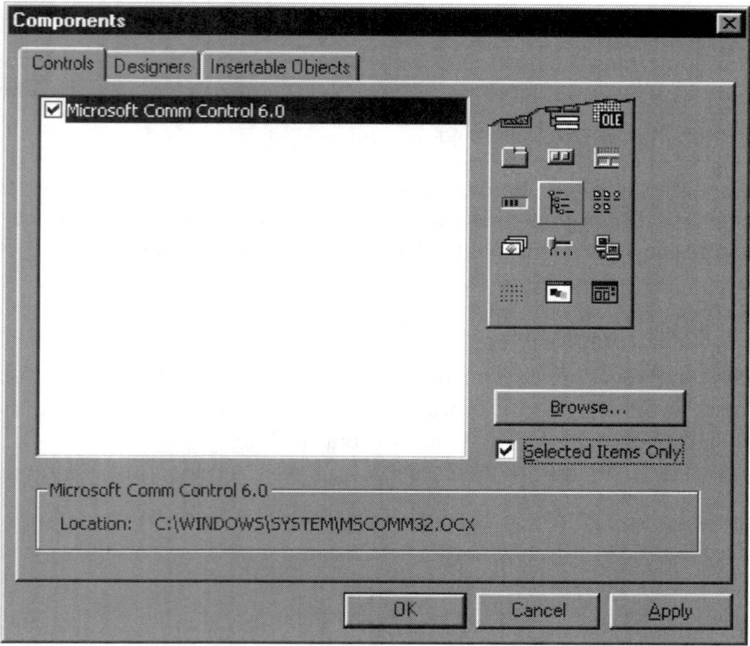

Figure 5.39 Addition of Microsoft's Comm Control Component.

```
1. Private Sub Command1_Click()
2.     On Error GoTo CommError
3.     SMSComm.PortOpen = True
4.     SMSComm.Output = "AT" & Chr(13) & Chr(10)
5.     Text2.Text = Text2.Text & SMSComm.Input & Chr(13) & Chr(10)
6.     SMSComm.Output = "AT+CMGF=1" & Chr(13) & Chr(10)
7.     SMSComm.Output = "AT+CMGS= " & Chr(34) & "+" & Trim(Text3.Text)
          & Chr(34) & ",129" & Chr (13) & Chr(10)
8.     SMSComm.Output = Trim(Text1.Text) & Chr(26)
9.     Text2.Text = Text2.Text & SMSComm.Input & Chr(13) & Chr(10)
10.     SMSComm.PortOpen = False
11.      Exit Sub

12.     CommError:
13.      Text2.Text = Text2.Text & "Comm Error " & CStr(Err) + Chr(13) +
          Chr(10)
14.      Resume Next
15. End Sub

16. Private Sub Command2_Click()
17.     Unload Me
18. End Sub

19. Private Sub Form_Load()
20.     On Error GoTo InitError
21.     SMSComm.CommPort = 2
22.     SMSComm.Settings = "9600,N,8,1"
23.     SMSComm.InputLen = 0
24.    InitError:
25.     Text2.Text = Text2.Text & "Comm Error " & CStr(Err) + Chr(13) +
          Chr(10)
26.      Resume Next
27. End Sub
```

Figure 5.40 Ch05c.vbp program.

Line 8 sets and sends the actual message itself.

Line 9 accepts the response code and sets the window variable to display the result.

The application will produce the window shown in Figure 5.41. Enter the SMS message desired in the Message body area, the receiver's telephone number in the *Send Message to* area and press the Send SMS button. The bottom portion of the window will show the responses from the device, including all the AT commands.

Once again, the telephone number used is fictitious. You'll have to use a real number in your tests.

SMTP

This option was so obvious that it was only a matter of time before the carriers would offer it. The Simple Mail Transport Protocol (SMTP) method of sending SMS-based

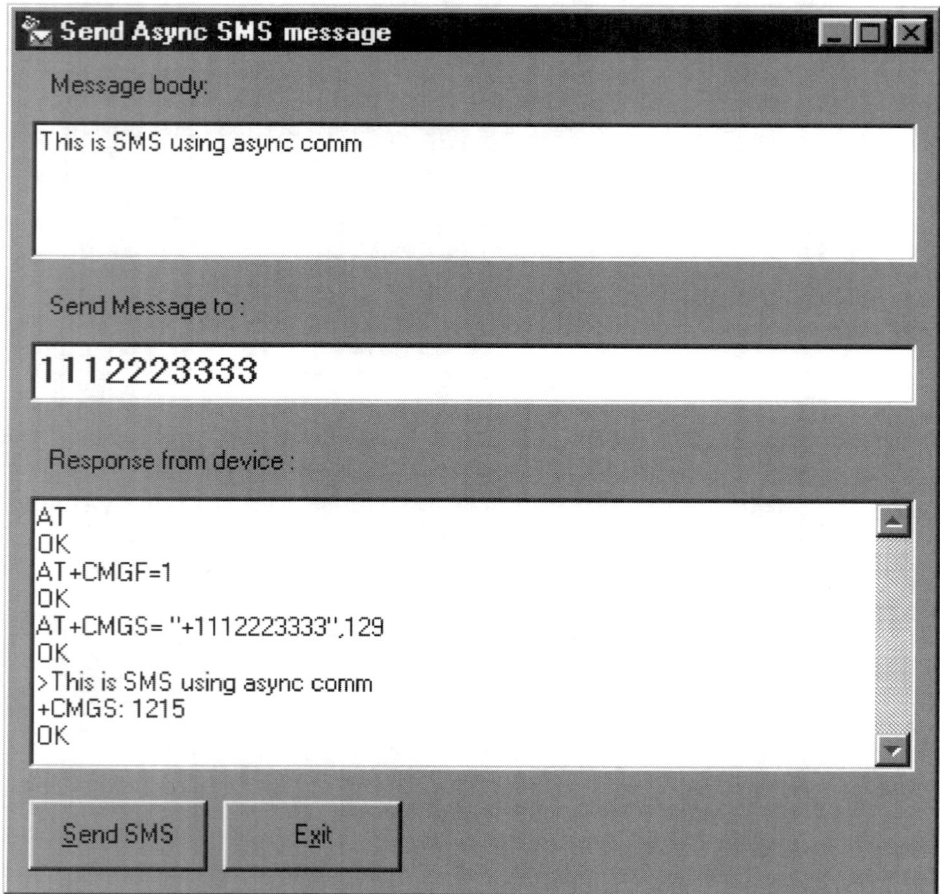

Figure 5.41 Resulting window from program Ch05c.vbp.

messages uses a traditional SMTP gateway. Carriers install, within their facilities, an SMTP gateway that serves as a bridge between the wireless networks and Internet mail systems.

A specific email address is created for each SMS-enabled cell phone using the cell phone's telephone number, for example, 2221113333@mobiledomain.net. To send the person an SMS message, simply send a message to the special email address. The carrier's email server will convert the email address to the proper SMS telephone number of the destination receiver.

```
1.  <% @LANGUAGE="VBSCRIPT" %>
2.  <% Response.Buffer = True %>
3.  <%
4.  Set SMSMail = Server.CreateObject("Perits.MailSender")
5.  SMSMail.Host = "smtp.mobiledomain.net"
6.  SMSMail.IsHTML = False
7.  SMSMail.From ="authors@wavedev.com"
8.  SMSMail.AddAddress = "2221113333@mobiledomain.net"
9.  SMSMail.Subject = "SMS over SMTP!"
10. SMSMail.Body = "It really Works!"
11. SMSMail.Send
12. %>
```

Figure 5.42 Ch05d.vbp program.

Figure 5.42 is a small ASP program that will send a simple message to a subscriber. In this example we use a third-party component called ASPMail from Persits Software (free component).

The program is very straightforward whereby all the email components are set up with the final command on line 11, sending the email as seen earlier in this chapter.

WAP Personalization

All examples presented in this chapter have been developed and tested using Openwave's (Phone.com) WAP toolkit, UP.SDK 4.1, unless stated otherwise. For more information on WAP toolkits, refer to the Development Toolkits (SDK) section in Chapter 1.

Every line of program code in this chapter is numbered for easy reference. Code on the CD is identical but without the numbers, making it easy to simply copy and execute.

This chapter describes WAP personalization. We'll show multiple mini-applications, which all fit together into one large personalized dynamic menu system. We start off by looking at WAP usage on Web phones and how to create personalized individual menus. Then, to bypass constantly logging into the application and having to reenter the userID and password, we introduce cookies and create a special cookie application. To further enhance functionality with personalized menus, we introduce the Pull concept and present how it can be used in direct advertising. As an advanced system, we show an application-created Push system to notify Web phone users of incoming messages (or whatever they choose). As usual, all program code in this chapter are functional and can also be found on the CD that accompanies this book.

Dynamic Personalized Menu

There has definitely been some wonderful new technological advancement in the wireless industry in the past few years that will be the basis of a future wireless society. But the success of the wireless industry will depend on user experience and acceptance. If no one uses or wants to use the service, investors will not fund research ventures or content providers, and this will slow wireless advancements.

Rather than leaving new Web phone users without direction, and to jump-start WAP enthusiasm, carriers have included default WAP menus on all Web phones. By having something to immediately see, touch, and use, people can quickly begin using their new gadgets with minimum confusion, hopefully. Of course, the main reason for purchasing a Web phone is still for its phone abilities, but that will soon change.

As in any competitive business, carriers want people to use their service, manufacturers want the public to buy their Web phones, microbrowser creators want their microbrowsers to become the most popular, and content providers want their content to be first on everyone's minds, especially if it's an m-commerce application. So, carriers and Web phone manufacturers got together and worked out deals where the carrier would market a particular cellular phone from a particular manufacturer. Then manufacturers got together with microbrowser creators and worked out the same type of deal whereby the microbrowser creator would supply their browser technology to the manufacturer for their Web phones. Then, of course, the microbrowser folks hooked up with content providers to supply great WAP sites.

CONTENT PROVIDER NOTE

If you have a great WAP site, do get in touch with the microbrowser creators (Openwave, Nokia, Ericsson, Motorola, and others), because they'd really like to hear from you. Who knows, your site could be the next big hit!

Once all the deals are done, we end up with wireless WAP technology on Web phones with default content already in place. A great start indeed. When NTT DoCoMo's iMode Web phones were released in Japan, everyone hurried to purchase one. The main thrill of these devices, other than a new gadget to play with, was that they were all ready to go. Buy the phone, register for services, and voila—instant new technology at your fingertips (literally) with lots of preset services, games, and many more features all built into the device. Kids loved these new Web phones and would sit side by side and send SMS messages to each other rather than having face-to-face conversations. Isn't it amazing how technology can change our lives so quickly!

This preset menu concept also applies to software development toolkits (SDKs). Many WAP toolkits have preset WAP sites added for developers to review. Since SDKs usually allow the viewing of WML code, having these WAP sites preset in the toolkits allows developers to view existing and functional WAP sites as well as most code behind the scenes, which is a great start for developers. I have many years in the computer industry, mostly all technical with a lot of programming and design knowledge, and if there's one main point I've learned over the years, it is to never reinvent the wheel. If you have a program already developed that can be used as a template for another new program, use it, because it will save a lot of development effort. It's the same idea with the SDK samples: Use them to view the source code and learn how others perform certain programming tricks.

Figure 6.1 shows Openwave's default menu on its SDK. As you can see, this is an excellent starting point for developers. Simply press the F5 key on the phone emulator, and all the code for each window will be displayed in the information window.

The next question is: What should the content provider include in the menus? Or, perhaps from a user's point of view, the next question should be: What do users want on their menus? To answer this, we looked at recent polls and found that most people, in general, want what the applications they already use on their PCs. Users want communications features as in email or games. When stuck in public transportation or while waiting for someone and away from a personal computer, the typical user wants to play quick games. Others, such as business people, want access to financial information such as stock quotes and want the ability to trade stocks. And kids, well, kids just want to have fun and talk with each other about almost anything. As seen in Figure 6.1, Openwave has set up typical general categories such as financial, traffic, travel, weather, sports, and so on from many content providers around the globe to show how these items can be set up and coded.

Carriers, manufacturers, and microbrowser creators are all trying to find that killer application that everyone could and would use regularly. Manufacturers want to have the best darn menu (meaning content) they can to attract customers and to attract carriers to market their devices. This inevitably means revenues and profits. As with anything else, if the group (carriers, manufacturers, and microbrowser creators) has a good following, it then has a captive audience and can profit with advertisements and commercials. This is much like what AOL currently does (and what CompuServe did). Companies provide content, easy access, free software, and whatever they can to attract individuals. Most users don't know the technical details or intricacies of surfing the Web, so companies create the easy user experience by providing easy access and simplicity. Bring up the Web page, click on Start, and off you go with lots of information at your fingertips with no hassles. It's a great idea, and companies like AOL have made a fortune by making the Internet user experience simple and fun. For the more advanced user, there are no boundaries. If users know what they are doing, they can certainly figure out how and where to type in any desired URL address and surf the Net without preset categories. The same process will happen with the wireless mobile industry, giving the individual user a personalized dynamic system that is also open to add any Web site desired.

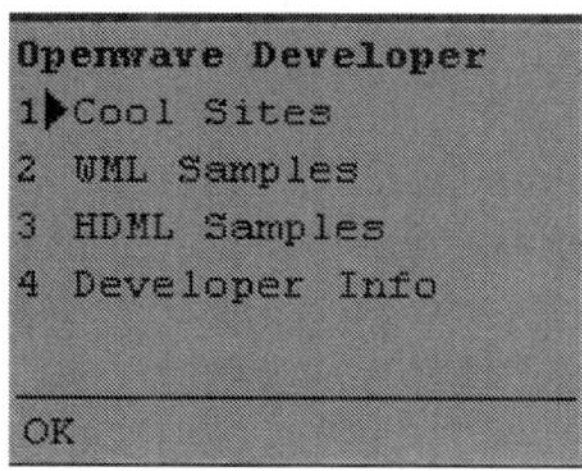

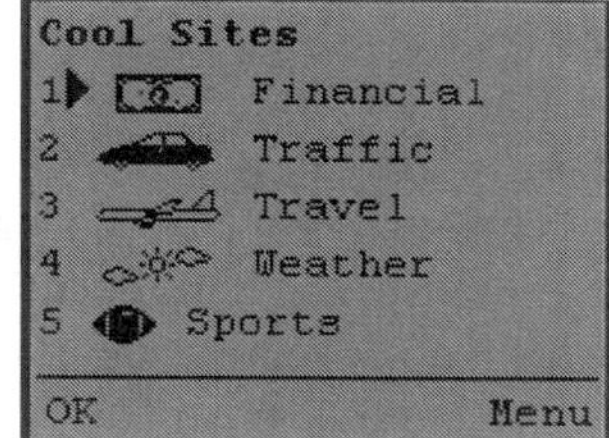

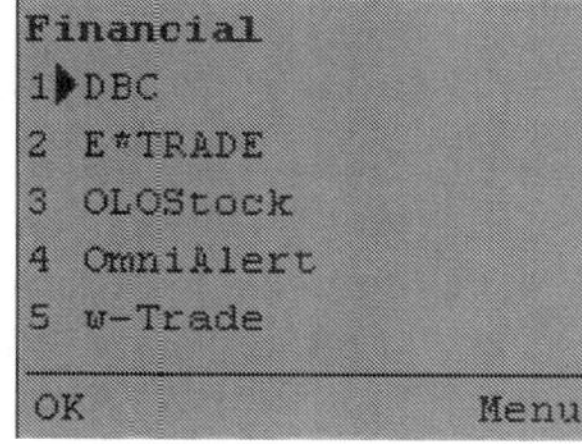

Figure 6.1 WAP menus.

Limitations

What many carriers initially did with Web phones was they created menus but did not allow users to leave the confines of these preset menus. So, similar to AOL on the Web, these carriers decided to preset menu items on the WAP device default menu. This gave the user access to many great sites and topics but really enclosed the user into a sort of walled garden, as they say. You can do whatever you like but only with the information we supply, and there's no way out. What do you think happened? Of course, the industry received complaints from frustrated users who spent lots of hard-earned income on a Web phone and suddenly became aware that they couldn't go to any sites other than the preset sites. The frustrations were heard far and wide.

But there was a reason for this preset limitation other than simply to acquire a captive audience; it was initially to help the individual users avoid manual input. Even though Web access is available from WAP devices, it is quite difficult to browse via current handheld units. The keypads on cellular phones were designed for numeric input. Trying to type a large URL address is very frustrating, and one mistake could drive the user absolutely nutty due to the extra effort needed to correct an error. If you've tried typing a URL on most Web phones, you know that it's difficult and frankly not worth the effort. Surfing the Net for information is fast, simple, and at times fun via a personal computer but not from a Web phone, mostly because of this typing restriction.

Because of these problems and complaints, the industry has realized the importance of providing a simple, comfortable, and low typing interface to the Web from wireless devices, which is called the *Personalized Solution*.

Personalized Solution

To start with, at this early stage in the wireless Internet age, WAP sites have to be designed and written for specific languages and so there are not that many WAP sites out there compared to regular HTML Web sites. Of those that do exist, there are few worth searching. More sites are becoming available, but they usually have quite long URLs since many do not use browser detection or site redirection, as explained in Chapter 5. For these reasons, many portals have emerged whereby individuals can pre-build their personal WAP menus via the Web to be used later on wireless devices.

The idea is that since typing URLs on a Web phone is difficult and surfing the Net via the same type of device is not an easy task, the avid user would create a personalized WAP menu system via the Web from his or her personal computer. The WAP menu application would then be immediately available on the wireless WAP device. The problem with these types of portal sites is that once again the content is limited to specific content provider categories with the end result being a preset menu with little flexibility. Many portals offer this type of service, but they all differ in content, setup, and availability. If you want specific content from one site and some other content from another portal site, it can't be done since each offers its own distinct menus, and they can't be merged.

The concept in general is quite good. Register with a specific Web site via your personal computer and build your own tailored WAP menus as you see fit. The built menu would then be available on the Web phone or wireless device, allowing the user to quickly access the information rather than constantly retyping the URL on the wireless unit. Of course, the Web-side menu creation process would allow the freedom to select from both the content provider's specific URLs and categories as well as allow for free-hand URL additions. In addition, since the users are creating a menu system, users should be allowed to create their own menu titles and create the menu structure in any fashion they desire. Since the menu items can be updated via the regular Web, users have the freedom to select any number of WAP sites, either provided by the Web site or manually entered.

A great addition to this flexibility would be to allow menu creation directly from the wireless device. This would be a great project but, so far, I'm not aware that anyone has successfully achieved this task, but it won't be long before someone does. If the menu could be created via voice recognition commands, the wireless mobile device would be quite the tool. Chapter 7 discusses VoiceXML and voice-enabled applications—perhaps there is a possible business application mix here!

WaveDev offers a completely free open system and was created specifically to solve the preceding menu creation problems. The same URL, http://wavedev.com, is used for both Web and WAP sites since redirection logic has been added to the application, similar to that detailed in Chapter 5. The dynamic personalized menu service is offered free of charge and is very flexible. WaveDev's Do-The-Wave, or DTW, allows the individual to freely add any WAP URL they wish to their menus, choose from a list of existing WAP URLs, pick any menu name they fancy, and organize their own menu structures in any manner desired. The entire concept was built on Window's file manager (now called Explorer), which allows files within directories, directories within directories, renaming, deleting, moving directories to any level of any other directory, and so on.

Figure 6.2 shows WaveDev's DTW menu creation page on the Web side; the resulting WAP menu on the WAP side is shown in Figure 6.3.

Figure 6.2 shows the menu creation screen on the Web side. All menus in this application on the Web side appear in blue, and on the WAP side, the menus are preceded by a plus sign as seen in Figure 6.3. Menu names can be whatever the user desires, and any menu can be moved to any place in the structure even beneath or above another menu. Specific WAP sites are the individual items, nonblue entries in the application, and can be added at any menu level. Item 5 in Figure 6.2 is an item having the description WorldJobMart (not seen in the WAP menu in Figure 6.3 because of screen size constraints).

Once entered on the Web side, the entire setup is immediately available on the WAP side, since all entries are stored in a back-end database. Each screen on the WAP side is dynamically generated with values retrieved from the back-end database, hence making the application available instantaneously. Dynamic WAP is fully explained in Chapter 4, so we'll leave the general dynamic retrieval details to that chapter.

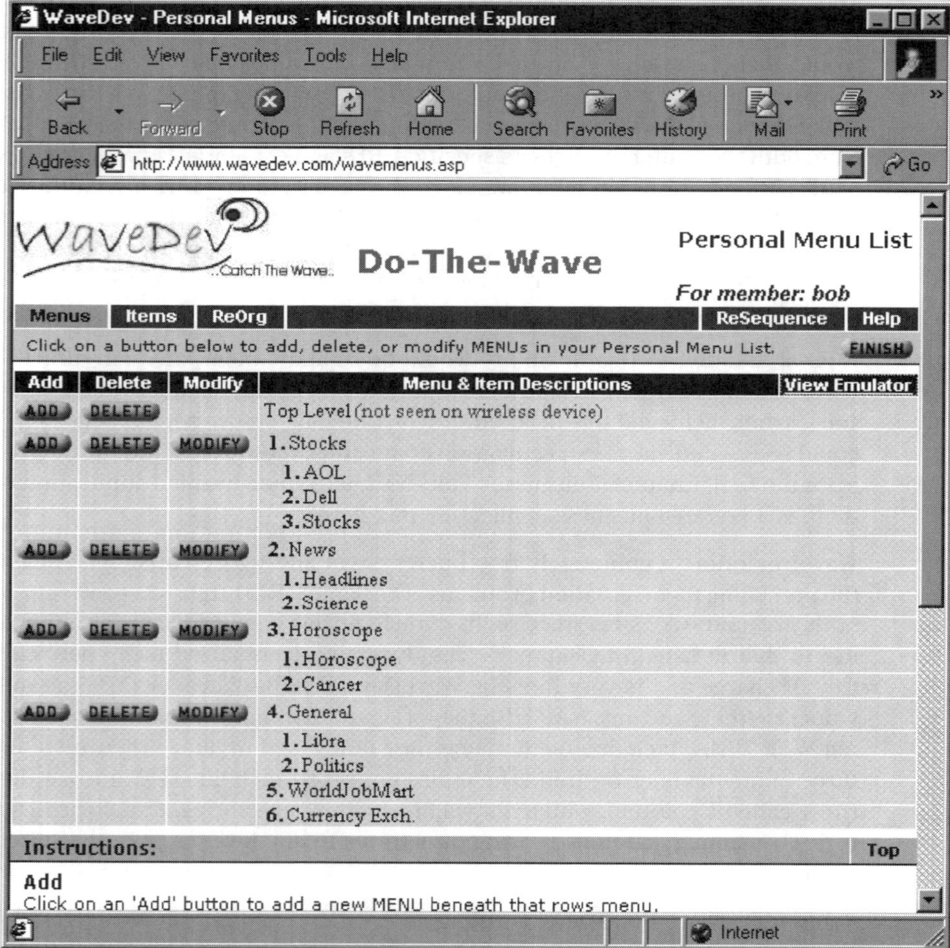

Figure 6.2 Web side, dynamic personalized menu.

Benefits

The best type of dynamic WAP application is one where everybody can benefit. WaveDev allows both the end users and content providers to register free of charge. We already mentioned the benefits to the individual users, which is the ability to create their own WAP menus by selecting from either a list of preset WAP sites or by adding their own WAP URLs themselves. Content providers also benefit because they can register their WAP sites (URL and description) in WaveDev and categorize it accordingly. This allows the individuals to easily find the content they wish when building their personalized menu system.

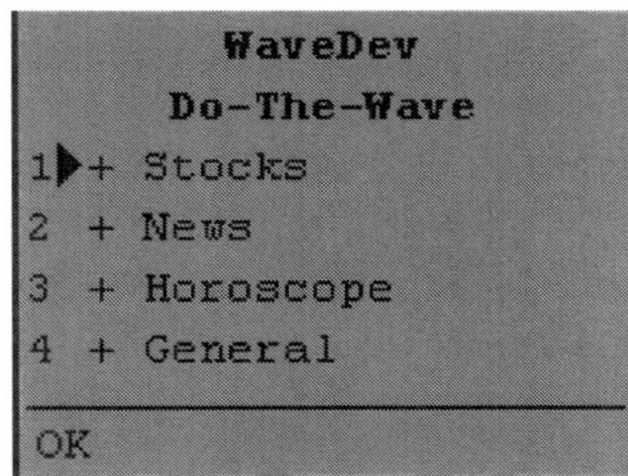

Figure 6.3 WAP side, dynamic personalized menu.

As mentioned, another great feature is the ability to reorganize the menu structure as desired. No longer is an individual forced to use a content provider's specific menu layout. If the person wants a menu called Stocks as the first entry on the first menu level, so be it. If a user desires a special work-related topic as the second entry, again he or she can easily do that. Flexibility was and will remain the primary focus behind the creation of WaveDev's Do-The-Wave service.

The industry and WaveDev are still fairly new, but both are advancing nicely. As a free system, one cannot complain, yet efforts are under way to improve the application on both the Web and WAP sides. Push and Pull applications are being created whereby the individual can select scheduled or parameter-based Push applications as a regular feature on the site. If you want to be notified at a certain time, simply select the feature, enter the parameter, and a notification will be sent to your Web phone at the desired time. Isn't technology wonderful!

Example—Dynamic Personalized Menu Paging

Keeping with our main goal of having a personalized WAP menu system, one of our top priorities is to generate and maintain a certain level of simplicity in building the dynamic application and in using the application once built. Since most Web phones have only 10 keys and since items on the screen display can be invoked with the touch of one of these keys, it's good practice to code no more than nine items in a selection menu. This allows for the user to press any key from 1 to 9 to invoke the numbered menu items. The tenth key, being 0, is not usually used as a standard in the industry as a whole. But give the 0 button a try; sometimes it maps to the tenth item and it's a lot quicker to use than scrolling to the bottom of the current page. Having only nine items on a menu requires some sort of paging logic. If more items exist on any particular menu level, simply page to the next screen to view the remaining items.

Let's have a look at an entire working dynamic personalized menu application with full paging back and forth as well as up one full level. Figure 6.4 shows a typical menu in two screens since the SDK being used only shows a certain number of lines per screen.

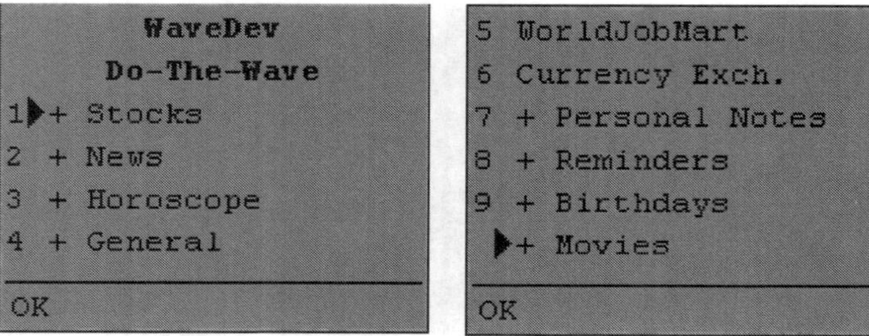

Figure 6.4 Personal dynamic menu before paging.

Both screens are considered to be the same menu level since scrolling down from the first screen shows the remaining entries on the same level. Notice the tenth item, Movies, has no associated number on its left. This is because it is past the ninth menu entry. This menu item should really be on another page as seen in the third frame of Figure 6.5.

Figure 6.5 is the result of a proper paging menu application. Frame 2 shows the tenth entry as More.., which replaces the prior Movies entry. When the user invokes the More.. option, a third window now appears as seen in the third frame. Here Movies is on its own page and another item, Back.., is created to navigate backward to the second frame, if desired.

In our example, we require a database to hold the dynamic entries. For this we've created a database called Paging.mdb (an Access database), which has only one table called MenuTable. The table is very simple and is defined in Figure 6.6.

Imagine that we've already visited a Web application similar to WaveDev's DTW, and have already created all our menu items. Figure 6.7 shows all the entries in the database MenuTable table, which parallels our resulting WAP screen shots in Figure 6.5. Even though we haven't shown all the lower menu levels in Figure 6.5, you can see from the entries in the database that more do exist (Figure 6.7 items with IDs of 11, 12, and 13). The first menu item, Stocks, has two entries itself (ID=11—AOL and ID=12—Tech submenu). Submenu item 12 (ID=12) is itself a menu which has its own entry called Blue

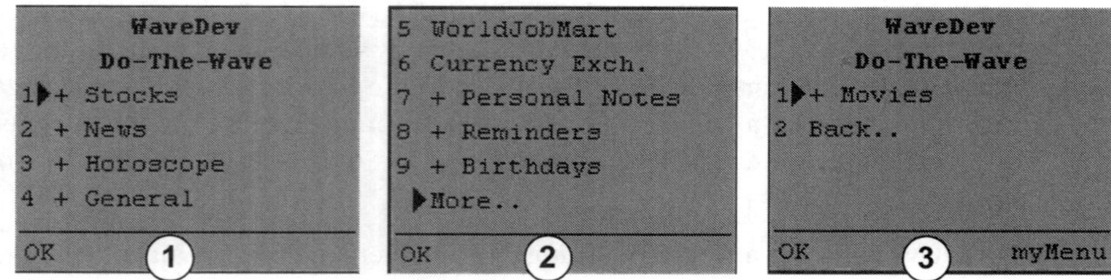

Figure 6.5 Personal dynamic menu with paging.

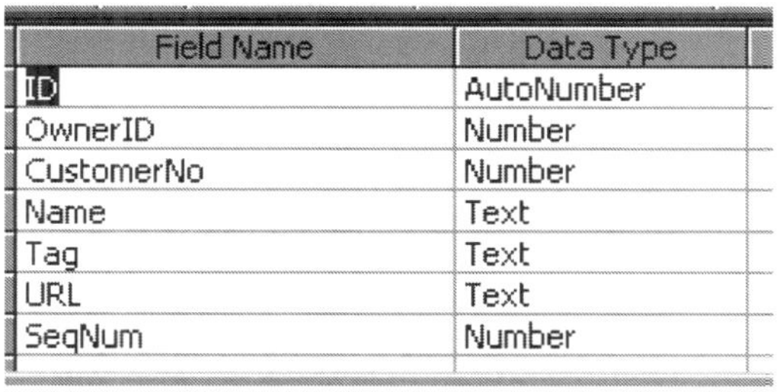

Field Name	Data Type
ID	AutoNumber
OwnerID	Number
CustomerNo	Number
Name	Text
Tag	Text
URL	Text
SeqNum	Number

Figure 6.6 Paging.mdb table layout.

Chips (ID=13). You can see how this can be quite flexible and is easily customizable by the specific user.

Having a menu within a menu within a menu, and so on, requires unique logic. We've achieved this by simply creating a secondary column in the table called OwnerID. See Figure 6.7. This is step-referencing architecture that allows any item to contain the ID of its parent item. Top menu level entries have a zero OwnerID since there is no owner to the top level. Items within a submenu have the ID value of its parent menu in the OwnerID column, and so on. This allows for a simple mul-

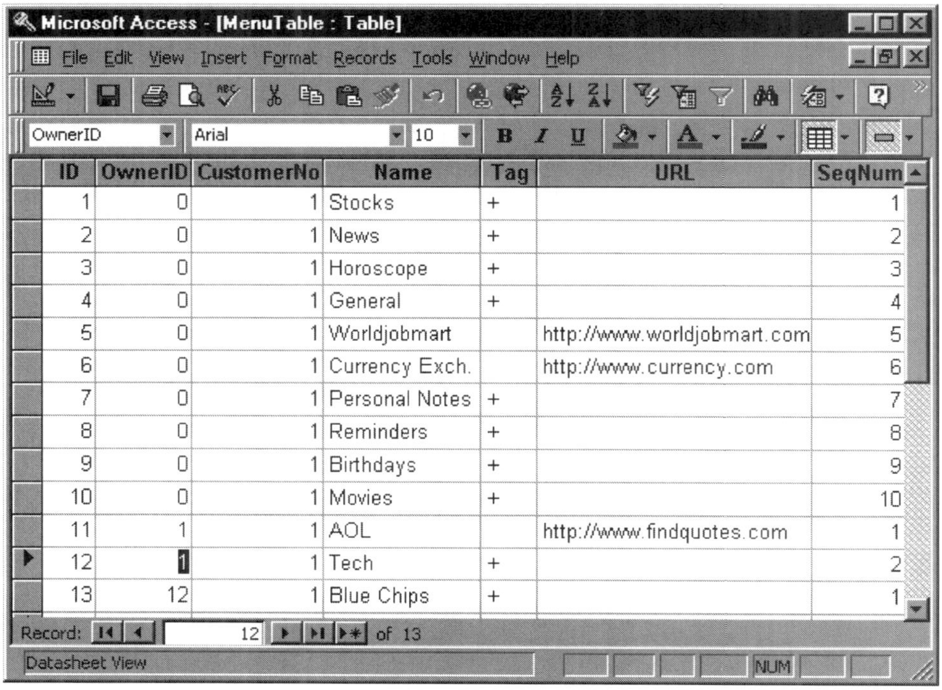

ID	OwnerID	CustomerNo	Name	Tag	URL	SeqNum
1	0	1	Stocks	+		1
2	0	1	News	+		2
3	0	1	Horoscope	+		3
4	0	1	General	+		4
5	0	1	Worldjobmart		http://www.worldjobmart.com	5
6	0	1	Currency Exch.		http://www.currency.com	6
7	0	1	Personal Notes	+		7
8	0	1	Reminders	+		8
9	0	1	Birthdays	+		9
10	0	1	Movies	+		10
11	1	1	AOL		http://www.findquotes.com	1
12	1	1	Tech	+		2
13	12	1	Blue Chips	+		1

Record: 12 of 13

Figure 6.7 Paging.mdb database.

tiple menu level design and for the application to easily move up and down different levels.

Another added feature is the ability to reorganize the menus and especially items within a menu level. This is easily achieved with the addition of another column called SeqNum, which allows the ordering of all items within each menu level.

From a technical point of view, having a proper paging system reduces the burden on the network and database since the application only retrieves one menu level at a time, thus making the database query very efficient. Since only small amounts of data are retrieved, minimum traffic exists and the network will not be overly congested, especially if the site becomes popular.

Our main program in this example, DTW.asp, does 99 percent of the work. It retrieves the required menu items from the back-end database and formats the output with added navigational features. It consists of an ASP program with VBScript additions. The second program, DTWUpOneLevel.asp, gives the application the ability to jump up one menu level making the system's functionality very user friendly.

We recommend having a security front end whereby the user signs in to the WAP application. Then IIS could maintain an ASP session with the member's customer number for the duration of the session. The next section in this chapter discusses the use of cookies for just this purpose. For this stage, the example application is completely functional as is with the inclusion of the customer number as part of the invoking URL as seen in Figure 6.8. Simply copy the programs to your Web site and change the www.wavedev.com to your personal site name. The rest of the URL should remain as is.

Let's begin a detailed look at the main DTW.asp program, as shown in Figure 6.9. This program builds the entire dynamic personalized WML menu system based on data within the back-end database. It is very important to ensure the database entries are properly created or this program will not function correctly. Many programming specifics have already been described in previous chapters and hence will not need to be explained here.

Line 1 sets up the VBScript language.

Line 2 states that output is to be buffered before being sent to the device.

Line 3 expires all code in cache after it has been written.

Lines 6 through 13 determine the relative physical path to the database directory from the current directory.

```
http://www.wavedev.com/dtw.asp?txtCustNo=1&txtOwnerID=0
```

Figure 6.8 Invoking code.

```
 1. <% @LANGUAGE="VBSCRIPT" %>
 2. <% Response.Buffer = True %>
 3. <% Response.Expires = 0 %>
 4. <%
 5. '---- Open DSNless connection to database
 6. DB    = "database/Paging.mdb"
 7. Dir   = Request.ServerVariables("SCRIPT_NAME")
 8. Dir   = StrReverse(Dir)
 9. Dir   = Mid(Dir, InStr(1, Dir, "/"))
10. Dir   = StrReverse(Dir)
11. Path = Server.MapPath(Dir) & "\"
12. file = "database/Paging.dsn"
13. DSNa = "filedsn=" & Path & file & ";DefaultDir=" & Path & ";DBQ="
    & Path & DB & ";"

14. dim Conn, RS, sql
15. dim strOwnerID, strOwnerMenu, strCustNo
16. dim NumRowsPerPage, ScrollAction, PageNo, strNoRows

17. if request("txtOwnerID")="" then
18.    strOwnerID=0
19. else
20.    strOwnerID= request("txtOwnerID")
21. end if
22. strCustNo= request("txtCustNo")

23. Set Conn = Server.CreateObject("ADODB.Connection")
24. Set RS   = Server.CreateObject("ADODB.RecordSet")
25. Conn.Open DSNa
26. sql = "select id,ownerid,customerno,name,tag,url,seqnum from
    MenuTable where customerno="& strCustNo &" and ownerid="&
    strOwnerID &" order by seqnum"
27. RS.Open sql, Conn, 1,1

28. strNoRows="N"
29. if RS.EOF or RS.BOF then
30.   strNoRows="Y"
31. else
32.   NumRowsPerPage=9
33.   RS.PageSize= NumRowsPerPage
34.
35.   if request("PgNo")="" then
36.        ScrollAction=0
37. else
38.        ScrollAction=Cint(Request.QueryString("PgNo"))  '--
           Read in page number.
39. end if
```

Figure 6.9 DTW.asp paging program.

```
40. if ScrollAction < 1 then
41.     PageNo=1
42. elseif ScrollAction > RS.PageCount then
43.     PageNo=1
44. else
45.     PageNo=ScrollAction
46. end if
47. RS.AbsolutePage=PageNo   '-- Set current page number
48. end if

49. response.Buffer = TRUE
50. response.ContentType = "text/vnd.wap.wml"
51. response.write "<?xml version="+chr(34)+"1.0"+chr(34)+"?>"
52. response.write "<!DOCTYPE wml PUBLIC "+chr(34)+"-//PHONE.COM//DTD
    WML 1.1//EN"+chr(34)+"
    "+chr(34)+"http://www.phone.com/dtd/wml11.dtd"+chr(34)+">"
53. response.write "<wml>"
54. response.write "<card id="+chr(34)+"card1"+chr(34)+">"

55. if strNoRows="Y" and strOwnerID=0 then
56.   response.write "<do type="+chr(34)+"accept"+chr(34)+"
      label="+chr(34)+"Home"+chr(34)+">"
57.   response.write "<go
      href="+chr(34)+"../mainmenu.wml"+chr(34)+"/>"
58.   response.write "</do>"
59.   response.write "<p mode="+chr(34)+"nowrap"+chr(34)+">"
60.   response.write "<b><br/>Not Available</b>"
61. else
62.   response.write "<do type="+chr(34)+"accept"+chr(34)+"
      label="+chr(34)+"OK"+chr(34)+">"
63.   response.write "<prev/>"
64.   response.write "</do>"
65.   if strOwnerID <> 0 then
66.       if strNoRows="N" then
67.         response.write "<do
            type="+chr(34)+"accept"+chr(34)+"
            label="+chr(34)+"Level Up"+chr(34)+">"
68.         response.write "<go
            href="+chr(34)+"DTWUpOneLevel.asp?txtCustNo="&
            strCustNo &"&amp;txtID="& strOwnerID +chr(34)+"/>"
69.         response.write "</do>"
70.   else
71.       '-- Empty menu page
72.         response.write "<do type="+chr(34)+"accept"+chr(34)+"
            label="+chr(34)+"Back"+chr(34)+">"
73.         response.write "<prev/>"
74.         response.write "</do>"
```

Figure 6.9 Continued DTW.asp paging program.

```
75.  end if
76.  end if
77.  if not (strOwnerID=0 and PageNo=1) then
78.      response.write "<do type="+chr(34)+"accept"+chr(34)+"
         label="+chr(34)+"myMenu"+chr(34)+">"
79.      response.write "<go
         href="+chr(34)+"DTW.asp?txtCustNo="& strCustNo
         &"&amp;txtOwnerID=0&amp;txtOwnerMenu=&amp;PgNo="+chr(34)+"/>"
80.      response.write "</do>"
81. end if
82. response.write "<p align="+chr(34)+"center"+chr(34)+">"
83. if request("txtOwnerMenu")="" then
84.     strOwnerMenu=""
85.     response.write "<b>WaveDev<br/>Do-The-Wave</b>"
86. else
87.     strOwnerMenu= request("txtOwnerMenu")
88.     response.write "<b>WaveDev<br/>" & strOwnerMenu & "</b>"
89. end if

90. if strNoRows="N" then
91.     response.write "</p><p align="+chr(34)+"left"+chr(34)+"
        mode="+chr(34)+"nowrap"+chr(34)+">"
92.     response.write "<select>"
93.     MaxNum = 1
94.     do while MaxNum < NumRowsPerPage+1
95.     if RS(4) = "+" then
96.         '-- this is a menu
97.         response.write "<option onpick="&
            chr(34) &"DTW.asp?txtCustNo="& strCustNo
            &"&amp;txtOwnerID="& RS("ID")
            &"&amp;txtOwnerMenu="& RS(3) &"&amp;PgNo=1"&
            chr(34) &">+ "& RS(3) &"</option>"
98.       else
99.           '--no parm, so just show wapurl
100.          response.write "<option
              onpick="+chr(34) & RS(5) & chr(34) &">  "& RS(3)
              &"</option>"
101.      end if
102.      RS.MoveNext
103.      if RS.EOF then
104.          exit do
105.      end if
106.      MaxNum = MaxNum + 1
107.   loop
108.   if MaxNum = NumRowsPerPage+1   then
109.         '-- More rows ahead
110.          response.write "<option
```

Figure 6.9 Continued　DTW.asp paging program.

```
                      onpick="+chr(34)+"dtw.asp?txtCustNo="& strCustNo
                      &"&amp;txtOwnerID="& strOwnerID
                      &"&amp;txtOwnerMenu="& strOwnerMenu &"&amp;PgNo="&
                      PageNo+1 & chr(34)+"> More..</option>"
111.    end if
112.    if PageNo > 1  then
113.          '-- More rows behind
114.          response.write "<option
                      onpick="+chr(34)+"dtw.asp?txtCustNo="& strCustNo
                      &"&amp;txtOwnerID="& strOwnerID
                      &"&amp;txtOwnerMenu="& strOwnerMenu &"&amp;PgNo="&
                      PageNo-1 & chr(34)+"> Back..</option>"
115.    end if
116.    response.write "</select>"
117. else
118.        response.write "</p><p align="+chr(34)+"center"+chr(34)+">"
119.        response.write "<br/>Empty Menu"
120.   end if
121. end if

122. response.write "</p></card></wml>"
123. Conn.Close
124. set RS = nothing
125. set Conn = nothing
126. %>
```

Figure 6.9 Continued DTW.asp paging program.

Certain line explanations are skipped in hopes that you, the reader, are already familiar with the basics.

The following if statement is important since it determines the ownerid being passed to the program as a parameter in the URL address. This will determine which menu level to retrieve from the database and hence determines our navigational requirements.

Lines 23 through 27 are the database connectivity and query execution statements. As you can see, the SQL statement uses the customerno and ownerid parameters and orders the results using the seqnum column.

If there are many rows in the queries result set, lines 32 through 47 will set the number of rows per page, normally set to nine, and using another passed parameter, will set the page number. RS.Absolute is basically a window on the result set based on the number of rows per page. If there are 90 rows in the result set, and the rows per page are nine, then there are ten pages. Paging logic will allow the user to page from the first to the tenth (in this case).

Line 49, response.Buffer = TRUE, once again buffers all output before sending everything at once to the output device.

Line 50, response.ContentType = "text/vnd.wap.wml", sets the MIME type. Refer to Chapter 1 for more information on MIME types.

Lines 51 through 54 set up the initial WML deck tags.

Lines 56 through 60 are invoked if there are no menu items for the very first menu. This may never happen, but code is required as a fail-safe.

The first thing to do in the WML coding is to set up the option Softkeys. Of course, the first is option is OK, which is set to <prev/>.

Next, if we're not on the first menu level, and there are menu entries, we set up the Level Up feature. This allows the user to jump up one menu level. If there are no menu items and we are not on the first menu level, then a simple Back feature is created instead of the Level Up feature.

Line 68 is the Level Up feature call itself. Here the DTWUpOneLevel.asp program is called with customer number and the ID of the current menu's parent item. This will allow us to easily jump up to the parent menu.

Lines 77 through 81 are specially coded to quickly allow the users to jump back to their initial personalized menu. If the user is not on the first page of the first menu level, this navigational feature will show up. Basically, we just reinvoke the main program for this customer number using a 0 ownerid, which represents the top menu level.

Lines 83 to 89 are the if statement that sets up a title on the screen. If the user is on the initial top menu level, Do-The-Wave will appear after the WaveDev name. If the user is on any other menu level, that menu's name will appear as the menu title again after the WaveDev name. This creates a very user-friendly application by letting the user know which menu he or she is on.

Now we begin to fill the screen with menu items. If there are no menu items, we simply send a message, Empty Menu, to be displayed. If entries do exist, we loop through them one by one, placing a plus sign before submenu items. The looping logic is dependent on the number of rows per page specified earlier on line 32. For nonmenu entries, we simply create an underlying link to the WAP URL and show that site's title on the WAP device as the menu item. Once the corresponding button is pressed, control is passed to that underlying URL. For submenus, we simply create a URL to reinvoke the dtw.asp program with all the required parameters.

Lines 108 to 111 will produce the forward paging feature. This section of code will produce another menu entry on the screen called More... Rather than having all menu items on the menu, this feature will allow the user to page to the next screen of menu items for the same menu level. Notice the PageNo is simply increased by 1.

Lines 112 to 115 produce the backward paging feature. This bit of code creates the Back.. menu item. It allows the user to page to the prior page in the result set where each page has as many items on it as defined by line 32, NumRowsPerPage.

The rest of the program is code to close all open WML tags and to close the database connection before the program ends.

That's it. There's not much to the program, and it can be altered based on the database table column definitions, rows per page requirements, and so on.

The program in Figure 6.10 is used to jump up one menu level. If the next higher menu is the top menu level, the program will take this into consideration. The only tricky part in this program is that in jumping to a higher menu level, the higher menu level's parent menu must be accessed to determine the menu title on the higher menu.

If the txtID parameter is equal to 0 (line 17 and 18), meaning the higher menu is the top menu, line 35 is invoked with a txtOwnerID parameter set to 0.

If not, lines 19 to 33 are executed. First the database is connected to and a query is run to obtain the parent menu's name and its parent ID value. If the grandparent's ID is 0, meaning it is the top menu level, then we simply set the OwnerID to 0 as seen on line 24. If not, then we obtain that grandparent's menu title via lines 26 through 29.

Then the database connection is closed, and the program ends.

Now we have a working dynamic personalized menu level application with full navigation.

Future

Currently, the WAP world has many languages and therefore many incompatibilities among WAP sites and devices. We anticipate a general standardization of WAP languages in the future, but for now WAP sites are very much incompatible at times. Users should take caution in building a personalized menu and choose only sites that will function on their particular device. There is nothing more frustrating than creating a great menu with the anticipation of sites delivering wonderful information only to discover that the site only functions on a particular device, for example, HDML devices.

WaveDev has plans for just this scenario and more. In the future, upon registration, users will specify their exact device model and only sites that are viewable on that device's microbrowser will appear for selection on the Web side. This method will guarantee that any site choices will function on their specific wireless device.

Another advancement will be the ability to register, create, and update the dynamic WAP menu from the WAP device. To avoid the tedious task of manually typing a URL, the application will offer multiple select types, category-based sites, browser-based sites (for instances when the browser has been upgraded), and the basic manual entry option. This will create a well-rounded application from the Web and to the WAP points of view.

Cookies

Without cookies, every time a user returns to a Web or WAP site requiring a sign-on, he or she must reenter a userID and password information. This is quite a pain, especially

```
 1. <% @LANGUAGE="VBSCRIPT" %>
 2. <% Response.Buffer = True %>
 3. <% Response.Expires = 0 %>
 4. <%
 5. '---- Open DSNless connection to database
 6. DB      = "database/Paging.mdb"
 7. Dir     = Request.ServerVariables("SCRIPT_NAME")
 8. Dir     = StrReverse(Dir)
 9. Dir     = Mid(Dir, InStr(1, Dir, "/"))
10. Dir     = StrReverse(Dir)
11. Path = Server.MapPath(Dir) & "\"
12. file = "database/Paging.dsn"
13. DSNa = "filedsn=" & Path & file & ";DefaultDir=" & Path & ";DBQ="
     & Path & DB & ";"
14. dim Conn, RS, sql
15. dim strCustNo, strID
16. strCustNo=request("txtCustNo")
17. strID=request("txtID")
18. if strID > "0" then
19.     Set Conn = Server.CreateObject("ADODB.Connection")
20.     Conn.Open DSNa
21.     sql = "select ownerid,name from menutable where customerno="&
        strCustNo &" and id="& strID
22.     set RS = Conn.Execute(sql)
23.     if RS(0)=0 then
24.       response.redirect
          ("http://www.wavedev.com/dtw.asp?txtCustNo="& strCustNo
          &"&txtOwnerID=0&txtOwnerMenu=")
25.     else
26.       strOwnerID=RS(0)
27.       sql = "select name from menutable where customerno="&
          strCustNo &" and id="& strOwnerID
28.       set RS = Conn.Execute(sql)
29.       response.redirect
          ("http://www.wavedev.com/dtw.asp?txtCustNo="& strCustNo
          &"&txtOwnerID="& strOwnerID &"&txtOwnerMenu="& RS(0))
30.     end if
31.     Conn.Close
32.     set RS = nothing
33.     set Conn = nothing
34. else
35.     response.redirect ("http://www.wavedev.com/dtw.asp?txtCustNo="&
        strCustNo &"&txtOwnerID=0&txtOwnerMenu=")
36. end if
37. %>
```

Figure 6.10 DTWUpOneLevel.asp program.

if the user selected a lengthy userID or password and especially if input is via a cellular phone. To avoid this hassle, the application can use cookies, which would maintain the userID and password information over time over many sessions.

Unfortunately, in the wireless world, cookies are not generally supported in anything less than WAP version 1.2, which is not generally supported. Until it is, we're stuck with ASP session variables. These are similar to cookies but only last for the duration of the current application session. An exception to the WAP 1.2 rule is Openwave's (and Infinite WAP server's) ability to accept cookies via their gateway server (Cookie Proxy on WAP gateway). Openwave's gateway (Up.Link Server) and their SDK both store persistent cookies. The SDK manages cookies in HTTP direct mode and stores them in a CookieCache file on the developer's computer. When in Up.Link mode, the server completely manages the cookie, and they are never delivered to the SDK on the user's PC.

An enhancement to our dynamic personalized menu application would be to add a security sign-in feature. It would be great if the member could sign in once and every time he or she revisited the site, be it the same day or a week later, the system would remember and automatically bypass the sign-in process. This is essentially what can be accomplished with cookies. Unfortunately, cookies are not 100 percent available in the WAP world. We could use a regular ASP session, but this is temporary and only lasts for as long as the user is logged in. The next visit would still require a completely new sign-in again.

For our dynamic menu application, we'll assume everyone is accessing the application via an Openwave Up.Browser microbrowser and therefore can use cookies. This will make our application very user friendly and efficient.

What Are Cookies?

Before we continue, let's have a closer look at cookies themselves. Without getting too technical, *cookies* are used to temporarily hold variables across application sessions. *Temporary* means that the variables are available throughout the current session up until the session ends, at the least, and up to a predefined date set on the server, which is somewhere in the year 2038 (but don't quote me here).

The individual cookie is a small piece of information sent to a browser by the WWW server and therefore is available to the application. Cookies have primarily two main components: a variable name and its value. Any name and value can be used, for example, CustNo=123. Cookies can also have other qualifiers such as expire date, if it's secure or not, a path name, and domain name. Programs can set as many cookies as desired. Cookies are part of the HTTP Cookie collection (Active Server Pages term) and are usually set via the <META> tag definition:

```
<META HTTP-EQUIV="Set-Cookie" Content="...">
```

There are other methods of creating cookies as we'll see later on. Cookies were initially designed for use with Web browsers such as Netscape and Microsoft Internet Explorer and have the following basic syntax:

```
Set-Cookie: NAME=VALUE; expires=DATE; path=PATH; domain=DOMAIN_NAME;
secure
```

NAME=VALUE

- Name and value are the only required attributes. The name refers to a variable name and the value is that of the variable. These are basically character value strings with the exception of comma, semicolon, and a blank space. An application would refer to the cookie name to obtain its value, for example, CustNo=123.

expires=*DATE*

- Expires is an optional attribute.
- The date has specific limitations with the earliest date allowed being some date early last century. Its upper limit is somewhere in the year 2038.
- If this option is not set or set for the current date, the cookie expires when the user's session terminates. If the date is set in the past, the cookie expires immediately. To remove an existing cookie, simply modify its expires date to be in the past.
- The format for this attribute is in GMT format: Wdy, DD-Mon-YYYY HH:MM:SS GMT.

path=*PATH*

- Path is also an optional attribute.
- It specifies the part of the URL of the domain attribute for which the cookie is valid.
- Default value is the same path as the document for which the Set-Cookie header has been delivered.

domain=DOMAIN_NAME

- Domain is another optional attribute.
- Domain is used to validate the cookie being used with a given domain name.
- Default value is the host name of the server that sent the Set-Cookie HTTP header. Some specific rules do apply for the matching pattern. For example, the domain name will require two periods if it ends with one of the following: COM, EDU, NET, ORG, GOV, MIL, or INT. Any other case will require three periods.

secure

- Secure is another optional attribute.
- Default value for this attribute is not secured, which allows the cookie to be sent as clear unencrypted text over an unsecured connection. If it is marked as secure, the cookie is still sent unencrypted but only over a secure HTPS (SSL) session connection.
- This is a Boolean variable. Its presence signifies a true or on value. If it does not appear, the option defaults to false.

Limitations

Consider the following limitations before sending cookies to the client browsers:

- Cookie size cannot be larger than 4K.
- The Set-Cookie response header should never be cached (some proxy servers do this).
- Multiple Set-Cookie headers can be issued in a single server response.

Cookie Samples

Cookies are sent to the requesting user's browser in the form of an HTTP header. There are two basic types of cookies: Persistent and Temporary (also known as a *session cookie*).

Following is an example of a session cookie. These are the basis to Microsoft's ASP Session command. Notice that the Date and Expires fields below are identical, which means the cookie will expire as soon as the application session ends (manually or via timeout).

```
HTTP/1.1 200 OK
Server: Microsoft-IIS/5.0
Date: Mon, 21 Jul 2001 20:00:00 GMT
Content-Length: 2048
Content-Type: text/html
Expires: Mon, 21 Jul 2001 20:00:00 GMT
Set-Cookie: ASPSESSIONIDQQASDWER=TYRFEDFVVVBGHJKKHTYGCFFD; path=/
Cache-control: private
```

The next example shows a persistent manually created HTTP header cookie example on the client side. Notice in this example that the Date and Expires fields are different. This cookie expires one week in the future according to the date specified in Expires. This particular cookie has a variable called BOOK_NAME , which has a value of WIRELESS.

```
HTTP/1.1 200 OK
Server: Microsoft-IIS/5.0
```

```
Date: Mon, 21 Jul 2001 20:00:00 GMT
Content-Length: 2048
Content-Type: text/html
Expires: Mon, 28 Jul 2001 20:00:00 GMT
Set-Cookie: BOOK_NAME=WIRELESS; path=/
Cache-control: private
```

Cookies can be used for a variety of reasons, such as maintaining variables across application sessions spanning days, weeks, or longer. They can also be used strategically in applications as bookmarks. Since cookies can be retrieved and read, an entire bookmarking application could be created giving the user a very flexible system.

Baking Cookies

Creating a cookie has been coined *Baking Cookies*. Each programming language has its own method of generating, updating, and removing cookies. The following shows three basic methods: ASP, Perl, and JavaScript.

ASP

To create, modify, or delete a cookie, use the Response.Cookies. To read cookies, use the Request.Cookies command.

Response.Cookies

If the cookie exists for the given domain, then doing a Response.Cookies for any variable will result in the modification of the existing cookie. If the cookie does not exist, it will be created.

Response.Cookies(Name){(Key)|.Attribute]=Value

```
<%
Response.Cookies("myCookie")("BOOK_NAME") = "WIRELESS"
Response.Cookies("myCookie")("Authors") =
"RobertLaberge/SrdjanVujosevic"
%>
```

To delete a cookie simply set the Expires attribute to a date in the past:

```
<%
Response.Cookies("myCookie").expires = #01/01/1999#
%>
```

Request.Cookies

This ASP method will allow access to the values stored in the cookie. There is only one required attribute and that's the cookie name. Note that a cookie can only be retrieved from the domain on which it was created.

Request.Cookies(Name){(Key)|.Attribute]

```
<%
strBookName = Request.Cookies("myCookie")("BOOK_NAME")
strAuthors = Response.Cookies("myCookie")("Authors")
%>
```

To retrieve each variable and its corresponding value in a cookie, try the following code. To view the results on a WAP device, simply change the <br> to <br/>.

```
<%
For each CookieVar in Request.Cookies
    Response.Write CookieVar & "=" & Request.Cookies(CookieVar) &
"<br>"
Next
%>
```

Perl

Creating a cookie in Perl is also fairly simple and can be accomplished as follows:

```
#!/usr/local/bin/perl
...
print "Content-type: text/html\n";
print "Set-Cookie: BOOK_NAME=WIRELESS; expires=10-Oct-01 GMT\n\n";...
```

Deleting a cookie is just as easy, set the cookie's Expires date to a date in the past:

```
print "Set-Cookie: BOOK_NAME=WIRELESS; expires=04-Jul-61 GMT\n\n";
```

JavaScript

To post the cookie to the client with JavaScript, it's as simple as executing:

```
<script language="JavaScript">
<!--
document.cookie="BOOK_NAME=WIRELESS";
//->
</script>
```

To set the cookie expires date to 1 month in the future, use the GMT format, toGMTString() function.

```
<script language="JavaScript">
<!--
var Bookexp = new Date ();
Bookexp.setTime (Bookexp.getTime() + (24 * 60 * 60 * 1000 * 31));
document.cookie="BOOK_NAME=WIRELESS; expires=" +
Bookexp.toGMTString();
//->
</script>
```

To read our cookie example with JavaScript, use the following routine. For this very quick example, we're assuming the only variable in the cookie is BOOK_NAME.

```
<script language="JavaScript">
<!--
var NameStart = document.cookie.indexOf("BOOK_NAME=");
var NameEnd = document.cookie.indexOf(";",NameStart);
var BookName = document.cookie.substring(NameStart+10,NameEnd);
document.write(BookName);
//->
</script>
```

To delete this cookie in JavaScript, as with any other language, simply repost it with an Expires date in the past.

Example—Member Sign-on

Continuing with our dynamic personalized menu application, let's add a member sign-in process that makes use of cookies. This mini add-on application will allow a member to initially sign on using his or her userID and password. In the future, whenever the person returns to the application and as long as the cookie exists, the person will automatically bypass the sign-in process and jump directly to a personalized menu.

The first part of the process involves a sign-on program that checks whether a sign-on cookie currently exists. If one does, program control is sent directly to the dtw.asp program using the person's customer number stored in the cookie. If, however, a sign-on cookie does not exist, then control will be passed to the WAP sign-on screen/routine. The member will enter his or her userID and password, which will be validated against a back-end database. If either is incorrect, a warning screen will appear for 3 seconds, followed by control being returned to the WAP sign-on screen/routine.

Remember, this example will not function on all WAP microbrowsers since not all vendors support the use of cookies until WAP version 1.2, which is not yet in wide use. At the end of this example, we'll show a more generic approach to maintaining the customer number throughout the application session, but, unfortunately, since this method uses a regular ASP session variable, the value will be lost after the user exits the application. The member must reenter his or her userID and password each time he or she uses the application.

Figure 6.11 shows the overall flow of the sign-on application. The first time the user signs on, the Signon.asp program will create a cookie. All future accessing will result in direct program flow to DTW.asp, since the cookie already exists. For testing purposes, we've included the Reset.asp program. This program will remove an existing cookie and invoke Signon.asp. This will help in the development process since a simple program execution will reset the entire system.

Remember the redirection examples from Chapter 5 where the browser type determined which program to invoke? Well, instead of invoking the DTW.asp program for

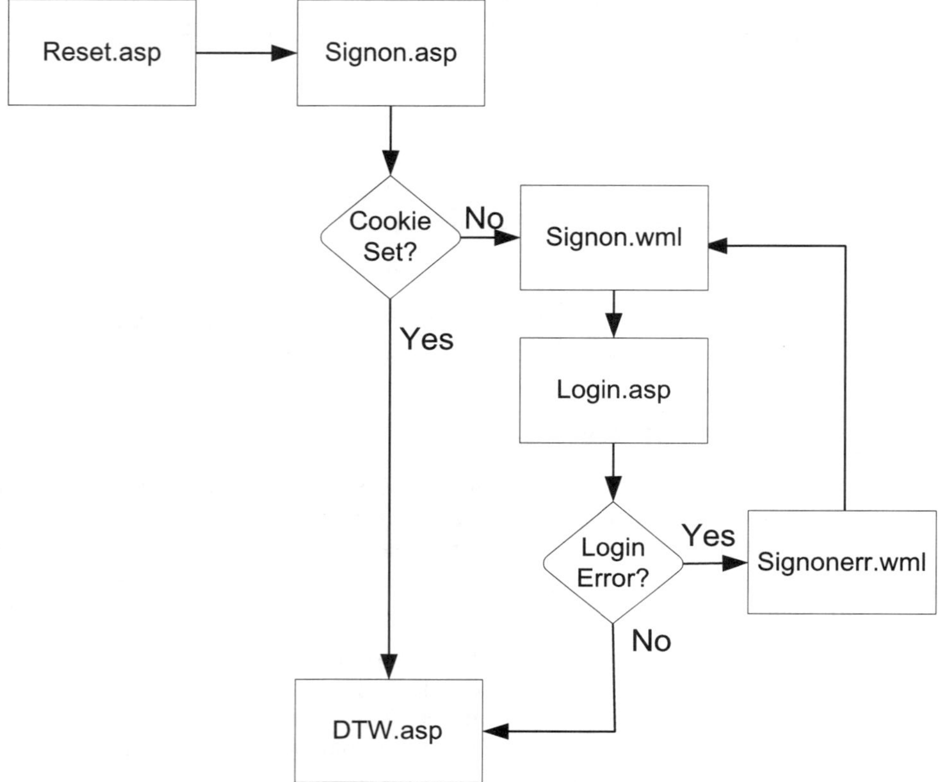

Figure 6.11 Sign-on flowchart.

Up.Browser microbrowsers, the Redirect.asp program would now point to Signon.asp. This ensures that the user used the new cookie security feature.

To begin, a new table has been added to the Paging.mdb Access database. This table, called Members, has only three columns, the MemberID and Password to be supplied by the sign-on screen (Signon.wml), and CustomerNo, which is the internal representation of our customer. The CustomerNo on this new security table joins the original MenuTable. See Figure 6.12.

For our demonstration and testing purposes, only one member needs to be set up. We've set up a MemberID of *bob* with the same password, as shown in Figure 6.13. Of course, it would have been wiser to choose numeric values since entering characters on a Web phone is a cumbersome task, but the deed has been done.

From a planning point, all we need now is the look and feel of the application. Figure 6.14 shows our anticipated results with the first screen being the user sign-on. The second screen shows the password entry, which is really the same program, but

Members : Table

	Field Name	Data Type
🔑▶	CustomerNo	Number
	MemberID	Text
	Password	Text

Figure 6.12 Members table.

since the language prompts for the two input fields on separate windows, this is what it looks like. The third screen is a view of what the user will receive from Signonerr.wml. This screen simply tells the user that his or her userID and password combination was not found in the back-end database. As shown in the application flow, if this last screen is seen, program flow will return to Signon.wml for another input try.

That's about all we require before we get going with the actual programs. Let's begin with the first program in our mini-application, Signon.asp, as shown in Figure 6.15. This program simply checks for an existing cookie and, if not present, will redirect control to the Signon.wml program for user input. If a cookie is present, it directs the flow to the member's personalized menu, which is created by program DTW.asp.

Line 6 checks the value of variable CustNo in the DTWCookie. If the value is null, we assume the cookie doesn't exist and proceed to Signon.wml for input.

If the cookie's variable is not null, execution continues with lines 9 and 10. Line 9 reads the CustNo value into a program variable, and line 10 will include it in the redirection command to program dtw.asp.

The next program, Signon.wml (Figure 6.16), is pure WML and is used to gather the userID and password.

Line 5 is a meta option used in the <head> tag statement. This command sets the Cache-Control variable in the HTTP header to max-age=0. In other words, it tells the system not to keep the contents in memory.

Line 9 is the redirection to the third program, login.asp. This program, along with its parameters (User and Smart) is invoked once the user presses the key associated with the Softkey label Login.

Members : Table

	CustomerNo	MemberID	Password
▶	1	bob	bob
*	0		

Figure 6.13 Data for members table.

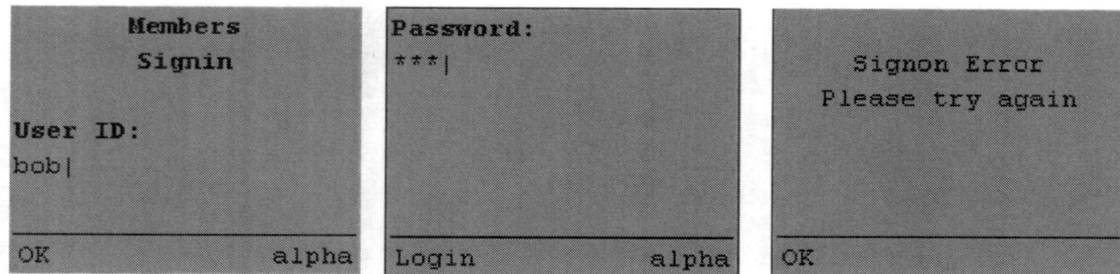

Figure 6.14 Sign-on screens.

Lines 14 and 16 define the input parameters, User and Smart, respectively. Instead of using the word *password*, we prefer to call it something else just in case. Having been in the computer industry for many years, there are a lot of things we do for security or efficiency reasons, and we've come to call them "just-in-case" reasons. As you can see, the first parameter can only be 15 characters long and the password has a maximum of 10 characters. Both fields must have a value as the emptyok is set to false, meaning something must be entered.

The next program in the process is login.asp, as shown in Figure 6.17. It checks the userID and password combination against the new Members table in the Paging database. If not found, control is sent to Signonerr.wml. If it is a valid combination, a cookie is baked with the CustomerNo and an Expires date of January 1, 2002.

Lines 5 and 6 read in the program variables after setting them to lowercase. This ensures a valid comparison test with the values in the database and also falls into our just-in-case category.

Lines 7 through 15 set up the database and DSNless ODBC connections.

```
1.  <% @LANGUAGE="VBSCRIPT" %>
2.  <% Response.Buffer = True %>
3.  <% Response.Expires = 0 %>
4.  <%
5.  dim strCustNo
6.  if request.cookies("DTWCookie")("CustNo") = "" then
7.     response.redirect ("http://www.wavedev.com/signon.wml")
8.  else
9.     strCustNo = request.cookies("DTWCookie")("CustNo")
10.    response.redirect ("http://www.wavedev.com/dtw.asp?txtCustNo="&
       strCustNo &"&txtOwnerID=0")
11. end if
12. %>
```

Figure 6.15 Signon.asp program.

```
1.  <?xml version="1.0"?>
2.  <!DOCTYPE wml PUBLIC "-//PHONE.COM//DTD WML 1.1//EN"
    "http://www.phone.com/dtd/wml11.dtd">
3.  <wml>
4.     <head>
5.         <meta http-equiv="Cache-Control" content="max-age=0"/>
6.     </head>
7.     <card>
8.         <do type="accept" label="Login">
9.             <go href="login.asp?User=$(User)&amp;Smart=$(Smart)"/>
10.        </do>
11.        <p align="center"><b>Members<br/>Signin</b><br/></p>
12.        <p align="left">
13.            <b>User ID:</b>
14.            <input name="User" maxlength="15" type="text"
               emptyok="false"/><br/>
15.            <b>Password:</b>
16.            <input name="Smart" maxlength="10" type="password"
               emptyok="false"/><br/>
17.        </p>
18.     </card>
19. </wml>
```

Figure 6.16 Signon.wml program.

Lines 16 through 19 connect to the database and execute the SQL query on line 18.

If the userID/password combination is not found in the database, line 25 directs control to the error program. If the combination is valid, the database is closed, lines 27 to 29, and the cookie logic follows.

Line 32 sets the Expires variable date for a cookie named DTWCookie. If the cookie doesn't exist, it's created; if it does exist, it is updated.

Line 33 creates a cookie variable called CustNo and sets it to the value of strCustNo from the database for the current user.

Line 34 sends control to dtw.asp, the dynamic menu program, with its required parameters, one being the customer number from the cookie.

Figure 6.18 shows the contents of the DTWCookie taken from the information page of Openwave's UP.SDK 4.1. Notice the cookie name and a variable called CUSTNO in the value field with its own value of 1. Also the TTL or Time To Live is set to a high number of seconds. If the Expires variable date was set to 01/01/2002, subtract the number of seconds in the TTL and you'll get the current date and time. For this example, you'd get the date that I created the cookie.

For development purposes, we have supplied the Reset.asp program. As seen in Figure 6.19, this program merely resets the Expires variable date for the DTWCookie, which

```
1. <%
2. Response.Expires = 0

3. dim Conn, RS, sql
4. dim strMemberID, strPassword, strCustNo

5. strMemberID = lcase(request("User"))
6. strPassword = lcase(request("Smart"))

7. '---- Open DSNless connection to Access database
8. DB = "database/Paging.mdb"
9. Dir = Request.ServerVariables("SCRIPT_NAME")
10. Dir = StrReverse(Dir)
11. Dir = Mid(Dir, InStr(1, Dir, "/"))
12. Dir = StrReverse(Dir)
13. Path = Server.MapPath(Dir) & "\"
14. file = "database/Paging.dsn"
15. DSN = "filedsn=" & Path & file & ";DefaultDir=" & Path & ";DBQ=" &
    Path & DB & ";"
16. Set Conn = Server.CreateObject("ADODB.Connection")
17. Conn.Open DSN
18. sql = "select CustomerNo from Members where MemberID='" &
    strMemberID & "' and Password='" & strPassword & "'"
19. Set RS = Conn.Execute(sql)

20. if RS.EOF or RS.BOF then
21.   Conn.Close
22.   set RS = nothing
23.   set Conn = nothing
24.   response.redirect ("http://www.wavedev.com/signonerr.wml")
25. end if
26. strCustNo = RS("CustomerNo")

27. Conn.Close
28. set RS = nothing
29. set Conn = nothing

30. '-------baking a cookie ----Mmm, delicious!!--------------
31. '--make the date current date and it auto expires.
32. response.cookies("DTWCookie").expires = #01/01/2002#
33. response.cookies("DTWCookie")("CustNo") = strCustNo

34. response.redirect ("http://www.wavedev.com/dtw.asp?txtCustNo="&
    strCustNo &"&txtOwnerID=0")
35. %>
```

Figure 6.17 Login.asp program.

```
Name:       DTWCookie
Value:      CUSTNO=1
Version:    0
TTL:        22153279 seconds to live
Path:       /
Domain:     www.wavedev.com
Comment:
```

Figure 6.18 DTWCookie contents.

deletes the cookie and then redirects control to the first program in our application. This small program, as shown at the beginning of the application flow diagram in Figure 6.11 is only for development purposes, not to be used in a working production environment.

As mentioned earlier, at this point in the overall WAP timeline, since most micro-browsers and gateways do not support WAP 1.2, it might be a good idea to create one application specifically for Up.Browser devices and another for other microbrowsers. Since Up.Browser gateways do support cookies, the examples you just read will function without any problems. For other browsers, use an ASP session variable instead of a cookie for the user information.

The programs in our examples in this chapter send the customer number as a parameter in all places it's required. We could have simply accessed the cookie (or session variable) as needed and not sent the variable as a parameter, but we thought we'd follow a certain standard.

Without cookies, the first program, Signon.asp, is not necessary since the user will have to sign on every time he or she returns to the application. So we can simply change the login.asp program, lines 32 and 33, to refer to a session variable rather than a cookie. However, in the design or our application logic, we could simply comment out lines 32 and 33 in the login.asp program and continue as is since the customerno is retrieved at only this one spot from the database.

Another method to use for sessions is to create the session variable in login.asp at lines 32 and 33 and not pass the strCustNo variable in the URL. In each program requiring the variable, simply replace a typical request("txtCustNo") with session("txtCustNo"), since the session variable is really a short-term cookie available to all programs within the user's application session.

```
<%
response.cookies("DTWCookie").expires = #19/04/2001#
response.redirect ("http://www.wavedev.com/signon.asp")
%>
```

Figure 6.19 Reset.asp program.

Real Life

Although technology removes a lot of hassles from our lives and makes us more productive in our work and in our spare time, there are downfalls. Suppose you lose your WAP device and all the important items stored on it. If the WAP device actually holds persistent cookies with userIDs and passwords, you're in trouble. Normally, a person remembers his or her specifics until they are entered on the device. Then they are promptly forgotten because we rely solely on our computers and WAP devices. Personally, when I removed all my cookies from my PC, I had a heck of a time trying to remember what all my passwords were. Life is easy when all is functioning properly, but one small glitch and bills aren't paid, meetings are missed, and so on.

On the other hand, the person who finds your WAP device or has your personal computer can access all your private matters since the cookies allow him or her to bypass any sign-on security.

So, does the ease of use and enjoyment override security issues? Well, marketing and sales people would say it does somewhat. Wouldn't you prefer to sign on once and have the system plop you directly where you want to be any time you access a particular site? I sure would. Less hassle, quicker response times, and a higher fun factor.

Pulls (Polling)

WAP applications are either dynamic or static. Static applications are basically hard-coded results within the programs. Press a button, and the program always displays the same results, such as general company information, instructions, or logos, that sort of thing. The basic premise is that there is no back-end database access or any type of other changing data access. Dynamic applications, on the other hand, retrieve information on the go, so to speak. With supplied parameters, programs can retrieve information from a back-end database or another source, resulting in changing data on the WAP device screens.

Pull applications follow the same idea as dynamic applications with the major difference being the ability to poll information. *Polling* is the simple task of requesting data. Dynamic applications also request information and hence can be considered polling or pulling results. However, the concept of polling here is to automatically pull information without the user having to constantly press the same button over and over again. This concept is called *smart pulling*.

Figure 6.20 shows the result of manual polling and smart polling. The first screen is a basic program invoked and reinvoked by the end user continuously pressing the Softkey button labeled Again. The screen display on the right side of Figure 6.20 is the same application with a polling feature. It automatically refreshes itself without the continuous manual intervention.

The second screen shows the Auto-Refresh title along with the refresh minutes or seconds remaining. Simply set the refresh rate and invoke the option. Once invoked, the

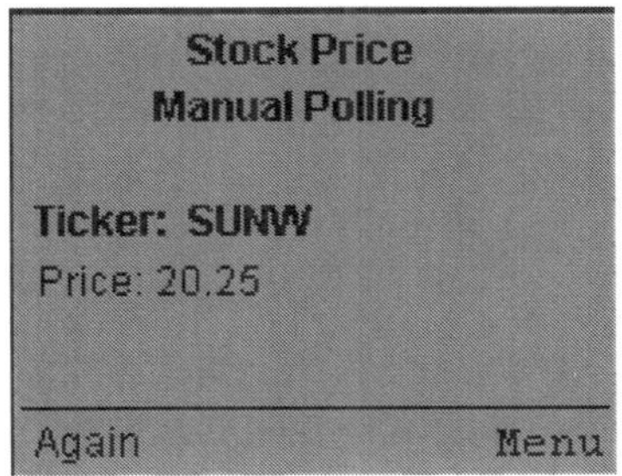

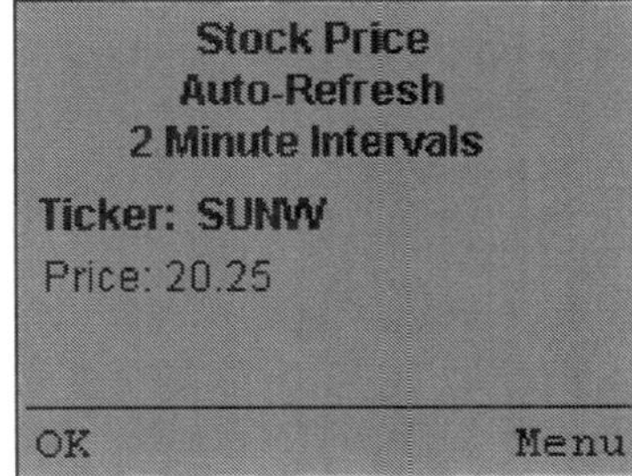

Figure 6.20 Manual and smart pull results.

screen will automatically refresh itself whatever number of minutes is set by the refresh rate. This allows the user to view, in this example, the price of a particular stock in real time (or as specified by the application).

In a client server environment, pulling can be done at either the client side or the server side. In this case, the client side is the WAP device and therefore any refresh invoking routine must be based on the WAP language being used, which in our examples is WML. If the polling is left to the server, ASP would reinvoke the data fetching and result-display routines.

Either way, pulling information automatically is application driven and hence easily maintained. And since the program is polling the same backend system over and over again, there are few complications other than the Refresh command itself.

Limitations

Although pulling information seems efficient and a useful feature for many WAP applications, there are limitations. The first and foremost is the fact that the WAP pull program must always be on. This means the screen on the Web phone must always be executing the pulling program. The user cannot use any another application while this feature is running. In our example, we get stock quotes every 2 minutes, but we can't do anything else. If we could set the notification parameters and have the stock price sent to the Web phone every refresh rate while having the ability to continue on with other options or applications, we'd really have a nice system.

Another smart pulling limitation is the network capabilities and costs. Many cellular network providers in many countries only charge for data being sent back and forth over the cell network to the WAP device. In this case, any type of polling is relatively cheap since a small amount is being sent over the network. The network connection can remain on for as long as the WAP device's battery allows and charges only apply every few minutes when the polling feature invokes the data transfers. However, if the carrier is billing for every minute that the user is logged on to the Internet, then pulling information every 2 minutes (or whatever time frame) would have an associated cost, which could add up quite quickly.

With messages being sent to the device periodically, the user can base important decisions on these dynamic results. However, the user cannot react to the particular message directly. Sure, an application can be built into our example where the user can press a button to buy or sell stocks, but this means the user must continuously watch the results before invoking another action. If the person's attention is distracted, he or she may miss the opportunity to react quickly to a specific bit of news. There are no alerts built in unless the programmers specifically add a feature that can test a parameter for a certain value and then display a new screen. And, since many devices do not support WMLScript commands, this would have to be done on the server side.

From a content provider's point of view, there are many pieces still required to allow pull notification responses to be used with many types of applications and to allow users to respond to the pull messages immediately. However, since the processes at all steps are purely application driven, anything is possible.

Advantages

Pulling information from a back-end database or application can be very useful. Once a user signs into an application, such as our personalized dynamic menu system, the first thing that could be done is for the application to initiate a lookup program. This program could query a back-end application or database for personalized notifications such as emails, notices, reminders, and so on.

Regular pulling is usually a manual task; however, smart pulling can be somewhat automated. For example, it can activate a chain of procedures based on a specific user reaction. Suppose a person signs into the dynamic menu application as described at the beginning of this chapter. The first thing that the application does after checking security is to check personal notifications. If the person chooses to continue, the personalized menu system appears. However, if the person wants to react to a notification category, a completely new application could be invoked.

Suppose the notification program shows the user that three new unread emails exist in the user's inbox. Well, the program could dynamically build a response to a selection list so that once the person scrolls to the email notification, the underlying Softkey label could invoke a goto or linkto type of action, thus invoking a completely new application or, at a minimum, jumping to a specific application. Figure 6.21 shows the possible program flow potential.

In this scenario, the notification feature would always show up as the first item on the primary personal menu. The member would not see this in the menu creation system on the Web site (Figure 6.2), but it would show up on his or her personal menu, as seen in Figure 6.22. To get this going, the SeqNum column of table MenuTable in database Paging.mdb (Figure 6.7), would have to be changed to allow for one decimal place (maybe two). The content provider could then add entries to the database with sequence number values less than 1. When the database query ran (Figure 6.9, line 26), the order by seqnum statement would place the system-defined menu item (Notifications) first on the member's first personal menu level.

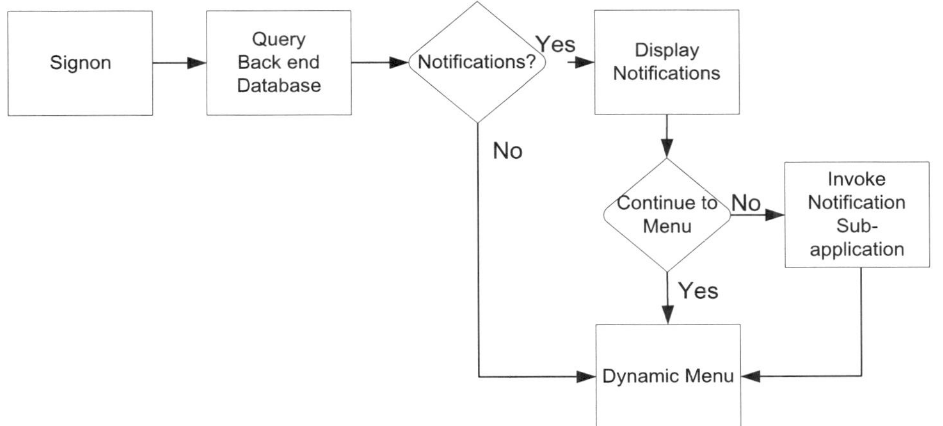

Figure 6.21 Notification pulling flow.

The up side of this is, of course, content control. This would allow the content provider the ability to provide notifications including emails, reminders, and so on. The down side is that the personal menu would not completely reflect the member's menu numbering layout. But then again by introducing paging to the application, personal menu numbering would change as soon as any page other than the first is presented. Is this a feature or a nuisance? Why not leave it up to the individual member to decide? If the user wants the feature, it can be enabled from the Web side.

Another enterprising use of polling, on initial sign-on or whenever, is to pull specific advertisements to be displayed to the user. The smart-polling feature here, as with the notification subapplication, would be that if the user did not continue on, after a number of seconds, a new advertisement would be presented. This is a dynamically generated advertisement system polling from a back-end marketing or sales database. The content provider could tailor advertisements to specific user profiles based on initial registration information or on the individual's selection of menu items. There are many possibilities.

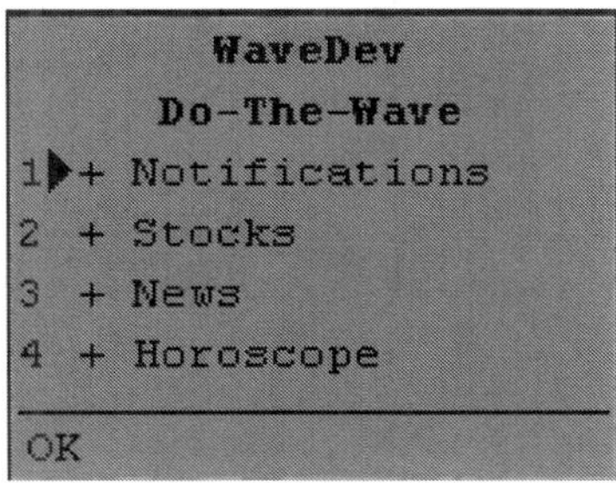

Figure 6.22 Notifications menu item addition.

Example—Pulling Advertisements

Let's look at one of our three presented scenarios, the advertisement example. This application is a client side refresh, meaning the WAP device will continuously invoke the refresh. To initiate the program, the user must execute the program directly either manually or via another program. In our example, the application is invoked once the user signs into the dynamic personalized menu system. The advertisement routines will be executed just before the main DTW.asp program is initiated.

A simple back-end database is required that contains several tables: Members, Categories, and the Ads table for the advertisements themselves. See Figure 6.23. This example will only be programmed for the general WML WAP language and so the description column in the Ads table will contain the advertisement already in WML format. All the application must do is to present the code directly as is from the Ads table to the device. This routine has many possible areas of potential enhancements, and we'll leave that to your imagination and business requirement.

The advertising database, an Access database called *Advertisement.mdb*, has the three necessary tables: Ads, Categories, and Members. The Category table is not used in our programs and is only included for ease of understanding and integrity definitions.

Figure 6.24 shows the data used in the database for our example. In our scenario, we'll be using a customer number, CustomerNo, of 1. As seen in the Members table, this person has two entries, which means the member will be shown advertisements for two categories: category 1 and category 2. To obtain the specific advertisements tailored to our specific CustomerNo, the CategoryID field from the Members table will be joined with the same column in the Ads table.

Ads : Table

Field Name	Data Type
ID	AutoNumber
CategoryID	Number
Priority	Number
AdDescription	Text

Categories : Table

Field Name	Data Type
CategoryID	Number
CategoryDesc	Text

Members : Table

Field Name	Data Type
CustomerNo	Number
CategoryID	Number

Figure 6.23 Advertisement database tables.

⊞ Ads : Table			
ID	**CategoryID**	**Priority**	**AdDescription**
1	1	99	`<p align="center"> <img src="http://www.worldjobmart.com/wireless/UpBrowser/wjmbig.bmp" alt="Jobs"/>  <b>WorldJobMart</b></p>`
2	1	2	`<p align="center"><b>Global Financial Newspaper</b>  Visit us at <b>www.GlobalFin.com</b></p>`
3	2	1	`<p align="center"><b>XY Financial Planners Worldwide Call Anytime</b> www.XY.com 1-212-555-1234</p>`
4	3	99	d
5	4	99	e

⊞ Categories : Table	
CategoryID	**CategoryDesc**
1	financial
2	news
3	weather
4	movies

⊞ Members : Table	
CustomerNo	**CategoryID**
1	1
1	2
2	1
3	4

Figure 6.24 Advertisement data.

Individual advertisements can be assigned a specific priority and the extraction query will sort all the advertisements in an ascending order based on the Priority column in the Ads table. From a marketing point of view, the first advertisement will definitely be seen, the second advertisement may be seen, and the others may go unnoticed, as most users will probably skip most other advertisements. So advertisers will have to pay a premium for these two top positions, which hold the highest visibility.

Many different algorithms could be created to position certain advertisements first or in specific orders, but we'll leave that to your imagination. We simply use the ascending order for the Priority column in the Ads table. The default Priority value is 99, and the highest priorities have values of 1 and 2. Our extraction query is as follows:

```
Select a.AdDescription from Ads a, Members m where m.CustomerNo = 1
and m.CategoryID = a.CategoryID order by a.Priority asc
```

Again, notice the AdDescription column in the Ads table of Figure 6.24. The exact WML code that will be used on the WAP device is stored directly in the database. All the extraction program has to do is to take the AdDescription column and place it in the WML deck and we're done.

The database query result set will contain three advertisements, row IDs of 3, 2, and finally 1, in that specific order. To make things interesting, our program will create a WML deck with two cards, each containing one advertisement. After 3 seconds, the first card will pass control to the second card in the deck. Then, after another 3 seconds, the second card will call an ASP program, which will create and display another deck with another two new advertisements. When the end of the advertisements is reached and if the deck is not full (in our case only one card), a last specific advertising card will be included noting our (content provider's) advertising potential [Figure 6.25, deck 2, second card (right-most card)]. The user may invoke the Skip button found on each advertisement at any time, which will send him or her directly to the personal menu to avoid any further advertisements. If the person does not skip the advertisements, the system will go on to display all possible advertisements for that person at 3-second intervals until none remains for that particular user. Finally, after the last advertisement has been displayed for 3 seconds, the advertising application will redirect control to the personalized dynamic menu application, showing the member his or her personalized menu.

Figure 6.25 shows the result of two dynamically generated WML decks. The first deck would show the top two advertisements, and the second would display the last two advertisements.

The dynamically generated WML code for the two advertisements marked with a 1 in Figure 6.25 is featured in Figure 6.26. As you can see, it's a straightforward WML program with the ontimer option on the <card> tags, lines 4 and 11, followed by the <timer> tag on lines 5 and 12, respectively. We've created the Skip option to jump to the person's dynamic menu as seen on lines 6 through 8 and 13 through 15 on the second

Figure 6.25 Advertisement examples.

card. Lines 9 and 16 were taken directly from the AdDescription column in the Ads table of our database.

An important design feature in this program is the ontimer parameter on the last card, line 11. This particular parameter shows how control is passed to the main advertisement program Adverts.asp. As this main program produces and displays more decks, the page number (PgNo) parameter value is constantly increased so that the next few advertisements are picked up the next time the user signs on. The WML program is built to hold two advertisements at a time, and we do this by simply paging through only two rows per execution. If you'd like to add more advertisements per deck, simply increase the number of rows per page variable and repeat the card creation code. The Adverts.asp program is explained in Figure 6.27.

The Adverts.asp program, which generates the above WML code is shown in Figure 6.27.

As usual, many basic lines of code will be skipped, since you should know their usage by now. We'll highlight the important lines and concepts only.

Line 20 shows the database query. Here, the customer number (CustomerNo) is read from the URL parameters, line 16, and stored in a program variable (strCustNo). This variable is then substituted into the select statement.

```
1.  <?xml version="1.0"?>
2.  <!DOCTYPE wml PUBLIC "-//PHONE.COM//DTD WML 1.1//EN"
    "http://www.phone.com/dtd/wml11.dtd">
3.  <wml>
4.      <card id="card1" ontimer="#card2">
5.          <timer name="time" value="30"/>
6.          <do type="accept" label="Skip">
7.              <go href="dtw.asp?txtCustNo=1&amp;txtOwnerID=0"/>
8.          </do>
9.          <p align="center"><b>XY Financial
            Planners<br/>Worldwide<br/>Call
            Anytime</b><br/>www.XY.com<br/>1-212-555-1234</p>
10.     </card>
11.     <card id="card2" ontimer="Adverts.asp?txtCustNo=1&amp;PgNo=1">
12.         <timer name="time" value="30"/>
13.         <do type="accept" label="Skip">
14.             <go href="dtw.asp?txtCustNo=1&amp;txtOwnerID=0"/>
15.         </do>
16.         <p align="center"><b>Global
            Financial<br/>Newspaper</b><br/><br/>Visit us
            at<br/><b>www.GlobalFin.com</b></p>
17.     </card>
18. </wml>
```

Figure 6.26 Dynamically generated WML deck.

```
1. <% @LANGUAGE="VBSCRIPT" %>
2. <% Response.Buffer = True %>
3. <% Response.Expires = 0 %>
4. <%
5. '---- Open DSNless connection to database
6. DB       = "database/advertisement.mdb"
7. Dir      = Request.ServerVariables("SCRIPT_NAME")
8. Dir      = StrReverse(Dir)
9. Dir      = Mid(Dir, InStr(1, Dir, "/"))
10. Dir     = StrReverse(Dir)
11. Path = Server.MapPath(Dir) & "\"
12. file = "database/advertisement.dsn"
13. DSNa = "filedsn=" & Path & file & ";DefaultDir=" & Path & ";DBQ="
    & Path & DB & ";"

14. dim Conn, RS, sql
15. dim strCustNo
16. strCustNo=request("txtCustNo")

17. Set Conn = Server.CreateObject("ADODB.Connection")
18. Set RS   = Server.CreateObject("ADODB.RecordSet")
19. Conn.Open DSNa
20. sql = "select a.AdDescription from Ads a, Members m where
    m.CustomerNo="& strCustNo &" and m.CategoryID=a.CategoryID order
    by a.priority asc"
21. RS.Open sql, Conn, 1,1

22. if RS.EOF or RS.BOF then
23.   Conn.Close
24.   set RS = nothing
25.   set Conn = nothing
26.   response.redirect
      ("http://www.wavedev.com/dtw.asp?txtCustNo="&
      strCustNo &"&txtOwnerID=0")
27. else
28.   NumRowsPerPage=2
29.   RS.PageSize= NumRowsPerPage

30.   if request("PgNo")="" then
31.       ScrollAction=0
32.   else
33.       ScrollAction=Cint(Request.QueryString("PgNo"))   '--
          Read in page number.
34.   end if
35.   if ScrollAction < 1 then
36.       PageNo=1
```

Figure 6.27 Adverts.asp program.

```
37.    elseif ScrollAction > RS.PageCount then
38.         Conn.Close
39.         set RS = nothing
40.         set Conn = nothing
41.         response.redirect
              ("http://www.wavedev.com/dtw.asp?txtCustNo="& strCustNo
              &"&txtOwnerID=0")
42. else
43.      PageNo=ScrollAction
44. end if
45. RS.AbsolutePage=PageNo   '-- Set current page number

46. response.Buffer = TRUE
47. response.ContentType = "text/vnd.wap.wml"
48. response.write "<?xml version="+chr(34)+"1.0"+chr(34)+"?>"
49. response.write "<!DOCTYPE wml PUBLIC "+chr(34)+"-
    //PHONE.COM//DTD WML 1.1//EN"+chr(34)+"
    "+chr(34)+"http://www.phone.com/dtd/wml11.dtd"+chr(34)+">"
50. response.write "<wml>"

51. MaxNum = 1
52. do while MaxNum < NumRowsPerPage+1
53.      if MaxNum = 1 then
54.             response.write "<card
                id="+chr(34)+"card1"+chr(34)+"
                ontimer="+chr(34)+"#card2"+chr(34)+">"
55.             response.write "<timer
                value="+chr(34)+"30"+chr(34)+"/>"
56.             response.write "<do
                type="+chr(34)+"accept"+chr(34)+"
                label="+chr(34)+"Skip"+chr(34)+">"
57.             response.write "<go
                href="+chr(34)+"dtw.asp?txtCustNo="& strCustNo
                &"&amp;txtOwnerID=0"+chr(34)+"/>"
58.             response.write "</do>"
59.             response.write RS(0)
60.             response.write "</card>"
61.      else
62.             response.write "<card
                id="+chr(34)+"card2"+chr(34)+"
                ontimer="+chr(34)+"Adverts.asp?txtCustNo="& strCustNo
                &"&amp;PgNo="& PageNo+1 & chr(34)+">"
63.             response.write "<timer
                value="+chr(34)+"30"+chr(34)+"/>"
64.             response.write "<do
                type="+chr(34)+"accept"+chr(34)+"
                label="+chr(34)+"Skip"+chr(34)+">"
65.             response.write "<go
```

Figure 6.27 Continued Adverts.asp program.

```
                          href="+chr(34)+"dtw.asp?txtCustNo="& strCustNo
                          &"&amp;txtOwnerID=0"+chr(34)+"/>"
66.               response.write "</do>"
67.               response.write RS(0)
68.               response.write "</card>"
69.       end if

70.       RS.MoveNext
71.       if RS.EOF then
72.             if MaxNum = 1 then
73.                   response.write "<card
                          id="+chr(34)+"card2"+chr(34)+"
                          ontimer="+chr(34)+"Adverts.asp?txtCustNo="&
                          strCustNo &"&amp;PgNo="& PageNo+1 & chr(34)+">"
74.                   response.write "<timer
                          value="+chr(34)+"30"+chr(34)+"/>"
75.                   response.write "<do
                          type="+chr(34)+"accept"+chr(34)+"
                          label="+chr(34)+"Skip"+chr(34)+">"
76.                   response.write "<go
                          href="+chr(34)+"dtw.asp?txtCustNo="& strCustNo
                          &"&amp;txtOwnerID=0"+chr(34)+"/>"
77.                   response.write "</do>"
78.                   response.write "<do
                          type="+chr(34)+"accept"+chr(34)+"
                          label="+chr(34)+"Call"+chr(34)+">"
79.                   response.write "<go
                          href="+chr(34)+"wtai://wp/mc;1-212-555-
                          1234"+chr(34)+"/>"
80.                   response.write "</do>"
81.                   response.write "<p
                          align="+chr(34)+"center"+chr(34)+"><b>Call
                          Now<br/>Advertise<br/>Here<br/><br/>1-212-555-
                          1234</b></p>"
82.                   response.write "</card>"
83.             end if
84.             exit do
85.       end if
86.       MaxNum = MaxNum + 1
87.   loop

88.   response.write "</wml>"
89.   Conn.Close
90.   set RS = nothing
91.   set Conn = nothing
92. end if
93. %>
```

Figure 6.27 Continued Adverts.asp program.

Line 21 shows the database query execution command by way of a record set, rather than a one-time query, thus allowing a cursor result set.

If the query returns an empty result set, then line 26 will redirect flow to the dynamic menu main program. If, however, there are advertisements to display, control will continue with the else statement on line 27.

Lines 28 to 45 are the basic paging setup code to determine the number of rows per page on the output and to set up the absolute page for the result set paging. There is one major change to this code for our example. Normally, we scroll the result set and if the page number requested is higher than the result set number of pages, we reset the page number. In this example, we take a different approach and redirect control to the menu program, lines 38 to 41.

Program flow continues, and we enter the loop logic where output is created. In the example, there are two types of cards for our logic, the non-last cards and the last card. Since we're only displaying two cards per deck, we don't have to worry too much about semi-empty decks.

The first card, lines 54 to 60, is generated with the ontimer parameter directing flow to the next card, card2. Line 59 is the advertising code, which is retrieved directly from the database query.

Lines 62 to 68 represent the last card in the deck. The ontimer parameter on line 62 reinvokes the same program but with a new page number, which is one higher than the current page. And again, the advertising code is retrieved from the database as seen on line 67.

Line 70 advances the cursor on the result set. If no more rows exist and we haven't created the second and last card (since we use only two cards per deck for this example), a last advertisement card is created. This last card is an advertisement of our own.

Since we're only using two cards per deck, we set line 73's card name to card2 since the first card's ontimer has already been set. If more cards were added per deck, we'd have to substitute the current counter number plus 1 for the card name number, similar to page numbers.

That's it: a very simple nearly standalone application to retrieve and display multiple advertisements, which can be hooked up to any other application. The application is all client-driven, since the refresh (ontimer) mechanism is on the WAP device.

To incorporate the advertisement application into our dynamic menu system, we only have to change two programs from the cookie applications. Change line 10 of program Signon.asp (Figure 6.15) and line 34 of program Login.asp (Figure 6.17) to redirect control to the Adverts.asp program instead of directly to the DTW.asp program. If no advertisements exist, control automatically will jump to DTW.asp. If advertisements do exist for the specific member, the Adverts.asp program will run and then flow to DTW.asp until no more advertisements exist or until the user presses the Skip Softkey button.

Both lines will change from:

```
response.redirect ("http://www.wavedev.com/dtw.asp?txtCustNo="&
strCustNo &"&txtOwnerID=0")
```

to:

```
response.redirect ("http://www.wavedev.com/adverts.asp?txtCustNo="&
strCustNo &"&PgNo=").
```

A detailed program flowchart of the entire system as presented in this chapter is shown in Figure 6.28. Also included is the Redirect.asp program from the browser detection section in Chapter 5. With the Redirect.asp program set as the primary page for your Web site, rather than, say, index.html, once a person inputs your URL from the Web or WAP device, the Redirect.asp will pass the user to the proper application. If entering the URL on a WAP device, the Redirect.asp program would send control to Signon.asp, and the application system is under way.

Push

Automated notifications to mobile users will become more important in our daily lives as the technology grows and more and more people come to depend on them. Not only will we expect typical financial information pushed to our wireless devices but also information in other areas such as traffic jams, flight arrivals and departures, hotel bookings, and much more. These are just a few of the personalization features that we'll have available around the clock with our wireless WAP devices in the near future.

Unlike the earlier pull examples, push information deals with data being sent directly to our Web phones without user interaction. The user, for example, will set up his or her requirements such as stock price and when the price is hit, a notification will be immediately sent to that user's wireless WAP device, regardless of whether the user is using another feature, option, or application. When the notification is received, the phone will beep, chirp, vibrate, or whatever it has been set up to do. Then the user simply selects the notification option to view the received message details.

The push mechanism has been completely set up on Openwave's Push Proxy Gateway. The gateway requires little development effort from the content provider, because it is a fairly easy system to tap into. However, the actual pushing application that sends the push message to the push gateway is still left to the developers.

Figure 6.29 shows a typical push scenario. An application on the Web server sends a push message via the Push Access Protocol (PAP) to the Push Proxy Gateway, which, via the push Over-the-Air (OTA) protocol, sends the notification to the end user device. The device can then respond to the message by selecting the message option, which is associated with an underlying URL also received with the message. The WML program on the client side can then request that application and the drilling continues as any normal WAP application.

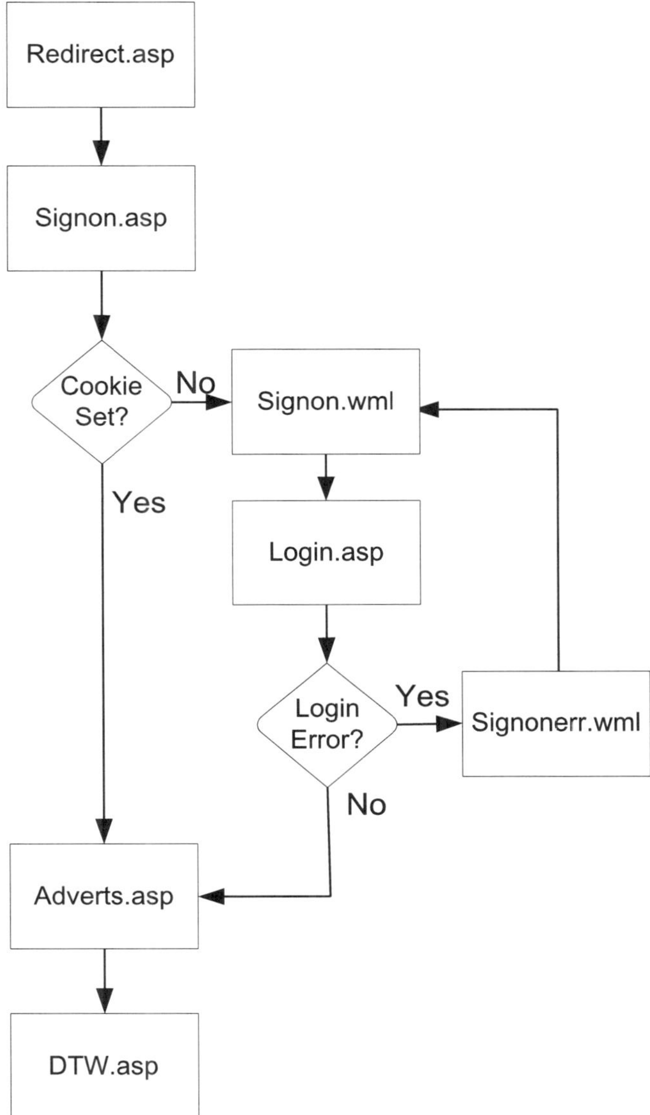

Figure 6.28 System flowchart.

Push Access Protocol is used by a Push Initiator (it can be any custom-built application or server) that resides on the Internet or corporate Intranet with its main task being to access the Push Proxy Gateway (PPG). For you network folks, the Push Access Protocol is totally independent of the underlying transport protocol. PAP is implemented over HTTP and may include other definitions in the future, such as

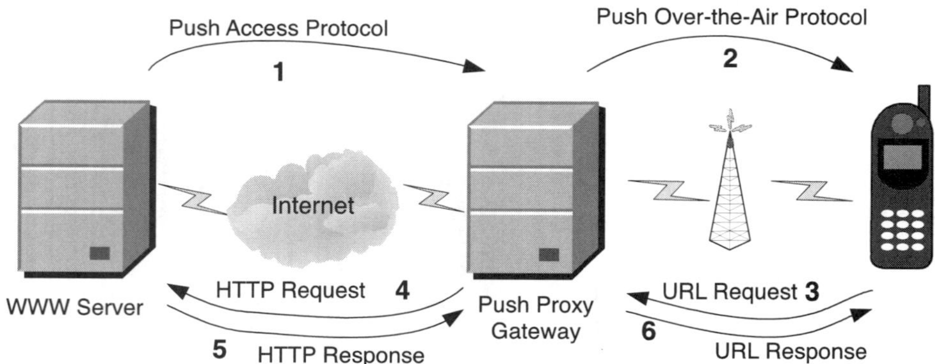

Figure 6.29 Push overview.

SMTP. It allows the Push Initiator to perform several operations to the Push Proxy Gateway such as submit, cancel, and query the status of a push query for wireless device capabilities. On the another hand, in response, PPG can send resulting notifications to the Push Initiator. Actually, this is one of the main premises of PAP: request/response operations.

Push Over-the-Air protocol is the delivery of content to a WAP client from a WAP server. It's an application layer protocol built on top of the WSP layer. The basis of the push OTA architecture is a distributed client-server application where the push initiator resides on the Push Proxy Gateway and the client is the mobile device. This protocol addresses the delivery of push contents to the WAP clients, defines the server-initiated asynchronous push, defines bearer types, and authenticates the push initiator (PPG) and application addressing.

There is quite a bit of information on push architecture at Openwave's Web site. We're only interested in presenting the topic and a working helpful application to learn the fundamental details. For more detailed information, visit www.openwave.com.

Disadvantages

Currently, not all carriers support the push architecture; hence, the feature is not available to everyone. This is simply due to the fact that the WAP industry is in its early stages. WAP 1.21, which not every carrier is using yet, does accommodate the push architecture. These specifications can be found at http://wapforum.org/what/technical.htm. All the major gateway vendors are expected to include the push architecture in their upcoming gateway releases. This means that any applications currently being built to use the Openwave technology will be available only to devices using their Up.Browser microbrowser. This may change in the future, but for now it's a limiting factor. Although there are many carriers worldwide using this microbrowser, there are many that are not. The push mechanism will not function on Nokia microbrowsers, eliminating many users worldwide.

Another disadvantage, or not, depending on your point of view, is that content providers must supply their own pushing application mechanism. By this we refer to automating a continuous pushing application such as the one featured in our example in Figure 6.30. Here we must build our own timer or scheduler, which basically forwards notifications to the WAP device. It's not the scheduling application that is the problem but the fact that to run it, the developer must have his or her own WWW server. For larger firms this is not a problem, but for smaller and medium-size firms having to solicit the services of an ASP to share a server with dozens if not hundreds of other customers and running a server-side application may be a bit daunting.

A special application would have to permanently run on the server, and shared service administrators really don't like this sort of thing. They much prefer the basic active server pages or Perl programs. Nonetheless, we've developed and will demonstrate with our example how to write a Visual Basic application to continuously execute on the server side.

Another main disadvantage is the potential for receiving spam on the personal WAP device. With push technology, content providers could obtain individual device and gateway information and easily send unsolicited messages just as many currently do with emails. Since the Openwave push technology has limits, such as the device only being able to receive nine push messages, if spam uses them up, there will be no room for true authorized messages. Openwave has a limit of 160 bytes per message and URL link with nine total messages. This gives a grand total of 1500 potential bytes available for all push messages. The idea behind this limit is that users would normally send a message with a small title and an underlying URL link for the user to respond. Even though these limitations exist, Openwave did quite a nice job with the overall push architecture and availability.

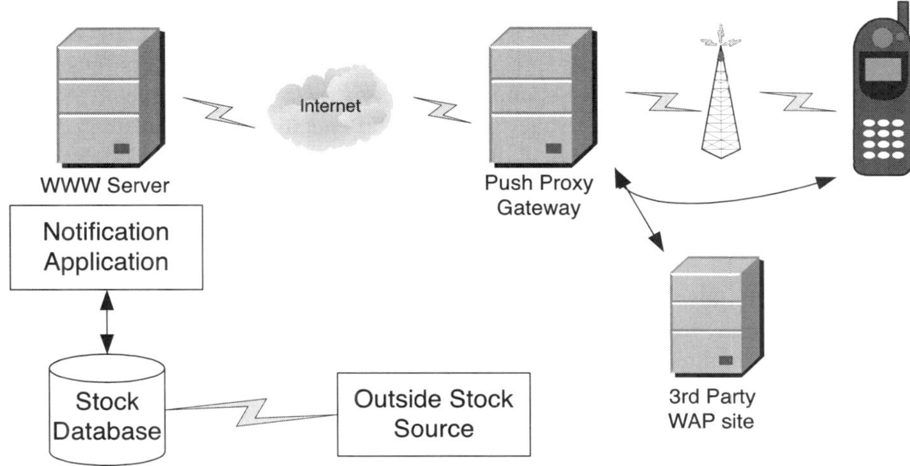

Figure 6.30 Push Application overview.

Advantages

Pushing messages to the Web phone is a highly important and personalized concept. While there are current limitations, the industry is still young and advances will come about. Having a mobile wireless communication connection to the Internet, and hence to the world, is wonderful, but the original concept of cellular phones was to receive calls as well as to send calls (make a call). The same idea applies to the wireless technology; we should not only be able to pull Internet information but also to receive information via pushes.

The pulling concept presented earlier is a great feature but is only available while the user is focused on a particular screen or application. The push concept allows the freedom to be doing some other online task and still have messages arrive at any time. With a back-end database application, arriving messages can be intercepted and stored in a database for later retrieval, historical or logging purposes, or whatever the content developer's imagination provides.

As with pulling applications, pushing messages can have associated URL links. This means the user can perform specific tasks or invoke specific applications per individual message. If a stock alert is received, the message could be associated with a BUY/SELL link, whereby the user clicks on the link and is then able to immediately buy or sell the stock in question.

This type of messaging can be used for all sorts of applications, stock alerts, reminders, appointment notifications, beeper type messages, and many more advanced potentials such as alerts when your bank account goes below a certain amount, etc. The example in the next section is based on stock alerts. All programs including the scheduler can be changed and applied to any other application.

Example—Pushing Stock Alerts

The example application enables the user to set a high or low trigger value on a particular stock. A continuously executing program will run on the content provider's Web server, checking every 30 seconds to see if any trigger values have been reached. If one has been obtained, a message is sent to the specific user requesting the notification. This type of application will allow a typical stock guru to always be in reach of the latest stock market happenings. At the beach, on public transportation, or in a restaurant, the wireless mobile device user will always remain in touch with the latest stock movements.

Our stock alert application is behind the scenes, running on an application server and through Openwave's Up.Link Push Proxy Gateway server. The database is continuously being fed by another application that is grabbing specific stock prices from an outside stock source. We'll leave the possibilities to your imagination and creativity.

The notification application is self-reinvoking every 30 seconds and queries the database for high or low trigger values to be compared to the latest stock price in our database. If a user wants to know when a particular stock reaches $50, he or she can set a high trigger if the stock is currently below that price and vice versa for a low trigger setting. For example, the first time a stock value is equal to or greater than a trigger value (for high triggers), a message is pushed to the user's WAP device. Device information is also stored in the stock database. Once the user receives the message, he or she can erase the message or invoke the accompanying URL, which may transfer control to a third-party WAP site for any number of possible reasons such as buying or selling the stock.

The example is based on Openwave's UP.Link 4.3.2 specifications, which can be found at http://phone.com/products/uplink.html. Openwave notifications are defined as asynchronous messages, which WML services send to UP.Link subscribers. The following are types of notifications that can be sent from the WML service:

- Alerts that beep, vibrate, or display a visual message
- Cache action that removes one or more URLs from the UP.Browser cache
- Images
- Decks
- Digests

In our stock alert example, we'll use the *alert* notification. This notification includes a short notification message and usually a URL, which serves to extend the alert's usability. Any of the following features can be used in combination with an alert in order to notify the user:

- Device will beep, vibrate, or signal the device's light.
- Screen will display a pop-up message card.
- Screen will display an alert icon.

The UP.Phone device adds each alert message it receives to its special Inbox card. The Inbox card option is shown as a Softkey icon, usually strategically added to the user's home or primary menu as seen in the lower right-hand corner of the left-hand image in Figure 6.31. Once the associated key is pressed, the Alert Inbox is shown, right image in Figure 6.31. Up to nine alert titles and accompanying URL links can be stored in the Inbox for this scenario. In most cases, a total of 1500 bytes are allocated for this purpose. Users therefore limit the size of each message, alert title, and URL to a combined 160 bytes (9 x 160=1500 bytes).

The generic Inbox icon code to add to your application to make the Alert Inbox messages available is shown in Figure 6.32. We've also added the code to our DTW.asp dynamic personalized menu program as seen later on in this section.

Let's begin our Stock Alert push application. We have to create our own application to run on our Web server to pull and check our back-end database for high and low stock trigger values. Then the application will push a message if required to the specific user's Web phone. The Web phone application will have the special Alert Inbox application and icon as just described.

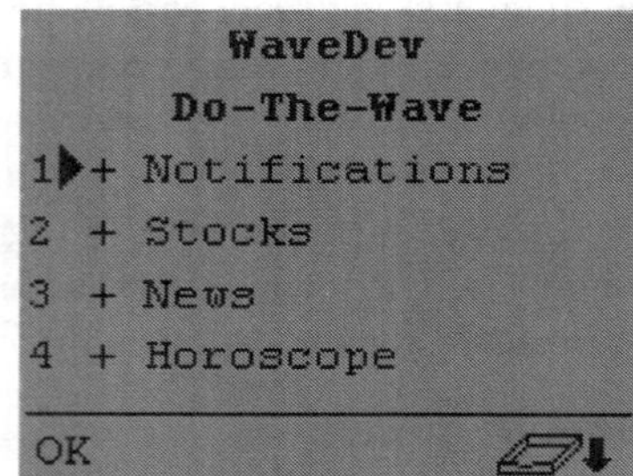

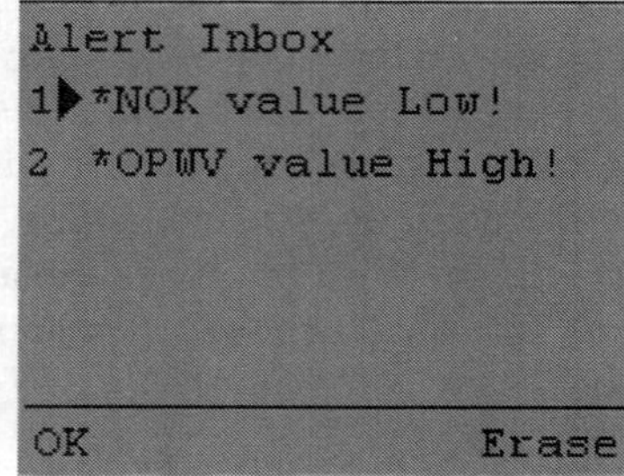

Figure 6.31 Inbox example.

The application running on the server is a one-program application written in VB6. The back-end database is an Access database with three basic tables. We'll add the stock alert application to our existing dynamic personalized menu system where it will be available on every menu level.

Before we begin, we must set up our development environment. To push the message we must have access to Openwave's Developer Up.Link Server. We must register on the gateway so it can recognize our device (Up.Simulator), which will be the UP.SDK 4.1 running on our PC. In real life, the user's mobile device will be preregistered since it comes with the Up.Browser microbrowser and has its own unique identification. For everything to run smoothly, you must ensure that your Internet connection allows communication via TCP ports 3356 and 4445.

To register our PC with Up.Link's Server, the server must recognize our IP address. To begin, you must register with Openwave at http://developer.openwave.com/gateway/provision.html. If your IP address changes every time you log on to the Internet, you'll have to perform these steps every time you want to use the Up.Link server. In this scenario, it would be best when registering your client ID to register a dummy address. Then, every time you reconnect to the Internet, you simply synchronize (Sync) your phone (dynamic IP address) with the Server.

Go to the next page on the Openwave Web site, as shown in Figure 6.33.

Once on this page, select the Login button to log in to the Up.Link Provisioning system if you're already signed up. If not, sign up and then log in. Then, as shown in Figure 6.34,

```
<do type="options">
  <spawn href="device:status">
   <catch/>
  </spawn>
  <img localsrc="inbox" src="" alt="InBox"/>
</do>
```

Figure 6.32 Inbox WML code.

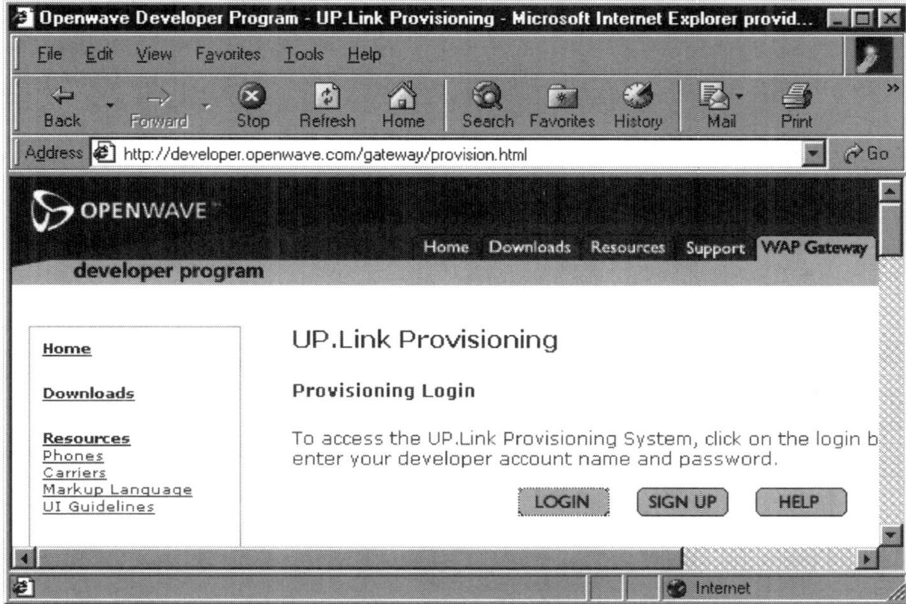

Figure 6.33 Up.Link provisioning.

select the Find Subscriber button on the left of the page to display the subscriber form. Click on the Submit button to view all your subscriber entries. One should have been set up when you registered. When the results return, click on the Client ID pertaining to WAP if you're using the UP.SDK 4.1 simulator or click on HDTP for version 3.2 or earlier. You may have to click on all entries until you find the proper Client ID format. The Client ID is your computer's IP address.

Here you will find all the information that the Developer UP.Link Server has pertaining to your subscriber account. Now you must synchronize your PC with this server information. This is simply a process whereby your Internet connection IP address is recorded in the UP.Link Server so it knows where to send the notifications (messages). Click on the Developer Utilities button on the left and then choose the Sync Phone utility. This will automatically synchronize the Server and your PC.

Now the gateway knows who you are, or rather it recognizes your IP address. Now, go into UP.SDK 4.1's UP.Simulator. Click on the UP.Simulator and once it has started, select the Settings option followed by the UP.Link Settings option. See Figure 6.35.

The default setting is HTTP Direct, which bypasses any UP.Link Server and goes directly to a WAP site. Since we want to use the features on Openwave's production development UP.Link Server, choose any UP.Link radio button and click on OK. This automatically unselects the HTTP Direct choice and connects your UP.Simulator to an UP.Link Server. The UP.Simulator will show a security message as shown in Figure 6.36.

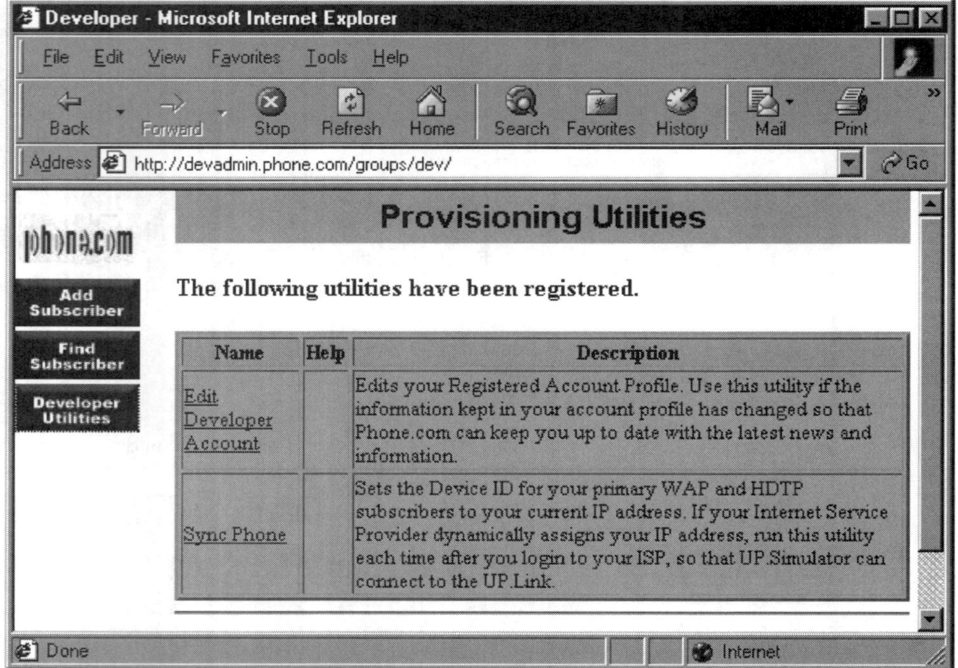

Figure 6.34 Sync phone utility from Openwave.

Select Yes to set up your device. If done successfully, you should be in sync with the UP.Link Server and ready to use all the available features provided by Openwave's Developer production gateway. If you have any problems, refer to their UP.SDK Tools and APIs Reference manual at http://developer.openwave.com/htmldoc/41/tools/.

Now to test sending (pushing) an alert message through the UP.Link Server to the UP.Simulator on your PC, which is connected to the Internet, select the SendNtfn Tool in the UP.SDK 4.1 developer kit. See Figure 6.37.

To get this working, enter the Subscriber ID from the Web page after you synchronized your IP address with the UP.Link Server in the Subscriber ID input area as seen in Figure 6.37. If you don't remember it or have reconnected to the Internet, simply go back to Openwave's site and resync your phone via the Developer Utilities option button. When entering the Subscriber ID in the SendNtfn tool, don't remove the gateway information (_devgate2.uplanet.com as seen previously). Just replace the zeros with your specific Subscriber ID number.

Now to test a push alert, type something in the Alert Title in the Additional Alert Information area and press Send Alert. If a message is received on your UP.Simulator, you'll hear a beep. The message will then be available in the Alert Inbox area if one is set up on your simulator. If you don't have one specifically in your application, go to

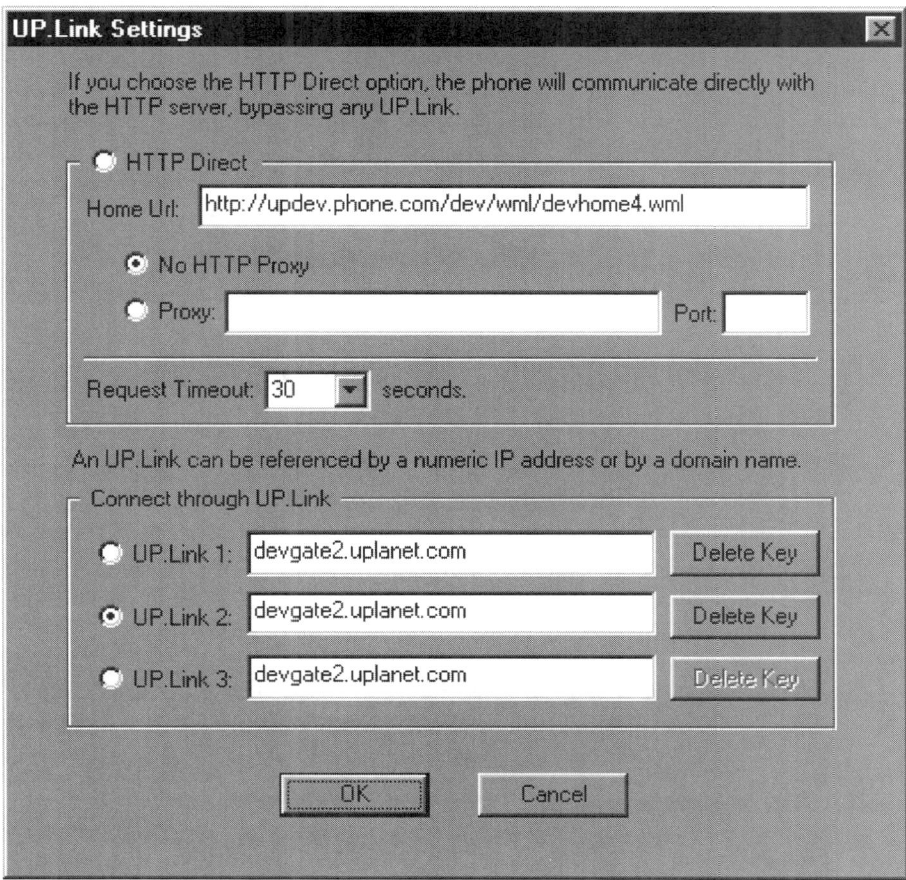

Figure 6.35 UP.Link settings in UP.SDK 4.1.

Advance from Openwave's main menu on the UP.Simulator, click on the Menu button, and then select the Home button. This action will bring you to Openwave's Gateway Menu, http://developer.phone.com/dhome.cgi. From there, on the right-hand side of the simulator screen, an Inbox tray icon should be visible. Select it, and you'll be able to see your sent alerts.

Now all the system pieces are set up, and we have connectivity of sending and receiving messages so we're ready to go. All we require is our VB6 push application and the back-end database. As we mentioned earlier, we'll be using an Access database with three tables.

We will be using a new database because this push example is its own application. We can always create an application to validate the data's integrity across this database—Customers table with the Members table in the Advertising database as well as the

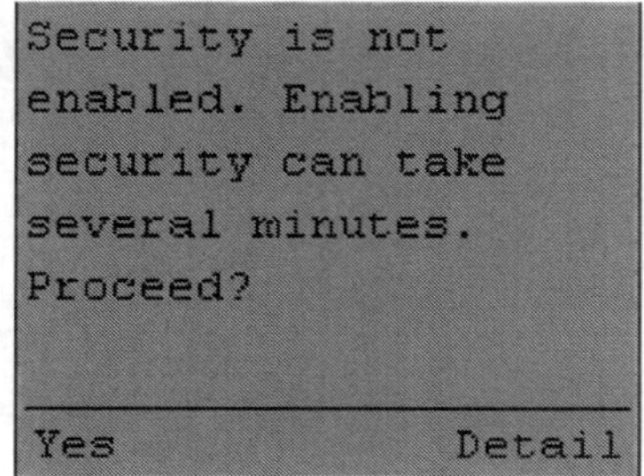

Figure 6.36 UP.Simulator security screen.

MenuTable in the Paging database—but for simplicity we have left all that out. See Figure 6.38.

The Customers table is for registered customers and contains their customer number, subscriber identification number, UP.Link Server gateway information, and an alert column flagging whether or not the person has any alerts set.

The Stocks table is to register each individual stock with the stock price or current value. Our application will be referring to this table for the source for the stock price.

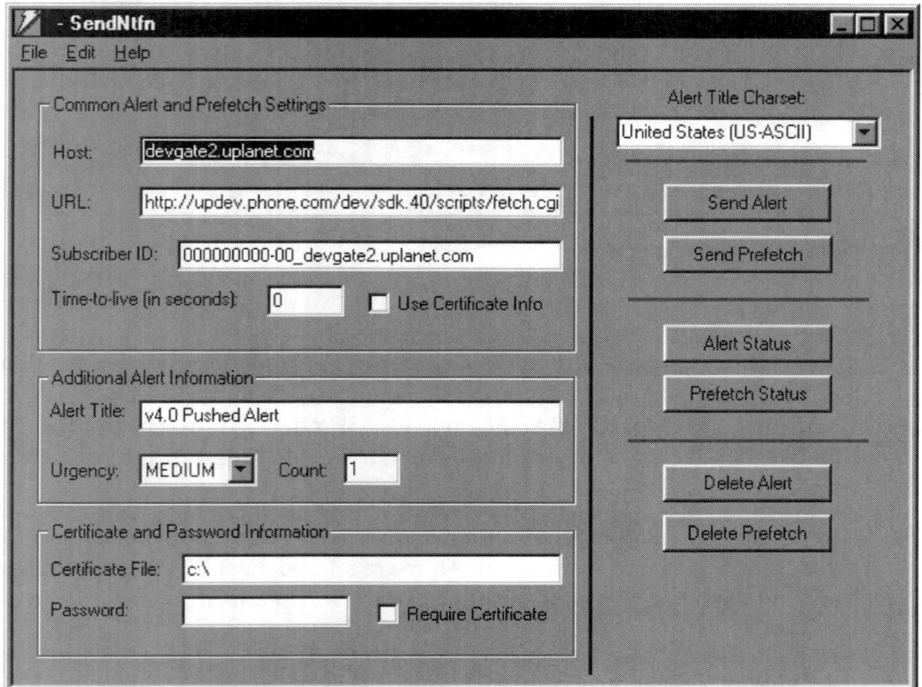

Figure 6.37 SendNtfn tool in UP.SDK 4.1.

Alerts : Table

Field Name	Data Type
AlertID	AutoNumber
CustomerNo	Number
Ticker	Text
LowTrigger	Currency
HighTrigger	Currency
Frequency	Number
Created	Date/Time

Customers : Table

Field Name	Data Type
CustomerNo	AutoNumber
CustomerName	Text
CustomerSubscrNo	Text
CustomerGateway	Text
CustomerAlerts	Yes/No

Stocks : Table

Field Name	Data Type
Ticker	Text
Price	Currency
TimeValued	Date/Time

Figure 6.38 SendPush.mdb database table definitions.

We could have built another program that checked stock prices directly against a well-known stock source such as Bloomberg or Reuters, but this is not the point of our example and so we decided to simply access a database table as our stock price source.

The Alerts table contains the trigger values. A user decides which stock to set a high or low trigger on, selects a specific stock price, and the frequency of the alert. For our example, alerts can only be in intervals of 30 seconds since our notification program is only reinvoked every 30 seconds. In our example, the user wants to be alerted if the price of NOK reaches a high of $120 or a low of $80. For simplicity, the program only checks for values greater than or equal to the high or less than or equal to the low trigger values. See Figure 6.39.

The VB6 application will have the task of querying the database and, based on the rules set by the customer and stored in the Alerts table (high and low trigger values for specific stocks), will push an alert to the WAP device. When the alert is received, the device will beep, vibrate, or the WAP device light will flash, notifying the user of the message arrival. For our development environment, the UP.Simulator, whenever a message arrives you will hear a beep.

The VB application code is compiled and an .exe file is created, which, when run, will appear on the application Web server, as shown in Figure 6.40. Of course the informa-

Alerts : Table

	AlertID	CustomerNo	Ticker	LowTrigger	HighTrigger	Frequency	Created
▶	2	1	NOK	$80.00	$120.00	100	07/04/01
	3	3	NOK	$40.00	$110.00	300	19/04/01
	4	1	OPWV	$30.00	$40.00	100	20/04/01

Customers : Table

	CustomerNo	CustomerName	CustomerSubscrNo	CustomerGateway	CustomerAlerts
▶	1	Srdjan	984796135-10037	devgate2.uplanet.com	☑
	2	Bob	984796135-10036	devgate2.uplanet.com	☑
	3	Albert	984796135-10035	devgate2.uplanet.com	☑

Stocks : Table

	Ticker	Price	TimeValued
▶	MSFT	$65.00	
	NOK	$50.00	
	OPWV	$45.00	

Figure 6.39 Database table data.

tional comments and arrows will not appear since they've only been added for documentation purposes.

The VB code specifics are as shown in Figure 6.41.

This VB6 program contains just the basics. Let's run through each line of code. The first thing to know about VB is that there are two parts: the GUI section and the underlying

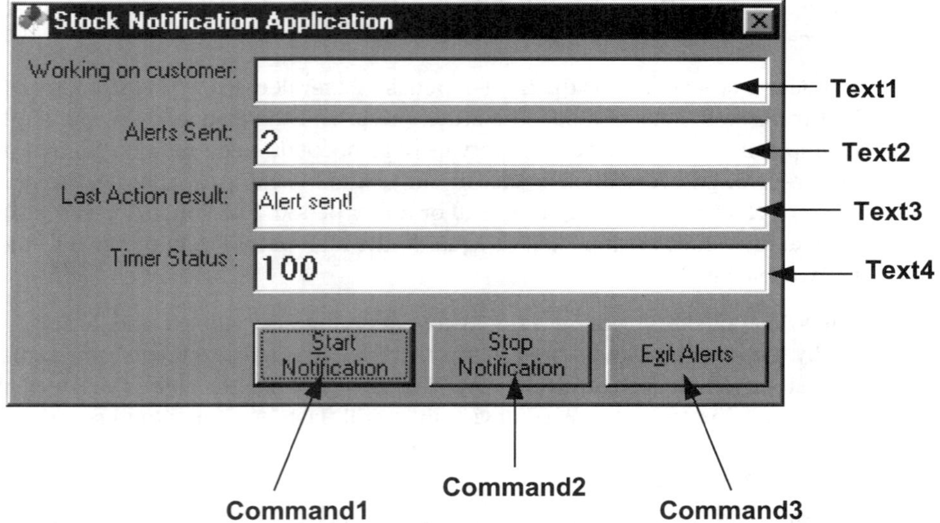

Figure 6.40 Stock notification application GUI.

```
1.  Private Sub Command1_Click()
2.      Timer1.Enabled = True
3.  End Sub


4.  Private Sub Command2_Click()
5.      Timer1.Enabled = False
6.      Text4.Text = 0
7.      Text4.Refresh
8.      Text2.Text = 0
9.      Text2.Refresh
10. End Sub


11. Private Sub Command3_Click()
12.     End
13.     Unload Me
14. End Sub


15. Private Sub Form_Load()
16.     Timer1.Enabled = False
17.     Timer1.Interval = 30000
18. End Sub


19. Private Sub Timer1_Timer()
20.     Text4.Text = Val(Text4.Text) + 30
21.     Text4.Refresh
22.     Data1.RecordSource = "select C.CustomerNo, C.CustomerName,
        C.CustomerAlerts, C.CustomerSubscrNo, C.CustomerGateway,
        A.Ticker, A.LowTrigger, A.HighTrigger from Alerts A, Customers C
        where A.CustomerNo = C.CustomerNo and C.CustomerAlerts = True"
23.     Data1.Refresh
24.     If Data1.Recordset.EOF And Data1.Recordset.BOF Then
25.         Text3.Text = "Nothing to send at this time"
26.         Text3.Refresh
27.     Else
28.         Data1.Recordset.MoveFirst
29.         Do While Not Data1.Recordset.EOF
30.             Data2.RecordSource = "select Ticker, Price from Stocks
                where Ticker = '" &
                Trim(Data1.Recordset.Fields("Ticker")) & "'"
31.             Data2.Refresh
32.             If Val(Data2.Recordset.Fields("Price")) >=
                    Val(Data1.Recordset.Fields("HighTrigger")) Then
33.                 Text2.Text = Val(Text2.Text) + 1
```

Figure 6.41 CH06Alert.exe VB program code.

```
34.                    Call SendAlert(Data1.Recordset.Fields("CustomerNo"),
                       Data1.Recordset.Fields("CustomerName"),
                       Data1.Recordset.Fields("CustomerSubsCrNo") & "_" &
                       Data1.Recordset.Fields("CustomerGateway"),
                       Data1.Recordset.Fields("CustomerGateway"),
                       Data1.Recordset.Fields("Ticker"), "High")
35.                    Text1.Text = Data1.Recordset.Fields("CustomerName")
36.                    Text1.Refresh
37.               End If
38.               If Val(Data2.Recordset.Fields("Price")) <=
                       Val(Data1.Recordset.Fields("LowTrigger")) Then
39.                    Text2.Text = Val(Text2.Text) + 1
40.                    Call SendAlert(Data1.Recordset.Fields("CustomerNo"),
                       Data1.Recordset.Fields("CustomerName"),
                       Data1.Recordset.Fields("CustomerSubsCrNo") & "_" &
                       Data1.Recordset.Fields("CustomerGateway"),
                       Data1.Recordset.Fields("CustomerGateway"),
                       Data1.Recordset.Fields("Ticker"), "Low")
41.                    Text1.Text = Data1.Recordset.Fields("CustomerName")
42.                    Text1.Refresh
43.               End If
44.               Data1.Recordset.MoveNext
45.          Loop
46.       End If
47. End Sub


48. Private Sub SendAlert(CID, CN, CS, CG, CT, CD)
49.       Dim sendResult As Long
50.       Dim ntfn As New Ntfn3Client
51.       ntfn.NtfnSetHost CG
52.       ntfn.NtfnSetCharset "US-ASCII)"
53.       ntfn.NtfnPostAlert CS,
          "http://www.wavedev.com/StockAlert.asp?CustNo=" & CID &
          "&Ticker=" & CT & "&Value=" & CD, 60, "D---", CT & " value " &
          CD & "!"
54.       lngResult = ntfn.NtfnGetLastResult
55.       If lngResult = 204 Then
56.          Text3.Text = "Alert sent!"
57.          Text3.Refresh
58.       Else
59.          Text3.Text = (Str(sendResult))
60.          Text3.Refresh
61.       End If
62. End Sub
```

Figure 6.41 Continued CH06Alert.exe VB program code.

code. The GUI section defines the application front end and defines variables, as shown in Figure 6.40. The VB code is sectioned into subroutines as defined on lines 1, 4, 11, 15, 19, and 48. These routines are associated with buttons on the GUI definition. For example, Figure 6.40 shows the Start Notification button and has Command1 variable defined to it. Once this button is pressed, it invokes the first subroutine in Figure 6.41, lines 1, 2, and 3. This essentially sets the timer value to on and begins the Stock Notification application.

This application will send notifications every 30 seconds if several conditions are met. First the customer must request alerts, which is done through the CustomerAlerts field in the Alerts table. If this is set to TRUE, alerts are possible. Second, the customer must set a high and/or low stock trigger, which, as the name implies, triggers the alert.

The subroutine, Command2_Click, on lines 4 through 10 will be invoked when the Stop Notification button is pressed. It simply resets the Alerts Sent (Text2) and Timer Status (Text4) variables.

To end the routine, press the Exit Alerts button, which invokes subroutine Command3_Click on lines 11 through 14. This will end and unload the application.

In order to achieve the automatic sending, the VB application must have timer control logic added. And for the application to connect and send the notifications, the application must include the UPNotify Type Library DLLs as seen in Figure 6.42.

Line 17 sets the timer control to 30-second intervals, which is disabled during this Form_Load routine on lines 15 through 18.

Once the form is loaded, an active Alert cycle will start when the Start Notification button is clicked. Again, this button refers to Command1, which refers to the Command1_Click subroutine on lines 1 through 3.

Now the program waits for 30 seconds.

Once the predefined interval has been reached, the counter (shown in Text4) is increased for 30 more seconds, line 20 for the setting and line 21 for the refresh.

Then the real business starts on lines 22 and 23. The database is queried (every 30 seconds) to obtain all customers who have alerts.

If query returns an empty Recordset, line 24, the Text3 variable is set to an administrative message, line 25, and the Last Action result display (Figure 6.40) will be refreshed with the result, line 26.

If there are customers with alerts, control continues after the else statement on line 27.

The first item in the Recordset is obtained, line 28, and the Do loop statement begins, lines 29 through 45. While rows exist in the Resultset, each trigger value for every record is checked against the stock price from the Stocks table for the specific stock, lines 30 and 31.

Line 32 checks if the stock price is greater than or equal to the high trigger value. If it is, the Alerts Sent display (Figure 6.40, Text2)) is called on line 33 and the SendAlert

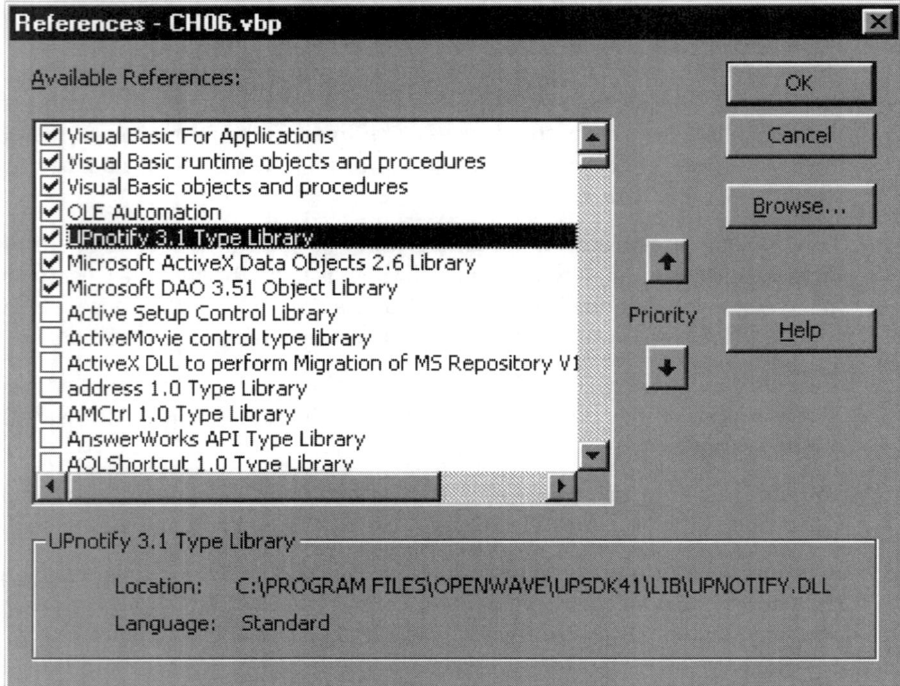

Figure 6.42 Referencing UPNotify DLL library in VB 6.

subroutine is called on line 34. When the routine ends, the customer name is written to the screen, Text1 on line 41.

The same thing happens for the low trigger values except it obviously checks for less than or equal to on line 38.

If no trigger value conditions are met, the stock is still between the high and low trigger values, no action is taken, and the loop will continue on with the next customer and alert scenario. Once done, the program will wait another 30 seconds and then start all over again.

The SendAlert subroutine on lines 34 and 40 call the main routine of this program. In doing so, several important parameters are passed. Each has a specific role as follows:

- **CID.** The Customer Identification which is from the CustomerNo.

- **CS.** The customer subscriber number, or CustomerSubscrNo for the UP.Link Server (made up of both the subscriber number and gateway name with a dash in the middle).

- **CG.** Customer Gateway. If using the UP.Simulator, this will be devgate2.uplanet.com.

- **CT.** Stock Ticker value, for example, NOK for Nokia, for our underlying message title.

- **CD.** An ASCII word, *Low* or *High*, to be passed to WML deck.

This brings us to our core program subroutine, SendAlert, on lines 48 to 62.

After defining several variables on lines 49 and 50, the UP.Link Server gateway is set with the CG parameter, line 51, from the Call command. Line 52 sets the notification variable character set required by the server.

The actual notification is sent from line 53. We'll explain all the parameters in a moment.

Line 54 obtains the result of the sending.

Line 55 will test the sending result for a 204 value, which means it was successfully sent as seen. If this happens, a message is sent to the screen in the Text3 variable (Last Action result), which is refreshed on line 57.

If the sending was not successful, line 59 will send the resulting error message to the Text3 variable.

To better understand the notification process, let's dissect line 53, the notification posting alert statement.

```
53. ntfn.NtfnPostAlert CS,
"http://www.wavedev.com/StockAlert.asp?CustNo=" & CID & "&Ticker=" &
CT & "&Value=" & CD, 60, "D---", CT & " value " & CD & "!"
```

The CS parameter is the SubscriberID made up of the customer subscriber number, a dash, and the gateway, for example, 1111111-111_uplink.foo.com.

The next part "http://wavedev.com/StockAlert.asp?CustNo=" & CID & "&Ticker=" & CT & "&Value=" & CD is the underlying notification URL to be used when the user clicks on the message, for example, Buy/Sell Softkey label.

The 60 defines the notification's Time-To-Live (TTL). This means that if the server hasn't been able to send the notification message for 60 seconds, the message will not be sent and the result will be an error message.

The next parameter, D---, is the alert type in the following form: Device-dependent signal, Sound, Visual Signal, Vibration. The following are the possible values for each signal:

- **Device-dependent signal.** -, D
- **Sound.** -, 1, 2, 3, 4
- **Visual signal.** -, 1, 2, 3, 4
- **Vibration.** -, 1

The D value represents the default signal, and the dashes turn the specific options off.

The last entries—CT, values, and CD—are used for the alert message title.

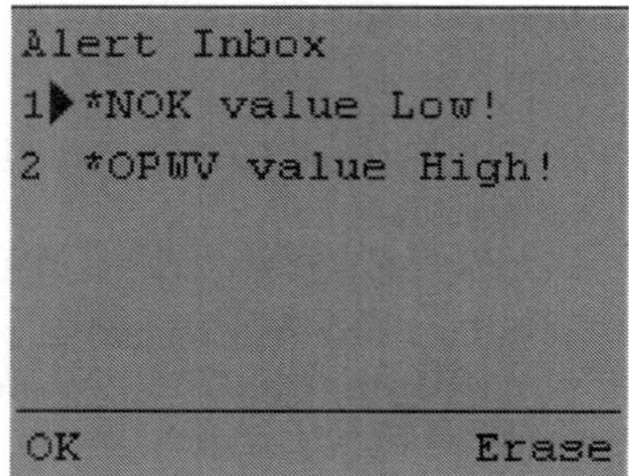

Figure 6.43 StockAlert.asp program results.

After the notifications are sent, a new cycle starts. The application will run tirelessly until manually interrupted by clicking the Stop Notification button.

 The previous code will generate the push alerts on the customer's microbrowser. Once the InTray icon on the menu page is selected, the Alert Inbox page (Figure 6.43) will be displayed. And once a generated stock notification message is selected, program control will link to the underlying URL. This URL was sent from the VB application as part of the message and once selected will display a page with the entire message (Figure 6.44) generated from the ASP program, Figure 6.45.

The underlying URL page can display whatever the content provider decides. Now outside the confines of the alert message, the WML page can be a regular WAP application capable of anything. In our example, we simply show a Buy/Sell Softkey label, signifying the possible ongoing application potential. We do not show that application since it is outside the scope of our application.

There is no need to explain this ASP program since all aspects have been explained many times in this chapter and in other examples. Linking to the next application can be through the ASP program in the GO statement on line 20 with whatever parameters are required. Of course a simple text message, with or without instructions, can be included on the generated WML page as was done on lines 22 and 23.

To upgrade the dynamic personalized menu program, DTW.asp from Figure 6.9, to include an Inbox icon on every menu level, simply add the code from Figure 6.32

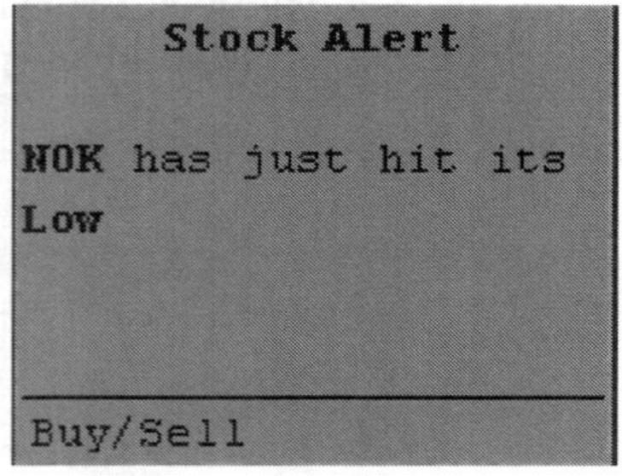

Figure 6.44 StockAlert.asp program results.

```
1. <%@ LANGUAGE="VBSCRIPT" %>
2. <%
3. Response.Expires = 0


4. Dim strCustNo
5. Dim strTicker
6. Dim strValue


7. strCustNo = request("CustNo")
8. strTicker = request("Ticker")
9. strValue = request("Value")


10. Response.Buffer = TRUE
11. Response.ContentType = "text/vnd.wap.wml"
12. response.write "<?xml version="+chr(34)+"1.0"+chr(34)+"?>"
13. response.write "<!DOCTYPE wml PUBLIC "+chr(34)+"-//PHONE.COM//DTD
    WML 1.1//EN"+chr(34)+"
    "+chr(34)+"http://www.phone.com/dtd/wml11.dtd"+chr(34)+" >"
14. response.write "<wml>"
15. response.write "<head>"
16. response.write "  <meta http-equiv="+chr(34)+"Cache-
    Control"+chr(34)+" content="+chr(34)+"max-age=0"+chr(34)+"/>"
17. response.write "</head>"
18. response.write "<card>"
19. response.write "<do type="+chr(34)+"accept"+chr(34)+"
    label="+chr(34)+"Buy/Sell"+chr(34)+">"
20. response.write "   <go href="+chr(34)+"buysell.asp?Ticker="+
    trim(strTicker) +"&amp;CustNo="+ strCustNo +chr(34)+"/>"
21. response.write "</do>"


22. response.write "<p align="+chr(34)+"center"+chr(34)+"><b>Stock
    Alert</b></p>"
23. response.write "<p align="+chr(34)+"left"+chr(34)+"><br/><b>"+
    strTicker +"</b> has just hit its  <b>"+ strValue +"</b></p>"


24. response.write "</card>"
25. response.write "</wml>"
26. %>
```

Figure 6.45 StockAlert.asp program.

between lines 64 and 65 in DTW.asp. Lines 65 through 70 are the newly entered code as shown in Figure 6.46.

This completes the Push Stock Notification application. The code is also included on the CD. Feel free to modify it as you see fit for your own scenario or project. This application can be used as the basis for many different applications, including mail notifica-

```
55. if strNoRows="Y" and strOwnerID=0 then
56.   response.write "<do type="+chr(34)+"accept"+chr(34)+"
      label="+chr(34)+"Home"+chr(34)+">"
57.   response.write "<go href="+chr(34)+"../mainmenu.wml"+chr(34)+"/>"
58.   response.write "</do>"
59.   response.write "<p mode="+chr(34)+"nowrap"+chr(34)+">"
60.   response.write "<b><br/>Not Available</b>"
61. else
62.   response.write "<do type="+chr(34)+"accept"+chr(34)+"
      label="+chr(34)+"OK"+chr(34)+">"
63.   response.write "<prev/>"
64.   response.write "</do>"
65.   response.write "<do type="+chr(34)+"options"+chr(34)+">"
66.   response.write "   <spawn
      href="+chr(34)+"device:status"+chr(34)+">"
67.   response.write "    <catch/>"
68.   response.write "    </spawn>"
69.   response.write "   <img localsrc="+chr(34)+"inbox"+chr(34)+"
      src="+chr(34)+chr(34)+" alt="+chr(34)+"InBox"+chr(34)+"/>"
70.   response.write "</do>"
71.   if strOwnerID <> 0 then
72.       if strNoRows="N" then
```

Figure 6.46 Addition of Inbox icon into DTW.asp.

tions, ticket purchase notifications, up-to-the-minute traffic notifications, and whatever else you can dream up.

Additional

There are many other types of push application possibilities, such as bids on auction sites and games. I'm sure there will be many clever applications in the future that will perhaps generate millions of dollars in revenues. Push is the next major addition to wireless mobility—for WAP or any other underlying technology.

The examples in this chapter were simple but did explain the topics and demonstrated how WAP can be personalized. Individuals currently purchase cellular phones based on a specific color, size, or weight, and soon the choice will be based on content. Those offering content with push systems, which personalize applications to the individuals, will definitely benefit.

CHAPTER 7

VoiceXML

Al examples presented in this chapter have been developed and tested using Motorola's Mobile ADK version 2.0. Every line of program code in this chapter is numbered for easy reference. Code on the CD is identical but without the numbers, making it easy to simply copy and execute the code.

This chapter presents an overview of VoiceXML with some basic components such as tags and their usage. First we'll introduce the topic with its history and then present an overview of the unique architecture.

VoiceXML deals with voice rather than vision; hence, Web browsers are replaced with telephones. To help the business architects and developers build an application without the help of any visual end products, *dialog documents* and *state diagrams* are used. We'll have a look at these and follow up with the full code to a functional VoiceXML application. Our goal is to help you, the reader, quickly understand, develop, and deploy voice-enabled Web applications.

VoiceXML is not that popular as of mid-2001, but it will become as widely used as WAP and other wireless technologies within the next several years. In addition to viewing that little screen on a Web phone, VoiceXML will allow users to talk to Web sites. Being able to speak to an application and have it respond is quite an achievement in technology. Voice communication between machines and people is definitely a marvel of today's age.

Introduction

Voice Extensible Markup Language (VoiceXML) is the latest addition to the Internet anywhere. This new Internet technology is based on the XML subset called VoiceXML, which functions in cooperation with Voice Browser technology.

VoiceXML is a language for creating voice-user interactive interfaces. It uses telephone-style speech recognition and/or Dual-Tone Multi Frequency (DTMF) touch-tone (keypad entry) for input and prerecorded digitized audio and synthesized text-to-speech for output. This is not voice-over IP or long distance over the Internet as advertised by Internet providers. This is voice-enabling Internet Web sites for interactive voice response applications based on the Worldwide Web Consortium's (W3C) Voice Browser Working Group. W3C can be thought of as a sort of regulating body that ensures the foundation of Web technology is standardized, portable, and developed in as much of an open architecture style as possible.

VoiceXML technology can be used in two particular applications. The first is by granting voice access to a Web site and the second is to build and enable nonproprietary Interactive Voice Response (IVR) services over the Internet.

When developing applications using VoiceXML, the Web's basic components and infrastructure remain the same. The main difference is that instead of using a Web browser such as Internet Explorer or Netscape, a Voice Browser is used. Unlike a Web browser, which sits on the client PC, a Voice Browser resides on a highly specialized remote server. To make a connection, simply pick up a telephone and dial a specific number that connects to the VoiceXML interpreter. The interpreter then connects to the Internet as explained in the architecture section that follows.

History

Changes in today's computer technologies, especially in how we are using and accessing information available over the Internet, are occurring at a rate that very few imagined possible 10 years ago. When President Bill Clinton was elected in 1992, there was only a handful of Internet Web sites. When George W. Bush became president 8 years later, there were over 25 million Web sites—an incredible increase. The next phase of expansion is interactive voice-controlled Internet, all beginning with VoiceXML.

VoiceXML, the *dialog markup language* as it's referred to by the VoiceXML forum, is a fairly new subset of XML. XML was itself only first presented in November 1996.

Initial attempts to create a phone (or dialog) markup language started with AT&T Bell Laboratories with a research project called *PhoneWeb*. But efforts were delayed when AT&T was forced to split up into AT&T and Lucent Technologies back in 1995. Not much happened until September 1998 when Motorola announced a new method to merge telephony (wire and wireless technologies) with the Internet via a new XML subset called VoxML. Motorola realized early on the importance of hands-free Internet voice commands, and an integral part of their strategy was to focus on speech recognition as that input mechanism. VoxML is currently in use and is quite a nice and easy XML subset tag language. For perspective, think of it as VoxML is to VoiceXML as HDML is to WML.

On March 2, 1999, AT&T, Lucent Technologies, and Motorola joined forces in the formation of a new Voice Extensible Markup Language Forum called *VXML Forum*, which was later renamed *VoiceXML forum*. The forum is a centralized area that specializes in the VoiceXML dialog markup languages and related concerns. Visit them at www.voicexml.org.

As recently as April 2000, the VoiceXML Forum announced that the World Wide Web Consortium, regulators of Web standards, acknowledged the submission of version 1.0 of the VoiceXML specifications. And at the May 2000, meetings in Paris, the W3C's Voice Browser Working Group agreed to adopt VoiceXML 1.0 as the basis for the development of a W3C dialog markup language—a big step in voice technology acceptance.

As of early 2001, along with the forum's founding members (AT&T, Lucent Technologies, Motorola, and later IBM), membership in the VoiceXML forum has grown to nearly 400 members.

Architecture

In order to enable communication between the telephone devices (wired and wireless), as seen in Figure 7.1(1) and (2) and the Internet, a specialized mixture of hardware and software called the VoiceXML gateway is required [Figure 7.1(3, 4, 5)].

The VoiceXML gateway is basically a computer server running an interpreter called a *Voice Browser*. Voice Browsers understand and interpret VoiceXML dialogs. In simple terms, the VoiceXML gateway facilitates communication between the dialogs and the Internet by controlling certain specific resources such as Automatic Speech Recognition (ASR), digitized voice recording and playback, Text-To-Speech (TTS), Dual-Tone Multifrequency (DTMF) tone recognition, and Public Switch Telephone Network (PSTN) network connectivity.

The ASR engine, TTS engine, system dictionaries, and Internet interface all form part of the Voice Browser and Interpreter. Motorola's VoiceXML gateway also includes the VoxML interpreter. Many ASR engines include support for multiple languages, as is

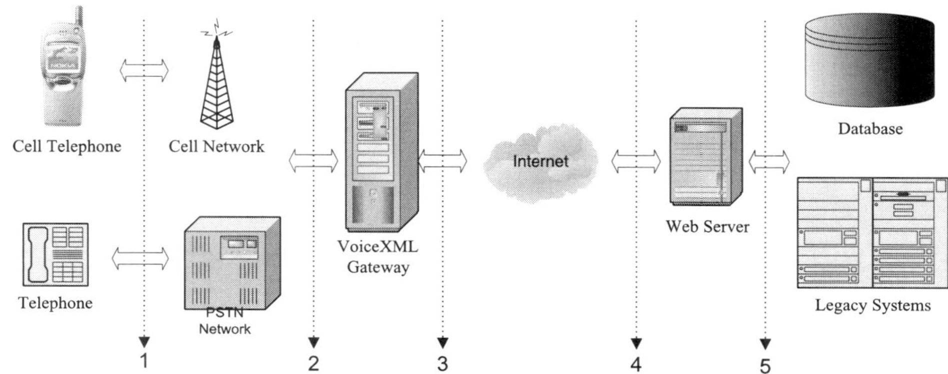

Figure 7.1 VoiceXML high-level overview.

the case with Nuance's Voice Browser, which supports more than 15 different languages.

Figure 7.2 represents three main Internet connectivity methods. Figure 7.2(A) depicts a classic personal computer with a Web browser. Figure 7.2(B) shows the major connection points for mobile WAP microbrowsers via Web phones. It's important to note that in both cases the Web browser physically resides on the client side located on the PC or WAP-enabled wireless device such as a Web phone or PDA. Usually, most code execution for these two scenarios runs on the client side.

It's a completely different story for Voice Browsers. Voice Browsers reside within the VoiceXML gateway [Figure 7.2(C)] or can be integrated within the telephone network. These server-side browsers allow users to place calls from any telephone and navigate through the VoiceXML application by selecting options on voice menus and executing simple voice input commands. Navigation can also be done by keypad or touch-tone input. The voice browser interprets the sounds of pressed keypad buttons, thus allowing either voice or touch-tone input.

Voice Browser program code resides on Web servers and on VoiceXML gateways and is therefore a server-side browser similar to execution of active server page (ASP) programs. This simplicity allows VoiceXML developers to easily maintain the source code in the same fashion as they would regular HTML or ASP code. It also allows developers to write applications that will be platform independent. Web developers must

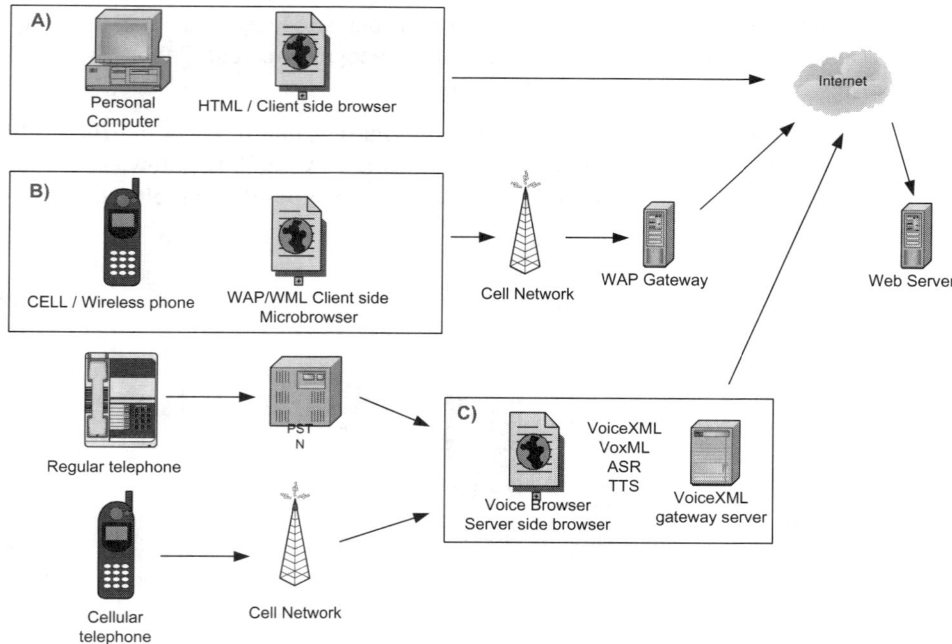

Figure 7.2 VoiceXML connectivity overview.

ensure that their HTML code correctly functions on Netscape and Internet Explorer browsers, WAP developers must ensure that their WML code correctly functions on Up.Browser and Nokia microbrowsers, but VoiceXML developers only have to worry about one VoiceXML gateway. In short, it should be easier to develop and maintain a VoiceXML application than a Web or WAP application. At the same time, there is no need for new MIME types to be added to the Web server in order to be able to serve VoiceXML code.

Overview

If you've had previous experience programming HTML, XML, or an XML subset, you shouldn't have any problem picking up the VoiceXML language. This chapter doesn't cover all VoiceXML tag details with all possible tag attributes but will explain the basic layout of a working application with basic tag introductions. For a detailed explanation of VoiceXML tags, visit http://voicexml.org and refer to Appendix D at the end of this book.

VoiceXML programs are called *documents* based on XML terminology. In a VoiceXML document, the user is always in a conversational state called a *dialog*. There are two types of dialogs, *forms* and *menus*. A document can contain any number of dialogs as the programmer sees fit. Each dialog determines the flow to the next dialog, all depending on which selection is chosen or which command is given. In Web programming, execution is halted when a screen is displayed; the user then enters information and clicks OK (or whatever), selects a hyperlink, or chooses a form item to continue. In VoiceXML, instead of a screen being presented, the system tells the user navigational information or a selection to take, and execution is then paused until the user returns either a voice command or presses a keypad button (depending on the application). When the dialog pauses, it's said to be in a *wait* or *input* state. Of course there are attributes to a paused dialog, enabling execution to continue or end automatically as the tags will later explain.

From the program's point of view, transitions to new dialogs are specified via Universal Resource identifiers (URIs). All URIs must be fully qualified, meaning that the entire site path must be included in the program name. If no specific dialog is specified on the URI, the first dialog in the document is assumed, similar to specifying which card in a deck to jump to via the URL. Execution of a dialog is terminated when no further dialog is specified or if a stated element explicitly exits the conversation.

PROGRAMMING NOTE

Always guide the user by letting him or her know exactly what's next in the application flow. Without visuals, one must take care in designing the application so that the user is notified of all possible choices at any given moment. Try not to leave the person hanging on the phone, unsure of what to do next.

Let's have a peek at a couple of really simple VoiceXML programs.

Figure 7.3 shows a simple, basic program. Once dialed, this program would greet the caller with the "Hello .." message, and execution would then end. All the basics are here.

Line 1 states that the document is an XML subset, and line 2's start tag, along with the ending tag on line 8, defines the XML subset as VoiceXML. The <form></form> tags define a form dialog, and the <block></block> tags tell the interpreter to say the encapsulated "Hello..." message when a customer calls.

The next program, Figure 7.4, has several more useful and common tags. It starts in the same manner as the previous example, but then an input field is defined on line 7 via the <field> tag. This tag defines a field called CustNo, which can only contain digits as defined by the type attribute.

The program executes as follows: Upon entry to the program, the caller is greeted with the Hello message. Then the system prompts the caller for a customer number via the message within the <prompt> </prompt> tags on line 9. Once something is said, which could be anything at this point, and that something is recognized as digits, then the input field is essentially filled and control is passed to the ValidateCustomer.asp program via the URI specified by the *next* attribute of the <submit> tag on line 12. The CustNo field is implicitly passed to the ValidateCustomer.asp program.

If, however, the caller says something like "apple," the VoiceXML interpreter will recognize that the caller did not say a numeric number and will reprompt the caller via automatically redirecting control back to line 7. The Voice Browser on the VoiceXML gateway automatically handles all the voice recognition and program redirection back to the input field. This allows the developer to deal with the application requirements rather than the voice recognition logic and coding.

Of course, this is a simple example using only basic tag attributes. There's a lot more that could be done to handle program flow, caller instructions, and so on, which we'll explain as we proceed.

Step by Step

Rather than explaining each and every tag in the language, this chapter introduces the language basics via a working and functional application. As we go, we'll explain the

```
1. <?xml version="1.0"?>
2. <vxml version="1.0">
3.    <form>
4.       <block>
5.          Hello, and welcome to e Cigars, the cyber cigar store with
             the best e cigar selections.
6.       </block>
7.    </form>
8. </vxml>
```

Figure 7.3 VoiceXML program.

```
1.  <?xml version="1.0"?>
2.  <vxml version="1.0">
3.     <form>
4.         <block>
5.             Hello, and welcome to e Cigars, the cyber cigar store with
                the best e cigar selections.
6.         </block>
7.         <field name="CustNo" type="digits">
8.             <prompt>
9.                 Please say your customer number to enter the system.
10.            </prompt>
11.            <filled>
12.                <submit next="ValidateCustomer.asp"/>
13.            </filled>
14.         </field>
15.     </form>
16. </vxml>
```

Figure 7.4 VoiceXML program.

basic usage of certain key tags with certain key attributes. Not all tags or attributes will be explained, as the goal here is to introduce the language and get you developing as quickly as possible.

This chapter's example is based on the imaginary company called eCigars, which sells cigars via a VoiceXML application behind a 1-800 toll-free telephone number.

Our examples use a Microsoft Access database on a Web server (either Internet- or Intranet-based), a VoiceXML development tool (we used Motorola Mobile ADK 2.0), and VBScript scripting language. Perl, JavaScript, or C++ could also have been used, but we prefer the simplicity of VBScript.

Dialog Definition

The first step in creating an interactive voice-enabled Web application is to define the conversation between the user and the computer system. This conversation is called the *dialog*.

Designing a voice application is nothing more than predefining the dialog flow within the application. Think of this process as writing down the anticipated and optimistic conversation between your salesperson and the client. Direct the conversation and only allow predefined responses, thus maintaining control over the execution flow.

Figure 7.5 shows the general anticipated conversation flow for the interactive eCigars' voice application:

Notice in the conversation flow that different scenarios are presented. In our example, it's rather important to handle certain events such as orders over the 20-box limit or

```
← Start of dialog →
System: Hello, and welcome to e Cigars, the cyber cigar store with
        the best e cigar selections.
System:  To purchase cigars, you must be a registered e Cigars
         member. Please say your customer number to enter the
         system or for more information say help.
User:    12345
System:  Sorry, I didn't hear exactly 6 digits.
System:  To purchase cigars, you must be a registered e Cigars
         member. Please say your customer number to enter the
         system or for more information say help.
User:    123456
System:  Welcome back John Puff.
System:  Please select one of the following cigar types:
         Say Cohiba for a box of 25 Cohiba cigars at the price of
         50 dollars.
         Say Dominico for 20 number two Dominico cigars per box at
         the price of 40 dollars.
         Say Local for a box of 25 Locally rolled cigars at the price
         of 25 dollars.
User:    Dominico.
System:  Please select the quantity in increments of one box.
         Maximum quantity is 20 boxes per order.
User:    21

← Customer has requested more than 20 boxes for this order →
System:  Sorry, you have selected more than 20 boxes for this
         order, please try again.
System:  Please select the quantity in increments of one box.
         Maximum quantity is 20 boxes per order.
User:    Ten

← Customer has requested more than is currently available in stock →
System:  Sorry you have requested more cigars than we currently
         have available in stock, so we've given you all we have.
System:  You have placed an order for 8 boxes of Dominico cigars
         for a total cost of 320 dollars.
System:  Please say yes to commit this transaction or say no to
         cancel and start over.

← Quantity ordered is available in stock →
System:  You have placed an order for 10 boxes of Dominico cigars
         for a total cost of 400 dollars.
System:  Please say yes to commit this transaction or say no to
         cancel and start over.
User:    Yes

← Order delivered to address on file for registered customer →
System:  Your order will be delivered to: John Puff living at 21
         Smoke Circle.
System:  Thank you for shopping at e Cigars, bye bye.

← End of dialog →
```

Figure 7.5 Dialog conversation flow.

when inventory is less than a requested amount. The dialog document should have these significant scenarios highlighted for documentation purposes.

State Diagram

Once you have a firm understanding of the anticipated dialog flow, we highly recommend that you create a *State Diagram*. A State Diagram will help you visualize the flow of information through your application, which is the key to a successful design. The diagram will help you notice possible shortcomings in your conversation designs as well as possible logical improvements before you start the actual program coding.

As with the dialog conversation flow document, the State Diagram will be used as your system documentation once you've completed the application. Since you cannot see your program results on a Web browser or in a development tools program such as Front Page, the only tangible items you'll have after the application is completed will be these two documents, so keep them up to date.

As seen in Figure 7.6, every general step of the application is highlighted. Developers can easily see the breaking points, the conversation flow, and overall logical flow. Rather than reading through the dialog definition in the programs, one can simply glance at the State Diagram to quickly understand the individual programs and overall application.

The initial step in creating a State Diagram is to simply highlight each major point. Then section the points into blocks based on conversation and processing. Next, create your programs based on the sectioned blocks.

HINT

Always begin your VoiceXML applications with a .vxml program rather than, say, an .asp program. We suggest this because many automated robots will scour the Web looking for specific program extensions in attempts to discover and categorize new applications for their search engines. By making your first program a .vxml extension, you'll allow your application to be properly categorized into popular Internet search sites. With few VoiceXML applications and/or sites out there at the moment, having your system properly categorized in the major search engines will definitely bring in the hits.

Database Design and Connectivity

What kind of dynamic VoiceXML application would we have if we didn't connect to some sort of back-end database? In our application, we're using a Microsoft Access database to hold all information pertaining to customers (Customers table), available stock (Cigar table), and customer orders (Transactions table).

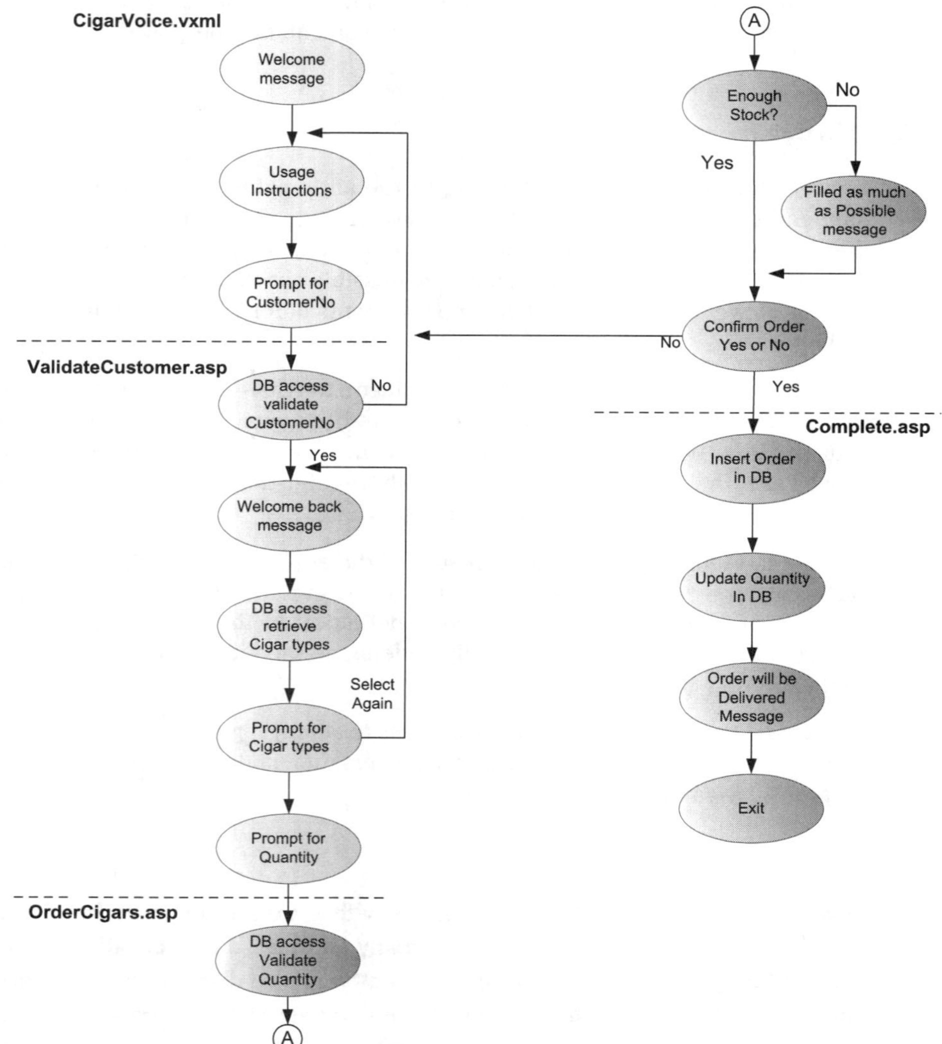

Figure 7.6 eCigars State Diagram.

Figure 7.7 shows the database table layouts along with referential integrity. Figure 7.8 details each table definition used in our database.

Our database is called eCigars.mdb and is placed, along with its DSN file, in the Web server's root directory. If either of these files is located in another directory, remember to modify the program code and the DSN contents to reflect the proper location.

In order for our ASP programs to connect to a back-end database, a connection string is required. The string can be hardcoded in the program logic, defined within the DSN

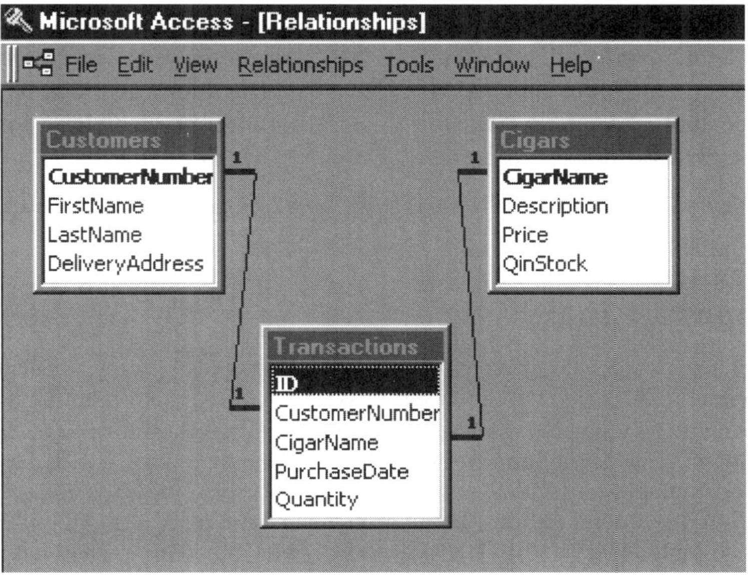

Figure 7.7 eCigars database layout.

file that we use, or created by using the ODBC administrator (from your PC click on Start → Settings → Control Panel → ODBC Data Sources application, and you'll be guided through the ODBC creation process).

```
Table: Customers
        Column Name                     Type                    Size
        Customer Number                 Long Integer            4
        Last Name                       Text                    50
        First Name                      Text                    50
        DeliveryAddress                 Text                    50

Table: CigarType
        Column Name                     Type                    Size
        CigarType                       Text                    50
        QinStock                        Long Integer            4
        CigarPrice                      Currency                8

Table: Transactions
        Column Name                     Type                    Size
        DiaperType                      Text                    50
        PurchaseDate                    Date/Time               8
        CustomerNumber                  Long Integer            4
        Quantity                        Long Integer            4
        ID                              Long Integer            4
```

Figure 7.8 eCigars database table definitions.

NOTE

The default location for the "File DSN" tab entries is in "C:\Program Files\Common Files\ODBC\Data Sources." If you don't specify a fully qualified path to the DSN file location as we do in Figure 7.12, lines 4 through 11, you'll have to place the eCigars.dsn file in this default location.

Figure 7.9 shows the DSN file that we'll be using in our ASP programs to connect to the back-end database.

Development Tool

In order to develop a VoiceXML application, you'll require a special VoiceXML development tool. Once the tags are understood, putting the programs together via an editor such as Notepad is a handy, fast development method for the accustomed developer. But to test, debug, and run the application on the spot you'll require an application development kit (ADK) such as the free Motorola mobile ADK 2.0. It's more or less an all-in-one integrated development environment for VoiceXML. As a bonus, Motorola also includes a VoxML ADK for earlier voice applications as well as a WML SDK for building WAP application within the ADK 2.0 software.

Motorola mobile ADK 2.0 is a nicely packaged tool that will run on Win98, NT, or Windows 2000. Figure 7.10 is a typical screen image of the tool as it's being used to develop the eCigars application.

It's important to utilize tools that will help shorten the development and test life cycle of your applications, and Motorola's mobile ADK 2.0 fits the bill. A great feature of the

Figure 7.9 eCigars.dsn file.

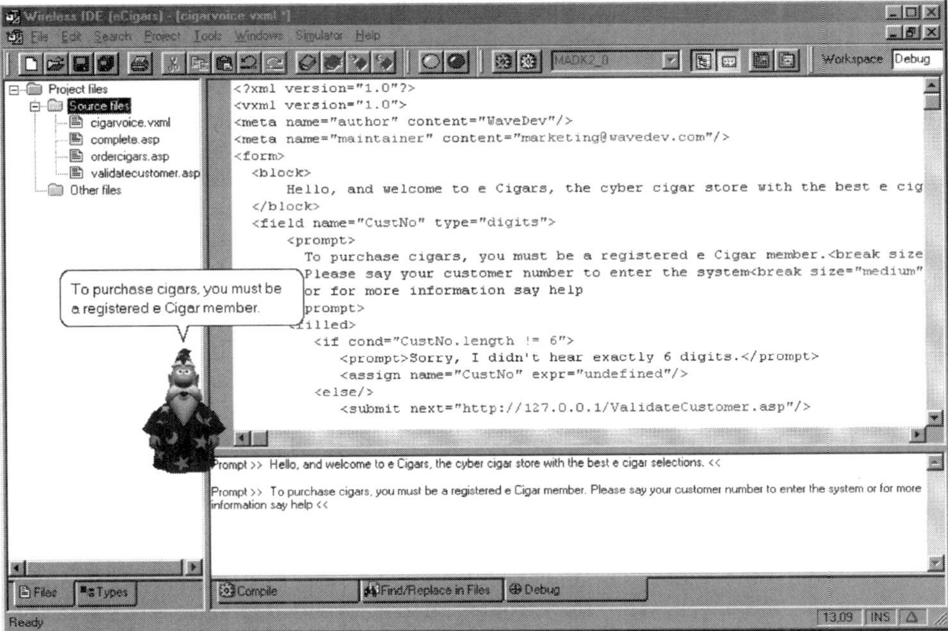

Figure 7.10 Motorola mobile ADK 2.0.

product is the little wizard seen in Figure 7.10, which appears on the screen. When the tool is in voice mode, the little guy actually talks, making the entire development process quite fun and fairly realistic.

Basic Tags

As with other development languages, VoiceXML has all the basics: input, output, navigation, and processing commands. The only difference with this language is that output is a voice rather than a visual. Being a tag-based language, VoiceXML has limited functionality and hence requires another processing language to allow all the basic data manipulation. Our preference is to use the VBScript programming language in our programs.

All input and output including Text-To-Speech recognition, translation, and presentation are handled by VoiceXML, which saves a bunch of development time. Let's have a quick look at some of the basics for input and output, along with other functions, before we jump into the programs.

When one thinks of voice, we think of hearing and talking or talking and hearing, depending on your perspective. In VoiceXML, input and output come from several commands. First we have the basic <block></block> tags used in forms to encapsulate a message. Normally, the <block> tag is used once per form and primarily used to give some type of greeting or initial instruction. Secondly, the <prompt></prompt> tags, while primarily used to ask questions, may seem like an output type command but are really used in anticipation of (usually) audio input. This tag forms the basis for much of the VoiceXML language.

Prompts are used in conjunction with forms, which are made up of fields. Both have their own tags, <form></form> and <field></field>. Fields, like on any form, exist to be filled; hence the existence of the <filled></filled> tags, which describe what to do when the form field is filled. Fields are filled via an end user's audio input. This audio input is really a reply to a prompt in a particular dialog (or form). When we say audio input, we are also including touch-tone keypad entries, which won't be included in our examples, but are well defined in the vendor documentation.

The next big piece is navigation. Navigation in VoiceXML is limited to two similar commands: <goto> and <submit>. The <goto> and <submit> tags are basically the same since they both allow the transfer of control to another dialog. The only difference between the two is that <goto> does a simple transfer while <submit> has many attributes and basically allows the transfer with variables. Variables, by the way, are fields themselves or individually defined variables—<var> tags.

Although the <goto> and <submit> commands are used extensively to direct program (or dialog conversation) flow, VoiceXML has a second level to it to catch conversation stoppers called events. The VoiceXML interpreter residing on the VoiceXML gateway is always listening in the background. So if the user gets confused and doesn't answer the question or doesn't know what to do next and says "help" the <catch></catch> tags will kick in and direct the flow to a special routine coded by the developer.

That's about the entire language in a nutshell. Of course there are more tags and more attributes, but these are the basics. Let's have a look at our eCigars application to see how all these tags can be put together to form a fully functional interactive dynamic voice application.

eCigars—VoiceXML Application

In this system we'll assume that eCigars members have already been preregistered into the database via some sort of Web-based application. The VoiceXML portion is simply for members to order their favorite cigars via the telephone. So at this point the dialog conversation flow is created, the State Diagram is designed, the database is in place and populated with some test data, and our VoiceXML development ADK is ready to go. Now we're all set to start coding our eCigars application.

The first two programs in our application—CigarVoice.vxml and Validate Customer.asp—introduce most of the VoiceXML tags described previously. The last two programs—OrderCigars.asp and Complete.asp—close the application, thus making it a fully functional system, which can be a great starting point for you to enhance as you wish for your own usage. Our goal is not to ramble on about each program but to introduce the programming aspects and practical usage of VoiceXML.

The first program is a pure static VoiceXML program as denoted by its extension—.vxml. The second program will demonstrate dynamic VoiceXML code and back-end database connectivity from an ASP program. The third will check that stock exists and report any inventory problems. The last program in our application will place the order in the database, relay a confirmation message to the end user, and then disconnect.

As mentioned earlier, we highly suggest that the first program in your application should always be a pure VoiceXML program ending with the .vxml extension. This is to ensure that crawlers and robots (programs that automatically index Web pages) will discover your application program and properly categorize it as a voice application in their indexed database search engine, for all the world to see.

Program One—CigarVoice.vxml

The VoiceXML program in Figure 7.11 initiates the application with an introduction to the caller followed by a prompt for the user to say his or her customer number. This application assumes the user is preregistered with eCigars.

The first line in the program in Figure 7.11 defines the program as an XML document. Following this is the <vxml></vxml> tag pair (lines 2 and 32). This defines all encapsulated code to be VoiceXML.

Lines 3 and 4 are simple meta tags similar to HTML meta tags. Line 3 defines the author's name, and line 4 documents the email address of the person maintaining the code.

Lines 5 and 31, the <form></form> tags, are key components since they define a dialog in a VoiceXML document.

Lines 6 through 8 define a (usually) one-time executed block of code. Line 7 within this block is the initial application greeting to the end users. Unless specifically stated, blocks of code execute a one-time message. After the block has executed, reinitiation of the form will not rerun the block message.

Lines 9 through 30 define an input field for the form. This is a very important part of the program since this is how we'll gather the customer number from the end user. The field type attribute defines the CustNo field as digits only, which will be edited by the <filled> statements on lines 15 through 22. The digits attribute will accept user input such as "one two three four five six" but will not accept "one hundred twenty three thousand and four hundred and fifty-six."

As mentioned earlier, prompt commands are used to gather input from the end user into the form field. Since VoiceXML has no visuals, think of these prompt commands as the input lines for a form on a Web page. Lines 10 through 14 define the <prompt></prompt> tags. In our case, line 11 gives an audio message to the user followed by a programmed medium pause or break (hence the use of a <break> tag) and then a direct request to capture the customer number. We've also included the high-level HELP instructional message. If the user says "help" at this point, the VoiceXML interpreter context will catch this event as seen on line 23.

```
1.  <?xml version="1.0"?>
2.  <vxml version="1.0">
3.  <meta name="author" content="WaveDev"/>
4.  <meta name="maintainer" content="marketing@wavedev.com"/>
5.  <form>
6.    <block>
7.        Hello, and welcome to e Cigars, the cyber cigar store with
          the best e cigar selections.
8.    </block>
9.    <field name="CustNo" type="digits">
10.       <prompt>
11.           To purchase cigars, you must be a registered e Cigar
              member.<break size="medium"/>
12.           Please say your customer number to enter the system <break
               size="medium"/>
13.           or for more information say help
14.       </prompt>
15.       <filled>
16.           <if cond="CustNo.length != 6">
17.               <prompt>Sorry, I didn't hear exactly 6
                  digits.</prompt>
18.               <assign name="CustNo" expr="undefined"/>
19.           <else/>
20.               <submit next="http://127.0.0.1/ValidateCustomer.asp"/>
21.           </if>
22.       </filled>
23.       <catch event="help">
24.           Please provide your six digit customer number.
25.       </catch>
26.       <catch event="nomatch noinput" count="3">
27.           <prompt>Sorry too many invalid attempts to login.
              Connection ended, Goodbye.</prompt>
28.           <throw event="telephone.disconnect.hangup"/>
29.       </catch>
30.    </field>
31.  </form>
32.  </vxml>
```

Figure 7.11 CigarVoice.vxml.

OK, so what happens once the end user responds to the customer number prompt? As detailed on lines 15 to 22, <filled></filled> tags are used. These specify what action to perform when the CustNo field is filled by our end user's audio reply. Filled tags can be used at the individual field level or at the higher form level. Our example uses them at the field level.

Within the filled tags is some basic processing <if> <else> </if> tags. In our case, line 16 tests the input field's length once it has been filled. If the field is not exactly six digits long, the user will be prompted with an error message from line 17 and the assign tag on line 18 will reinitialize the CustNo field to undefined. This reinitialization will send control back to line 9 where the user will be, once again, prompted from line 10.

If, however, the CustNo length is exactly six digits, control will be rerouted to our second program via the submit command on line 20. The CustNo variable from the field tag will be automatically sent to this second program.

Lines 23 through 29 have been coded to capture events. In the first <catch> tag, if the user says "help" the message on line 24 is spoken by the system, giving the user more precise instruction on what to say. Control is then returned to the input field on line 9, and the entire process starts over.

If the user says an unrecognizable customer number more than three times, line 26 will relay our exit message to the user and disconnect the application by hanging up as seen on line 28. The unrecognizable customer number is just that, a mumbling, nondigit reply, or fewer or more than six digits spoken by the user.

This is a simple, uncomplicated VoiceXML program with all the basics components. For more information on VoiceXML tags and their attributes, visit the VoiceXML forum at www.voicexml.org.

Once valid input is accepted in the CustNo field, from the voice interpreter's point of view, control is passed to a second program called ValidateCustomer.asp as documented in the State Diagram, (see Figure 7.6).

NOTE

To commercialize this main program we could change the initial block command slightly. We could have placed our greeting message between <prompt> </prompt> tags within the block tags and included the *bargein=false* attribute. This would force the user to hear the entire message without being able to bypass the message. Bypassing an audio message is always possible by simply responding to the prompts before or while the audio is being heard. Forcing the caller to listen to a prerecorded message is a great way to place some sort of advertisement.

Program Two—ValidateCustomer.asp

The first thing our second program does, Figure 7.12, is to validate the customer number passed from the first program against our back-end database customer table. If the number is invalid, control reinvokes the first program, CigarVoice.vxml. This time around, since the initial block message was already said on the last entry, it will be skipped and the user will hear the prompt message from line 11. If the CustNo is valid, we continue on with our second program.

```
1.  <%@ LANGUAGE="VBSCRIPT"%>
2.  <%response.write "<?xml version="+chr(34)+"1.0"+chr(34)+"?>"
3.  '---- Open connection to database
4.  DB      = "eCigars.mdb"
5.  Dir     = Request.ServerVariables("SCRIPT_NAME")
6.  Dir     = StrReverse(Dir)
7.  Dir     = Mid(Dir, InStr(1, Dir, "/"))
8.  Dir     = StrReverse(Dir)
9.  Path    = Server.MapPath(Dir) & "\"
10. File    = "eCigars.dsn"
11. DSN     = "filedsn=" & Path & file & ";DefaultDir=" & Path &
                ";DBQ=" & Path & DB & ";"
12. dim sql, Conn, RS
13. dim strFirstName, strLastName, strDeliveryAddress
14. dim strCustNo
15. strCustNo = request("CustNo")
16. Set Conn = Server.CreateObject("ADODB.Connection")
17. Set RS  = Server.CreateObject("ADODB.RecordSet")
18. '---- See if customer exists
19. sql = "Select FirstName, LastName, DeliveryAddress from Customers
                where CustomerNumber = " & request("CustNo")
20. Conn.Open DSN
21. RS.Open sql, Conn, 1,1
22. if RS.EOF or RS.BOF then
23.     WrongCustomer = true
24. else
25.     WrongCustomer = false
26.     strFirstName=RS("FirstName")
27.     strLastName=RS("LastName")
28.     strDeliveryAddress=RS("DeliveryAddress")
29. end if
30. Conn.Close
31. set RS = nothing
32. set Conn = nothing
33. %>
34. <vxml version="1.0">
35. <meta name="author" content="WaveDev"/>
36. <meta name="maintainer" content="marketing@wavedev.com"/>
37. <var name="SelectedType"/>

38. <form id="init">
39.   <%if WrongCustomer then%>
40.     <block>
41.         <prompt bargein="false">
42.             Customer <%=strCustNo%> does not exists please try
                again.<break size="large"/>
```

Figure 7.12 ValicateCustomer.asp.

```
43.            </prompt>
44.            <goto next="http://127.0.0.1/CigarVoice.vxml"/>
45.        </block>
46.  <%else%>
47.     <block>
48.        <prompt bargein="false">
49.           Welcome back <%response.write strFirstName & " " &
              strLastName%><break size="large"/>
50.        </prompt>
51.        <goto next="#SelectCigarType"/>
52.     </block>
53.  <%end if%>
54. </form>

55. <form id="SelectCigarType">
56. <help> Please select from the list of cigar types.</help>
57. <noinput>I didn't hear anything, please select from the list of
    cigar types.</noinput>
58. <error>Sorry I did not understand, please select from the list of
    cigar types.</error>
59. <%
60. Set Conn = Server.CreateObject("ADODB.Connection')
61. Set RS  = Server.CreateObject("ADODB.RecordSet")
62. sql = "select CigarName, Description, Price from Cigars where
    QinStock > 0"
63. Conn.Open DSN
64. RS.Open sql, Conn, 1,1
65. %>
66.     <field name="CigarType">
67.        <prompt>Please select one of the following cigar
           types:<break size="large"/>
68.           <%RS.MoveFirst
69.           do while not RS.EOF%>
70.                 Say <%response.write trim(RS("CigarName"))%> for
                    <%response.write RS("Description")%> at the price
                    of <%response.write RS("Price")%> dollars.<break
                    size="medium"/>
71.                 <%RS.MoveNext
72.           loop%>
73.        </prompt>
74.        <%RS.MoveFirst
75.        do while not RS.EOF%>
76.              <option value="<%response.write
                 trim(RS("CigarName"))%>"> <%response.write
                 trim(RS("CigarName"))%></option>
77.              <%RS.MoveNext
```

Figure 7.12 Continued ValicateCustomer.asp.

```
78.          loop%>
79.          <filled>
80.              <assign name="SelectedType" expr="CigarType"/>
81.              <goto next="#CigarQuantity"/>
82.          </filled>
83.      </field>
84. <%
85. Conn.Close
86. set RS = nothing
87. set Conn = nothing
88. %>
89. </form>

90. <form id="CigarQuantity">
91.    <field name="CigarQty" type="digits">
92.        <prompt> Please select the quantity in increments of one box.
           Maximum quantity is 20 boxes per order.<break size="large"/>
93.        </prompt>
94.        <filled>
95.           <if cond="CigarQty > 20">
96.              <prompt>Sorry, you have selected more than 20 boxes,
                 please try again.</prompt>
97.              <assign name="CigarQty" expr="undefined"/>
98.           <else/>
99.              <submit
                 next="http://127.0.0.1/OrderCigars.asp?CustomerNo=<%=st
                 rCustNo%>" namelist="CigarQty SelectedType"/>
100.          </if>
101.       </filled>
102.       <catch event="help">
103.           Please choose the quantity of cigars for your order.
104.        </catch>
105.        <catch event="nomatch noinput" count="3">
106.           <prompt>Sorry I did not understand what you said.
                 Connection ended, Goodbye.</prompt>
107.           <throw event="telephone.disconnect.hangup"/>
108.        </catch>
109.     </field>
110. </form>
111. </vxml>
```

Figure 7.12 Continued ValicateCustomer.asp.

This second program has three steps for three distinct user interactions. The first step is to welcome the user back if the CustNo is valid or send the control back to the first program if not. The second step is to offer the user all possible cigar choices that eCigars sells. Of course if there are no cigars in stock for a particular cigar type, the program will refrain from listing that particular cigar type in the selection list; hence it will not be available to the user for purchase. Then, finally, the third step prompts the user for the quantity of cigars desired. Once all data is acceptable, control moves on to our third program to ensure inventory and to confirm the order before we commit the order to the database via our fourth program.

The first section of this second program is to connect to a back-end database and validate the customer number. Lines 1 through 33 do this simple task with a predefined MS Access database. Notice the DSN file logic, lines 4 through 11. The logic here will determine exactly where on the Web server machine to find the DSN file, wherever this machine is located in the world. We could have simply defined an ODBC connection to the database via the ODBC administration utility, but we prefer this method since we have more control over the dataset name and location.

The next minor but important section is the setting up of the VoiceXML header and meta tags, lines 34, 35, and 36, which is identical to our first program setup. Notice that the second line of the program sets up the XML header type. It's placed at the top of the program due to the default buffer setting in ASP. As the program is coded, each line of code is sent directly to the VoiceXML interpreter as produced. If this line were moved to after line 33, the program would abend on anticipation of the header line not being present. So, we set it on line 2 of the program, and all is well.

Line 37 defines a global variable called SelectedType to be used in a later form. Variables can be defined directly via the <var> tag or via a <field> tag where the attribute *name* is the variable name. By using the <var> tag as we did here, the variable is now globally available to all forms within this program.

The first form called *init*, lines 38 through 54, is used to reply to the customer number request. If the number is valid, the program will welcome back the member by name and proceed to the next form. If the number does not exist in the database, the user will be told an error message and control will return to the invoking program.

Notice the use of the *bargein* attribute for the prompt tag on lines 41 and 48. As mentioned earlier, this forces the application to play the entire message in the prompt without any interruptions from the caller.

The second form called *SelectCigarType* on lines 55 to 89 will prompt the user to select the type of cigar he or she wishes to purchase from the presented list of cigars.

Lines 56, 57, and 58 define three events. In the first program, Figure 7.11, lines 23 to 25 defined a catch event. If the user said "help," the catch event would trap control, play a message, and return execution to the input field command. Another method of coding the same event catching is as specified on these lines in our second program. Line 56 will do the same logic as the three lines from Figure 7.11.

Lines 60 through 64 set up the database connection and the SQL query similar to the code at the beginning of this program.

Lines 69 to 72 show a while loop used to build the prompt statement, which tells the caller of all the cigar types available. This is the dynamic database and VoiceXML portion. For each cigar type, the user will hear a prompt as follows:

Say *cigarname* for *cigar.description* at the price of *cigar.price* dollars.

In this simplified example taken from line 70, the italic words are replaced with values returned from the database query from line 62. This is very simple phrasing but quite effective.

Lines 75 to 78 hold the logic to another loop using the same database result set. This time the <option> tag is used to set values to the CigarType field variable from line 66. When the user responds to the original field prompt, the system will query the option list created by this loop, looking for a match to fill the field variable.

Once this input field, *CigarType*, is filled, lines 79 to 82 will assign to the defined variable SelectedType. Then line 81 will pass control to our next step via a <goto> command. Since the variable SelectedType is a global variable in the VoiceXML program, it will be accessible in the next form.

The last form, *CigarQuantity*, on lines 90 through 110, will again prompt the user but this time for the quantity of desired cigars. This form has a field called CigarQty, which is defined as digits on line 91. The first thing that happens in this form is that the user is prompted with an instructional message to select a quantity. Once the input field is filled, the if statement checks the value of CigarQty. If the value is less than or equal to 20, control is passed to another program via a <submit> tag as is done in the previous program. If the quantity is greater than 20, the user is told an error message and the field is reinitialized to undefined, thus forcing VoiceXML to reinvoke the input field logic, automatically passing control to line 91.

Line 99 uses a <submit> tag rather than a <goto> tag because we wish to pass variables to the next program. First, we explicitly set the CustomerNo to the input value CustNo passed from our first program. We also pass the CigarQty and SelectedType variables. This is done with the namelist attribute, which merges the two variables into a one-time array. The receiving program can then request these variables individually as required. The CustomerNo variable could also have been included in the namelist but was omitted to show differences in variable passing.

The last two catch events will trap the help condition and the nomatch or noinput conditions. If the user says help, a brief instructional message is told and execution returns to line 91. As with the first program, if three invalid attempts are performed, a final message is spoken, and the application terminates by hanging up via the <throw event="telephone.disconnect.hangup"/> command on line 107.

Program Three—OrderCigars.asp

Figure 7.13 shows the flow in our State Diagram. You can see that our third program queries the database to determine if there's sufficient inventory to satisfy the user's purchase request. If not, we give all we have in stock to satisfy the order. Then, either way, we ask the user to confirm the purchase. If confirmation is denied, we return to the first program in our application to start all over again. If the user does confirm the order, execution flow continues on to our fourth program to commit the order into the system.

```
1.  <%@ LANGUAGE="VBSCRIPT"%>
2.  <%response.write "<?xml version="+chr(34)+"1.0"+chr(34)+"?>"
3.  '---- Open connection to database
4.  DB      = "eCigars.mdb"
5.  Dir     = Request.ServerVariables("SCRIPT_NAME")
6.  Dir     = StrReverse(Dir)
7.  Dir     = Mid(Dir, InStr(1, Dir, "/"))
8.  Dir     = StrReverse(Dir)
9.  Path    = Server.MapPath(Dir) & "\"
10. File    = "eCigars.dsn"
11. DSN     = "filedsn=" & Path & file & ";DefaultDir=" & Path & ";DBQ="
            & Path & DB & ";"
12. dim sql, Conn, RS
13. dim strFilledOrderQty, strCustNo
14. strCustNo = request("CustomerNo")
15. Set Conn = Server.CreateObject("ADODB.Connection")
16. '---- Get cigar information
17. sql = "Select Price, QinStock from Cigars where CigarName = `" &
    request("SelectedType") & "'"
18. Conn.Open DSN
19. Set RS = Conn.Execute(sql)
20. strQuantityInStock = RS("QinStock")
21. strCigarPrice = RS("Price")
22. Conn.Close
23. set RS = nothing
24. set Conn = nothing
25. %>


26. <vxml version="1.0">
27. <meta name="author" content="WaveDev"/>
28. <meta name="maintainer" content="marketing@wavedev.com"/>


29. <form id="init">
30.     <field name="Corder" type="boolean">
31.     <%if (strQuantityInStock - request("CigarQty")) < 0 then
32.        strFilledOrderQty = strQuantityInStock%>
33.        <prompt bargein="false">Sorry you have requested more cigars
            than we have in stock, so we've given you all we have.
34.          <break size="large"/>
35.        </prompt>
36.     <%else
37.        strFilledOrderQty = request("CigarQty")
38.     end if%>
39.     <prompt>You have placed an order for <%=strFilledOrderQty%>
            boxes of <%response.write request("SelectedType")%> cigars
            for a total cost of <%response.write (strFilledOrderQty *
            strCigarPrice)%> dollars.
```

Figure 7.13 OrderCigars.asp.

```
40.            <break size="large"/>
41.            Please say yes to commit this transaction or say no to
               cancel and start over.
42.        </prompt>
43.        <filled>
44.          <if cond="Corder">
45.            <submit next="http://127.0.0.1/Complete
             .asp?CustomerNo=<%=strCustNo%>&amp;CigarName=<%response
             .write request("SelectedType")%>&amp;CigarQty=
             <%=strFilledOrderQty%>"/>
46.          <else/>
47.            <goto next="http://127.0.0.1/CigarVoice.vxml"/>
48.          </if>
49.        </filled>
50.        </field>
51.        <catch event="help">
52.          Please respond with either  yes or no.
53.        </catch>
54.        <catch event="nomatch noinput" count="3">
55.          <prompt>Sorry I did not understand what you said.</prompt>
56.        </catch>
57. </form>
58. </vxml>
```

Figure 7.13 Continued OrderCigars.asp.

As with the program in Figure 7.13, the first part of the ASP program in Figure 7.14 is to connect to the back-end database and retrieve the requested information. In this case, we're looking for the quantity on hand for our client's selected cigar type.

Lines 1 through 25 show the entire database access, including setting VBScript variables to the value of our retrieved database fields on lines 20 and 21.

Following is the dynamic generation of a one-form VoiceXML program on lines 26 to 58.

Line 30 is the field definition, but this time we're using the *boolean* type attribute. This is self-explanatory in that the expected reply for this field is either yes or no.

The next several lines, 31 through 38, show how VBScript coding is used to generate our VoiceXML code. Line 31 does a VBScript test to see if the database cigar quantity value (stored in a variable because the database connection is now closed) minus the requested quantity from the previous program is less than zero. If yes, line 32 sets another VBScript variable to the quantity in stock and lines 33 through 35 send a message to the user explaining the lack of inventory on hand.

If our inventory levels can accommodate the requested order, the logic on line 37 will simply set the same VBScript variable to the quantity requested.

```
1.  <%@ LANGUAGE="VBSCRIPT" %>
2.  <%response.write "<?xml version="+chr(34)+"1.0"+chr(34)+"?>"
3.  '---- Open connection to database
4.  DB      = "eCigars.mdb"
5.  Dir     = Request.ServerVariables("SCRIPT_NAME")
6.  Dir     = StrReverse(Dir)
7.  Dir     = Mid(Dir, InStr(1, Dir, "/"))
8.  Dir     = StrReverse(Dir)
9.  Path    = Server.MapPath(Dir) & "\"
10. File    = "eCigars.dsn"
11. DSN     = "filedsn=" & Path & file & ";DefaultDir=" & Path & ";DBQ="
               & Path & DB & ";"
12. dim sql, Conn, RS
13. Set Conn = Server.CreateObject("ADODB.Connection")
14. Conn.Open DSN
15. '---- Get Customer information
16. sql = "Select FirstName, LastName, DeliveryAddress from Customers
    where CustomerNumber = " & request("CustomerNo")
17. Set RS = Conn.Execute(sql)
18. strFirstName = RS("FirstName")
19. strLastName = RS("LastName")
20. strDeliveryAddress = RS("DeliveryAddress")
21. %>

22. <vxml version="1.0">
23. <meta name="author" content="WaveDev"/>
24. <meta name="maintainer" content="marketing@wavedev.com"/>

25. <form>
26.     <block>
27. <%
28. '---- Insert new transaction into Transactions table
29. sql="insert into transactions (CustomerNumber, CigarName,
    PurchaseDate, Quantity) values (" & request("CustomerNo") & ", '"
    & request("CigarName") &  "', date(), " & request("CigarQty") &
    ")"
30. Set RS = Conn.Execute(sql)
31. '---- Update available quantity in Cigars table
32. sql = "update Cigars set QinStock = QinStock - " &
    request("CigarQty") & " where CigarName ='" & request("CigarName")
    & "'"
33. Set RS = Conn.Execute(sql)
34. %>
35. <prompt>Your order will be delivered to :   <%response.write
    strFirstName + " " + strLastName%> living at <%response.write
    strDeliveryAddress%>.
```

Figure 7.14 Complete.asp.

```
36.              <break size="large"/>
37.              Thank you for shopping at e Cigar, bye bye.
38.          </prompt>
39.          <disconnect/>
40.      </block>
41. </form>
42. </vxml>
43. <%
44. Conn.Close
45. set RS = nothing
46. set Conn = nothing
47. %>
```

Figure 7.14 Continued Complete.asp.

Next is the confirmation message. Line 39 will set a prompt command to tell the caller of the exact order details using our VBScript variables to complete the sentence. Then we simply ask the user to say yes or no to commit the transaction.

Using the filled tag on lines 43 to 49, the code checks the field value. If the value is true, the flow continues to the next and last program in our application. We use the <submit> command on line 45 and set our variables to be used in the next program. We could also have used a <goto> here because we're using set variables within the URI program rather than a namelist.

If the user responds with a no to the confirmation, line 47 will send control back to the very first program in our application, CigarVoice.vxml (see Figure 7.11).

The last two command chunks are set to capture help, nomatch, and noinput events. If the user says help during this program, line 52 will say the coded message and return control to line 29. If there is no input or no match from the user reply with true or false, then line 55 message will be spoken and control returns to line 29. There is no exit strategy in this program; the user must say yes or no.

Program Four—Complete.asp

The last program, shown in Figure 7.14, is straightforward. It accesses the database to obtain user information, and uses it with the order information to commit the client order by inserting a row into the transactions table. We end by telling the client his or her shipping information, and we then disconnect. Our application is complete.

Again, initial code in the program is geared toward database connectivity and data retrieval. Here we start by obtaining the customer's information using the customer number passed from the previous program. Then the VoiceXML code is generated as in the other programs: the voicexml definition on line 22 and the meta tags on lines 23 and 24.

Lines 29 and 30 commit the order to our system by inserting a row into the Transactions database table.

Lines 32 and 33 reduce the available inventory for the selected cigar type by updating the Cigars table.

We then tell the client where the order will be delivered, thank the person for shopping at eCigars, and finish by disconnecting the phone (hanging up).

The application is completed.

With this application we tried to show the fundamental use of VoiceXML tags, dynamic VoiceXML code generation, back-end database connectivity and access, along with VBScript mixed into the code. Of course this application is far from being production ready, but the basics are all here. An important point to note is that since VoiceXML deals with user interaction, as would any interactive application, consideration must be made for quantity on hand. There may be a discrepancy between the time the user selects the desired quantity and the time the database is updated, so be sure to include such logic in your own application if using our template.

Related Links

To learn more about VoiceXML, visit the VoiceXML forum at www.voicexml.org. They have a great language reference manual available to anyone wishing to download it. Also, we highly recommend visiting Motorola's site and obtaining their Mobile ADK 2.0 development toolkit. With these two items and our examples, you should be able to put together your own application in a very short time.

For more information on VoiceXML, visit the following Web sites:

http://studio.tellme.com

http://www.motorola.com/MIMS/ISG/spin/mix/

http://www.alphaworks.ibm.com/tech/voiceserversdk

http://extranet.nuance.com/developer/

http://www.generalmagic.com

http://www.voicexmlcentral.com/

http://www.xml.org/

http://www.voicexml.org

http://www.voicexml.org/voicexml1-0.dtd

http://www.w3.org/TR/2000/NOTE-speechobjects-20001114

http://www.alphaworks.ibm.com/tech/voicexml

http://www.oasis-open.org/cover/sable.html

CHAPTER 8

Wireless Trends

This chapter discusses wireless trends of the future. Of course we can't tell the future, but because we are aware of today's popular wireless technologies with an understanding of how they all came about, we can certainly extrapolate the future of the wireless industry as it relates to information transmissions and other generalities. We also did quite a bit of research into the findings of the major vendors and influences in the industry with firms and organizations such as Nippon Telegraph and Telephone Corporation (NTT), Institute of Electrical and Electronics Engineers (IEEE), Openwave, Symbian, and W3C.

There is so much happening today, and many people are working in many different areas of the wireless industry, although some results will not be revealed for years. Research is being done in every area, not only wireless, and everything will merge to form a brilliant technological future.

Remember when Spock would give Captain Kirk information on a small diskette in the first *Star Trek* television show? That's just common practice today with diskettes. The *Star Trek* crew also used a communicator—today it's called a cellular phone. And remember when the crew would speak to the ship's computer and ask it a question? Well, as we saw in Chapter 7, that is nearly a reality. What's next? Using a transporter to beam people to different locations? (Notice how all these examples are wireless in nature.) We've come a long way, but we're still in the initial stages of the wireless Internet spectrum, and we still have a long way to go before Scotty can beam us up.

Current Situation

In the future, wireless communication will become an essential part of everyday life. It will allow the daily flow of information not only around the globe but also between planets, without our even being aware that we're using the technology. The first step in this development is arguably via WAP.

WAP has been very successful so far mainly because it's a global standard for wireless Internet transmissions. Because of this widespread standardization, manufacturers, cellular providers, and developers have all been working together to build one main infrastructure from the wireless units, to cellular networks, and all the way to specific content.

The main point here is that WAP is a global standard. Even in Japan, operators such as DDI/IDO are finding much success with WAP with more than 3 million subscribers. Of course NTT DoCoMo's iMode has been very successful, but iMode is not a global standard. NTT DoCoMo is a very large company with a magnificent customer base, which allowed NTT to quickly profit through its single national telecomm company and development language derived from HTML rather than creating a completely new language. Imode has had great financial and technological success (being the first always on or always connected protocol in the world). However, the fact remains that WAP is a globally accepted standard whereas iMode is used mostly in Japan with very little European and North American penetration.

At the moment WAP (versions 1.2.1 and early 2.0—as of the writing of this book) is the only de facto global mobile standard. Almost every major mobile device manufacturer includes a WAP microbrowser in their latest mobile cellular units. At the same time, more than three-quarters of the mobile device manufacturers are WAP Forum members and supporters and in one way or another are deeply involved in the evolution of WAP.

Evolution

The future of WAP depends on several areas and as each grows, its momentum will push and pull the others. We have illustrated the basic layers of expansion in Figure 8.1.

Networks and Infrastructure

The need for the type of infrastructure that will exist in the future will be driven primarily by the network bandwidth requirements as wireless subscribers from around the globe demand high-end quality services using voice, video, and high-speed data transmissions. In order to provide these types of services, broad frequency bands will be necessary. Some examples of these high frequencies called *wireless broadband* are microwave, millimeter-wave, and Ka-band.

Remember the term *wireless broadband*; you'll hear a lot about it, as it'll be the future of high-quality and/or high-speed wireless IP-based networks. Don't confuse *wireless broadband* with the generic terms *broadband networking* or Broadband Integrated Services Digital Network (BISDN). These refer to the Internet backbone's fixed access network technologies (fiber-optic-based) implemented to achieve data transmission speeds upward of 155 Mbps.

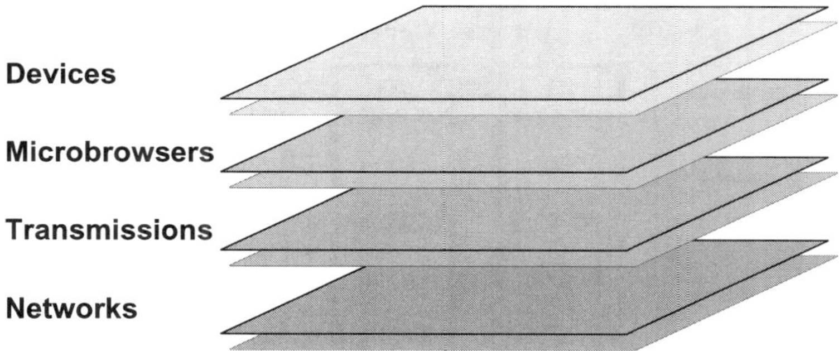

Figure 8.1 Wireless expansion layers.

Wireless broadband is not compulsory for high-end quality services, as we know since these services are beginning to be available in 2.5 and 3G. But when we do achieve the wireless broadband infrastructure, the high-end quality services, as well as others, will become the norm with fast and reliable data transfer rates. Television experienced a similar evolution. Originally, the transmission was in black and white, which was fine but color was better and more appealing to customers, who were increasing in number. The same thing is happening with the physical wireless devices. To obtain more television channels, one would simply set up a larger and higher antenna; today we have cable and satellite TV. Wireless trends are following the same evolutionary concept with wireless broadband, allowing for a larger frequency and thus more potential information to pass through at quicker rates, which will attract more users who will demand more, and advancements will continue to grow.

To get a bird's-eye view of the evolution of wireless infrastructures, including transmission rates and cellular systems, see Figure 8.2. This diagram shows the major milestones of each G, or generation, of cellular systems and where we're going. For more information on the first three Gs, refer to Chapter 1. The fourth and fifth generations are still way in the future. For these generations to efficiently exist, the following must take place:

- IPv6 and supporting infrastructure must be in place. IPV6 is briefly explained separately in the next section.

- Networks must transition from circuit-switched to wireless packet-switched data networks. It's estimated that packet-based third-generation (3G) system infrastructures will exceed circuit-switched systems by the mid 2000's.

- Flawless roaming between wired and wireless systems must be the norm. Current roaming obviously exists but quicker, more efficient hand-over of calls is required, especially with cellular usage about to skyrocket.

Fourth-generation (4G) systems are expected to be in place soon after 2010 and will hopefully attain their anticipated minimum transfer rate of 2 Mbps. This minimum rate is mostly for moving or roaming units such as when used in moving vehicles, which tend to

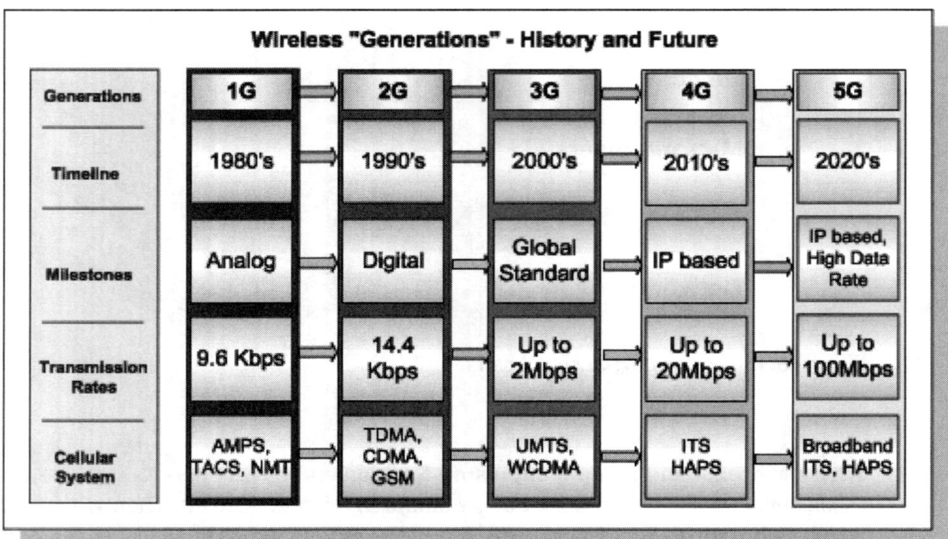

Figure 8.2 Wireless generations.

receive slower transfer rates due to roaming within or outside providers' cellular regions. The capacity of 4G systems will be at least 10 times higher than their predecessor, and the cost per bit will most likely drop to encourage usage and attract consumers and content providers. Top transfer rates for 4G should reach 20 Mbps, which will be the basis for fifth-generation (5G) systems. Fifth generation should top out hopefully around 100 Mpbs. Imagine the types of applications and content we'll be able to access at these speeds. Imagine the possibilities of the capabilities of the individual units!

Another parameter that differs from the current 3G systems is the geographic coverage area of cellular networks. Since 4G and 5G systems will produce much higher data transfer rates, more towers will be required that are much closer to each other primarily to handle the large coverage areas of the past generations. This, of course, raises the issue and importance of smooth hand-over (or transferring) from cell to cell and cell to LANs.

A very futuristic method of delivering substantially high data access rate networks is with High Altitude Stratospheric Platform (HASP). This proposed concept would have 600-MHz bandwidth in the 47/48-GHz band allocation and will be based on a network of large airships maintaining altitudes of 20 km above the ground and relaying transmissions from there. This would certainly cover a wider geographic area and eliminate the need for many cellular towers.

IPv6

IPv6 is a new definition and infrastructure of IP addresses and will most likely be required for higher generation levels to come.

Currently, the world is sitting at IPv4, or IP version 4, which uses a 32-bit address, meaning that there are only 2^{32} (4,294,967,296) IP addresses available. IP addresses are the four-octet numbers used for Web sites, for example, 255.255.255.255. A Web site translates directly to a unique IP address.

Here's an interesting insight into IP addresses. Take the binary representation of each octet, that is, 255 is 1111111 (8 bits turned on), and string them all together—in this case we'd have 32 1's. On your scientific calculator, convert the number to decimal; the result is 4,294,967,296. This figure represents the maximum number of IP addresses available in the world using IPv4, and we're running out of them. It's been obvious for many years now that the number of available IP addresses on the Internet is shrinking. Back in 1981 the TCP/IPv4 was standardized in ARPANET RFC, and who would have thought that 20 years later nearly 4 billion addresses would exist. It sure seems like a lot of addresses, but wait until the wireless momentum picks up. Soon, with technologies such as Bluetooth, almost every electronic device will be connected to the Internet so as to communicate with other machines. This means a huge boom in IP addresses and IPv4 just won't be able to handle the demand. The Internet Engineering Task Force (IETF) estimates that the current reserve of IP addresses under the IPv4 structure could run out by 2010. So IPv6 is a must.

IP version 6 is based on a 128-bit address space, which is four times wider than the 32-bit address space in IPv4. This represents an estimated 340 undecillion IP addresses (or 340,232,366,920,938,463,463,374,607,431,768,211,456 addresses, to be precise). That's 2 to the power of 128 and it's a heck of a lot of IP addresses, which should last far beyond needs during our lifetimes and beyond (unless there is some unforeseen technology development that will take up all the IP6 addresses in the next 20 years). Another point of interest is that security is mandatory in IPv6 and includes encryption of packets and authentication of the sender.

Having IPv6 globally implemented will definitely influence the spreading and growth of the wireless Internet and all advancements in the wireless area.

Imagine that your refrigerator is connected to the Internet and is automatically maintaining your milk inventory. When you run low, it could either send you an email reminder or add an item to your shopping list, which would already be scheduled on your weekly agenda. Or imagine your washing machine recommending a new detergent on your weekly shopping list because the manufacturer has sent out notices to all its latest Internet washers. Technologies such as Bluetooth could easily wirelessly connect appliances to a central home unit or HomeHub, which could be continuously connected to the Internet to send or receive communications.

The only problem to overcome with IPv6 is that the Internet backbone routers must maintain full Internet routing information. Over recent years, routing tables have experienced exponential growth, and the long-term solution can no longer be to simply throw memory to the routers for expansion. With IPv6, many components of the Internet backbone must be upgraded *worldwide*.

Transmissions (Bluetooth)

Bluetooth, previously known as MC Link (and named after a tenth-century Danish king who unified his kingdoms in Denmark and Norway), was conceived by Ericsson in 1994 and is being developed by a group of corporations (Ericsson, Nokia, IBM, Intel, Toshiba, Motorola, and Palm). It's a technology specification that describes how devices (mobile phones, computers, PDAs, and other electronic devices) can interconnect with each other using short-range wireless transmissions.

The wireless transmission distance can be up to 100 meters, but most transmissions would be within the range of 10 meters, resulting in a reliable data transfer rate of approximately 720 Kbps. Line of sight is not necessary, and transmissions can pass through walls, partitions, and nearly any solid object in its path. Enabled devices require the inclusion of a special low-cost transceiver chip to receive and transmit signals in the 2.45-GHz band spectrum, which was previously underutilized and globally available. Each Bluetooth unit has a preassigned unique 48-bit address set by the IEEE.

There is no doubt that the number of Bluetooth-enabled devices will grow considerably in years to come, as everyone sees the benefits and freedom of wireless connections and transmission. This technology will allow users of cellular phones, pagers, computers, and PDAs to transparently connect to data networks and other wireless devices directly. Users can then perform ad hoc user groupings (by using multipoint connections, for example, several people sitting in a restaurant can all connect to each others' devices), easily sync-up information from personal mobile devices with desktop or notebook computer, send and receive faxes, and all while the individual is placing an online order from his or her favorite pizzeria wirelessly. And if you've ever had to find a specific proprietary cable so that you could connect your peripheral devices, you'll really appreciate this technology as it does away with most types of cables.

Also apart from being convenient, the data exchange rates are much higher than currently available cell transfer rates. Transmission speeds for the first Bluetooth generation are approximately 1 Mbps with up to 2 Mbps in the second generation, making connectivity seamless.

So what's beyond Bluetooth? NTT is currently performing a pilot program in Tokyo called Biportable as seen in Figure 8.3. The program deals with wireless broadband technology with broadband networks of optical fiber access lines, which interface with Advanced Wireless Access (AWA) at speeds of up to 36 Mbps. The pilot program, currently under way, tests AWA wireless access points (minibase stations), which are being installed in homes, offices, shops, and other facilities in specific trial service areas. Users are supplied with AWA-enhanced PDAs and PC cards for specific wireless devices and are asked to test the systems' capabilities. With the system in place, end users can access systems without cables or wires through walls, partitions, and most solid objects sitting between the units and their access points, allowing fast and reliable transmissions of video, audio, and data.

Microbrowsers

The reason we included microbrowsers as a specific category in wireless trends is because microbrowsers are the basis for the end user experience. No matter what happens on the network side or the magnificent transmissions potentials, if the micro-

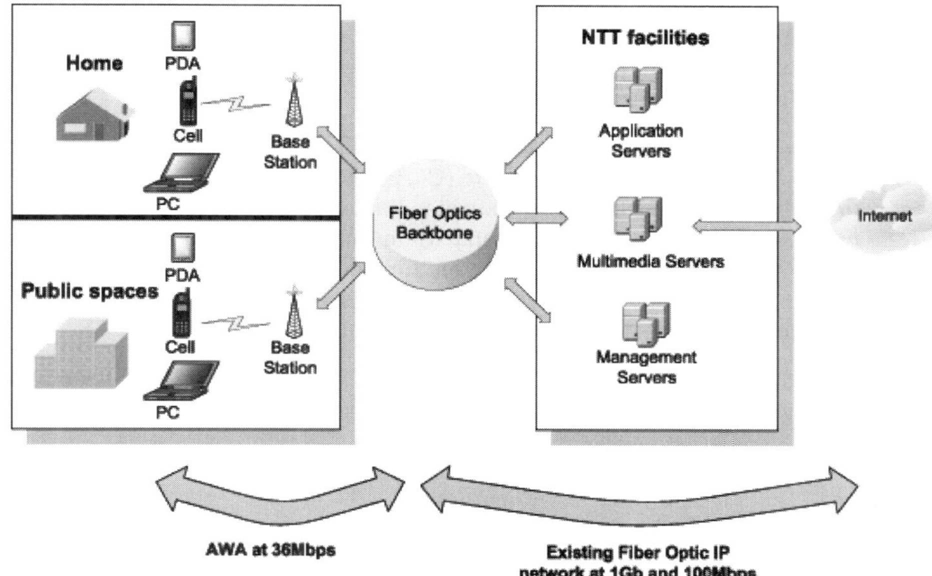

Figure 8.3 NTT biportable pilot program.

browser only handles a single language and remains black and white, the entire wireless Internet future is at risk. Therefore, we included microbrowsers as a short topic in itself.

Leaving the James Bond-style device capabilities and physical units for another section, let's have a quick look at microbrowsers and their reach.

These tiny browsers are currently only available on cellular phones and PDAs. Having a microbrowser on a cellular phone instantly turns it into a Web phone because it has the ability to interact with the Internet. The majority of units today have a specific microbrowser either by Openwave (Up.Browser) or Nokia. There are others but these are the two most popular versions. Microbrowsers (or just browsers) usually handle a WAP flavor of their own, making applications difficult to create since the programmer must always be aware of the many irregularities among the browsers. With the future of WAP heading toward centralized and integrated language, microbrowsers will soon be able to handle many more tag-based languages, including WAP, cHTML (iMode), XHTML, and regular HTML.

Openwave's WAP browser can already handle HDML and WML and has just announced its new GUI-based microbrowser that supports WML, cHTML, and XHTML. Microsoft's Microsoft Mobile Explorer (MME) can support pure HTML (but not the full tag set) and WAP. Symbian is also going the same route with their Smartphone reference design, running the Symbian platform version 6.2.

On January 26, 2001, the W3C recommended the Extensible Hypertext Markup Language (XHTML), which is to supersede HTML 4.0. XHTML is an XML-based content description language and is compatible with current HTML. The WAP Forum is introducing WML into XHTML with the cooperation of W3C, which will form the basis for the next generation of WAP. In the future, users will have the ability to access content regardless of the physical device (such as PCs or mobile phones).

Although still under development, XHTML will incorporate a function called the *composite capability/preference profile* (CC/PP) to recognize differing device characteristics. This new ability will allow downloading of content to be done in an optimal manner keeping the specific unit's capacity in mind. For example, when access is made from a mobile phone, content sufficient for display on that specific device will be downloaded. If access is from a PDA with lots of memory and a larger screen, content sufficient for that particular unit will be made available.

XHTML will also provide for enhanced security, larger downloads for mobile devices, data synchronization, and location-based services.

Devices

The physical device creates the User Experience. Japan's iMode was a big success for many reasons but primarily because of the gadget itself. People adored using those new tiny devices, with which they could talk, write, and see images with little to no technical knowledge required. Just turn it on and there it is. People really like gadgets. The television show *Star Trek* captured our attention with their wireless mobile devices from phasers to communicators. Of course you remember the James Bond movie where Mr. Bond drove his BMW car from his cellular phone screen's touch pad while hiding in the back seat. Wireless mobile devices are here to stay and will definitely be in our immediate and long-term future.

It won't be long before you find yourself in a wireless store with the salesperson asking if you would like the phone, computer, organizer, MP3 player, video and television, or camera features on your new personal wireless unit. Would you like voice-enabled, thumb mouse, squeeze trigger, or the new remote device for your wireless mobile device? We'll each have one, and it'll be as common as our personal wallets. Of course each unit will have a location-based system and email included. Buy the latest upgrade package for your unit and receive 1 month of free long distance or a free intercommunication translation package.

The FCC has already been talking about including location-based software into every new cellular phone for emergency purposes. Emergency telephone operators must know where your phone is located if you call and can't relay that information. Image the potential uses for this type of phone capability!

So how do we get there? Well, phones are like computers in that they have microprocessors, screens, power supplies, memory chips, and added components like digital signal processors and radio frequency power sectors.

The future will bring smaller units with increased power and abilities similar to the evolution of the personal computer and laptops. Twenty years ago, we were thrilled to get a Commodore 64 and today we have cellular phones with Internet connections and the ability to email anyone from almost anywhere in the world.

All the components will increase in capacity and abilities. The CPUs will become smaller and faster; screens will become larger, be available in color, and have more resolution. Back in February 2001, the Sony Corporation announced the development of a large-scale Active Matrix Organic Electroluminescence (OEL) display driven by thin film transistors (TFT) for mobile devices. This will bring vivid colors with high resolution to mobile devices.

Here's an interesting note on how the wireless industry is affecting other areas in the world. Investments in a precious metal called Tantalum are increasing as the wireless industry grows. In the past 3 to 4 years, the price of this metal has risen over 600 percent—not a bad investment! Why is this, you ask? Well Tantalum is used in the creation of electronic (passive) capacitors for wireless devices. With the use of this metal, cell circuitry components can be made smaller, and this leads to smaller physical device sizes.

Memory will increase and be interchangeable like the Memory Stick from Sony products. Batteries will be smaller and allow for more up time. As with computers, the mobile devices will have integrated systems with plug-and-play features for add on, all with superb security features.

The computer was the first phase, wireless Internet and communications are the second phase, and the name of the next phase is going to be *User Experience*.

The Future

Today's wireless services and applications are character- or text-based with some voice-based systems and only a small portion of information is multimedia-based. This is going to change in the following ways.

- Wireless devices will advance and eventually be able to store, display, and interact with bandwidth-hungry multimedia applications.
- Content providers will offer more multimedia-rich content (music, video, conferencing, advertising).
- Wireless operators will have the networks and abilities to transmit and receive high-bandwidth transmissions.

It's evident that the future of the wireless industry will include the merging of multiple technologies in many areas. It won't be as much a question of who will prevail in these mergings, but how they will merge. For example, NTT DoCoMo uses its proprietary wireless application protocol called iMode. Openwave uses HDML and WML with its own extensions while the WAP Forum tries to globalize their standard WAP language (similar to Openwave's WML). On the other hand, the WAP Forum is advocating the merger of WML and HTML into XHTML. There will be mergers of languages, and there will be greater standards as time goes on.

Add to the picture more advancements such as short-distance; high-speed interfacing among devices, especially via Bluetooth; much higher data transfer rates to and from base stations, along with autosynchronization of personal information, and it's not difficult to imagine the following scenarios.

Figure 8.4 shows how an individual can purchase items online via his or her personal wireless device, as is done today. But, thanks to Bluetooth and other advancements, the physical device will then instantly download the purchase to the person's home financial management software such as Quicken or MS Money. A further advancement would be if the home software would then call the person's financial institution and credit card company and synchronize entries and balances. So, for example, every time an online transaction is approved, your smart wireless device will send a message to the software on your PC and have it update your financial records if you're within range of the PC. If not, the unit will store the transaction until it senses the PC is within transmission range. You'll never have to balance your checkbook again.

Another possible scenario could be a patient with a specific medical condition that requires continuous monitoring. As the patient performs various daily activities, a portable medical monitoring device attached directly to the patient could regularly monitor his or her biometric parameters. The device would be in constant transmission range to a Bluetooth base station and would regularly transmit critical information directly to the hospital systems. If the medical system notices any unusually high or low values for any of the dozens of monitored signs, it could react within minutes (if not seconds) of receiving the signal from the patient and alert the proper medical personnel.

The wireless aspects of this scenario would allow the patient the freedom to be mobile and yet still be within moment's contact of a doctor knowledgeable of his or her specific situation. And with a two-way system, healthcare providers could interact directly with the patient and go so far as instantly change a medical dosage remotely. Imagine

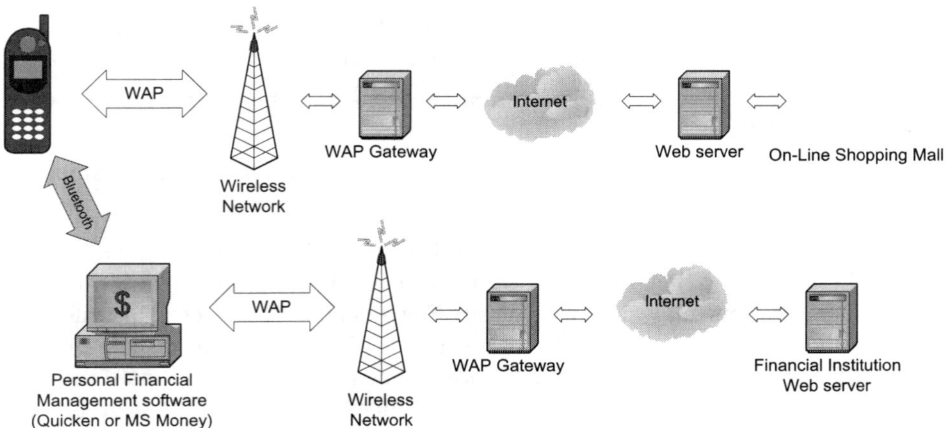

Figure 8.4 Autosynchronization of information.

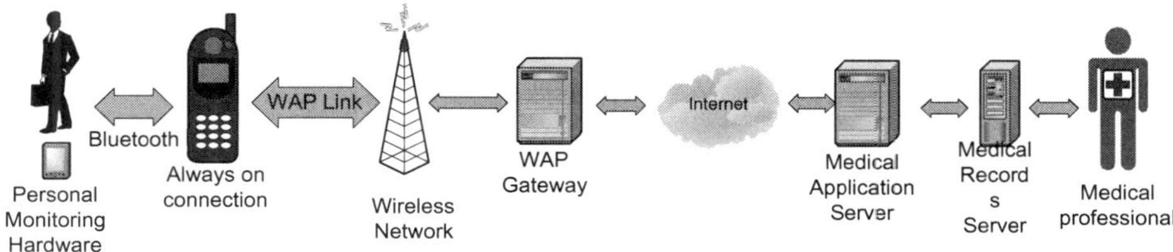

Figure 8.5 Remote wireless medical monitoring system.

the potential benefits to the patients. Figure 8.5 shows the potential connection points to the remote wireless medical monitoring system.

These scenarios are still hypothetical, but in time any part of our lives where interaction between a customer and a service provider exists will be an opportunity for wireless application solutions.

And Beyond...

Let us not forget the most important part of the future, which are the people who make it all happen: the entrepreneurs, architects, developers, and all others intrigued by this new technology. If you're reading this book, then you probably fit in one of these categories and you'll be one of the many involved in building some aspect of this wireless Internet technology. Infrastructures, tools, and business needs are either in place or becoming available and waiting for you to provide new and innovative content and services to the wireless world.

Our only limitation is our own imagination with our only barriers being today's hurdles. Yesterday we created computational machines and interlinked them worldwide. Today we can perform many tasks remotely due to wireless technology. Tomorrow, well...beam me up, Scotty!

HDML Elements

HDML tags

<-- ... -->

Makes comment in the code.

```
...
<-- This is comment  -->
...
```

<!-- ... -->

Makes comment in the code.

```
...
<!-- This is comment  -->
...
```

<A>

Anchor tag.

The attributes for this tag are:

LABEL	{key label} The label name and it should be no more than five characters.
ACCESSKEY	{key number} A number (0-9) that will be shown on the left side of the screen.
TASK	{task type} The task to execute. Values can be: go, gosub, return, cancel, prev, call, noop.
DEST	{url name} The URL that will be requested in GO/GOSUB type of tasks.
REL	NEXT It instructs phone to prefetch next url that is defined by DEST.
METHOD	{submit method} The method used to request URL. Can be GET or POST. If not specified, default method would be GET.
POSTDATA	{data} The data to be posted to target URL if POST method has been selected.
ACCEPT-CHARSET	{character set} Defines the character set which the HDML application expects.
VARS	{var pairs} Defines list of variables.
RECEIVE	{var list} List of variables to store return values from GOSUB delimited by semicolon.
RETVALS	{value list} List of values that an activity returns to the invoking activity.
NEXT	{next url} The URL to be invoked post nested activity completion.
CANCEL	{cancel url} The URL to be invoked post GOSUB tasks cancellation.
FRIEND	{boolean} A TRUE or FALSE value specifying whether the nested action.
SENDREFERER	{boolean} A TRUE or FALSE value specifying whether the microbrowser should provide the URL of the current deck.
CLEAR	{boolean} A TRUE or FALSE value specifying whether a RETURN.
NUMBER	{number} The method of calling the telephone number.

```
...
<A attributes>link text</A>
...
```

<ACTION>

Marks the beginning of the ACTION statement.

```
<ACTION TYPE=ACCEPT TASK=GO DEST=#MyCard>
```

The attributes of this tag are:

LABEL	{key label} The label name and it should be no more than five characters.

TYPE	{key value} The key to associate the task with:

       ■ ACCEPT - LABEL not required

       ■ HELP - LABEL *required*

       ■ PREV - LABEL ignored

       ■ SOFT1 - LABEL *required*

       ■ SOFT2 - LABEL *required*

       ■ SEND - LABEL *required*

       ■ DELETE - LABEL *required*

TASK	{task type} The task to execute. Values can be: go, gosub, return, cancel, prev, call, noop.
DEST	{url name} The URL that will be requested in GO/GOSUB type of tasks.
REL	NEXT It instructs phone to prefech next url that is defined by DEST.
METHOD	{submit method} The method used to request URL. Can be GET or POST. If not specified, the default method would be GET.
POSTDATA	{data} The data to be posted to target URL if POST method has been selected.
ACCEPT-CHARSET	{character set} Defines the character set which the HDML application expects.
VARS	{var pairs} Defines list of variables.
RECEIVE	{var list} List of variables to store return values from GOSUB, delimited by semicolon.
RETVALS	{value list} List of values that an activity returns to the invoking activity.
NEXT	{next url} The URL to be invoked post nested activity completion.
CANCEL	{cancel url} The URL to be invoked post GOSUB tasks cancellation.
FRIEND	{boolean} A TRUE or FALSE value specifying whether the nested action specified in a GOSUB task is "friendly."
SENDREFERER	{boolean} A TRUE or FALSE value specifying whether the microbrowser should provide the URL of the current deck.
CLEAR	{boolean} A TRUE or FALSE value specifying whether a RETURN or
CANCEL	task from a nested activity clears all of the variables.
NUMBER	{number} The method of calling the telephone number.
SRC	{image url} The image URL to display instead of the Softkey label.

ICON{icon name} The local image name that will be displayed instead of the Softkey label.

```
<HDML VERSION=3.0>
<ACTION TYPE=SOFT1 TASK=CANCEL LABEL=Cancel>
<DISPLAY NAME=Wave>
  <ACTION TYPE=ACCEPT TASK=GO DEST=#WJM>WaveDev deck
</DISPLAY>
<DISPLAY NAME=WJM>
  WJM deck
</DISPLAY>
</HDML>
```

<CE>

Choice entry define items that can be selected in a choice card (see <CHOICE>).

```
<CE LABEL=Stocks>OpenWave stocks
```

The attributes of this tag are:

VALUE {val} An optional value stored to the variable specified by the KEY option.

LABEL {key label} The label name, which should be no more than five characters.

TASK {task type} The task to execute. Values can be: go, gosub, return, cancel, prev, call, noop.

DEST {url name} The URL that will be requested in GO/GOSUB type of tasks.

REL NEXT It instructs phone to prefetch next url that is defined by DEST.

METHOD {submit method} The method used to request URL. Can be GET or POST. If not specified, default method would be GET.

POSTDATA {data} The data to be posted to target URL if POST method has been selected.

ACCEPT-CHARSET {character set} Defines the character set which the HDML application expects.

VARS {var pairs} Defines list of variables.

RECEIVE {var list} List of variables to store return values from GOSUB delimited by semicolon.

RETVALS {value list} List of values that an activity returns to the invoking activity.

NEXT {next url} The URL to be invoked post nested activity completion.

CANCEL {cancel url} The URL to be invoked post GOSUB tasks cancellation.

FRIEND {boolean} A TRUE or FALSE value specifying whether the nested action specified in a GOSUB task is "friendly."

SENDREFERER	{boolean} A TRUE or FALSE value specifying whether the microbrowser should provide the URL of the current deck.
CLEAR	{boolean} A TRUE or FALSE value specifying whether a RETURN or.
CANCEL	task from a nested activity clears all of the variables.
NUMBER	{number} The method of calling the telephone number.

```
...
<CHOICE IKEY=ch>
<CE LABEL=NOK>Nokia
<CE LABEL=OPW>OpenWave
</CHOICE>
...
```

<CHOICE>

Choice cards display header text followed by a list of items. User can select single item from the list of items.

The attributes of this tag are:

NAME	{card name} Name for the card.
MARKABLE	{boolean} TRUE or FALSE value, specifying whether the card can be bookmarked.
TITLE	{card title} The default bookmark name.
BOOKMARK	{bookmark URL} The URL added to the bookmark list.
KEY	{var name} The name of the variable that stores the value.
IKEY	{var name} The name of a variable, specifying index number of the default item.
METHOD	{choice method} The choice method.
DEFAULT	{default val} The default value of the variable defined by the KEY attribute.
IDEFAULT	{default number} The index of the default entry.

```
...
<CHOICE KEY=ch IKEY=num IDEFAULT=3>
<CE ...>
<CE ...>
</CHOICE>
...
```

<DISPLAY>

Display cards display formatted text.

The attributes of this tag are:

NAME	{card name} Name for the card.

TITLE	{card title} The default bookmark name.
MARKABLE	{boolean} TRUE or FALSE value, specifying whether the card can be bookmarked.
BOOKMARK	{bookmark URL} The URL added to the bookmark list.

```
<HDML VERSION=3.0>
<DISPLAY>
</DISPLAY>
...
</HDML>
```

<ENTRY>

An entry card that displays content followed by an entry line. This is used for user entries.

The attributes for this tag are:

NAME	{card name} Name for the card.
TITLE	{card title} The default bookmark name.
MARKABLE	{boolean} TRUE or FALSE value, specifying whether the card can be bookmarked.
BOOKMARK	{bookmark URL} The URL added to the bookmark list.
FORMAT	{fmt specifier} Format designators.
FILL	{right or left} Direction of text appearance.
DEFAULT	{default value} A default value of the string that will be presented to the user.
KEY	{var} The name of the variable that will store user entries.
NOECHO	{boolean} Used for password fields when NOECHO=TRUE the phone will hide entered text.
EMPTYOK	{boolean} Allows for empty input if TRUE. Default is FALSE.

```
...
<ENTRY KEY=state FORMAT=AA DEFAULT=CA>
<ACTION TYPE=ACCEPT TASK=GOSUB DEST=?state=$state>
State:
</ENTRY>
...
```

<HDML>

An HDML deck is used to transport and cache sets of HDML cards.

The attributes for this tag are:

| VERSION | {version number} The version of the HDML language. |

TTL	{cache time} Time to live is the number of seconds the microbrowser should cache the deck.
MARKABLE	{boolean} TRUE or FALSE value, specifying whether the card can be bookmarked.
PUBLIC	{boolean} Defines whether deck access control is to be used.
ACCESSDOMAIN	{domain} Defines what domain can access the deck.
ACCESSPATH	{path} Defines the path of URLs that are allowed to request cards within the deck.

```
<HDML VERSION=3.0>
...
</HDML>
```

<IMG>

Specifies an image that appears in formatted text.

```
<IMG ICON="trademark" ALT="TM">
```

The attributes for this tag are:

ALT	{alt text} Text to be displayed if the image is unavailable.
SRC	{image url} The URL of the image to display.
ICON	{icon name} The name of a local image.

```
...
<DISPLAY>
Here is my trademark <IMG ICON="trademark" ALT="TM">
</DISPLAY>
...
```

<NODISPLAY>

Type of card that does not appear on the phone, it immediately executes the ACCEPT or PREV action.

```
...
<NODISPLAY>...</NODISPLAY>
...
```

The actions are given in the following table:

TASK	NO-DISPLAY ACTION
GO	ACCEPT
GOSUB	ACCEPT
RETURN	PREV
PREV	PREV
CANCEL	PREV
RETURN or CANCEL with DEST	ACCEPT
RETURN with the NEXT	ACCEPT
RETURN with the CANCEL	ACCEPT

WML Elements

Mime Type Requirements

The MIME content type for WML of any source is: text/vnd.wap.wml.

WML 1.2 tags

<a>

Establishes a link to another URL.

The attributes for this tag are:

Accesskey	number representing a button on the phone keypad.
Href	specifies the destination URL (use #cardname for another card in the same deck).
Title	specifies a brief text string, identifying the link that shows up in the Softkey area.

```
...
<a href ="url" accesskey ="1">Press one to link</a>
<a href ="#card2">Click here for card 2</a>
<a href="url" title="Next">Press the Next button</a>
...
```

```
<a href="URL or #cardname" accesskey="char" title="short text">
```

<access>

Specifies access control for the entire deck via domain and path. Specified within the header tag and can only appear once.

If not specified, cards from any other deck can access this deck.

The attributes for this tag are:

domain	domain name of allowed referring pages that can access the deck.
path	path name prefix of allowed referring pages that can access the deck.

```
<head>
<access domain= "wavedev.com" path= "/wireless/">
...
</head>
```

```
<access domain="domain" path="path">
```

<anchor>

Specifies an anchor tag similar to <a>.

The attribute for this tag are:

title	text string identifying the link.

```
...
<anchor title= "Titles" ><go href= "title.wml" />Search by Title</anchor>
...
```

```
<anchor title="name">task and/or text</anchor>
```

<b>

Denotes bold text.

```
...
<b>This will appear bold</b>
...
```

```
<b>...</b>
```

<big>

Specifies large font text.

May not be available for all microbrowsers.

```
...
<big>This will appear big</big>
...
```

```
<big>...</big>
```


Denotes a line break.

```
...
<br/>
...
```

```
<br/>
```

<card>

A deck contains one or more cards. Each card represents a single user interaction. Cards are displayed one at a time.

The attributes for this tag are:

id	name of the card.
title	title for the card.
newcontext	true/false; if true, browser context is reinitialized.
onenterfoward	initiated if card is invoked explicitly.
onenterbackward	initiated via a prev command.
ontimer	url invoked once timer expires.

```
<wml>
<card id="card1">
 <p>
   Simple card
 </p>
</card>
</wml>
```

```
<wml>
<card id="name" title="label" newcontext="boolean" onenterforward="url"
onenterbackward="url" ontimer="url">
    content
</card>
</wml>
```

<do>

Invokes an action to take for the current card. Can be at the card level or deck level, which would apply to all cards unless overridden.

The attributes for this tag are:

type	action to be taken, accept/prev/help/reset/options/delete/unknown.
label	text showing in the Softkey area. Default is OK.
name	if same as deck do statement, card level statement will override.
optional	if true, the browser may ignore this Do statement.

```
...
<do type="accept" label="Back">
  <go href="mainmenu.wml"/>
</do>
...
```

```
<do type="type" label="label" name="name" optional="boolean">
  task
</do>
```


Emphasizes text.

```
...
<em>This text emphasized</em>
...
```

```
<em>text</em>
```

<fieldset>

Allows the grouping of related fields and/or text within a card.

```
<fieldset title="label">content</fieldset>
```

<go>

Specifies a navigation path to a URL.

The attribute for this tag are:

href	url or card name. Cards are preceded by a # sign.

sendreferer   true sets the http_referer to the relative url of the requesting deck.

method   get/post.

accept-charset   specifies character set.

```
...
<do type="accept" label="Search">
  <go href="queryjobM.wml"/>
</do>
...
```

```
<go href="url" sendreferer="boolean" method="method" accept-
charset="charset"
   content
</go>
```

<head>

Specifies the optional header tag for the deck.

```
...
<head>...</head>
...
```

```
<head>content</head>
```

<i>

Specifies italicized text.

```
...
<i>This text italicized</i>
...
```

```
<i>text</i>
```

<img>

Specifies that an image is to be included.

The attributes for this tag are:

alt   alternative text to display if no image source is found.

src   url of the image to display.

localsrc   local known icon.

Align   top/middle/bottom.

height	height of the image.
width	width of the image.
vspace	vertical white space, above and below image.
hspace	horizontal white space, left and right of image.

```
...
<img alt="scissor picture" localsrc="scissors" src="" />
<img alt="WJM" src="http://www.worldjobmart.com/wjmbig.bmp"/>
...
```

```
<img alt="text" src="URL" localsrc="icon" align="alignment" height="n"
width="n" vspace="n" hspace="n"/>
```

<input>

Allows for user input.

The attributes for this tag are:

name	input variable name.
title	label text.
type	text or password. Password text is not shown on the device.
value	default value.
format	data format of the entered text.
emptyok	boolean, true means field is optional.
size	length of visible input field.
maxlength	maximum number of characters allowed for input.
tabindex	same idea as in HTML, order of tab input.

```
...
<b>UserID:</b>
<input name="User" maxlength="15" type="text" format="XXXNN*m" emptyok="false"/>
...
```

```
<input name="variable" title="title" type="type" value="value"
format="format" emptyok="boolean" size="n"
maxlength="n" tabindex="n"/>
```

The format is:

A	no numbers, any uppercase character or symbol.
a	no numbers, any lowercase character or symbol.
N	any numeric character.
*N	any numeric of numeric character.
X	any numeric, symbol, or uppercase character - can't change to lowercase.
x	any numeric, symbol, or lowercase character - can't change to uppercase.

M	any numeric, symbol, or uppercase character for many input characters, changeable to lowercase and first character defaults to uppercase.
*M	any number of any characters, but treated as uppercase.
m	any numeric, symbol, or lowercase character for many input characters, changeable to uppercase and first character defaults to lowercase.
*f	any number of any type of characters.
nf	any n integer number of any characters.
\c	display the character after the slash in the display.

<meta>

Allows meta information for the deck within the header. Not all attributes are always supported.

The attributes for this tag are:

name	meta data name.
http-equiv	instead of the name attribute, sets an HTTP header variable.
content	value associated with name or http-equiv (max-age is set in seconds).
scheme	form or structure used to interpret data value.
forua	boolean, true means meta data is intended to reach the user. Default is true.

```
...
<head>
     <meta http-equiv="Cache-Control" content="max-age=0"/>
 </head>
...
```

```
<head>
<meta http-equiv="Cache-Control" content="max-age=time" forua=true/>
...
</head>
```

<noop>

Nothing to be done task.

```
<noop/ >
```

<onevent>

When an event occurs, the task will take place.

The attribute for this tag is:

type   sets the type of event being waited upon. Onpick/onenterforward/onenterbackward/ontimer.

```
...
<onevent type="onenterforward">
  <refresh>
      <setvar name="jobtype" value="" />
  </refresh>
</onevent>
...
```

```
<onevent type="type">task</onevent>
```

<optgroup>

Allows the grouping of <options> thus forming submenus.

The attributes for this tag is:

title   name of submenu

```
...
<select name="cars" title="Select your car">
  <optgroup title="Available cars">
    <option value="ford">Ford</option>
    <option value="chev">Chevrolet</option>
  </optgroup>
</select>
...
```

```
<optgroup title="label">content</optgroup>
```

<option>

Specifies a single choice option in a select element.

The attributes for this tag are:

title   name of option to appear on Softkey.
value   value of variable specified in select element.
onpick   URL to jump to if option is selected.

```
...
<select name="cars" title="Select your car">
  <optgroup title="Available cars">
    <option value="ford">Ford</option>
    <option value="chev">Chevrolet</option>
  </optgroup>
</select>
...
```

```
<option title="label" value="value" onpick="url">content</option>
```

<p>

New paragraph with alignment and line wrapping.

The attributes for this tag are:

align	left/center/right; default is left.
mode	wrap/nowrap—text wrapping mode defaults to last set mode.

```
...
<p align="center">
  This text is centered
</p>
...
```

```
<p align="align" mode="mode">content</p>
```

<postfield>

Method to post variables via a URL request.

The attributes for this tag are:

name	names a variable.
value	value of named variable.

```
...
<go href="SendEmail.asp">
  <postfield name="T" value="$(to)"/>
  <postfield name="F" value="$(from)"/>
</go>
...
```

```
<postfield name="name" value="value"/>
```

<prev>

Used to navigate back to the previous URL in the history stack. Use <prev/> if no content is used.

```
...
<prev>
  content
</prev>
...
```

```
<prev>content</prev>
```

<refresh>

Specifies a refresh task, which refreshes the specified variables.

```
...
<refresh>
  <setvar name="abc" value=""/>
</refresh>
...
```

```
<refresh>content</refresh>
```

<select>

Allows a user to select from a list of options.

The attributes for this tag are:

title	label for select list.
multiple	true/false, whether multiple selections are possible.
name	name of select variable.
value	default named variable value.
iname	index variable name assigned the index value of the selected option.
ivalue	default named index variable value.
tabindex	allows the user to tab to ordered selection values.

```
...
<select>
  <option onpick="jobS.wml">Category Search</option>
  <option onpick="jobM.wml">Manual Search</option>
</select>
...
```

```
<select title="title" multiple="boolean" name="variable" value="default"
iname="index_var" ivalue="default" tabindex="n">
content
</select>
```

<setvar>

Sets a value to a variable.

The attributes for this tag are:

name	names a variable.
value	value of named variable.

```
...
<setvar name="abc" value="123"/>
...
```

```
<setvar name="name" value="value"/>
```

<small>

Specifies a small font text.

May not be available for all microbrowsers.

```
...
<small>This will appear small</small>
...
```

```
<small>...</small>
```


Specifies a strong font text.

May not be available for all microbrowsers.

```
...
<strong>This will appear strong</strong>
...
```

```
<strong>...</strong>
```

<table>

Specifies a table.

The attributes for this tag are:

align	left/center/right alignment.
title	names a table.
columns	number of columns.

```
...
<table columns="2" align="c" title="Grades">
<tr>
    <td>Name</td>
    <td>Number</td>
</tr>
<tr>
    <td>Albert</td>
    <td>55</td>
</tr>
</table>
...
```

```
<table title="title" align="align" columns="columns">rows and columns
</table>
```

<td>

Defines a table column.

```
<td>content</td>
```

<template>

Deck level code, which is added to every card, but can be overridden at the card level by respecifying the same event code.

The attributes for this tag are:

onenterfoward	initiated if card is invoked explicitly.
onenterbackward	initiated via a prev command.
ontimer	url invoked once timer expires.

```
<wml>
<template onenterforward="/wireless/mainmenu.wml">
  content
</template>
...
```

```
<template onenterforward="url" onenterbackward="url"
ontimer="url">content</template>
```

<timer>

Sets a timer countdown. Used to automatically invoke a task after a period of time.

The attributes for this tag are:

name	names a variable.
value	value of a named variable in 1/10th seconds.

```
...
<card ontimer="#card2">
  <timer name="timer" value="10"/>
...
</card>
...
```

```
<timer name="url" value="url"/>
```

<tr>

Defines a table row.

```
<tr>
  <td>content</td>
</tr>
```

<u>

Specifies underlined text.

```
...
<u>This text will be underlined</u>
...
```

```
<u>...</u>
```

<wml>

Specifies a WML deck. Decks can have one or more cards.

```
<wml>
  <card>
    ...
  </card>
</wml>
```

```
<wml><card>...</card></wml>
```

Openwave WML extensions

<catch>

Specifies an exception handler.

The attributes for this tag are:

name	exception name.
onthrow	what to do when exception occurs.

```
<catch name="name" onthrow="displayerr.wml">...</catch>
```

<exit>

Specifies an exit task, indicating that the current context should be terminated.

```
<exit>...</exit>
```

<link>

Specifies a link in the head element.

The attributes for this tag are:

href	url of link.
sendreferer	true/false, Default false; if true, sets an HTTP header variable.
rel	relationship between the link containing deck and the card being navigated to.

```
<head><link href="href" rel="rel"/></head>
```

<receive>

Receives data sent from another context.

The attribute for this tag is:

name	names the variable to be received.

```
<receive name= "name"/>
```

<reset>

Resets variables in current context.

```
<reset/>
```

<send>

Specifies a value to be included in a parameter block.

The attribute for this tag is:

value	names the variable to be received.

```
<send value="name"/>
```

<spawn>

Makes a spawn task, creates a child context, and invokes a URL within it.

The attributes for this tag are:

href	URL name.
onexit	URL to invoke on exit of completion of child context.

sendreferer	true/false, default false; if true, sets an HTTP header variable.
method	get/post HTTP request method.
accept-charset	specifies character codes.

```
<spawn href="url" onexit="name"/>..</spawn>
```

<throw>

Declares a throw task - indicates an exception should be raised.

The attribute for this tag is:

name	name of the exception.

```
<throw name="name"/>content</throw>
```

iMode Elements

Mime type requirements

MIME content type for Compact HTML is the same as for HTML and text/html.

W3 submission

W3 submission can be found at http://www.w3.org/TR/1998/NOTE-compactHTML-19980209/.

iMode (chtml) tags

! --

1.0. This tag will be used to comment the code.

```
<!---This comment will not appear on the browser screen -->
<!-- -->
```

&XXX;

1.0. Designates a value as follow.

```
&amp; = &
&gt; =
&lt; =
&quot; = "
 
&#0;~#127;
```

A

1.0. This tag establishes a link to another URL and sends email or phone the number.

The attributes for this tag are:

name	"marker name"
href	"URL#marker name"
accesskey	"char"

```
...
<A href ="TryThis.htm" accesskey ="1">Press on to Try</A>
<A href ="tel:14412984681">here</A>Enquiries by phone
<A href="mailto:marketing@wavedev.com">here</A>Enquiries by e-mail
...
```

```
<A name="">
<A href="URL#marker name" accesskey="char">
```

BASE

1.0. The BASE tag designates a URL that is used as the base path in an HTML file.

The attribute for this tag is:

href	"Base URL"

```
<HTML>
<HEAD>
<TITLE>BASE</TITLE>
<BASE href="http://www.xxx.co.jp/">
</HEAD>
<BODY>
This tag designates the base URL that relative paths in an HTML file are based on.<BR>
<a href="./base.htm">From relative to absolute
</BODY>
</HTML>
```

```
<BASE href="URL">
```

BLINK

2.0. The <BLINK> tag blinks a tagged character string at intervals.

```
...
<BLINK>Blinking alert</BLINK>
...
```

`<BLINK>...</BLINK>`

BLOCKQUOTE

1.0. Creates a text block and displays a quote mark. It is used to indent text block.

```
...
Financial News:
<BLOCKQUOTE>
Wall Street sky rocketed for the first time above 20,000 mark.
</BLOCKQUOTE>
...
```

`<BLOCKQUOTE>...</BLOCKQUOTE>`

BODY

1.0. Designates text content to be displayed as a page.

```
...
<BODY>
The page content comes here.
</BODY>
...
```

`<BODY>...</BODY>`

2.0. The <BODY> tag defines color designation.

The following is the hex list of supported colors (only for the models that support color displays):

Black	"#000000"
Gray	"#808080"
Maroon	"#800000"
Purple	"#800080"
Green	"#008000"
Olive	"#808000"
Navy	"#000080"
Teal	"#008080"
Silver	"#C0C0C0"
White	"#FFFFFF"

Red	"#FF0000"
Fuchsia	"#FF00FF"
Lime	"#00FF00"
Yellow	"#FFFF00"
Blue	"#0000FF"
Aqua	"#00FFFF"

The attributes for this tag are:

bgcolor	"hexadecimal color representation or color name"
text	"hexadecimal color representation or color name"
link	"hexadecimal color representation or color name"

```
...
<BODY bgcolor="white" text = "black" link="red">
Background is white.
Text is black.
Link is red.
</BODY>
...
```

```
<BODY bgcolor="color choice" text="color choice" link="color
choice">...</BODY>
```

BR

1.0. Designates the line change. Designates cancellation of wraparound after the tag.

The attribute for this tag is:

clear	"left, right or all"

```
<BR>
<BR clear="Part of screen (left, right or all) wraparound is canceled">
```

CENTER

1.0. Centers character strings, images, and tables.

```
...
<CENTER>Equipment</CENTER>
...
```

```
<CENTER>... </CENTER>
```

DD

1.0. The DL, DT, and DD tags are used to create definition lists.

```
...
List of large rivers
<DL>
 <DT>Europe
   <DD>Danube
   <DD>Main
   <DD>Rain
</DL>
...
```

```
<DL>
<DT>Title
<DD>Details
</DL>
```

DIR

1.0. Creates a list of menus or directories. Lists are nested between <DIR> and </DIR> tags. Each item in the list must start with <LI> tag.

```
...
WaveDev goals<BR>
<DIR>
<LI>Application Design
<LI>System Integration
<LI>Wireless Personalization
<LI>Management Consulting
<LI>Article and Book writing
</DIR>
...
```

```
<DIR>...
<LI>...
</DIR>
```

DIV

1.0. Aligns the tagged text block at left, right, or center.

The attribute for this tag is:

align   "left, center or right"

```
...
<DIV align =" center " >Sport Results</DIV>
...
```

```
<DIV align= "left, center or right">...</DIV>
```

DL

1.0. DL tag is used in combination with DD and DT tags to create lists. Please read DD tag for an example.

DT

1.0. Designates the list heading and aligns the character string at left. DL tag is used in combination with DD and DT tags to create lists. Please read DD tag for an example.

FONT

2.0. The <FONT> tag designates the color of the font.

The attribute for this tag is:

color   "hexadecimal color representation or color name"

```
...
<FONT color="blue">This time font color is blue.</FONT>
...
```

```
<FONT color="color selection"> ... </FONT>
```

FORM

1.0. Encloses an area to be shown as a data input form. The tag should be followed by the URL or email address (mailto). Defines method to send data to server to either GET or POST.

The attributes for this tag are:

action   "URL"
method   "get or post"

```
...
Please enter search keywords.<BR>
<FORM method="post" action="http://www.worldjobmart.com/imode/search.htm">
<INPUT type="text" name="Words" size="14" maxlength="30"><BR>
<INPUT type="submit" value="Submit"><BR>
<INPUT type="reset" value="Clear">
</FORM>
...
```

```
<FORM method="get or post"action="URL">... </FORM>
```

HEAD

1.0. Designates the information that is used as the page title. This tag directly follows HTML tag.

```
<HTML>
<HEAD>
<TITLE>Select provider</TITLE>
</HEAD>
<BODY>
...
```

```
<HEAD>...</HEAD>
```

Hn

1.0. Designates the alignment and size of the header.

The attribute for this tag is:

align   "left, center or right"

```
...
<H1>Header example</H1><BR>
<H4 align="center">Centered header example</H4><BR>
...
```

```
<H1 align="left, center or right">...</H1>
```

HR

1.0. The HR tag inserts a horizontal rule. It also defines attributes of the rule like alignment, length, and thickness.

The attributes for this tag are:

align	"left, center or right"
size	"number of pixels"
width	"number of pixels or %"
	Default line across display: <HR>
	Control the thickness of the line: <HR size=6>
	More control: <HR align="left" width="50%">
<HR align	"location of horizontal line" size="number of pixels" width="number of pixels or %">

HTML

1.0. Indicates start and end of an HTML document.

```
<HTML>
<HEAD>
<TITLE>HTML Works</TITLE>
</HEAD>
<BODY>
This must be an HTML document.
</BODY>
</HTML>
```

```
<HTML>...</HTML>
```

IMG

1.0. Designates an image file (obligatory attribute). Defines the way the image and character string are laid out, and how the character string wraps around the image. Sets image attributes like width, height, and blank space left of the image and between image and preceding line. It also defines alternative text to be shown if image is not available.

The attributes for this tag are:

src	"file name"
align	"top, middle, bottom, left or right"
width	"number of pixels or %"
height	"number of pixels or %"
hspace	"number of pixels"
vspace	"number of pixels"
alt	"character string"

```
...
<IMG src="logo.gif" align="bottom" alt="Company Logo">WaveDev
<br clear="all">
<IMG src="logo.gif" widht="65" height="65" alt="Company Logo">
Another version of the same.
<br clear="all">
...
```

```
<IMG src="file name" width="number of pixels or %" height="number of
pixels or %" align="top, middle, bottom, left or right"
vspace="number of pixels" hspace="number of pixels">
```

INPUT

1.0. The input tag defines settings for text input boxes, checkboxes, radio buttons, submit buttons, reset buttons, and others.

The attributes for the <INPUT> tag control behavior of this tag are:

type	"text, password, checkbox, radio, hidden, submit, or reset"
name	"name of field"
value	"data"
size	"number of characters"
maxlength	"maximum number of characters" checked
accesskey	"char" directkey function

The following shows how to submit a character string example:

```
...
Please enter search keywords.<BR>
<FORM method="post" action="http://www.worldjobmart.com/imode/search.asp">
<INPUT type="text" name="Words" size="14" maxlength="30"><BR>
<INPUT type="submit" value="Submit"><BR>
<INPUT type="reset" value="Clear">
</FORM>
...
```

The following shows how to submit a password field example:

```
...
Please enter your password.<BR>
<FORM method="post" action="http://www.worldjobmart.com/imode/login.asp">
<INPUT type="password" name="WJMPWD" size="14" maxlength="14"><BR>
<INPUT type="submit" value="Submit"><BR>
<INPUT type="reset" value="Clear">
</FORM>
...
```

For a text input box:

```
<INPUT type="text" name="name of field" value="data" size="number of
characters" maxlength="maximum number of characters" accesskey="char">
```

For a submit button:

```
<INPUT type="submit" name="name of field" value="data" accesskey="char">
```

For a reset button:

```
<INPUT type="reset" name="name of field" value="data" accesskey="char">
```

For a password input box:

```
<INPUT type=" password" name="name of field" value="data" size="number
of characters" maxlength= "maximum number of characters"
accesskey="char">
```

LI

1.0 and 2.0. The LI tag is used for list items. Please refer to <OL> tag for more details about version 2.0.

Attributes:

Type	"1, a or A"
value	"number"

```
...
Countrys and states of North America
<OL>
<LI>Canada
<LI>USA
<LI type="a">Arizona
<LI>Texas
<LI>Alaska
</OL>
...
```

```
<LI type="label type" value="number">...
```

MARQUEE

2.0. The MARQUEE runs a character string between the <MARQUEE> and </MARQUEE> tags on the screen. There can be only 64 bytes in one MARQUEE tag. There can be maximum of four MARQUEE sets on the same screen.

Attributes:

Direction	"left or right"
Behavior	"scroll, slide or alternate"
Loop	number of times

```
...
Marquee example<BR>
<MARQUEE behavior="slide" direction="left">Lets scroll right to left
</MARQUEE>
...
```

```
<MARQUEE> direction="left or right" behavior="scroll,  slide or alternate"
loop=number of times>...</MARQUEE>
```

MENU

1.0. Creates a menu list in combination with <LI> tag.

```
...
IMode Bank Services<BR>
<MENU>
<LI>Balances
<LI>Transfer
```

```
<LI>Bill Payment
<LI>i-mode mail
<LI>Other
</MENU>
...
```

```
<MENU>...
<LI>...
</MENU>
```

META

2.0. The <META> tag makes it possible to set the text encoding to SHIFT-JIS.

```
<META http-equiv="Content-Type" content="text/html ; charset=SHIFT_JIS">
```

OL

1.0. Creates a numbered list.

```
<OL>...
<LI>...
</OL>
```

2.0. The OL tag automatically labels items in a list with numbers or letters.

The attributes for this tag are:

type	"1, a or A"
start	"starting number"

where
1   labels with numbers
a   labels with lowercase letters
A   labels with uppercase letters

```
...
Some European Countries
<OL type="a">
<LI>France
<LI>Germany
<LI>Slovenia
<LI>Italy
<LI>Yugoslavia
</OL>
...
```

```
<OL type="label type" start="starting number">...
<LI>...
</OL>
```

OPTION

1.0. Designates the selected (initial value). This tag should immediately follow <SELECT> tag. Please see SELECT tag for more details.

```
<OPTION value="value" selected>...
```

P

1.0. The <P> tag creates a text block.

The attribute for this tag is:

align   "left, center or right"

```
...
Sample text
<P>This is sample text.</P>
...
```

```
<P align="position of text block">...</P>
```

PLAINTEXT

1.0. This tag displays a text file exactly as entered. If the source text has more lines than can fit on the screen, it will be broken into multiple lines.

```
...
<PLAINTEXT>
All of the text will be preserved.
</PLAINTEXT>
...
```

```
<PLAINTTEXT>... </PLAINTEXT>
```

PRE

1.0. Displays a source text in exact format as original, including line feeds and blank spaces.

```
...
<PRE>
This format
    will be preserved.
</PRE>
...
```

```
<PRE>...</PRE>
```

SELECT

1.0. The <SELECT> tag creates a list of optional items (in combination with <OPTION> tag).

The attributes for this tag are:

name	"list name"
size	"number of lines"

```
...
<FORM method="get" action="cgi-bin/age.pl">
Select your age
<SELECT name="age">
<OPTION value="1">20 - 25
<OPTION value="2" selected>25 - 30
<OPTION value="3"> 30 +
</SELECT>
<BR>
<INPUT type="submit" value="Select">
<BR>
<INPUT type="reset" value="Clear">
</FORM>
...
```

```
<SELECT name="list name" size=number of lines
<OPTION>...
</SELECT>
```

2.0. The <SELECT> tag creates list of optional items. The multiple attributes allow multiple selections from a list of menu options. The maximum number of selections equals the number of options.

The attributes for this tag are:

name	"name of list"
size	"number of lines"

```
...
Please select favorite  food:
<BR>
<SELECT name="menu" size=1 multiple>
<OPTION value=1>Fish
<OPTION value=2>French Fries
<OPTION value=3>Lasagna
<OPTION value=4>Hotdog
</SELECT>
<BR>
...
```

```
<SELECT name="menu" size="1" multiple> <OPTION> </SELECT>
```

TEXTAREA

1.0. The <TEXTAREA> tag creates a textbox field for inputting a string that consists of multiple lines. A maximum of 512 bytes can be entered.

The attributes for this tag are:

name	"field name"
rows	"number of lines"
cols	"number of columns"

```
...
<TEXTAREA name="Comment" cols="12" rows="4">Please submit your
comment</TEXTAREA>
...
```

```
<TEXTAREA name="field name" cols="number of columns" rows="number of
lines">... </TEXTAREA>
```

TITLE

1.0. The <TITLE> tag designates the page title.

```
<TITLE>...</TITLE>
```

UL

1.0. The <UL> tag creates bullet point lists.

```
...
Book requirements
<BR>
<UL>
<LI>Great idea
<LI> Table of contents
<LI>Couple of great guys
</UL>
...
```

```
<UL>...
<LI>...
</UL>
```

VoiceXML Elements

VoiceXML tags

<assign>

Assigns a value to a variable.

The attributes for this tag are:

name	variable name
expr	value of variable

<audio>

Plays an audio message within a prompt.

The attributes for this tag are:

src	URI of audio message
caching	safe or fast caching methods
fetchint	prefetch, safe, or stream
fetchtimeout	time to wait for content to be returned

<block>

A container of executable code.

The attributes for this tag are:

name	form item variable name
expr	initial value of form item variable
cond	if true, form item can be visited

<break>

Inserts a pause in the output.

The attribute for this tag is:

msecs	milliseconds to pause

<catch>

Associates a catch with a document, dialog, or form item.

The attributes for this tag are:

event	event(s) to catch
count	event count
cond	condition used to test if event was caught by this element

<choice>

Used to specify speech/DTMF grammar fragments.

The attributes for this tag are:

dtmf	DTMF sequence for choice
next	next document or dialog URI
expr	expression to create next document or dialog URI
caching	safe or fast caching methods
fetchaudio	URI of the audio to play while fetch is being done
fetchint	prefetch, safe, or stream
fetchtimeout	time to wait for content to be returned

<clear>

Clears one or more form item variables.

The attribute for this tag is:

namelist	form item names to be reset

<disconnect>

Disconnects the interpreter context from the user.

<div>

Classifies a region of text as a particular type.

The attribute: for this tag is

type   sentence or paragraph

<dtmf>

Touch-tone key grammar.

The attributes for this tag are:

src	URI of location of grammar
scope	dialog or document to activate grammar scope
typeMIME	type of grammar
caching	safe or fast caching methods
fetchint	prefetch, safe, or stream
fetchtimeout	time to wait for content to be returned

<else>

Used in if element.

<elseif>

Used in if element.

<emp>

Emphasizes speech output.

The attribute for this tag is:

level   strong, moderate (default); none, reduced

<enumerate>

An automatically generated description of the choices available.

<error>

Short version for <catch event="error">.

The attributes for this tag are:

count   event count

cond   condition used to test if event was caught by this element

<exit>

Returns control to interpreter context.

The attributes for this tag are:

expr   return expression

namelist   variable names to be returned to the interpreter context

<field>

Input item to be filled by the user.

The attributes for this tag are:

name   field item variable name

expr   initial value of form item variable

cond   if true, form item can be visited

type   type of field

slot   grammar slot used to populate the variable

modal   if true, only the field's grammars are enabled

<filled>

Action to perform when fields are filled by the user.

The attributes for this tag are:

mode   all or any

namelist   fields to trigger on

<form>

Main component of VoiceXML documents.

The attributes for this tag are:

id   name of the form

scope   default scope of the form's grammar

<goto>

Links to another form item, dialog, or document.

The attributes for this tag are:

next   URI to which to transition

expr	URI is dynamically determined by evaluating the expression
nextitem	next form item to visit in current form
expritem	expression that yields the same as nextitem
caching	safe or fast caching methods
fetchaudio	URI of the audio to play while fetch is being done
fetchint	prefetch, safe, or stream
fetchtimeout	time to wait for content to be returned

<grammar>

Provides speech grammar.

The attributes for this tag are:

src	URI of location of script
scope	dialog or document, menu's grammar scope
type	MIME type of grammar
caching	safe or fast caching methods
fetchint	prefetch, safe, or stream
fetchtimeout	time to wait for content to be returned

<help>

Short version for <catch event="help">.

The attributes for this tag are:

count	event count
cond	condition used to test if event was caught by this element

<if>

Used for conditional purposes.

<initial>

Initially prompted for formwide information before individual prompts are done.

The attributes for this tag are:

name	variable name
expr	initial value of form item variable
cond	if true, form item can be visited

<link>

Redirection containing one or more grammars.

The attributes for this tag are:

next	URI to link to
expr	URI is dynamically determined by evaluating the expression
event	event to throw when one of the link grammars is matched
caching	safe or fast caching methods
fetchaudio	URI of the audio to play while fetch is being done
fetchint	prefetch, safe, or stream
fetchtimeout	time to wait for content to be returned

<menu>

Short hand for a form.

The attributes for this tag are:

id	menu identifier
scope	dialog or document, menu's grammar scope
dtmf	true- choices with no explicit DTMF elements

<meta>

Data about the document.

The attributes for this tag are:

name	name of the meta data property
content	value of name variable
http-equiv	HTTP header name

<noinput>

Short version for <catch event="noinput">.

The attributes for this tag are:

count	event count
cond	condition used to test if event was caught by this element

<nomatch>

Short version for <catch event="nomatch">.

The attributes for this tag are:

count	event count
cond	condition used to test if event was caught by this element

<object>

Access to platform-specific functionality.

The attributes for this tag are:

name	variable name
expr	initial value of form item variable
cond	if true, form item can be visited
classid	URI specifying the location of the object's implementations
codebase	base path of URI
codetype	data content type
data	URI of data location
type	content type of data in data attribute
archive	a prepared list of URIs for archives
caching	safe or fast caching methods
fetchaudio	URI of the audio to play while fetch is being done
fetchint	prefetch, safe, or stream
fetchtimeout	time to wait for content to be returned

<option>

Used to pass input values.

The attributes for this tag are:

dtmf	DTM sequence for the choice
value	string value to assign to the field item variable

<param>

Used to specify valued being passed to subdialogs or objects.

The attributes for this tag are:

name	parameter name
expr	computed value of name
value	literal string value with name
valuetype	data or ref
type	MIME type of result if valuetype is ref

<prompt>

Controls the speech and prerecorded audios.

The attributes of this tag are:

bargein	if a user can interrupt or not
cond	true if the prompt should be spoken

count	number of times to allow different prompts for a user doing repeated things
timeout	timeout value after user input

<property>

Sets a property value.

The attributes for this tag are:

confidencelevel	speech recognition confidence level
sensitivity	sets the sensitivity level
speedvsaccuracy	balance between speed and accuracy
completetimeout	speech timeout value
incompletetimeout	timeout value to use when no active grammar has been matched

<pros>

JSML element, which changes the prosody of speech output.

The attributes of this tag are:

rate	speech rate
vol	output volume
pitch	specifies the pitch
range	pitch range

<record>

Records from user input.

The attributes for this tag are:

name	variable to hold recording
expr	initial value of variable
cond	true will allow form item to be visited
modal	true, all higher-level speech and DTMF grammars are turned off
beep	if true, a beep is sounded before recording
maxtime	maximum recording time
finalsilence	amount of silence indicating end of recording
dtmfterm	if true, DTMF key press ends recording
type	MIME format of recording

<reprompt>

Do normal prompt processing on next form item visited.

<return>

Ends execution of a subdialog and returns to the calling dialog.

The attributes of this tag are:

event	return, then throw this event
namelist	variables to be returned to the calling dialog

<sayas>

Specifies how a word or phrase is spoken.

The attributes of this tag are:

phon	the Unicode IPA characters that are to be spoken instead of the contained text
sub	defines substitute text to be spoken
class	values area phone, date, digits, literal, currency, number, and time

<script>

Similar to HTML script, this allows client-side scripting language.

The attributes of this tag are:

src	URI of location of scrip
charset	character encoding of script
caching	safe or fast caching methods
fetchint	prefetch, safe, or stream
fetchtimeout	time to wait for content to be returned

<subdialog>

Invokes a called dialog.

The attributes for this tag are:

name	subdialog returned result
expr	initial value of form item variable
cond	if true, form item can be visited
modal	if false, grammars remain active
namelist	list of variables to submit
src	URI of subdialog
method	post/get
enctype	content type
caching	safe or fast caching methods
fetchaudio	URI of the audio to play while fetch is being done

fetchint	prefetch, safe, or stream
fetchtimeout	time to wait for content to be returned

<submit>

Invoke a document with a list of variables via HTTP get or post.

The attributes for this tag are:

next	URI to which the query is submitted
expr	URI is dynamically determined by evaluating the expression
namelist	list of variables to submit
method	post/get
enctype	content type
caching	safe or fast caching methods
fetchaudio	URI of the audio to play while fetch is being done
fetchint	prefetch, safe, or stream
fetchtimeout	time to wait for content to be returned

<throw>

Throws an event.

The attribute for this tag is:

event	event being thrown

<transfer>

Suspends the current session and transfers control to another.

The attributes for this tag are:

name	new session name
expr	initial value of form item variable
cond	if true, the form item can be visited
dest	URI of the destination
destexpr	expression yielding the URL destination
bridge	what to do once call is connected
connecttimeout	time to wait while connecting
maxtime	maximum time the call can last

<value>

Add the value of an expression to a prompt.

The attributes for this tag are:

expr	variable
mode	type of rendering, TTS (default) or recorded
recsrc	source URI of audio files

<var>

Declares a variable.

The attributes for this tag are:

name	variable name
expr	variable value

<vxml>

Defines a VoiceXML document.

The attributes for this tag are:

version	document version, current is 1.0
base	base URI
application	URI of the document's application root

WMLScript Elements

Libraries

- Console (debugging only)
- Dialogs
- Float
- Lang
- String
- URL
- WML browser

WMLScripts 1.1 Tags

Console Library

Console functions.

print   console.print(string), used for debugging to print a string

println   console.println(string), used for debugging to print a string and invokes a new line

Dialog Library

Typical user interface functions.

alert	dialog.alert(message), displays the message to the user
confirm	dialog.confirm(message, ok, cancel), displays message and prompts for OK or cancel
prompt	dialog.prompt(message, defaultInput), displays a message and prompts for input

Float Library

Functions to manipulate floating point numbers.

ceil	float.ceil(value), rounds a floating point number up the next larger integer value
floor	float.floor(value), rounds a floating point number down the next smaller integer value
int	float.int(value), returns the integer part of the value
maxfloat	float.maxfloat( ), returns the maximum floating point value that can be presented by the browser
minfloat	float.minfloat( ), returns the minimum floating point value that can be presented by the browser
pow	float.pow(value1,value2), raises value1 to the power of value2
round	float.round(value), returns the rounded integer value
sqrt	float.sqrt(value), returns the square root of the value

Lang Library

WMLScript core functions.

abort	lang.abort(variable), aborts execution and returns control to browser
abs	lang.abs(value), produces absolute value
characterSet	lang.characterSet( ), returns the character set
exit	lang.exit(value), stops execution of the script and returns a value
float	lang.float( ), returns true if floating point number is in use
isFloat	lang.isFloat(value), returns true if the value can be converted to a floating point number
isInt	lang.isInt(value), returns true if the value can be converted to an integer
max	lang.max(value1,value2), returns the higher value of the two
maxInt	lang.maxInt( ), returns the maximum integer value supported by the browser
min	lang.min(value1,value2), returns the lower of the two values
minInt	lang.minInt( ), returns the minimum integer value supported by the browser

parseFloat | lang.parseFloat(value), converts a string to a floating point number
parseInt | lang.parseInt(value), converts a string to an integer
random | lang.random(value), returns a random positive number
seed | lang.seed(value), sets a value for the random number generator

String Library

String functions. (Note: White space can be carriage return, form feed, line feed, blank space, horizontal tab, prvertical tab.)

charAt | string.charAt(string, number), returns the character at position number+1
compare | string.compare(string1,string2), compares both strings, 0 if equal, -1 if string1 < string2, 1 if string1 > string2
elementAt | string.elementAt(string, index, separator), returns all after position of index after separator from string
elements | string.elements(string, separator), returns number of separators in string
find | string.find(string, substring), returns the position of the first occurrence of the substring in the string
format | string.format(format, value), converts the value to a string by using the format
insertAt | string.insertAt(string, element, index, separator), returns a string with the element and separator inserted at the index position of the original string
isEmpty | string.isEmpty(string), returns true if the string length is zero
length | string.length(string), returns the length of the string
removeAt | string.removeAt(string, index, separator), a string with the element at the given index is removed
replace | string.replace(string, oldsubstring, newsubstring), substitutes the newsubstring for all oldsubstring
replaceAt | string.replaceAt(string, element, index, separator), replace the item at the index in the string with the element string
squeeze | string.squeeze(string), removes extra white space
subString | string.subString(string, startIndex, length), returns a substring starting at startIndex for length
toString | string.toString(value), converts a value to a string
trim | string.trim(string), removes leading and trailing white spaces

URL Library

Manipulates URLs.

escapeString | url.escapeString(string), replaces special characters with hexadecimal escape values

getBase	url.getBase(), returns an absolute URL
getFragment	url.getFragment(url), returns the fragment portion of the URL
getHost	url.getHost(url), returns the host portion of the URL
getParameters	url.getParameters(url), returns parameter's portion of the URL
getPath	url.getPath(url), returns the path portion of the URL
getPort	url.getPort(url), returns the port portion of the URL
getQuery	url.getQuery(url), returns the query portion of the URL
getReferer	url.getReferer(url), returns the relative URL of the calling script
getScheme	url.getScheme(url), returns the scheme portion of the URL
isValid	url.isValid(url), returns true if URL syntax is correct
loadString	url.loadString(url, contentType), returns the URL if of contentType
resolve	url.resolve(base, relative), Embeds the relative URL into the base URL
unescapeString	url.unescapeString(string), replaces hexadecimal escape values in the string with corresponding special characters

WMLBrowser Library

Functions to control the WMLBrowser.

getCurrentCard	WMLBrowser.getCurrentCard( ), returns relative URL of currently displayed card
getVar	WMLBrowser.getVar(name), returns the value of the named variable
go	WMLBrowser.go(url), links to the specified URL
newContext	WMLBrowser.newContext( ), clears the history stack and all variables
prev	WMLBrowser.prev( ), reinvokes the previous task
refresh	WMLBrowser.refresh( ), refreshes the card display and variables
setVar	WMLBrowser.setVar(name, value), true if the named variable has been set with the value

Glossary

1G First-generation wireless networks that provided analog service with speeds of 9.6 Kbps.

2G Second-generation wireless networks that provide digital service with speeds up to 14.4 Kbps.

3G Third-generation wireless networks that will provide global standardization and speeds up to 2 Mbps.

4G Fourth-generation wireless networks that will provide packet-switched service at speeds up to 20 Mbps.

5G Fifth-generation wireless networks; IP-based packet-switched network service that will provide speeds up to 100 Mbps.

Abend or ABEND Abnormal termination of program.

Access Line The circuit used to enter the communications network.

Address Translation The process of converting external addresses into standardized network addresses and opposite.opposite.

ADK Application Development Kit; the toolkit used to create wireless/voice applications.

ADO ActiveX Data Objects; an object-oriented programming interface from Microsoft.

AIN Advanced Intelligent Network.

AMPS Advanced Mobile Phone System; common type of first-generation analog cell phone network used mostly in the United States.

ANI Automatic Number Identification.

ANSI American National Standards Institute.

ANSI-136 The North American digital mobile standard used in TDMA systems.

Apache Web Server Open source, multiplatform Web server.

API Application Program Interface.

ARP Address Resolution Protocol (TCP/IP).

ARPANET Mainly military funded network of interconnected computers that has become what we know today as the Internet.

ASCII American Standard Code for Information Interchange; most common format for saving files in plain text.

ASP Active Server Pages.

ASR Automatic Speech Recognition systems; integral part of Voice Browser with the task of reliable voice recognition.

Asynchronous A form of concurrent receive and transmit communications with no timing dependencies between the two signals.

ATM Asynchronous transfer mode that utilizes high-speed, high-volume, packet-switching transmission protocol standard.

AUC Authentication Center.

AWA Advanced Wireless Access that provides speeds of up to 36 Mbps.

Base Station Core component of wireless (cell) network that serves as a bridge between wireless devices and wired part of the network. Two main components are Station transceiver system and Base station controller.

BISDN Broadband Integrated Services Digital Network; will enable speeds of 2 Mbps and up.

Bluetooth A short-range communications specification designed to enable all IP devices to share information and synchronize data. This technology requires a transceiver chip in each device. Bluetooth will enable data speeds of 720 Kbps within a 10-meter range.

BMP Bitmap image format used mostly in Windows and OS/2 environments.

Broadband A communication channel bandwidth higher than 2 Mbps.

CC/PP A function of XHTML called the composite capability/preference profiles; it will be used to recognize incoming device differences.

CD Compact disk; "write once, read many" mass storage media.

CDMA Code Division Multiple Access.

CDMA One (IS-95) A second-generation digital Code Division Multiple Access.

CDMA2000 3G system with roots in CDMA One.

CDONTS Collaboration Data Objects for NT; a set of APIs used to build messaging and collaboration application on Microsoft platforms.

CDPD Cellular Digital Packet Data with operating speed of 19.2 Kbps.

CDR Charging Data records.

CGI Common Gateway Interface; a method of transferring data to the Web server.

cHTML Compact HTML; a well-defined subset of HTML 2.0, 3.2, and 4.0 specifications. cHTML is designed for small information appliances.

Circuit switching Circuit connection between calling parties.

CPU Central Processing Unit.

CSD Circuit-switched data.

CTI Computer Telephony Integration.

DDI/IDO Largest provider of WAP in Japan.

DLL Dynamic Link Libraries.

DNS Domain Name Server resolves domain names to IP addresses.

DSN Data Source Name.

DTD Document Type Definition; used to define entities within XML documents.

DTMF Dual-Tone Multifrequency.

DTW Do-The-Wave; method for self-managing wireless content delivered to the users.

E911 A system that allows law enforcement to locate a caller. There is a regulatory requirement (FCC) for this service on U.S. networks.

EDGE Enhanced Data GSM Environment; intended as incremental step toward 3G services. It is also known as 2.5G and provides a communication rate of 384 Kbps.

EPOC The operating system for mobile devices developed by Symbian.

ETACS Enhanced TACS; an extension of the TACS analogue network.

FCC Federal Communications Commission; a governing body for communications standards in the United States.

FDDI Fiber Distributed Data Interface.

FDMA Frequency Division Multiple Access.

FM Frequency Modulation; modulation of the RF carrier frequency.

FSK Frequency Shift Keying.

GIF Graphics Interchange Format; image format that uses 2D raster data type and LZW compression.

GML Geography Markup Language.

GMT Greenwich Mean Time; known currently as Coordinated Universal Time (UTC); provides means of measuring standard time globally.

GPS Global Positioning System; a satellite-based system that can identify requested location within 10 meters.

GPRS General Packet Radio Service; upgrade for GSM networks.

GSM Global System for Mobile Communications; European standard that uses TDMA as the service basis.

GUI Graphical User Interface.

HASP High-Altitude Stratospheric Platform.

HDML Handheld Device Markup Language; predecessor to WML developed by OpenWave, previously known as Phone.com.

HDTP Handheld Device Transport Protocol.

HLR Home Location Register.

HTML Hypertext Markup Language.

HTTP Hypertext Transfer Protocol [RFC2068].

HTTPS Secured Hypertext Transfer Protocol [RFC2068].

IIS Internet Information Server; Microsoft platform for hosting Web services.

IEEE Institute of Electrical and Electronics Engineers.

IETF Internet Engineering Task Force; serves as standards setting body for the Internet.

IMT-2000 3G wireless service proposed by International Telecommunications Union.

i-Mode A packet-switched mobile phone service from Japan's NTT DoCoMo. I-Mode operates at 9.6 Kbps and supports code developed in cHTML.

IDE Integrated Development Environment.

IMAP4 The latest version of Internet Message Access Protocol; presents standard method for accessing email.

IP Internet Protocol.

IPv6 The latest set of standards and definitions for Internet Protocol proposed by IETF.

ISDN Integrated Services Digital Network; digital public telecommunications network.

ISO International Standards Organisation.

ITU International Telecommunications Union, based in Geneva.

IVR Interactive Voice Response; the method for accessing data by interacting with telephone users via touch-tone entries or voice recognition.

JAVA Programming language introduced by SUN Microsystems in 1995. It is specifically designed with the Internet in mind.

JPEG The graphic image format that uses the file format defined in ISO standard 10918.

LAN Local area network, computer data communications network.

LBS Locationbased services.

LES Location-enabled services.

LIF Location Interoperability forum; established by Motorola, Nokia, and Ericsson.

LIFO Last in, first out.

MADK Motorola's Mobile Application Developers Kit.

Mbps Data rate of 1 million bits per second.

MDA Mail Delivery Agent.

Microwave A signal in the generic frequency range from above 1 GHz to an upper end of perhaps 30 or 40 GHz.

MIME Multi-Purpose Internet Mail Extensions; provides means of extending the content types that are exchanged over the Internet.

MLS Mobile Location Server.

MME Microsoft Mobile Explorer; Microsoft's version of a microbrowser that supports WML and HTML formats.

Mobile Service A radio communication service between mobile and fixed stations, or between mobile stations.

Mobile Station A station in the mobile that will be used while in motion.

MP3 MPEG-1 Audio Layer 3; a standard format for compression of sound files into very small files while preserving reproduction quality. Resulting files can be 10 to 12 times smaller than original files.

MTA Mail Transfer Agent.

MTSO Mobile Telephone Switching Office; interconnects base stations.

MUA Mail User Agent.

Narrowband A communication channel bandwidth of 64 kbps or below.

NMT Nordic Mobile Telephone System.

NTT Nippon Telegraph & Telephone is the major carrier that provides i-Mode services.

ODBC Open Database Connectivity; an open standard API used to access the databases.

OEL Active Matrix Organic Electroluminescence displays are driven by Thin Film Transistors.

OLE DB Microsoft's program interface used for the access to many different data sources.

OSI Open Systems Interconnection; a standard reference model for communication between devices on the network.

OTA Over-The-Air protocol defined by WAP specification 1.21 (wapforum.org); used in wireless push applications for pushing the messages from WAP gateway to wireless devices.

PAP Push Access Protocol; defined in WAP 1.21 specification is used for message push from message initiator to WAP gateway.

Packet Switching A network transmission method that involves slicing information into "packets" of data. This method is going to be the basis for 3G and beyond wireless networks.

PC Personal computer.

PCN Personal Communication Network; short-range wireless service (30 meters to 1.5 km).

PCS Personal Communications Service.

PDA Personal Digital Assistant; a small handheld portable, personal device.

PDC Personal Digital Communications; the system used in Japan that utilizes packet-switched technology.

Perl Practical Extraction and Reporting Language; an interpreted scripting language that is supported on UNIX and Microsoft platforms.

POP3 Post Office Protocol 3; standard protocol for receiving email.

PSK Phase Shift Keying; a digital modulation of phase.

PSTN Public Switched Telephone Network; standard wired network.

RFC Request for Comments.

Roaming Ability of mobile phone user to travel from one cell to another without losing the established connections.

RTOS Real-Time Operating System; used in many portable wireless devices.

SDK Software Development Kit.

SGML Standard Generalized Markup Language.

SIM Subscriber Identity Module; smart card containing certification of user's identity and additional applications that can reside on the card (like an email program).

SMS Short Message Service; a text messaging service available on digital mobile phones.

SMPP Simple Mail Point to Point protocol.

SMSC Short Message Service Center.

SMTP Simple Mail Transfer Protocol.

Spread Spectrum A communication technique that spreads a communication signal bandwidth over a wide range of frequencies.

SQL Structured Query Language.

Symbian A joint venture established by Ericsson, Nokia, and Psion to develop an industry-standard operating system for mobile devices (EPOC).

Symmetrical Communications Two-way communications between mobile devices; typically used for videoconferencing.

SSL Secure Sockets Layer protocol used for secure data exchange over the Internet, originally introduced by Netscape.

TACS Total Access Communications; European analog network.

TCP Transport Control Protocol.

TCP/IP Data protocols used for Internet /Intranet communications.

TDMA Time Division Multiple Access; a form of digital multiplexing technique whereby each signal is sent at a repeating time slot in a frequency channel.

TFT Thin-Film Transistor used in liquid crystal displays. Every pixel on the display has a separate transistor.

TIA Telecommunications Industry Association.

TLS Transport Layer Security.

TTL Time to live; used to define amount of time that information will be available.

TTS Text To Speech engine; used to read text content of the files (or database fields) to the user connected via telephone.

UDP User Datagram Protocol.

UMTS Universal Mobile Telecommunications System; third-generation system developed in Europe and optimized for GSM operators.

URI Uniform Resource Identifier; a method to identify any possible content points available on the Internet.

URL Uniform Resource Locator.

URN Uniform Resource Name.

USSD Unstructured Supplementary Service Data.

VB Visual Basic; an IDE from Microsoft that enables rapid application development and quick deployment.

VB6 Visual Basic version 6.

VC++ Visual C ++ programming language.

VoxML Application of XML created by Motorola in order to provide voice access to Internet content.

VoiceXML Application of XML that allows interactive access to Internet content via regular or mobile telephone. Created by AT&T, IBM, Lucent Technologies, and Motorola.

W-CDMA Wideband Code Division Multiple Access; Japanese version of 3G system that builds on CDMA technology that could raise data transmission rates up to 2 Mbs. NTT DoCoMo has announced that W-CDMA will be implemented toward the end of 2001.

W3C World Wide Web Consortium.

WAE Wireless Application Environment.

WAP Wireless Application Protocol; open, global standard for wireless communication specification that enables mobile users with wireless devices to access and interact instantly with information.

WAN Wide Area Network.

WBMP Wireless Bitmap; an image format used to represent graphics on the wireless device.

WBXML WAP Binary Extensible Markup Language.

WDP Wireless Datagram Protocol.

WML Wireless Markup Language; a subset of XML used for application development in the wireless industry.

WMLScript Scripting language defined by WAP standard that is similar to Java in its structure.

WSP Wireless Session Protocol.

WTA Wireless Telephony Application.

WTAI Wireless Telephony Application Interface.

WTLS Wireless Transport Layer Security.

WTP Wireless Transaction Protocol.

WWW World Wide Web.

XHTML Extensible Hypertext Markup Language; expected to become the language used for WAP 2.0 specification.

XML Extensible Markup Language.

Index